Jackson County, Georgia TOMBSTONES

Jeannette Holland Austin
Dorothy Holland Herring

HERITAGE BOOKS
2008

HERITAGE BOOKS

AN IMPRINT OF HERITAGE BOOKS, INC.

Books, CDs, and more—Worldwide

For our listing of thousands of titles see our website
at
www.HeritageBooks.com

Published 2008 by
HERITAGE BOOKS, INC.
Publishing Division
100 Railroad Ave. #104
Westminster, Maryland 21157

Copyright © 1969 Jeannette Holland Austin/Dorothy Holland Herring

Other books by the authors:

***Jeannette Holland Austin*:**
Alabama Bible Records
Virginia Bible Records
North Carolina -- South Carolina Bible Records
1860 Paulding County, Georgia, Census
The Georgians Database, Genealogical Notes
DeKalb County, Georgia, Probate Records
Fayette County, Georgia Probate Records: Volume II, Annual Returns, Inventories, Sales, Bonds, 1845-1897
Georgia Obituaries, 1905-1910
Georgia Bible Records, Supplement, 1772-1940
Georgia Obituaries, 1740-1935
Masters of the Low Country, A History of the Georgia Colony

***Dorothy Holland Herring*:**
Company A of the Fortieth Georgia Infantry Regiment in the Confederate Service
Company C of the Twenty-Second Georgia Infantry Regiment in the Confederate Service

All rights reserved. No part of this book may be reproduced or transmitted in any form or by any means, electronic or mechanical, including photocopying, recording or by any information storage and retrieval system without written permission from the author, except for the inclusion of brief quotations in a review.

International Standard Book Numbers
Paperbound: 978-1-58549-710-2
Clothbound: 978-0-7884-7117-9

Preface

The authors made a thorough canvas of Jackson County, Georgia cemeteries in 1969. We located family cemeteries, church cemeteries, as well as, isolated cemeteries, that we were made aware of either by using a county map or word-of-mouth.

Although no burials are listed after 1969, this work is helpful today because many of those tombstones located in 1969 have been broken, vandalized, or disappeared completely.

Jeannette Holland Austin
Dorothy Herring Holland

HOSCHTON CITY CEMETERY, Hoschton

ADAMS

Osmers Jackson 1884-1965
Rose Preston 1888-

Jesse Curtis 12/17/1887-2/6/1938
Bessie M. 9/8/1903-
Julia Ann 12/22/1868-5/1/1933

Susie Effie, daughter of W. O. & J. A. Adams 5/14/1890-1896
Myra Lenora, daughter of W. O. & J. A. Adams 9/5/1896-6/14/1897
Alton 8/3/1900-5/17/19443

ALLEN

Virginia R., wife of Dr. Myron B. 1894-1935
Myron B., M. D. 1895-1953

L. C., Dr. 4/1/1862-3/6/1947
Isabelle C., wife of Dr. L. C. Allen 7/30/1892-8/2/1952
Alice E., wife of Dr. L. C., died 6/17/1923
Arpad Alvan, infant of Dr. L. C. & A. E. Allen 2/17/1894-9/3/1894
Alberta Elsse, infant of Dr. L. C. Allen 8/11/1896-9/8/1897

ANDERSON

Maude A. 10/20/1893-11/1/1942

Allen 1856-1915
Denie 1859-1899

ARNOLD

M. B. 4/23/1845-11/8/1902
Nancy J., wife of M. B. 10/19/1846-6/8/1915
Lena, daughter of M. B. & N. J. Arnold 5/20/1884-7/10/1885

BAILES

Harold C., Jr. 2/18/1956-2/19/1956

BAIRD

Evaline 10/15/1818-3/10/1903
Eliza Caroline 10/25/1820-5/28/1900
John A. 10/30/1811-3/13/1895
Rev. James 9/8/1815-55/25/1900
Tenie H. 8/15/1891-9/19/1939

HOSCHTON CITY CEMETERY

BELL

Nicholas A. 1902-1904
Cline 1907-1931
James F. 1869-1944
Mrs. C. Died 1965

BELGER

John Henry Belger, Georgia, PFC Btry F, 119 Field Arty, World War II
2/14/1894-10/5/1959

BLALOCK

John Bascom 11/27/1862-11/23/1902
Melissa Maynard 10/31/1867-6/30/1864

BROOKSHIRE

George M. 6/18/1886-12/19/1966
Sally 6/28/1896-6/21/1940

BURROUGHS

Julius C. 5/22/1889-10/31/1961
Catherine 2/24/1918-3/10/1918

CHESTNUT

John T. 1/3/1862-2/26/1898
Mary Vilula 2/11/1872-5/15/1957
Fred 10/17/1888-11/25/1904

Herschel G. 8/17/1891-6/5/1912
Juna Belle, daughter of J. T. & M. V. Chestnut died 5/17/1897,
aged 1 year, 4 months, 22 days

CLARK

Jewell W. 1919-1965
Tallulah, wife of M. W. Clark, 9/13/1855-7/31/1888
Willie A. 1/15/1895-9/16/1957
Emma Mae P. 4/3/1896-3/30/1959

HOSCHTON CITY CEMETERY, Hoschton

CRUCE

Charlie M. 10/14/1878-4/29/1960
Vesta F. 4/16/1886-4/26/1964
Clarence C. Died 6/20/1968, aged 55 years
Patrica Ann died 9/9/1941, aged 13 years

DARBY

James W. 6/5/1851-9/27/1927
Sallie Nowell 4/14/1855-1/18/1925

DE LA PIERRIERE

Herman Preston 8/7/1888-3/4/1951
William 10/19/1884-5/22/1915
Dr. Green Herschel 1/9/1882-6/14/1937
Homer Clarence 7/16/1894-11/24/1930
Otis Leon 3/1/1892-7/18/1892
Marie Belle 4/8/1887-6/3/1887
Bertrice Phillips 8/11/1892-4/3/1930
Mary Ann Smith, wife of Dr. W. P. 12/24/1853-5/30/1898
Dr. William Preston 1/1/1856-1/30/1917

FORRESTER

Infant of R. L. & M. J. 12/28/1897-1/5/1898
Flora 1898-1966

FREEMAN

Dr. Ralph Freeman 2/9/1884-4/13/1937

FRICKS

Robert Lee 1874-1924
Clara Adel 1888-1932
James Marius 10/19/1919-4/21/1921

GREEN

Martha Rebecca, wife of J. F. 1850-1928

HAWKS

Sarah Ruth 4/27/1884-5/13/1931

HOSCHTON CITY CEMETERY, Hoschton

HAYES

Martha H. 12/11/1858-1/4/1904

HEAD

Robert H. 1890-1962
Naomi 1917-

HILL

Elmer T. 5/20/1890-6/13/1890
Robert L. 4/17/1897-8/20/1897
Maggie N. 2/29/1872-9/16/1963
Olivia W. 1879-1957
Tyson 7/15/1898-6/20/1900
R. L. 9/23/1864-10/31/1912
Hugh W. 1874-1957
Elmer T. 5/20/1890-6/13/1890
Margaret E. 5/30/1919-6/3/1910
Annie Hugh 1919-1921
Margaret E. 1/1922-6/1923

HILDRETH

Walter A. 4/19/1875-12/20/1963

HOSCH

Matilda 12/7/1818-8/7/1898, aged 74 years, 10 months
Lt. Henry 12/23/1813, died in Richmond, Va. 7/7/1862
Fannie Camp 8/28/1854-5/28/1889
John R. 10/9/1850-1/14/1909
Infants of John and Fannie Hosch
Fronie Harris 11/10/1850-6/1/1898
Weldon H. 9/4/1892-4/6/1959
Asbury Camp 12/5/1880-5/19/1937
Flora t 2/21/1887-12/6/1939
Nancy, sister 6/10/1845-6/16/1889
Mary Ann 10/25/1838-5/29/1917
Henry Andrew 7/11/1853-10/5/1934, married 12/25/1879
Celestine Emma t, wife of Henry Adrew, 1/19/1867-7/2/1943
Paul A., Sr. died 5/17/1963, aged 71 years
Russell Brestone 3/17/1883-1/8/1950
Russell Angel 11/15/1855-12/25/1922
Tabitha Hill 9/2/1859-1/1/1924
H. Omer, son of R. A. & Tabitha 10/26/1878-9/20/1899
Mary 2/23/1900-6/14/1900

HOSCHTON CITY CEMETERY, Hoschton

HOSCH

John Henry 1901-1963
Mattie M. 1900 -

HUDGINS

Maude Bridges, wife of C. M. Hudgins 7/27/1879-12/22/1922
Carl M. 7/30/1872-9/25/1927

JACKSON

Arthur D. 1875-1949

JAILLETTE

Harriet C. 1933-1938
Ada A. 1934-1938
Betty L. 1935-1938
Mary E. 1936-1938

LANGFORD

Mollie S. 1/27/1886-10/17/1966
Thomas C. 2/1/1878-8/16/1850

LAWRENCE

Vesta, wife of M. T. 8/9/1863-2/12/1914

LEVANS

Mary 9/3/1851-5/9/1921

LILLY

James Rufus 2/28/1911-3/12/1912

LOTT

Ella H. -no dates
John H. -no dates
George W. -no dates
Jurelle G. 11/21/1910-11/3/1966
Dean S. 6/2/1900-3/14/1966
Lester Judd 4/30/1889-5/23/1968

HOSCHTON CITY CEMETERY, Hoschton

LOTT

H. J. 12/6/1855-11/3/1925
Olivia Bell 5/11/1859-2/5/1939
Leila, daughter of H. J. & Olivia 3/12/1898-5/31/1899
Ralph 6/18/1891-12/25/1947

McGANTS

Effie Eugenia, wife of William B. 9/21/1869-1/24/1893

McNEAL

William Ed 10/4/1880-4/23/1957

MARLOW

David J. 8/24/1874
Emma M. Moon 6/23/1879-3/30/1937

MANUS

Mary Jane, wife of J. B. 8/27/1839-1/21/1929
J. B. 1/5/1936-1/31/1917

MADDOX

William H. 10/25/1887-8/12/1958
Daisy Mae 6/27/1884-5/9/1926
Infant of Mr. & Mrs. W. H., born & died 2/2/1913

MAHAFFEY

James F. 3/18/1894-3/8/1966
Cornelia H. 3/22/1872-4/23/1950
John Spruell 11/13/1888-10/16/1926
Alexander M. 4/16/1857-2/14/1936

MOSS

Rev. N. A. 10/28/1836-6/20/1913
Celia Bell 1847-1940

NICHOLS

Louis, son of J. W. & Jessie 7/9/1908

HOSCHTON CITY CEMETERY, Hoschton

NOWELL

William F. 12/25/1871-10/4/1896

Matilda, wife of A. N. 8/12/1874-8/11/1905
Malvin, daughter of Matilda & A. N. 9/4/1896-6/29/1897

PARK

Mattie Mae 11/1895-3/19/1945
John Russell 1901-1956
Maude 1873-1959
M. W. 11854-1929

PATRICK

Miss Lola Drake died 2/5/1967, aged 42 years
Annie Bradley, wife of M. W. Park, 12/23/1865-8/5/1899

PEARCE

Jesse L. 11/20/1871-9/17/1897 married Mary Teague 12/29/1895

James W. 7/13/1832-5/12/1905
Martha A., wife of James W. 9/3/1838-8/27/1923
Carrie, daughter of James W. & Martha A. 11/15/1880-3/17/1896

PEPPERS

Son of M. W. & M. C. Peppers 12/22/1892-1/25/1898
Jesse, son of M. W. & M. C. 12/22/1897-1/25/1898
Davy, son of M. W. & M. C. 6/9/1894-8/5/1895

Emma 11/17/1845-2/26/1917

Rosella De La Pierrier 7/30/1828-2/8/1905

PIRKLE

P. Parks -
Oscar 1876-1949
Della 1879-1939
Green H., son of Oscar and Della 10/5/1901-11/16/1912

Avarilla 1884-1934

HOSCHTON CITY CEMETERY, Hoschton

QUATTLEBAUM

Harry C. 1/18/1867-6/5/1906
Mary E. 6/28/1868-5/28/1937
Fred, son of H. C. & M. E.
Paul, son of H. C. & M. E.
Stafford, son of H. C. & M. E. 2/16/1888-9/2/1894

REINHARDT

Jewell L. 1882-1956
S. Gertrude 1881-1/18/1968

ROBERTS

Ralph B. 5/1/1903-11/25/1917
Marcus A. 2/22/1873-3/8/1934

STOREY

Dorothy 3/2/1917-1/5/1929
Annis 5/16/1907-6/22/1908
Belle P. 1882-
James M. 1877

STRAYNGE

James A. 10/2/1809-10/9/1891
Emma E. 6/21/1847-7/30/1893

STONE

Cleo Evans 9/7/1896-
John F. 12/22/1890-3/14/1943

SMITH

Grover E. 8/30/1887-4/14/1967
Myrt Park 7/20/1887-9/20/1947

William M. 12/15/1849-8/25/1937

Paulina C. 3/10/1859-12/16/1925
Leila B. 1865-1952

George, son of G. M. & L. C. 7/10/1899-9/4/1913

HOSCHTON CITY CEMETERY, Hoschton

SELL

Dorothy Hill 1925-1925
Julia Anderson 1864-1931
Howell Jackson 1857-1946

THOMAS

Elizabeth C., wife of L. W. 9/5/1835-6/12/1891

THURMOND

Julian 7/14/1933-7/15/1933

TITSHAW

Pvt. L. W. C., 9 Ga Inf., C. S. A. 2/28/1833-12/21/1915

TRACY

S. T. 10/1/1859-10/13/1916

Baby Ruth 11/25/1904-5/5/1905

Sadie Darby 1/3/1877-1/26/1953

THOMPSON

Jasper Newton 3/14/1861-1/8/1933
Ida Anderson, wife of J. N. Thompson 7/28/1866-4/4/1955

TUGGLE

Sallie 3/7/1821-5/2/1891

WARD

William Lewis 8/10/1870-5/15/1950
Zimmer A., wife of W. L. 9/18/1872-4/1/1919

WATERS

Oma A. 7/26/1904 -

WIER

H. L. 1856-1889
Idalia 1862-1895

HOSCHTON CITY CEMETERY, Hoschton

Infant of H. L. & I.
S. B. 1823-1900
Mrs. S. B. 1836-1899

Lovic L. 1873-1919
Alice
Don E.

WILSON

Mae Maddox 1907-

Benjamin F. 1866-1957
Daisy Bean 1874-1938

WILEY

Mrs. M. C. 2/22/1828-12/25/1916

YOUNG

Loyd Kirby, son of F. B. & E. L. 6/15/1895-6/2/1896
Henry Velvin, son of F. B. & E. L. 9/11/1892-6/8/1894

BRASELTON FAMILY CEMETERY, BRASELTON, GA
Off Highway 124 (Established 1909)

BRASELTON

Royce G.
7/28/1892-11/1/1963
James Lewis, Jr. 10/1/1929-12/18/1944
Clyde Royce 1/22/1952
Steven W. 3/8/1950-11/24/1964
Mary Ann 10/30/1828-1833
Green B. 1/10/1833-11/1/1854
Sarah B. 10/15/1808-7/25/1893
Joe B. 12/30/1792-7/26/1848
W. H., Sr. 3/10/1835-11/10/1896
Susan F. 8/11/1846-1/3/1929
William MCKiney 7/14/1903-12/7/1966
Annette Maughon 7/14/1903-12/7/1966

Twin brothers, sons of Green & Mary 2/22/1904-6/9/1904 & 2/22/1904-6/18/1904
Infant son of Green and Mary 9/26/1916-10/15/1916
May Duncan, wife of Green 4/28/1880-7/12/1959
Green 9/29/1872-3/4/1953

BRASELTON FAMILY CEMETERY, BRASELTON, GA
Off Highway 124 (Established 1909)

William Henry 10/5/1868-5/25/1956
Pollie Darby, wife of William Henry, 9/16/1873-7/13/1949
Frances Newell, daughter of Pollie Darby and W. H. 5/15/1906-8/11/1924

Lena 8/20/1887-1/6/1954
John Oliver Sr. 3/31/1877-2/2/1951
Susan F. 8/11/1847-1/3/1929
W. H. Sr. 3/4/1835-11/10/1896

GILLESPIE

Charles Ridley, M. D. 9/29/1907-7/2/1964

HORGAT

Ludalia 1891-1936

JACKSON

Dr. John William, Jr. 11/29/11930-2/5/1961

MacKEAN

Maud Britton 6/20/1884-7/26/1962

McDONALD

Belle Braselton 3/27/1882-10/19/1959
Edward Monroe 1/1/1881-3/25/1961
Marian Lanelle, daughter of Belle B. & E. M. 8/30/1920-5/2/1921

PRUITT

R. D. (Bud) 5/31/1862-1/23/1950
Ruth L., wife of R. D. 12/3/1855-4/28/1926

WATLINGTON

Slover 1/11/1900-7/23/1962

ZION BAPTIST CHURCH, BRASELTON, GA.
Junction of Interstate #85, off Hwy 53, on a county road. (Established 1843)

ABBOTT

James Robert III died 2/24/1967, aged 21 years, 2 months, 10 days

ALEXANDER

James R. 12/20/1858-
Gazelle 12/10/1871-2/1/1938

ANDERSON

George E. 8/25/1869-8/17/1973
Thomas B. 12/19/1867-1/5/1936
Golden A. 7/17/1888-1/15/1957
W. D. 1/19/1861-8/31/1895

David W. 4/16/1830-12/15/1892
Martha A. 5/14/1830-6/27/1902

BAIRD

Joe Wilborn -Born & Died 9/19/1934
Infants, Almeta & Alberta, born & died 12/27/1909
Nancy Duck 7/24/1862-7/3/1877
Joseph Samuel 10/7/1874-10/24/1938

Arthur Belle, daughter of Mr. & Mrs. Arthur H. 10/24/1926-2/15/1927
Julia Carolyn, daughter of Mr. & Mrs. Arthur H. 10/24/1923-9/1/1926
Arthur H. 2/12/1894-11/14/1926

R. M.
Ida, wife of Jesse 2/22/1889-9/22/190-
Caroline S. 1855-1932
W. Billie 1853-1943
Fred H. 1904-1958
Jack Wayne 11/29/1939-3/22/1958

J. W. S.
Annie, daughter of J. W. S. & Minnie 8/4/1898-10/28/1916
Clarence, son of J. W. S. & Minnie 8/12/1896-4/20/1904
Infant of J. W. S. & Minnie 10/19/1900-1/2/1901
S. W. 5/18/1820-2/4/1899
Lucy 1836-8/1/1913, aged 77 years
Ritta C. 1872-1944
Henry F. 1872-1966

Infant son of J. S. & F. E. 6/24/1889

ZION BAPTIST CHURCH, BRASELTON, GA.
Junction of Interstate #85, off Hwy 53, on a county road. (Established 1843

BAIRD

Infant daughter of J. S. & F. E. 4/1/1893-4/2/1899
Frances R. 1873-1954
John O. 1867-1954
Nelia T. 9/22/1898-12/24/1961
Samuel B. 6/1/1870-6/4/1937
Mary Ann, wfe of S. B. 9/14/1872-10/25/1920
Infant daughter 10/9/1935
Jack Quillian 3/1/1927-10/28/1928
Sallie R. 1871-1926
James M. 1884-1961

ZION BAPTIST CHURCH, BRASELTON, GA.
Junction of Interstate #85, off Hwy 53, on a county road. (Established 1843)

BAILEY

Frank T. 10/11/1880-11/10/1936
Lizzie J. 5/17/1882-11/4/1948
A. T., infant of Mr. & Mrs. F. T. Born 7/20/1919

BARNETT

W. Andy 1873-1956
Omie M. 1886-1915

M. P. 7/9/1848-1/2/1929
Mrs. Mary, wife of M. P., born 1842, married 1866, died 9/26/1906

BELL

Pearl 1886-
Eddie 1885-1967

Trumon O. 12/8/1882-6/8/1962
Mae C. 9/20/1897-1/22/1946
Elise Mae 8/10/1893-12/28/1967

Martha M. 1868-1946
F. Cicero 1863-1943

BLANKENSHIP

Ruth A. 9/16/1824-9/16/1879

ZION BAPTIST CHURCH, BRASELTON, GA.
Junction of Interstate #85, off Hwy 53, on a county road. (Established 1843

BOND

Mary A. 1890-1932
William T. 1885-1944

BRADY

Infant of T. A. & M. M. 4/20/1901-3/19/1902
L. E., daughter of F. A. & M. M. 5/3/1889-5/9/1903

BREWER

Lillie 12/20/1902-12/9/1908
Dellie Mae 1909-1916

BRIDGES

Mary A., wife of Rev. H. 1/3/1845-1/13/1877

BROWN

John 6/18/1830-6/8/1889, aged 55
Mary E., daughter of John 11/16/1838-8/28/1920
Susannah 7/29/1818-7/21/1875, aged 57 years
Edward F. Died March 1879
Lydia J. 3/22/1848-12/31/1937

CARLYLE

C. Azalee 12/3/1882-5/14/1962
James M. 1/7/1885-12/8/1958
Grover Ansilum, son of J. M. & C. A. 9/15/1909-8/24/1915
Infant of J. M. & C. A. 1/24/1907

CARTER

Ora 8/4/1872-7/3/1948
M. V. 11/14/1861-4/9/1917
J. D. 9/29/1861-3/25/1946
Homer, son of J. D. & M. V. 10/27/1894-7/30/1909
J. D., son of Mr. & Mrs. W. J. 1/5/1930-11/20/1934

ZION BAPTIST CHURCH, BRASELTON, GA.
Junction of Interstate #85, off Hwy 53, on a county road. (Established 1843)

CASH

Lucy Ann, infant of Mr. & Mrs. B. W. 9/16/1934
Kay Broadus, infant of Mr. & Mrs. B. W. 11/16/1943

CHAMBERS

Sgt. Alga A. 1900-1965
Algia, Ga, Sgt, Med. Dept. World War I & II 10/25/1898-6/19/1965
Mollie Belle 9/6/1899-12/17/1963
Patsy A. 1963-1963

CHEEK

Freeman Virgil, son of William and M. A. 9/2/1893-4/9/1917

Rev. F. V. 3/8/1849-4/17/1907
Edney Isabelle Stephens, wife of Rev. F. V. 12/15/1844-10/16/1921

William C., Ga., Sgt. 453 AF Bomb G, World War II 6/4/1913-5/8/1944

Martha A. 1868-1948
Infant 1916-1916

William M. 1869-1951
Missouri A. 1869-1917

Lorena 1894-1960
Major G. 1891-

CLALK

Herman 12/10/1923-6/1/1963

COKER

C. Viola 2/4/1911
Emory H. 5/29/1911-3/30/1952

COOPER

Thomas Taylor 3/18/1849-5/25/1932
Martha Veal 11/15/1845-9/3/1909
Ann Elizabeth W. 7/26/1865-11/30/1960

ZION BAPTIST CHURCH, BRASELTON, GA.
Junction of Interstate #85, off Hwy 53, on a county road. (Established 1843)

COOPER

Marshall Tandy 8/2/1869-8/2/1965
Julia McEver 2/3/1869-11/13/1931
Son of M. T. & J. M., aged 1 year, 1 month, 12 days
Annie Maud, daughter of Mr. & Mr. M. T. 3/13/1912-7/18/1912
Lillie Belle 5/4/1895-4/26/1895

Ralph Monroe, infant son of J. O. & Julia 12/5/1914-6/4/191--

Dr. Hillyer 2/2/1866-8/3/1928
Martha E. 1/13/1863-7/12/1958
Infant of Dr. H. M. & Martha E. Born 1/1898
Early, son of Dr. H. M. & Martha E. 12/15/1892-7/14/1910

Claude R. 8/10/1900-4/7/1962

Infant son of J. C. & Lizzie 10/3/1893-10/6/1893
Infant son of J. C. & Lizzie 1/10/1896-2/20/1896
Florence, daughter of J. C. & Lizzie 6/25/1899-9/33/1899

Edna Cheek, wife of J. N. 3/21/1897-10/15/1916
Infant of J. N. & Edna, born and died 6/5/194

CRAFT

Colene, infant of J. E. & S. A. 3/7/1908-3/29/1909

CRUCE

John W. P. 7/18/1876-3/14/1957
Myrtice S. 12/8/1882-11/28/1967

CHRONIC

Rev. O. M. 8/12/1824-4/27/1902
Lewis, Co. A, 9 Ga. Inf., C. S. A., 1827-1904
Clarisa 9/9/1815-6/27/1901
Hazel 1801-1879
John H. 2/8/1830-6/28/1903, aged 73 years, 3 months

DAKES

Marshal B., son of W. & L. A. 10/6/1883-11/16/1883

ZION BAPTIST CHURCH, BRASELTON, GA.
Junction of Interstate #85, off Hwy 53, on a county road. (Established 1843)

DANIEL

Eulas 1923-1923

DAVIS

Esther, wife of J. M. 3/21/1881-9/24/1901
J. Manley 1877-1957
Mary S. 1885-1957
Infant of J. M. & Mary, born and died 12/14/1911
Chester A. 1902-1945

J. Marion 1898-
Mary F. 1918-
W. Lyndal 1924-1958
Flora B. 1897-1935
Pink
John H. 1850-1921
Martha 5/21/1882-6/21/1921
Omer F. 2/26/1886-8/13/1951
Jenie H. 7/10/1891-2/16/1958
Mary 1847-1921
Joseph E. 1853-1923
Minnie Bell 1882-1943
Joe Artis 1880-1908

DEATON

Amelia Emmett, wife of E. N. 9/18/1875-10/9/1911
Desa, infant daughter of E. N. & Amelia 12/31/1909-2/2/1910

DELAPERRIERE

Dr. Angel A. 2/23/1848-8/28/1899
Edward Lee 4/26/1873-12/20/1894

DUCK

Evelyn 3/31/1885-8/13/1947
Esther Allene 8/18/1906-8/27/1907
Infant 3/14/1910
Annie Kathleen 5/15/1937-5/13/1967
W. Branson 1914-1958
Bertie W. 1918-
Mae Cruce died 5/24/1958, 67 years, 10 months, 17 days
L. Gordon 1889-1957

ZION BAPTIST CHURCH, BRASELTON, GA.
Junction of Interstate #85, off Hwy 53, on a county road. (Established 1843)

DUCK

Branton J. 1914-1916
Annie 9/7/1870-8/23/1937

Rev. W. J. 6/3/1851-11/28/1925
Margaret, wife of W. J. 10/16/1855-12/26/1914

DUNCAN

Ola 1887-1904

Zeb 1875-1954

Children of E. M. & Sarah -
Bessie 2/17/1895-8/16/1901
Lena Belle 2/4/1897-8/15/1901

Mary F., wife of L. G. 6/22/1853-6/2/1879

L. F. 7/4/1830-2/18/1904
Mary M. 10/26/1827-11/12/1884

Anderson E. 8/24/1819-11/9/1898
Matilda 5/5/1819-1890

EDGE

Bartow T. 1878-1966
Cathrine Mc. 1876-1950

Ava, wife of J. C. 2/14/1883-2/19/1905

Catherine Ann 1/31/1913-9/13/1943

EMMETT

Charlie C. 7/10/1890-6/29/1959
Lillie L. 6/15/1889-11/6/1948

Robert Lea, Sr. 1880-1954
Martha Jane M. 1887 -

Grover, son of Mr. & Mrs. J. W. 7/1/1894-6/2/1895

ZION BAPTIST CHURCH, BRASELTON, GA.
Junction of Interstate #85, off Hwy 53, on a county road. (Established 1843)

EWING

James Homer 1902-
Martha Louise 1904-1966

Joseph W. 5/27/1944-3/2/1955
Infant son of Mr. & Mrs. J. W. 3/2/1937-4/2/1957

Mary Sue 12/15/1947-12/20/1949
Joseph 1944-1946

Joseph William 1909-1960

James B. 8/9/1885
Sarah 1/9/1878-5/23/1941

T. C., son of J. D. & S. I., 2/11/1917-4/30/1930

Infant daughter of J. B. & S. E.

Carrie B. Barton 8/8/1915-6/8/1917

Nancy S. 12/25/1868-11/28/1952
Noah C. 3/20/1873-6/18/1950

Joseph W. 5/27/1944-3/2/1966
Mary Sue 12/15/1947-12/20/1940

GABLE

C. E. (Bit) 1914-1963
Russell G. 1919-
J. R. died 1882

E. M. 1845-1904

GADDIS

Fred A., GA, PFC, Co. A,. 35 Inf., 25, Inf. Div., Vietnam 2/22/1945-11/4/1966

GEORGE

W. J. 1897-1962
Mattie E. 1894-

ZION BAPTIST CHURCH, BRASELTON, GA.
Junction of Interstate #85, off Hwy 53, on a county road. (Established 1843)

GRIER

Charlie J. 11/19/1877-1/5/1957
Hoke Smith 9/12/1907-12/21/1944
Birt 7/5/1882-4/16/1936
Mary I. 5/19/1851-11/18/1932
Joseph 1/10/1844-8/17/1920 "A Soldier of the Confederacy"

HARRIS

Hoke S. 2/26/1907-9410-8

HARRISON

Julious died 3/20/1907, aged 67 years

HARTLEY

Joe 8/11/1918-5/15/1919

HAYES

Maybell S. 6/25/1880
Dan I. 1/8/1877-3/30/1936

HOLLAND

Mary A. Hudson 1899-1919

Lillian M. Moon 1881-1919
Andrew Russell 1879-1965

John Henry Maefield 10/4/1866-1/15/1913, aged 47 years, 3 months, 11 days
Mollie 11/15/1867-5/21/1927

Joseph Henry 7/23/1849-8/22/1917
Mrs. J. H. 6/14/1849-44/19/1914
Chrissey Adeline, daughter of J. H. & N. D. 12/22/1869-6/14/1875

Dora Davis 1884-1951

J. William 1877-1950
Infant of Mr. & Mrs. J. W., born 1/2/1901
Infants of Mr. & Mrs. J. W. 8/13/1902-8/20 & 8/23/1902

S. M.

ZION BAPTIST CHURCH, BRASELTON, GA.
Junction of Interstate #85, off Hwy 53, on a county road. (Established 1843)

HOLLAND

Mary Ann

James Marion 1/23/1853-9/3/1856

HOGAN

Infant of I. T. & S. A. Born and died 8/19
W. T., son of I. T. & S. A. 11/22/1898-1899

HOLEAD

Eliza Emeline, daughter of J. H. & N. B. 12/21/18 -7/2/1886

HUDGINS

Beverly P. 1/11/1851-2/22/1915

IRVIN

Ava 1888-1931
Marshal 1874-1939
Lula H. 8/21/1875-7/5/1962
Charlie 2/27/1867-11/9/1918
George, husband of Eveline 10/5/1826-5/6/1909

ISAM

Delay, son of George Thomas & Sallie Johnson Isam 1884-1885
Jane Cosby 1828-1906

IVEY

George L. 1878-1959
Minnie A. 1886-1957

JACKSON

Charles Richard 10/25/1930-11/16/1968

ZION BAPTIST CHURCH, BRASELTON, GA.
Junction of Interstate #85, off Hwy 53, on a county road. (Established 1843)

JAMES

Henrietta 7/28/1880-8/8/1955
John L. 11/27/1868-1/19/1919
Jewell 6/30/1913-3/19/1934
Jesse E. 4/10/1898-12/11/1939
Jane E., daughter of Mr. & Mrs. John 6/19/1917-7/20/1917

JOHNSON

William Early 9/21/1893-9/9/1933
Annie C. 1866-1912
William C. 1866-1951
W. F. died 7/17/1895

Martha Anne, wife of Alexander 5/14/1829-5/6/1909
Alexander 2/17/1834-2/25/1886

Vera Mae 1914-1955
Freeman 1888 -
Louella 1892-1944
Paul Henry, infant son of Ralph and Nell 3/27/1951-4/11/1951
Ruby Davis 6/15/1907-
Ellis 7/12/1903-12/27/1965
Ellis R., son of Mr. & Mrs. Ellis 2/12/1933-3/3/1933

KENNEDY

Infant daughter of Mr. & Mrs. Howard 10/22/1931

KILEY

Jesse N. 1898-1961
Bertha B. 1905-
Clifford M., Ga, Pvt.210 Field Arty Bn, World War II 9/26/1926-1/5/1946

LANCASTER

Hannah H. 8/12/1803-12/27/1881
John 6/9/1804-6/24/1864

N. W. 10/5/1839-12/19/1907

ZION BAPTIST CHURCH, BRASELTON, GA.
Junction of Interstate #85, off Hwy 53, on a county road. (Established 1843)

LANCASTER

Parsada, wife of N. W., died 12/3/1892, aged 62 years

LUTHER

Henry A. 1889-1928
Maudie I. 1897 -

MADDOX

Charley 1879-1955
Julia A. 1879-1948

Margaret C. 1857-1941
John W. 1857-1944

MARLOW

Infant of D. J. & Emma died 1/13/1897

MAULDIN

Clarence L. 1905-1956

MOON

Georgia A. 1868-1927
William J. 1866-1931

Thomas J. 6/14/1841-11/30/1903
Ella D. 3/9/1844-3/18/1930

MORRISON

Annie P., wife of James 8/13/1869-2/6/1896, aged 26 years, 6 months

MUNDY

Z. T. 5/25/1847-11/28/1904
Isabelle Robert died 7/22/1952, aged 83 years

ZION BAPTIST CHURCH, BRASELTON, GA.
Junction of Interstate #85, off Hwy 53, on a county road. (Established 1843)

McEVER

Julia 7/11/1875-7/4/1936
C. C. 9/22/1873

Infant of Mr. & Mrs. R. B. born and died 2/9/1921
Fred 11/7/1898-10/6/1941
Lyman B. 7/1/1896-10/7/1945
Lillie M. 9/16/1897
Cora E. 1888-1962
Joe D. 1878-1949
A. R. 1/1/1854-1/26/1912

Andrew 10/1/1818-4/19/1890
Sallie Boyd, wife of Andrew, died 10/1874

Alis Cleo, daughter of P. A. & Laura 3/9/1895-11/25/1900

Walter W. 8/25/1895-5/27/1964
Minnie Craft 12/3/1895
William W. 11/10/1872 -
Ellen Roberts 12/21/1873-7/27/1930
Mary Haynes, wife of A. R. 8/22/1865-3/16/1924
Hugh 10/8/1891-10/14/1961
Ada M. 6/4/1894-11/11/1962
Miss Rossie Bell died 11/11/1968, aged 71
Robert A. 1866-1940
Laura S. 1871-1933
Annie E. 7/17/1901-12/15/1924
Caldonia, wife of John F. 8/26/1844-1/3/1919
J. F. 8/31/1844-10/14/1899

Joseph C. 10/2/1854-12/23/1906
Sarah Bell, wife of Joseph C. 9/26/1861-10/19/1936

Thomas E. 9/15/1893-12/28/1893
Joseph C. 1/13/1892-7/26/1892

Amanda, wife of J. D. 2/11/1811-1/21/1887
J. D. 8/4/1809-11/15/1872

W. T. 1/25/1832-4/22/1862
Sarah J. 1/24/1869-8/21/1948
Nicy J. 2/17/1839-3/23/1936
J. M. 10/12/1846-9/24/1915
Sallie White, wife of A. R., 5/8/1858-10/22/1887

ZION BAPTIST CHURCH, BRASELTON, GA.
Junction of Interstate #85, off Hwy 53, on a county road. (Established 1843)

NEAL

Augusta Ann, daughter of Mr. & Mrs. James T 8/4/1881-7/15/1897

OWEN

Barbara Sue 6/7/1947-8/2/1966

POTTS

Little Potts, infant son of Scina Barnett 10/5/1896-2/26/1897

QUEEN

Minnter Juel, daughter of S. J. & E. V. 10/29/1902-2/8/1903

RANDOLPH

Mollie, daughter of Mr. & Mrs. J. H. C. 10/13/1875-8/15/1876
Mrs. J. H. C. 11/16/1852-3/4/1916
J. H. C. 8/7/1847-4/22/1919

H. J. 9/15/1811-4/16/1887
Eliza, wife of H. J. 3/12/1816-5/29/1900

Hilliard J. 10/14/1886-8/24/1914

W. R. 8/2/1807-4/30/1861

REED

H. Grady 8/8/1896-11/11/1960
Dora I. 3/26/1895-4/8/1962

RICHARDSON

Infant of J. M. & N. C. 11/18/1905-1/7/1906

ROBERTS

W. J. 2/12/1831-8/5/1910
Georgia Ann Winston, wife of W. J., 12/17/1839-4/10/19--

ZION BAPTIST CHURCH, BRASELTON, GA.
Junction of Interstate #85, off Hwy 53, on a county road. (Established 1843)

RODGERS

W. M., wife of J. W. 5/10/1870-4/16/1894

ROUSE

Mattie E. 3/1/1895-12/24/1968

SAILORS

Cora 7/15/1895-5/1/1896

SALORS

Curtis C., son of C. C. & Ida 9/19/1909-6/13/1910

SHED

J. J., Sr. 3/28/1830-2/20/1907

SKELTON

Sarah E. 6/14/1832-2/4/1912, aged 79 years, 7 months, 20 days
G. W. 9/29/1865-2/4/1921, married to Tinie Murphy in 1888
W. J. 3/14/1833-11/20/1894
Mary Ann 5/21/1868-12/23/1942

SKELTON

Spurgeon 4/1/1903-12/18/1966
Eunice May 8/4/1896-1/25/1917

SMITH

J. R. died 9/1/1879
Lula Elizabeth, wife of S. P., 4/8/1877-9/22/1908
Milton 8/13/1870-5/3/1917
Venie, wife of A. E., 12/8/1866-4/21/1906
Lenora, daughter of G. M. & L. G. 1/15/1901-2/20/1901
H. N.
J. W.
Dee, son of J. H. 10/3/1887-12/8/1909

J. H. 3/23/1842-1/10/1917
J. Almond, son of Mr. & Mrs. H. C. 3/19/1916-5/27/1917
Cordelia, wife of A. N. 12/20/1845-10/7/1899

ZION BAPTIST CHURCH, BRASELTON, GA.
Junction of Interstate #85, off Hwy 53, on a county road. (Established 1843)

SMITH

Mittian Lola, daughter of Mr. & Mrs. J. H. 6/21/1879-6/13/1903
Antine, wife of A. N. 2/27/1832-7/11/1881
William P. (Baby)

SPAIN

Cynthia A. 9/24/1871-10/5/1925
Adeline 10/1835-12/20/1894
Roseller, daughter of Mr. & Mrs. F. A. 8/7/1909-12/19/191-
Thomas A. 8/7/1862-12/15/1943

SPEALMAN

Mary Antionette 6/4/1830-8/12/1907
Angel D. 2/20/1867-4/11/1921

SPRUELL

John W. 1/1/1836-11/6/1910

STEPHENS

Miss Julia 1901-1962
Levie E. 1874-1954
Joe W. 1873-1935

STEPHENS

Ray J. 12/29/1935-11/15/1953
Nolan, baby of Mr. & Mrs. Ellis 8/22/1833-10/21/1933
John Newton 1870-1951
Nancy Ann 1875-1952
Annie, daughter of Mr. & Mrs. J. N. 8/21/1908-5/17/1933
Etta J. 8/14/1965

Brisey A. White, wife of J. A. 5/9/1844-10/7/1931
Joseph A. 4/13/1842-9/13/1926
Julie E. Vaughlin 8/12/1887-10/3/1891

ZION BAPTIST CHURCH, BRASELTON, GA.
Junction of Interstate #85, off Hwy 53, on a county road. (Established 1843)

STEWART

Cammie A. 6/26/1887-3/27/1878
William Ed 3/27/1878-4/7/1952

STRANGE

John G. 3/15/1843-1/11/1875
Mary J. 10/3/1839-12/3/1886
Martha, wife of J. W. 9/25/1830-10/14/1903

THURMOND

Samuel Preston 2/16/1880-8/16/1929
Sarah Ella 2/24/1878-5/15/1962
Franklin W. 10/1/1913

TITSHAW

Little Mollie died 6/25/1879, aged 11 months
F. B. 1880-1881
S. W. & Mary A., infants who died 3/6/1879
J. T., son of E. M., 2/1/1908-3/6/1918
Fannie M. 1868-1942
James T. 1871-1949

TITSHAW

Serena, wife of L. W. C. 8/31/1836-10/8/1903

VAUGHN

Logan, son of Mr. & Mrs. W. A. 5/24/1897-7/10/1897
Albert, son of Mr. & Mrs. W. A. 10/11/1899-2/18/1900

VEAL

Virginia Elizabeth 9/29/1822-2/16/1925

VIDICE

George 1861-1865

ZION BAPTIST CHURCH, BRASELTON, GA.
Junction of Interstate #85, off Hwy 53, on a county road. (Established 1843)

WADDELL

James F. 7/1/1864-8/15/1930
Mollie, wife of J. F., 4/28/1872-6/26/1913
James A., Ga., Pvt. Base Hosp 110, World War I 7/1/1892-9/18/1959
Johnson, Infant son of C. E. & S. L. 9/12/1913-9/19/1913
Dursor, son of C. E. & S. L. 9/11/1892-6/26/1906
Ned, son of C. E. & S. L. 6/1/1899-8/4/1899
Lucille, daughter of C. E. & S. L. 8/4/1900-6/21/1905

WALL

Martha A. 1870-1944
H. Thomas 1877-1940

WATSON

R. L. 2/21/1867-12/5/1906
J. D. M. 1880 -
Jessie M., wife of J. H. 9/19/1836-12/24/1893

WEATHERLY

Frederick Elma 1880-1841
Ella Davis 3/25/1887-10/20/1964

WEATHERLY

Davis C., Jr., Capt., USMC 1939-1967
Davis C., Sr. 1914-1946

WHITE

Andrew Jackson A. 5/8/1863-10/7/1887

Polly Chamblee, wife of John 8/25/1819-1/31/1909
John Sr. 1/12/1812-3/12/1898
T. W. 3/7/1837-9/23/1913
Emma R., wife of T. W. 12/18/1840-8/17/1903

Hillie J. White 8/13/1878-3/28/1915
Nicie, daughter of T. W. & E. R. 11/5/1859-12/11/1860

ZION BAPTIST CHURCH, BRASELTON, GA.
Junction of Interstate #85, off Hwy 53, on a county road. (Established 1843)

WHITE

June W. 1899-1936
Thomas W. 1869-1941
Lucious 1911-1940
Joshua 4/22/1871-1/31/1924
Rillam 1875-1964
Nancy Mae 12/10/1873-2/6/1934

WILSON

Effie W., aged 72, died 11/24/1962
Paul 6/11/1938, aged 61, 2 months, 13 days

WOOD

Dee 6/6/1885-7/11/1968
Lillie J. 4/1/1890
Henry M., Sr. 1903-1958
Ruth Sykes 1902-1952

GALILEE CHRISTIAN CHURCH
6 miles from Jefferson, Ga (County Road Proceeds East after Hwy #124 ends)

ADAIR

Henry B.
9/4/1880-1/22/1912

Alice E.
3/26/1883-10/10/1911

Baby Annie Sue, daughter of H. B. & A. E., 9/8/1911-2/28/1912

ADAMS

Joseph 3/11/1814-3/7/1901
Caroline 10/2/1820-3/7/1901

J. Parks 6/5/1859-4/11/1941

J. T. , Jr. 5/17/1912-5/16/1919
Mary A., wife of J. T. 5/10/1860-11/25/1917

GALILEE CHRISTIAN CHURCH
6 miles from Jefferson, Ga (County Road Proceeds East after Hwy #124 ends)

ADAMS

J. Summie 11/19/1887-1/13/1964
Mattie A. 9/2/1856-2/12/1940
Ammar B. 9/23/1890-7/6/1965
Children of Parker & Mollie:
Infant son 4/23/1887-4/24/1887
Carrie 12/22/1890-10/14/1891
Clinton 7/26/1892-10/10/1896

ALEXANDER

Joe W. 1891-1935
Martha E. 1918-1929
Ella Freeman 4/28/1893
Russel 10/20/1925-10/20/19255
Jack 6/4/1917-10/15/1917

ANDERSON

Sarah F. 1935-1935
Annie J. 1936-1939

ANGLIN

Mary B. 12/7/1855-10/10/1937
James R. 6/4/1852-8/28/1929
Infant daughter of W. H. & M. D., born & died 10/31/1913

Darline S. 1/9/1897-1/20/1965
Willie H. 1/15/1891-11/1/1949

ARMSTRONG

Martin 10/7/1825-3/8/1896

BALEY

Mrs. Almar

BANKS

Ella E. 1896-1954
Hester V. 1894-19

GALILEE CHRISTIAN CHURCH
6 miles from Jefferson, Ga (County Road Proceeds East after Hwy #124 ends)

BLACKMON

Myrtle M., Elder
8/8/1897-5/15/1948

BLANKENSHIP

Donnie died 6/7/1966, aged 15 years

BONE

Homer 10/29/1910
Hilda E. 7/21/1920
Infant son of Mr. & Mrs. Homer 12/4/1937

BOON

Ratliff H. 6/1834-10/1879
Priscilla S. 8/1841-8/1895
Infants of R. C. & A., born and died 7/18/1907
Infant of Mr. & Mrs. R. C., 1/10/1909-2/8/1907

Edith 3/3/1907-10/25/1909

BOONER

Infants of Mr. & Mrs. Joe : Curley 4/3/1900 -Johney 1/27/1906

BONNER

Dollie 3/31/1911-9/4/1911

BROWN

Lillian A. 1926-1934

BRUCE

Roy 10/4/1906-1/8/1907

BULLARD

Nora 6/6/1905-2/10/1968

BURK

Hushel 9/11/1916-8/30/1921

GALILEE CHRISTIAN CHURCH
6 miles from Jefferson, Ga (County Road Proceeds East after Hwy #124 ends)

BURKE

Furd 12/10/1901-8/17/1921

BURRELL

Mary Louise 12/30/1933-1/31/1934
Andy L. 4/17/1905-4/9/1936

CANUP

Jessie L., daughter of Mr. & Mrs. H. L., 5/12/1922-5/23/1925

CARITHERS

Mrs. Clara Bell died 12/16/1968

CARRUTH

Bob Anthony 10/1/1954-10/1/1954

CHRISTIAN

A. C. 2/11/1844-3/4/1928
Sophie E., daughter of W. D. & M. E. Shields 1/23/1859-6/22/1901

COLEMAN

Clifford L. 2/14/1872-5/23/1929
William S. 2/1/1860-10/1/1934

COUCH

Esbon 4/8/1947, aged 16

DIAL

Lucy V. 10/7/1884-1/11/1931
Joseph S. 6/10/1997-3/31/1906

W. M. 7/2/1852-7/2/1927
Nancy F. Archer 4/20/1854-5/9/1911
Sarah Lucille, daughter of C. I. & Margaret 10/6/1914-9/3/1916

GALILEE CHRISTIAN CHURCH
6 miles from Jefferson, Ga (County Road Proceeds East after Hwy #124 ends)

DODD

Marcus M. 186-19
Nora N. 1888-1958
Johnie A., son of M. W. & M. N. 1912-1914

DUKE

C. D. (Deck) 1883-1958
Fannie J. 1885-19

ELDER

James C. 1922-1923

Elmer H. 9/30/1897-10/15/1952
Baby twins of Mr. & Mrs. E. H. -Martha & May, 6/6/1926

Eddie D. 1882-1933
George Knox 6/9/1854-12/4/1931
Susan Kittle 12/10/1857-7/18/1929
Nathan 11/17/1851-2/13/1929
America A. 1/12/1863-5/13/1950
Hettie, daughter of Mr. & Mrs. N. T. 3/14/1895-3/26/1896
Stephen, son of Mr. & Mrs. N. T. 9/24/1882-8/26/1883
Emma H. 1858-1898
J. Sidney 1849-1919
Ola 1886-1909
Beulah 1892-1911

Melvin C. 1892-1968, Ga, Pvt, 157 Depot Brigade, WW I, 4/24/1892-1/8/1968
Dr. John G. 1866-1921
Omer G. 1/18/1899-6/19/1900
Eula M. 4/10/1901-8/24/1902
J. Louis, son of G. K. 4/29/1887-10/18/1897

Lucy A. 9/5/1829-10/12/1894
John L. 9/18/1826-8/25/1889

Bertha Estelle 10/29/1885-1/17/1939
George Clifford 6/2/1881
Woodie Lee died 1/24/1913, aged 24 years
Infant 1915-1915
Infant 1945
Ernest E., son of Mr. & Mrs. D. O., 11/17/1892-9/16/1899
Sarah E. 1/12/1856-12/1/1931
David O. 6/2/1856-2/24/1930

GALILEE CHRISTIAN CHURCH
6 miles from Jefferson, Ga (County Road Proceeds East after Hwy #124 ends)

FITE

Infant son of Mr. & Mrs. H. S., born and died 11/23/1911
Henry Solomon 11/18/1883-6/13/1953

FIEVET

Mrs. M. E. 11/24/1856-10/7/1888

FINCH

Corine Shields 9/9/1911-8/26/1967
Thomas A. 8/31/1903-10/25/1964
Hoke S. 1/26/1909-
Mrs. Alma V. 11/7/1879-3/3/1915

FINTE

Carl Griffin 11/5/1882-3/6/1968

FREEMAN

Infant J. B. 1912-1913
Julius O. 4/5/1883-4/18/1918
Lula P. 1872-1939
Mozelle L., daughter of J. O. & Nettie 7/14/1909-7/1/1911
Emory 1895-1960
Nettie H. 2/6/1886-11/22/1967
Ada, wife of A. 2/4/1878-4/9/1897
John R. 11/16/1916-6/25/1918
Earley P. 5/11/1850-11/20/1933
Alice, daughter of Earley 11/29/1873-1/3/1955
Luther C. 1892-1962
Infant of Luther and Bertha
Louisa Neal, wife of William 12/10/1832-1/31/1915
Charles 1860-1941
Sadie Dell 1899-1910
Mollie 1864-1937
L. J. 1856-1920
Ruby M. 1934-
Alba 9/19/1871-5/28/1897
Cynthia S. 10/29/1852-7/4/1948
Sgt. W. Donald 1914-1944
Ruby Hanson, wife of A. Luther 1897-1930
Infant
Laura 1857-1890

GALILEE CHRISTIAN CHURCH
6 miles from Jefferson, Ga (County Road Proceeds East after Hwy #124 ends)

FREEMAN

Charles V. 1912-1967
Mell, daughter of Louisa N. 4/5/1861-4/16/1904

GRIFFIN

Edith L. 11/10/1915-9/19/1940
Infant son of G. W. & N. D. , born and died 4/13/1880
James L. 12/20/1885-12/23/1885
Alma M. 1892-
George Washington 8/10/1853-5/16/1936
Lucy E. 2/28/1891-6/17/1895
Nancy Davis Elder 4/9/1858-11/26/1931
Inus Edmond, son of G. W. & N. O., 11/19/1887-12/29/1901

GOLIA

James C. 12/29/1945

HALL

James 1/29/1884-2/16/1928

HAMMOND

James A., son of L. & Delia 11/8/1925-6/1/1930

HEARN

Elizabeth G. 1885-12/31/1892
Mary Lena, daughter of J. J. & M. L. 6/22/1900-6/19/1902

HINSON

Newton O. 1872-1951

HOPKINS

Kate Elder 9/3/1885-7/7/1944
Robert E. 5/9/1875-7/16/1926

JACKS

Willie N. 2/1/1878-6/24/1922
Herbert P. 1871-1925

GALILEE CHRISTIAN CHURCH
6 miles from Jefferson, Ga (County Road Proceeds East after Hwy #124 ends)

JACKS

Lunie Sheffield 5/23/1885-8/18/1963
Lena 1/31/1907
Lucy W. 1884-1953

JOHNSON

Nancy A. 6/5/1839-2/4/1927
Vinnie L. 2/16/1897-2/3/1899
J. C. 2/7/1914-9/3/1915

Leila 1875-1931
Fred, son of J. D. & Leila 8/26/1896-10/26/1919

Carlton E. 7/15/1881-10/22/1961
Resha 1883-1957
Safronia 6/17/1866-11/29/1899

Hattie 1878-1919
Farrie 6/26/1896-7/29/1896
Parilee 3/15/1901-7/26/1902
Joe A. 11/20/1914-12/16/1959
Roberta 10/23/1910-4/5/1916
Thomas S. 7/12/1853-7/8/1938
J. Monroe 9/22/1874-3/19/1900
Carey M. 1861-1942
J. D. (Matt) 1855-1936
J. A. 8/5/1879-6/15/1940
Henry G. 1883-1939
Nancey E. 11/28/1858-12/15/1936

JONES

J. T. 4/3/1898-5/21/1901

KESLER

Leota 7/17/1929-12/18/1932
Henry B. 5/21/1896-2/13/1960

KIZE

Eutha, daughter of A. D. & Lona 1/4/1921-11/18/1923

GALILEE CHRISTIAN CHURCH
6 miles from Jefferson, Ga (County Road Proceeds East after Hwy #124 ends)

LAMAR

Philip L. 11/14/1826-9/3/1878
Muller B., son of P. F. & Julia D. 6/18/1871-3/5/1896

MARTIN

Levi G. 1849-1885
Beatrice, daughter of Mr. & Mrs. H. L., 6/11/1917-11/4/1918
Elizabeth McCarty, wife of Malachi 1815-1891

MAULDIN

L. W. 10/22/1880-10/1/1952
Dora M. 1882-1957

MAXWELL

H. Douglas 1905-1959

McELHANNON

William Andrew, son of J. M. & M. H., 1/1/1883-1/19/1895
Martha Shields 1860-1942
John Monroe 1855-1931

MIZE

Joseph died 6/26/1925
Inez 1902-1914
Robert F. 1880-
Cora Lee 1900-1902

NIX

Howard M. 3/7/1919-3/11/1942
Infant son of Howard M. 4/25/1941
Infant son of Howard M. 4/16/1939
Jesse H., Ga Pvt. 36 Co. 157 Depot Brigade WW I 1/2/1895-2/19/1958
Joe W. 1903-1958
Martha A. 1909-

O'DILLON

Lillie Elder 1889-1950
James A. 1889-1919

GALILEE CHRISTIAN CHURCH
6 miles from Jefferson, Ga (County Road Proceeds East after Hwy #124 ends)

PATTON

Robert L., Jr. 1911-1932
Robert L. 1865-1951
Amanda A. 1874-1962

PORTER

William T. Died 1/1/1953, aged 82 years
Lena Mae, daughter of Mr. & Mrs. W. T. 10/24/1906-2/19/1912
Infant daughter of Mr. & Mrs. W. T. 8/24/1904
Infant son of Arthur N. & Ora B. 8/29/1908
Anna V., wife of J. H., 2/10/1871-1/22/1896

QUEEN

E. C. 5/20/1839-10/23/1904

RAIDEN

Docia F. 12/5/1869-7/15/1920
George B. 6/13/1870-11/11/1939

RAVENDER

Edna Mae, wife of J. L., 1893-1937

ROBERTS

Ellie May, daughter of Mr. & Mrs. R. L. 5/6/1909-8/8/1910
A. Scott 1884-1919
Essie E. 18887-1968
Infant 1912

SELF

Floella G. 10/28/1915
Lee Earnest 9/1/1934-4/5/1962

SHIELDS

Ola F. 8/2/1902-3/28/1925
Helen Anice 98/1905-6/19/1945
Sarah J. 6/14/1854-11/28/1916
Joseph R. 6/23/1856-2/2/1904
Infant son of J. T. & E. S., born and died 2/4/1893

GALILEE CHRISTIAN CHURCH
6 miles from Jefferson, Ga (County Road Proceeds East after Hwy #124 ends)

SHIELDS

Infant son of Mr. & Mrs. W. S. 4/16/1920
Emory H. 9/30/1874-11/27/1944
James T. 11/5/1852-4/5/1916
Lilly Alice 9/14/1877-7/9/1925
Emma S. 9/19/1873-2/15/1960
J. C. 9/14/1924-2/10/1938
A. S. 1868-1937
Annie Elder 9/1/1889

SIKES

Joe Talmadge 11895-8/11/1965
Exa F. 1890-1960

SWAN

Charlie V. 5/9/1879-6/24/1949
Corrie F. 5/15/1889-6/22/1940

TUCK

Lucile, daughter of Dr. J. A. & Neva 7/11/1891-3/20/1893
James M. 1869-1945
Lucy E. 1875-

VENABLE

Walter L. 1880-1956
Ethel 1884-

WHITE

Eula M. 1884-1934
Robert J. 1882-1934
Reba, daughter of R. J. & Eula 10/16/1905-7/17/1924

WHITEHEAD

Lizzie Wood 7/24/1887-12/7/1964
Stephen Theo. 11/15/1915-2/17/1918

GALILEE CHRISTIAN CHURCH
6 miles from Jefferson, Ga (County Road Proceeds East after Hwy #124 ends)

WILLS

J. W., Sr. 1885-1863
J. W., Jr. 1913-1944
W. M. 1/30/1881-12/14/1899
Lizzie 1860-1946

WILSON

Jessie Knight, wife of John L., 7/19/1862-3/5/1934
Martha J. 1848-1924
L. C. 6/17/1848-11/14/1916

WOOD

Cornelia A. died 3/12/1901
Green L. Died 12/17/1912, aged 74 years
James M. 1855-1921
Julia E. 1869-1962
Jeff, son of Mr. & Mrs. J. C., 10/15/1884-6/20/1886
Mary E., wife of J. G. 8/29/1855-7/2/1888

Maude J. 5/30/1888-
W. Tom 6/1/1889-8/31/1964
Dewitt 1/5/1912-10/16/1928
Mary A., wife of J. W. 10/8/1853-7/12/1921

Annie W. 1879-
James R., Co. C., 16 Ga. Inf., C. S. A.
Minnie Bell, daughter of R. L. & Maude, died 7/27/1902, aged 1 year
Julia 7/31/1848-11/12/1928
Marshall 1874-1913
J. W. 5/12/1856-12/8/1891
Mollie 5/14/1844-6/27/1929

YEARWOOD

George A. 4/10/1867-2/8/1897
Little A. T., son of W. C. & Lizzie 8/8/1896-8/21/1896

SHOCKLEY-PENDERGRASS FAMILY CEMETERY
Highway #124, Jefferson, Georgia (Easterly)

HOLDER

Ina Oblevia, daughter of T. R. & M. A. 2/16/1870-5/4/1871

JARRETT

3 infants of T. W. & Irene

PENDERGRASS

Nathaniel H. 10/24/1807-6/30/1879
Martha E., wife of N. H., born 7/10/1820, married 5/7/1838, died 6/21/1874
William Lane 8/13/1846-8/14/1870

ROBERTS

Miss Emily 10/27/1837-5/31/1917

SHOCKLEY

Irene 3/15/1815-1/23/1875
Sallie 1850
C. P. 9/7/1851-9/27/1922

HOWARD FAMILY CEMETERY
Highway #124 East, Jefferson, Ga.

Lola Fleeman 11/14/1872-8/31/1936
Robert Lee 5/17/1865-11/25/1929

Martha E., wife of Homer R., 1/25/1837-3/4/1910
Capt. Homer R. 12/10/1829-3/28/1903

Booge 1860-1934
Frank 1875-1927

Maebell 1892-
H. Thomas 1889-1954

HOWARD FAMILY CEMETERY
Highway #124 East, Jefferson, Ga.

HOWARD

Mrs. Almedia Carruth 9/23/1966, aged 65 years, 8 months, 22 days
Maude L. 12/28/1874-9/22/1960
J. Oscar 11/24/1866-12/22/1949

HOWARD FAMILY CEMETERY
Highway #124 East, Jefferson, Ga.

HOWARD

James Walter, Sr. 9/20/1867-4/2/1942
Ruth Jeanette 2/14/1890-3/15/1964
Beatrice 8/2/1918-7/7/1919
Sallie A. 1860-1956
Zack T. 1855-1930

HUFF

Mattie E. Howard 9/9/1885-1/8/1937

LUND

Agnes Cameron 2/21/1868-6/6/1933

WHITE PLAINS BAPTIST CHURCH, Braselton

ADKINS

Jay, Ga, AAOAM U. S. Navy 6/30/1935-3/9/1961

ALLEN

Eliza Skelton 1886-1942
Carlton Columbus 1885-1934

ANDERSON

Jack, Ga Pvt. Btry B, 29 Fld Arty BN 9/11/1911-7/18/1967
Ja. A. 8/1/1863-7/28/1931

ANGLIN

Clarence 9/17/1875-9/17/1957
Mellie 11/1/1890
Mrs. Ophelia 1838-1914

BANKS

P. F. C. Darrell Edge 5/6/1925-7/12/1944
Kateria Ann 7/17/1932-6/25/1934

BARRY

Diane, wife of Mr. & Mrs. Thomas 11/6/1951

WHITE PLAINS BAPTIST CHURCH, Braselton

BIRT

Master Billy 2/23/1957

BOONE, William Gilbert 3/16/1894-1/19/1962

BANNER

Shella Jeane 9/8/1938

BROOKS

E. D. 1923-1955
Gladys 1930-
Dorothy Ann died 4/21/1950
Evelyn Elain died 6/25/1948, aged 9
Joe Ira 4/26/1906-8/31/1966
Blondell H. 7/13/1908-8/31/1966

BROWN

J. H. 2/13/1858-2/20/1927
M. C. 1884-1941
Annie 1890-1966
Omie 1890-1966
Andrey, daughter of M. N. & A. B. 10/18/1920-12/16/1920
Ernest Harold, PFC Infantry WW II 12/14/1920-5/15/1963
Gladys D. 4/6/1912
May Ramsey 1913-1933
Mary A. 2/15/1855-9/13/1926
J. H. 2/13/1858-2/20/1927

BRYAN

J. R. 9/30/1847-5/9/1922
Nancy, wife of J. R., 2/14/1850-4/23/1925
Noah J. 1881-1852
Dora S. 1884-19

BRYANT

Rev. Wince 1887-1963
Jane 1894-1968
C. H. 3/21/1906
Caldoney 5/2/1914-4/29/1946
Martha J. Skelton, wife of W. B. 1879-1930
Dennis H. 11/10/1952-12/27/1953
Charlie 1869-1959

WHITE PLAINS BAPTIST CHURCH, Braselton

BRYANT

Julian P. 1878-19

CAIN

Hilda Grace 9/6/1948-6/11/1949

CAMPBELL

Rev. C. L. 1903-
Annie M. 1904-1963

CHILDERS

Lon F. 1875-1954
Goldie F. 1891-1968
Tom C. 1893-1/11/1968
Master Ted died 2/23/1968, 2 days

CHOCRAN

Amanda 1871-1844
J. Matt 1865-1944

COOPER

Thomas D. 1952
Hazel P. 8/4/1922-9/6/1965
J. E. (June) 1901-1957
Flora S. 1903-

CRONIE

Mrs. Joan Lavery 1949-1968

DOSTER

Clyde 1906-1963
Melvie 1909-
Mary E. 10/19/1858-8/24/1930
J. A. 3/1/1857
David L. 1878-1943
Neta C. 1880-1952
John L., Ga., Pvt. Med Dept. 6/3/1940
Henry Albert 6/27/1881-11/15/1924
Ida K. 1878-1957
William P. 1879-1955
Bart 1907-1958

WHITE PLAINS BAPTIST CHURCH, Braselton

DOSTER

R. Frank 1939-1964
Eli F., PFC 74 Gen. Hosp. WW II 3/28/1905-8/8/1955
James J. 1874-1953
Essie B. 1892
William H. F., Ga. PFC 115 Inf. 29 Inf. Div WWII 4/11/1922-8/4/1944
David L. 1878-1943
Neta C. 1880-1952

EVANS

David L. 1914-1969
Raymond 1898-1963
Ella F. 1898-19
Ellaease, daughter of Mr. & Mrs. Raymond 1926-1926
Hubert H. 1932-1966
Curtis E. 11/12/1910-7/8/1930
Calr

Carlton H. 1891-1955
Mollie R. 1893-1960
J. W. 8/14/1867-1/20/1933
Genie 7/26/1825-4/14/1950

FIELDS

Indianna 9/1/1968-5/16/1954
Ollie E. 8/8/1889-2/2/1965
Emma R. 1850-1950
James M. 1854-1942
Ollie E. 8/8/1889-2/2/1963

FORTNER

Pink, Ga. PFC 566, AAA AW BN CAC WWII 8/30/1909-6/4/1952

FREE
Mary Brown 1864-1935

GARRETT

Millie V. 1877-1943
Grand D. 1873 -
Mary Elizabeth 3/16/1881-8/25/1960
Jud Stephens 10/26/1878-7/31/1956

WHITE PLAINS BAPTIST CHURCH, Braselton

GLAZE

Connie B. 1955-1965
M. Florence 1927-1965
Grady G. 1927-1965

GOOCH

James Douglas died 7/29/1942, aged 6 months
John Allen 1940-1969
C. E., baby died 1918

Estell H. 1/7/1896
Carl S. 7/23/1894-9/19/1957
Ethel 12/17/1916
Maynard 1/1/1908-12/9/1958
Arvey 7/16/1879-6/18/1944
J. H. 9/5/1870-1/19/1948
Desma 1/4/1911-12/15/1957
Fred 4/28/1899-12/3/1965

GRACE

Bonnie C. 5/16/1927-3/13/1967

GRIFFIN

Claude Jr. 5/2/1927

GUINN

Fannie P. 7/25/1919-8/31/1957
William E. 7/8/1919

HACKETT

R. Jack 5/16/1948-3/28/1965

HALL

Ricky G. 12/13/1953-4/20/1967

HAMILTON

Infant daughter of Mr. & Mrs. Royce 1/27/1955

HAMMOND

Alvin Bryant 8/9/1950-8/10/1950

WHITE PLAINS BAPTIST CHURCH, Braselton

HAWKINS

Mattie 8/13/1885-11/14/1955
James B. 10/25/1861-19
Mary W. 10/4/1864-9/7/1929

HAYS

Infant daughter of D. E. & T. B. 1924

HEALAN

Donald Devins 1943-1946
H. William 1888-1963
Little Billy 8/21/1924-11/9/1936
Infant son of Mr. & Mrs. Royce 6/1/1949
H. William 1888-1963
Dovie S. 1891-

HOGAN

Lucy 1860-1940
C. A. 1/23/1858-6/26/1949
I. T. 2/23/1857-11/16/1933
C. D., wife of D. E., 7/26/1888-5/27/1924
W. E. (Dock) 1886-1945
E. M. 11/17/1875-9/12/1928
Dora D. 10/8/1884-5/2/1967
Willie J., son of Mr. & Mrs. W. T., 9/3/1933-10/16/1933
D. C. 1893-1966
Lilla M. 1898-1935

HOLDER

Grady Ben, son of Mr. & Mrs. Ben 5/31/1940-5/31/1940
Doris N. 1932-1965

HUDSON

Ormie 4/4/1913-1/5/1942

HUNSINGER

Sherley Ann 7/21/1947

WHITE PLAINS BAPTIST CHURCH, Braselton

HUTSON

William A. 1883-1962
Lizzie P. 1888-19
Stephen 6/10/1950-7/21/1950

IRVIN

Alice 2/2/1887-6/22/1922
J. (Nick) 1878-19
Mattie P. 1890-19

JOHNSON

Benjamin C. 1890-19
I. Sippie C. 1888-1958

JONES

C. 1878-1959
Lola R. 1879-19--

KING

Berry 1905-1965

LANCE

Caroline 1875-1945
W. Asberry 1875-1945

LEE

George W. 8/17/1902-7/19/1953
Lula Ann 3/29/1875
Emma M. 11/1/1891-3/28/1933

MALOCH

R. C. (Pat) 1/21/1906-11/13/1951
Sadie W. 7/13/1908-1/30/1966

MARLIN
Claypus Hope 4/4/1925-1/1/1928

MARLOW

Mrs. Roxie 6/16/1865-10/19/1953

WHITE PLAINS BAPTIST CHURCH, Braselton

MARTIN

Herby 7/8/1935-11/12/1965
Emma H. 1891-19
Hollis 1886-1964

Bert 1/15/1910-11/16/1963
Joyce Ann 10/22/1954-7/21/1962
Herby 7/8/1935-11/12/1965
Guy 7/12/1912-6/1/1968

McDANIEL

Julia Marie 5/11/1964-11/7/1965

McDOUGALD

Infant son of F. J. & Eddie 5/25/1928
Eddie 1906-
Floyd 1898-1950
William J. 9/16/1875-4/25/1950
Arminda 8/26/1875-4/28/1950
Alice 10/15/1909-8/4/1919

MITCHELL

Carrie M. 1924-1965

NIX

Edd 1908-1961
Dusty 6/18/1948-7/27/1948
Jessie 1918

PEEBLES

Albert, Jr. 1914
Jazel M. 1915-1968

PHILLIPS

Eddie B. 1/27/1898-6/12/1960
Elizabeth B. 12/5/19--
Frances M. 4/20/1932
Sanford J. 5/18/1926-3/17/1966
Tommie W. 9/28/1904

WHITE PLAINS BAPTIST CHURCH, Braselton

PHILLIPS

Reba S. 7/8/1906-8/20/1968

J. Homer 1881-1958
Fannie P. 1888-19

Bustell 10/25/1909-1/1/1969
J. H., Jr. 6/19/1933-3/17/1955

James 1/10/1856-8/10/1920
Mary J. 1855-1938

Laurabell, daughter of Mr. & Mrs. Thomas 3/17/1917-5/8/1919
Charles M., son of Mr. & Mrs. Pete 1952-1953
Martha Oralee 11/12/1883-12/6/1919
Albert W. 1895-1949
Mary W. 1903-19
Frank 1/3/1890-9/4/1955
Florence S. 1882-19
Tommie G. 1886-1952

POLLARD

Darlene 1913-1961
Vennie 1872-1950
Grady 1910
B. F. 1882-1941
Infants of Mr. & Mrs. Grady

PRESSLEY

Wiley Vandiver died 9/25/1965, aged 83
Roger 1951-1957
Rachel 12/24/1867-7/1-/1953
W. D. 1861-1945
Harvey S. 12/11/1947. Aged 68
Edd 9/3/1894-11/11/1948
Ida Mae 7/31/1894-8/5/1954
Martin, Jr. 3/21/1928-12/14/1956
Betty Ann 8/26/1933

RANDALL

Charles W. 1938-1942

REYNOLDS

Jeremiah 10/2/1875-1/23/1935

WHITE PLAINS BAPTIST CHURCH, Braselton

REYNOLDS

Fannie M., born 11/8/1874

Steve 9/14/1955-5/17/1957
Helen 4/14/1933-8/23/1949

RIVES

Ava Hogan 10/7/1900-8/27/1936

ROBERTS

Susie M. 1914-
Dave 6/3/1890-1/17/1960
Maude 7/11/1901-4/21/1965
Zilly 2/14/1859-12/17/1933
George D. 1914-1945
Charlie 2/4/1868-10/9/1935
Mrs. Sarah Eliza died 1/2/1961, aged 77
Josiah 6/5/1919-10/28/1921

SANDERS

Nellie A. 1891-1966

SATTERFIELD

Parents -Clyde and Pearl
Infant son and daughter, Ann 1947, Ray, 1950
William Clyde died 5/16/1954, aged 37
Henry W. 1894-1962
Infant son of Mr. & Mrs. H. W. 1942-1942

SELF

Ina Estelle 1894-1958
Stacy M. 1857-1950, aged 93

SHELTON

Berry 3/1/1883-1/20/1933
Mary 1920-1956

SHERIDAN

Marvin 1896-
Sinthia 1902-

WHITE PLAINS BAPTIST CHURCH, Braselton

SKELTON

Berry 3/1/1883-1/20/1933
A. Virgil 1889-1967
Nancy L. 1888-1959
John H. 10/10/1881-12/13/1928
Ila 4/23/1888-2/12/1956
Mary L., wife of John H. 8/31/1885-1/6/1918
Mary J. 1858-1934
J. W. 1858-1925
James S. 1863-1937
Estell 1923-1926
James Edward, son of J. V. & Lola 5/27/1966-11/7/1966

SMALLWOOD

Mary T. 1885-
Howard R. 1903-1953
Sargeant Howard R. died in the service of his country
Ruzell 1914-

SMITH

Claude P. 8/27/1903-11/7/1939
Ethel D. 10/10/1906
Michael Eugene 5/27/1966-11/7/1966

STARGEL

Iola R. 1879-
Jones C. 1878-1959

STEPP

Julian N. 1898-1951
Ralph, son of G. L. & D. E. 4/18/1916-6/18/1917

STEPHENS

Elizabeth F. 1878-1963

STREETMAN

Thomas C. 1934-1944
N. M. 2/7/1872-11/8/1937
Guf., wife, born 9/5/1882

WHITE PLAINS BAPTIST CHURCH, Braselton

STEWART

Ransom R., husband of Louisa Stewart 7/9/1903-12/14/1920, married to Louisa Fortner on 2/16/1919

TATE

Myrtle 1/27/1901-6/16/1925
Tobe died 12/8/1935, aged 70
Alvin C. 1882-1943
Sadie P. 1878-
Melvin C. 2/15/1887-4/14/1943
Mary J. 6/24/1904-3/29/1947
Infant son, born and died 1938

TURNER

Caroline M. 1870-1949

Iva L. 1896-1966
Homer J. 1890-

TWIGGS

Artie 1908-

WADE

Marion B. 4/16/1927-9/16/1956
Marion 4/15/1876-2/15/1956
Elizabeth S. 12/26/1882-8/8/1949

Hobson M. 5/9/1901-7/25/1927
Henry D., Sr. 5/14/1905-12/11/1959
Emmie 8/13/1927-8/13/1927

WALLACE

Lizzie 1882-1937
Henry 1886-1826
Lucy Brewer 1864-
G. A. 1859-1932

WATKINS

William S. 1884-
Lillia A. 1889-1943

WHITE PLAINS BAPTIST CHURCH, Braselton

WILSON

Columbus W. 10/19/1883-10/11/1968
Nora F. 6/1/1885

WOOD

L. Hinton 3/31/1884-5/3/1939
Lenora W. 7/1/1886
PFC Guy L. Killed in France 8/5/1944, 1923-1944

GUNNIN FAMILY CEMETERY, Off Hwy #15 North, Wilson Road (First dirt road to right off Wilson Road)

GUNNIN

J. J. 9/7/1836-3/27/1901
Georgia Ann R, wife of J. J., 2/8/1845-10/19/1897

POMEROY

Richard S. 10/15/1872-12/26/1906

McLESTER FAMILY CEMETERY, Wilson Road, off Hwy #15 North

ANDERSON

Lizzie C., daughter of O. L. & Nancy 8/24/1879-11/22/1896
Maggie 6/10/1885-12/5/1896

BERRY

Mrs. W. 1842-6/8/1866

CAIN
Thomas 2/28/1829-11/11/1896

CRABLIE

Little Melvin 3/2/1881-5/6/1882

CRISLER

Addison 11/5/1820-6/16/1899

McLESTER FAMILY CEMETERY, Wilson Road, off Hwy #15 North

LANGSTON

James Odel, son of R. L. & R. R. 11/24/1890-10/4/1891

LOGGINS

Maggie Montine 8/15/1891-8/4/1900

McLESTER

James G. 1/28/1812-12/6/1889
Cynthia 1/6/1806-1/3/1886
William M. 6/6/1820-11/26/1859

MORGAN

Elizabeth H. Dunson, wife of D. D. 7/21/1863-11/2/1909

NUNN

Martha 9/11/1800-6/3/1870

ORRA

Elizabeth K. 3/15/1822-1901

PRICKETT

J. F. Morgan, son of Fay & N. C. 3/26/1862-7/23/1866

SAILORS

Marton B. 10/15/1859-3/1/1885
Little Martha J., daughter of L. M. & V. A. 8/15/1873-9/25/1873
Little James, son of L. M. & V. A. 5/22/1864-7/3/1865
Joseph E., son of J. W. & T. G. 8/13/1889-9/18/1892
Little Linton, son of J. W. & T. G. 6/14/1897-7/1/1897

SMITH

Infant boy of J. N. & A. A. 7/16/1876-7/21/1876

WILCOX

Joseph Dillard 1877-1878, aged 1 year

WILSON

Lawson born and died 1896

McLESTER FAMILY CEMETERY, Wilson Road, off Hwy #15 North

YEARGIN

Martha E., daughter of J. C. & S. J. 1856-9/1873
John J. 5/25/1839-2/24/1898

APPLE VALLEY CHURCH, Hwy #15 North

ANDERSON

Infant of M. A. & D. B. 1895

ARTHUR

Cleo, daughter of M. C. & Rosa 10/1/1892-2/13/1914
M. C. 5/3/1863-6/5/1931
Rosa Da. 9/4/1869-5/1/1950

BARNETT

Ernest born and died 5/28/1895
Bunie M. 6/19/1869-12/16/1958
John W. 11/22/1860-2/18/1934

BARRETT

Lillie M. 1907-1951
Fred R. 1900-1969
Willie A. 11/8/1876-11/25/1936
Lillie M. 1907-1951

BECK

G. M. 1880-1945
Cordile 1884-1938
Ruby E. 1925-
Betty Jean 10/1/1838-9/17/1959
Robert 4/18/1940-2/9/1955
Manda Aarzela, wife of John 3/20/1873-6/23/1924
Harold L. 1924-1960

BENNETT

Agnes, daughter of Mr. & Mrs. C. L. 3/23/1903, aged 8 days

APPLE VALLEY CHURCH, Hwy #15 North

BENTON

J. P. Jr., son of J. P. & Alice 9/19/1906-12/24/1912
Alice M. 7/11/1879-7/3/1943
J. Pope 6/28/1873-4/5/1949

Lorenzo D. 8/16/1880-1/16/1953
Estelle H. 9/14/1904
Dell Blackstock, wife of D. D. 3/27/1889-7/7/1931
James Edwin, son of Mr. & Mrs. L. D. 3/20/1912, aged 8 weeks
Mrs. R. J. 9/27/1839-7/6/1906
T. W. 9/19/1831-7/25/1936
Harold L. 8/29/1905-4/10/1951
Myrtle M. 1/30/1872-3/31/1965
Barbara 12/7/1912-4/10/1942
Willie L. 1871-1952

BORDERS

Bessie G. Newman, wife of E. H. 7/19/1879-12/11/1903

BOWLES

W. H. 1853-5/7/1913
Mary R. 10/10/1854-10/4/1947

Martha I. 1924-1924
Curtis, son of Tommie & Ethel 4/19/1922-4/25/1922
Mary L., daughter of Tommie & Ethel 10/6/1918-1/16/1919
Garnett 11/6/1891-
Callie 1/12/1888-3/31/1963
Caroline Marie 1959-1962
Clarence E. 1915-1925

BROOKS

Curtis P. 8/18/1915-2/13/1941

CHURCHWELL

Edward P. 12/31/1869-3/28/1947

COLQUITT

E. C. 1872-1936
William J. 1/13/1829-10/29/1917
Birdie H. 1879-1959
Martha S. 7/4/1836-3/4/1929

APPLE VALLEY CHURCH, Hwy #15 North

DAVIS

Martha P., wife of Ephraim 7/4/1812-2/24/1892
W. C. 12/12/1843-11/2/1924, Co. C, 18th Ga (1861-1865)
L. M. 4/27/1829-8/31/1917

DAVISON

Caroline 1833-2/1/1913

DOUGLASS

Thomas S. 4/30/1836-2/6/1895

DOWDY

Thomas R. 1899-1958

EARHART

Mrs. L. C. 12/19/1861-1/19/1897

GARRETT

Virgil 1913-1967
Laura P. 1915-
Bessie W. 1902-
Louis G. 1929-1939
James A. 1889-1951

GLENN

Buford died 4/16/1953, aged 63 years, 9 months, 12 days
Amanda A. 10/20/1866-7/9/1953
Andrew D. 11/11/1861-12/18/1947

HARDY

Mary Ann 12/17/1829-8/24/1904

HAWKINS

Athea Vernon Christian, wife of J. M., 12/8/1845-6/14/1921
John Milner 9/1/1843-11/23/1929

Thomas I. 9/27/1870-2/22/1931
Annie G. 1879-1969
Charles A. 4/30/1875-1/7/1912

APPLE VALLEY CHURCH, Hwy #15 North

HAYES

Olin H. 1898-1967
Belah W. 10/30/1875-10/29/1939
Jane Boyd 12/13/1871 -

HUNT

Cortez O. 1872-1952
Eula S. 1876-1951
Nelson P. 1907-1908
Rhoda M., wife of W. J. C., 4/24/1839-7/6/1923
W. J. C. 12/23/1836-10/14/1898
Beulah B. 4/29/1882-8/29/1958
Tuc A. 3/30/1869-12/30/1936
Etta F., wife of Tuc A. 11/13/1876-
Opal K. 1909-
Brother Lavater 1866-1947
Ethyle D. 1893-19
Rhoda Lou 1912-1915
Sister Inez 1870-1955
C. Allie 7/10/1876-4/14/1951

ISBELL

Lenton H. 12/21/1882-3/20/1952
Leon B. 8/10/1885-4/15/1945

Infant son of L. B. & Daisy, 3/13/1912-3/14/1912
Levis E. 1880-1938
Daisy 1879-1962

B. M. 2/15/1844-4/22/1891
Lou E. Shirley, wife of B. M., 5/26/1848-10/15/1919

Willie Maud 12/13/1890-9/19/1914

JACKSON

Infant daughter of John & Beaulah 9/26/1907

JENNINGS

J. E. 4/25/1882-1/24/1910
J. M. 6/15/1851-6/5/1892
Lucy V. 11/7/1855-6/25/1941

APPLE VALLEY CHURCH, Hwy #15 North

JOHNSON

Carrie B. 1/10/1910-5/28/1946

JONES

Mamie L. 1892-1954
Roy H. 1891-1957

LOVE

George D. 19-3-1966
Cora L. 1901-

MALEY

J. H. 2/16/1852-2/3/1941
Sarah A. 5/9/1849-1/21/1933

Mattie 1/21/1880-2/12/1928

MATTHEWS

William S. 1/19/1842-12/2/1925
Sarah E. Glenn, wife of William S. 11/11/1875-7/28/1937

McDONALD

Edwin A. 4/15/1850-5/31/1932
Sarah Jane Nix, wife of Edwin A., 6/15/1852-9/27/1925

Dr. Thomas J. 3/7/1877-4/10/1957
Infant of Mr. & Mrs. H. H. born and died 3/14/1909
Alvin H. 3/9/1885-3/21/1925

MINISH

Victor B. 6/1/1903-12/27/1959
Sarah P. 3/12/1905-12/14/1964

Herbert Earl 1/13/1899-9/6/1907

Tinie Benton 3/29/1871-8/2/1933
William H. 8/7/1866-10/28/1936

Mollie Lee, daughter of J. W. & M. L. 12/20/1873-1/21/1910
John W. 2/15/1839-4/4/1913
Mary Nunn, wife of John W., 2/5/1845-3/15/1931

APPLE VALLEY CHURCH, Hwy #15 North

MINISH

Clombus P. 1/22/1868-11/20/1931
Della W. 9/23/1873-3/15/1948
Norman, son of Mr. & Mrs. L. G. 12/27/1896
Cumi, daughter of L. G. 11/3/1897-8/11/1901
Carlton, son of C. P. 7/17/1899-8/3/1899
Mary E., daughter of C. P. & Della born and died 4/11/1910

L. Gratt 2/12/1876-6/20/1963
Jessie B., wife of L. G. 10/12/1875-6/19/1910
Leola M. Benton, wife of L. G. 8/24/1880-2/12/1957
Jessie Blanche, daughter of L. G. & Jessie 6/10/1910-7/27/1910

Thomas Aubrey 3/23/1900-6/30/1948
Edman B. 11/6/1918-11/21/1918

NEWMAN

Francis A., Co. A, Roswell's Ga. Cav. C. S. A.

NIX

D. M. 2/16/1847-12/30/1904
Frances R., daughter of Mr. & Mrs. D. M. 11/6/1892-11/12/1895

Dilmus H. 10/11/1882-2/1/1929
Lillian M. 7/23/1887-10/22/1951
Permelia Jane Mitchell 8/10/1849-7/3/1935

Tennelle 1905-1907
Infant son 1904
Bonnie S. 1884-1963
Robert C. 1874-1933

Dora Bennett, wife of J. M. 12/25/1866-6/2/1938
John Morgan 6/7/1862-6/2/1950
Norma Lee, daughter of J. M. & D. B. 4/27/1895-4/18/1900
Lizzie Lurene, daughter of J. M. & D. B. 12/6/1893-7/29/1935
Lucile, daughter of J. M. & D. B. 3/4/1903-12/1/1968

PARK

Hiram L. 3/4/1866-7/20/1945
Lucius 12/25/1875-5/29/1960
Icie D. 10/8/1885-
Lorenza D. 8/19/1871-10/26/1903

APPLE VALLEY CHURCH, Hwy #15 North

PARKER

Lelia Hayes 10/27/1912-5/17/1964
George N. 11/15/1905 -

POE

Paul 1893-1960
Ethel G. 1891-

POTTS

Mrs. Mary E. 1928-1968

Sumner S., son of J. D. & E. F. 11/23/1886-6/14/1910
Infant daughter of Mr. & Mrs. J. D. Potts 12/13/1907-12/19/1907

William B. 3/23/1893-11/28/1954
John D. 3/17/1858-4/2/1931

C. G. 12/11/1874-8/15/1923
Florence S. 5/15/18680-6/26/1950
Jack 5/21/1929-4/26/1952 "Lost at Sea"

PRITCHETT

William Larry, son of Mr. & Mrs. Roy 1939-1940

PRUITT

James M. 1903-1948
Mollie T. 1903-

RICHEY

Mary Etta Nix, wife of E. W. 8/18/1859-12/6/1926
E. W. P. 6/10/1852-6/24/1922
Lydia Gertrude 3/1/1879-1/11/1919

Roy V. 1890-1963

SAILORS

Bessie G. Douglas 3/3/1868-2/12/1860

SHELNUTT

Lena H. 1875-1932
William M. 1867-1951

APPLE VALLEY CHURCH, Hwy #15 North

SHIRLEY

Thurza Ann 2/28/1854-4/5/1947
Jasper W. 9/9/1850-12/23/1934

Betty Colquitt 10/10/1857-1/5/1936
Richard Butler 5/28/1848-5/27/1921
Leo B. 7/18/1893-10/30/1944

Mary A., wife of B. T. 2/11/1826-5/21/1898
D. T. 8/23/1826, died 3/2/1893

SIMS

Henry C. 1/21/1880-7/25/1952
Alma R. 12/17/1883-

Carlton C. 8/24/1890-5/30/1964
Cora W. 5/12/1890-8/11/1962
Lammie C. 10/2/1895-11/16/1856

John Clark 11/16/1852-3/31/1934
Ella Colquitt 9/20/1855-2161921

Lawrence S. 11/15/1877-11/16/1940

SMITH

Grocer 1885-1935
Mary 1887-

Pvt. Joe Fred 4/26/1921 Killed in North Africa 8/2/1943, Co. B, 30 Signal Bn
Nettie Miller, daughter of Sam Smith 1/8/1876-2/12/1916
Patricia, daughter of Mr. & Mrs. Quillan 7/7/1948-7/16/1948

Robert D. 1975-1958
Daisy W. 1885-1968

STEVENS

Infant son of W. T. & M. E. 9/29/1900-10/10/1900

W. C. 2/2/1831-3/29/1897
Martha E. 3/3/1834-2/19/1908

W. T. 11/17/1863-7/8/1906
Mattie E. 10/28/1863-10/15/1900

APPLE VALLEY CHURCH, Hwy #15 North

SUTTON

Infant daughter of C. N. & E. L. 2/18/1906

THURMON

Ottico M. 2/27/1896-1/27/1949

TURNER

Joe J. 5/27/1880-3/29/1947
Minnie Lee B. 2/9/1884-7/2/1967

Robert Louis Jr. 4/25/1955-5/1/1955

VANDIVER

Cecil R., Ga. PFC US Army, WW II 1/19/1917-3/12/1965
Sarah L. 1920 -

WATKINS

Alford 8/10/1855-8/3/1930

WEST

Chester R. 1877-1950

WHITLOCK

Mrs. Nancy 1883-1956

Georgia Ann 1866-1930
Hiram M. 1862-1937

WILLIAMSON
Carl 1887-1952

WILSON

Summie 1891-1936
Martha Rosetta, daughter of Mr. & Mrs. Summie 8/19/1930-9/15/1930
Bessie B. 1902

WRIGHT

T. Frank 2/7/1877-8/10/1851

BETHANY METHODIST CHURCH, Hwy #335, Brockton

AARON

Lenard C. 9/3/1926-12/4/1926
Lonie J. 9/3/1926-11/22/1926
Willie M. 12/15/1919-11/23/1920
Mazie A.. 4/15/1917-4/8/1917
William M. 1997[1953
Maude F. 1894-
Clarence M. 7/18/1910-8/16/1958
Mack C. 1/12/1884-9/27/1958
Mamie F. 1894-

ANTHONY

Mack C. 1/12/1884-9/27/1958
Mae J. 11/10/1889-10/1/1968

BARDEN

Nida D. 3/30/1877-9/7/1918

BARNETT

Eloise T., wife of J. H. 10/4/1908-2/12/1957

BENNETT

Howell 10/20/1920-5/1/1921
DeWitt 10/7/1915-12/15/1915
Sammie Bascumb, son of J. W. & Effie 9/8/1910-10/18/1911

BOGGS

W. P. 12/20/1844-6/15/1921
M. A. 10/17/1856-8/16/1954
Ola May, daughter of J. H. & S. H. 8/3/1898-6/30/1901
Lona Ellen 12/20/1873-10/29/1894

BRAY

Willie R. 1909-1962

BROWN

James E. 1/4/1882-10/11/1932 Battery G, 14th C. A. C.

James V. 1855-1936
Ollie G. 1858-1927

BETHANY METHODIST CHURCH, Hwy #335, Brockton

BULLOCK

Vernie 3/30/1897-5/1/1948

BURNS

Maggie E., wife of R. B. 12/15/1871-7/12/1905

CAMPBELL

Elmer Carl, son of C. C. & Jaffie 9/28/1909-4/27/1911

CARROLL

James Lewis 3/17/1894-2/4/1951
Ernestine Barrett 11/11/1893-

Robert Verdell 7/7/1911-3/1/1957
Daisy C. 4/16/1928-

CHANDLER

G. N. 2/26/1849-1/4/1918
Mrs. G. N. 1/10/1851-3/10/1926

COLLINS

John H., infant son 5/14/1912
Lovie Aaron 1889-1943
R. M. Presley 1869-1936

Stanley B. 10/10/1894-2/16/1941
Allie E. 3/13/1893-55/23/1937

CRAWFORD

Infant son of Mr. & Mrs. W. D. 12/12/1934-12/14/1934

DALTON

Lola B. 1883-1956

DANIEL

Roy C. 5/3/1910-10/8/1960
Venie H. 1/12/1894-12/27/1956
Forrest C. 6/23/1870-7/2/1916
Lam H. 10/23/1896-6/18/1916
Bonnie Montine, daughter of P. A. & Mamie L. 8/25/1898-7/21/1906

BETHANY METHODIST CHURCH, Hwy #335, Brockton

DANIEL

Charley B. 10/23/1896-8/19/1897
Russell 1881-1902

DAVIS

Demaris Thurmond 1/26/1906-1/14/1944

DEADWYLER

Betty 1879-1940
H. C. 8/1/1854-9/8/1903

DEAVORS

Rev. W. C. 2/18/1823-7/26/1892

DENNIS

Sharon D. 7/4/1957-7/4/1957
Karen D. 7/4/1957-7/20/1957

DOWDY

Mr. Thelma 1900-1967
Infant son of Mr. & Mrs. Carl 8/1926
Fritz 8/26/1917-10/28/1918
Infant daughter of Mr. & Mrs. R. J. 6/19/1949
Mary Lou 1875-1934
Julia Denegan, wife of J. D., 3/31/1876-11/21/1918
James D. 9/18/1866-3/13/1934

DRAKE

Margaret M. 10/11/1875-
Frank S. 12/7/1874-1/5/1952

DUNCAN

Walter, son of J. R. & E., 8/2/1890-8/18/1890
Jesse, son of J. R. & E., 3/6/1887-3/18/1887
J. R. 7/5/1866-7/30/1947

DUNCAN

Mattie E. Martin, wife of J. R. Duncan, 3/23/1868-3/10/1927

BETHANY METHODIST CHURCH, Hwy #335, Brockton

EBERHART

Clyde 12/5/1887-12/11/1906

ECKLES

John Foster 12/6/1893-12/12/1950
John Douglas 11/29/1863-3/9/1950
Ellie Carter 9/17/1871-12/13/1957

FARMER

J. H. 7/21/1856-5/12/1927

FREEMAN

Susan 6/24/1820-1900
J. S. 11/27/1827-11/18/1883

GAILEY

Mrs. L. A. 8/29/1858-5/18/1912

GLENN

Talmade, son of Mr. & Mrs. W. R. 9/7/1909-4/25/1911
William R., Sr. 1874-1969
Mattie Venable 1888-1942

GLOSSON

Temple, wife of W. F. 11/21/1857-2/6/1897
Lounita 1913-
Roy Homer 1907-1957

GRIER

Nita Alline, daughter of Mr. & Mrs. W. H. 1934

GRIMES

Mae Omie 1884-1894
Gabriel W. 3/3/1836-4/10/1895

GUNTER

Levi C., Co. G., 16 Ga. Inf., C. S. A.
Infant of L. C. & Wooda, born and died 12/6/1908
Eliza, wife of L. C. 6/15/1842-3/24/1907

BETHANY METHODIST CHURCH, Hwy #335, Brockton

HARDY

J. Hubert 11/14/1891-4/14/1921
Laura C. 8/4/1885-

HARRIS

"Chris" C. 3/13/1876-3/17/1954
Ida Senora 1/23/1874-6/29/1918
Nora died 9/10/1918, 3 months
Qullian Booth, son of Mr. & Mrs. C. 2/8/1920-11/13/1929
Clara P. 12/21/1973-3/12/1951
John M., son of A. F. & N. Died 9/25/1905, 9 months, 8 days
James L. Jr. 11/17/1866-2/16/1941
Martha M. Morrison, wife of J. L. Harris, 9/15/1836-7/10/1917

HENDRIX

G. T., son of Gordon T. 5/14/1919-10/2/1921

HOUSE

W. H. 11/12/1867-12/20/1889
Margaret D., daughter of J. G. & S. J. 11/4/1903-7/20/1906
Samuel S. 6/21/1819-8/19/1896

HUMPHREYS

Elmer 1920-1925

HUNT

Infant daughter of Mr. & Mrs. L. A. 4/7/1943

HUTCHINS

W. W. (Bill) 1900-1928
Clara, daughter of D. W. & M. E. H. 8/16/1877-11/28/1908
Mary E., wife of D. W. 4/6/1847-10/6/1912
D. W. 1848-1936
Emma J. 1880-1959

JACKSON

Gussie 1910-1929
Julius L. 1865-1945
Edna 1919-1919
Ada V. 3/30/1885-1/13/1958

BETHANY METHODIST CHURCH, Hwy #335, Brockton

JACKSON

Candice S. 1868-1952
Jesse 1879-1957
Annie Lou 1905-
Elizabeth A. 1879-1862
Ned, son of H. S. & Mary 9/12/1892-8/13/1893
Anner B. 1886-
Charlie H. 1905-1953
John G. 1870-1962

JARRETT

G. Griffin 8/22/1875-7/17/1941
Ada V. 3/30/1885-1/13/1958
Ethel Lorena 3/11/1895-7/2/1896
Clifford 1896-1963 "A Loving Offering, Northwood Methodist Church, West Palm Beach, Florida"
Frances 4/3/1802-1/25/1891
Eula M., daughter of J. A. & S. E. 9/12/1885-7/13/1886

KELLEY

Clifford, wife of Peat, died 9/34/1910

KESLER

Frances Mary born 1/1/1847 married 8/15/1867 Henry Melvin Kesler, died 9/24/1910
J. P., M. D. 3/14/1870-4/3/1896
Boyd 3/4/1893-12/21/1963
Nancy M. 8/28/1868-1/6/1948
G. N., son of G. F & N. M. 8/23/1912-10/7/1922
Ruby M. 10/12/1892-10/28/1938
Ernest 9/3/1891-7/11/1948
George F. 2/1/1861-12/28/1938

KINZEY

Nellie P. 1/9/1870-11/15/1954
W. J. 3/16/1863-5/14/1925

LLEWELLYN

Joseph 8/7/1866-7/3/1941
Mrs. N. C. 1903-1961
Nannie M. 12/4/1876-9/10/1951
Maybell L. 11/4/1901-6/18/1919

BETHANY METHODIST CHURCH, Hwy #335, Brockton

MADDOX

Doris Daniel 4/20/1903-9/2/1944

MARTIN

Matilda 2/13/1842-5/11/1908
Lillie May 10/28/1904-2/28/1905

MASSEY

Leonia Bells, daughter of J. N. & M. L. 2/4/1898-10/17/1900
Walter J. 1892-
Vester F. 1924-1961
Ollie M. 1891-
Robert T. 1922-1944, Hero

MAULDIN

Fannie J. 1882-

McREE

Robert Lee 12/11/1868-12/2/1945
Clyde Walker Jr. died 4/18/1866, 25 years, 4 months, 5 days
Jessie V. 1880-1936
Caroline, wife of W. J. 11/24/1840-5/22/1932
Baby Boy died 9/11/1946
Frank W. 1874-1948
Marcus V., son of W. J. & L. M. 9/13/1892-12/6/1895
W. J., Co. B., Thomas Legion 61-65, C. S. A. 3/4/1831-5/9/1904

MILLIKIN
Mamie A. Chandler, wife of R. K. Millikin, 5/22/1873-7/7/1898

MITCHELL

A. Grady 4/14/1892-2/20/1962

PACE

E. O., son of Ewsial and Georgia 1858-1/1895
Georgia, wife of Ewsial, 2/26/1830-9/7/1909
Emma, wife of W. H., 1/8/1870-3/5/1888
W. H. 4/15/1862-

PARKER

Sara J. 11/12/1866-9/7/1946

BETHANY METHODIST CHURCH, Hwy #335, Brockton

PARKER

William M. Died 10/26/1960, aged 90 years, 8 months, 10 days

PAYNE

Carrie G. Gunter Payne 1876-1928
R. L., Jr., son of R. L. & Edna 9/8/1919-6/1/1921
William Brad 1877-1930
Alice B. 9/28/1878-8/14/1967
William Thomas, Ga. USNR WW II, 5/28/1927-12/1945
Nola Harriett, wife of Daniel, 6/17/1879-2/22/1914
Edna F. 3/22/1894 -
Myrtle 1902-1928

PIERCE

Mary Louise 4/3/1946-6/19/1947

PITTMAN

Charlie O. 7/7/1859-2/2/1939
Georgia F. 3/15/1860-11/13/1947

PORTER

Mary Lou Hayne 12/5/1869-5/16/1916
Carrie Sue, daughter of Mr. & Mrs. M. L. 2/3/1904-7/11/1904
Annis, daughter of M. S. & M. L. 8/10/1907-1/24/1909
M. S. Sr. 7/14/1866-
Venie Venable 8/18/1874-8/6/1937
Henrinelle, daughter of Mr. & Mrs. H. P. 9/6/1919-4/24/1926

POTTS

Amy Kathryn 8/23/1918-2/9/1932
Emily Mae 9/2/1923-10/20/1966
Lula Mae C. 1896-
Willie Ruth 2/10/1926-6/10/1940
Kate Eckles 3/12/1900
Sidney Walter 11/11/1919-1/12/1923
Leila Mae Eckles 9/2/1898-8/10/1967
Frank 1876-1962
Rockwell Eckles 9/15/1921-4/9/1959
James Rockwell 9/27/1889-7/9/1937
Ellie Myrtice 1/3/1927-2/3/1923
James M. 3/11/1851-11/13/1904
Martha A. 5/10/1851-8/28/1912
Katie, infant daughter of Mr. & Mrs. J. N. 12/1/1879-1/20/1880

BETHANY METHODIST CHURCH, Hwy #335, Brockton

POTTS

Homer O. 11/8/1877-6/30/1959
Frances Elizabeth 1/29/1833-9/8/1910
Bonnie B. 6/9/1884-12/26/1964
W. M. 8/15/1844-1/7/1914
G. L. 8/9/1880-10/31/1956
Thomas A. 11/3/1856-4/11/1950
Mary C. 3/16/1861-10/11/1917
Henry J., son of C. H. & Carrie 9/12/1915-5/24/1917
Julia C. Gathright, wife of C. C. Potts, 1/8/1824-5/29/1905
Lummie (no dates)

RAY

Nellie May, daughter of Owen & Harriet 6/8/1905-1/11/1906
Harriet A. Patton Ray 4/27/1863-
Olevie, daughter of O. G. & Margaret, 9/10/1895-11/16/1898
O. G. 10/26/1847-10/21/1920
Maggie L. Ragsdale, second wife of O. G. Ray, 6/28/1860-10/3/1894

William C. 1892-
Hugh 111898-7/21/1927
Ruby W. 1894-1933
Reba H. 1929-1947
Allene 11/5/1899-

REDD

William D. 1928-1956
Leah O'Donald 10/6/1890
Charles 9/11/1882-8/5/1954

REEVES

Eula V. 2/1/1892-
John Pittard, son of F. E. & Eula Lee 9/8/1917-6/2/1919
Emory E. 11/3/1884-9/4/1942

SARGENT
Mary Ray 1913-1968
Little Irene, daughter of D. D. & Benie 6/9/1912-6/23/1913
Maver I. 1896-
Shirley C. 1916-

SHARP

Edmond J. 1/9/1826-11/20/1888
Mary 1856-1949

BETHANY METHODIST CHURCH, Hwy #335, Brockton

SMITH

C. Eugene, son of Mr. & Mrs. R. C. 8/24/1951-8/24/1951
R. Earl, son of Mr. & Mrs. R. C. 12/5/1954-10/18/1957

STREETMAN

Edward B., Ga. Pvt. Bury B 489 Armd Fa Bn 5/27/1931-2/14/1953

STEVENS

Charlie O., son of C. M. & L. G. 12/19/1901-5/25/1902

STEWART

J. N. 10/24/1871-10/31/1932
Alice E. Hutchins 6/1/1875-

STROUD

Samuel J. Died 4/9/1909, aged 84 years
Martha M. 1844-1924

SWANGIM

(M. E. Eberhart), wife of K. E. Swangin, 6/3/1847-11/20/1911

THOMPSON

James M. 1869-1941
Plonia G. 1874-1961
Fred C. 8/22/1894-11/8/1946
Gordon G. 8/11/1887-9/3/1955
Mamie V. 11/4/1889-

THURMOND

Ollie I. Potts born 6/24/1885 married W. R. Thurmond 12/28/1904, died 11/8/1911

William Reuben 4/17/1885-
Gussie F. William born 1/5/1885 married W. R. Thurmond 7/18/1915, died 8/1/1947

TRAMMELL

Donna Marie died 1/23/1957, 2 months
Floyd A. 105/1900-7/8/1967

BETHANY METHODIST CHURCH, Hwy #335, Brockton

TRAMMELL

Mattie D. 7/30/1903-10/31/1966

VENABLE

Hoyt W. 5/21/1894-12/19/1962
Wiley 1864-1939
Zora 1872-1949
Mary 1831-1927
Martin 1808-1893
Lela 1890-1891
Mrs. Lona Mae 1901-1959
Richard 12/1860-6/11/1925
Martha J., wife of Richard, 4/3/1856-7/4/1915
E. M. 8/22/1855-6/9/1907
Jesse M. 8/15/1844-3/27/1914
Max, Ga GMI, US Navy WW II, Korea 11/15/1922-8/14/1960

Infant son of Fred and Ada born and died 6/14/1915
Fred 10/21/1889-12/27/1944
Ada J. 3/8/1893

Thelma M. 1908-
Gilber R. 1909-1948
Albert M. 4/1883-7/1950
Emma W. 2/1888-
Mrs. T. W. Died 4/7/1942, aged 29 years
Clara 9/24/1894-10/3/1968
Claud 3/18/1891-12/18/1860
Joe Richard 7/18/1924-9/22/1929
Emory Alva 1885-1957
Ida Elizabeth 1897-1957
Mays A. 7/25/1909-6/4/1968
Nelle 7/20/1912-
Iris Gayle 10/5/1939-10/9/1939
Mary Elizabeth 1875-1948
Robert Tuck 1870-1947
Cleo V. Register 1906-1948
Ned Jr. 10/29/1945-1/10/1952
Albert Ned, Ga. PFC Co. M. 124 Inf. WW II 12/7/1920-1/1/1959
James T. 6/17/1944-1966

WALLACE

Little Duncan 1886-1920

BETHANY METHODIST CHURCH, Hwy #335, Brockton

WALKER

Robert Joe 10/5/1887-2/25/1963
Lenora 4/3/1883-8/24/1967
Mary 12/20/1800-1/6/1885

WATERS

Candler G. 11/3/1884-5/13/1904

WEATHERLY

Walter R., son of W. F. & R. A. 4/10/1915-5/8/1916
Russie Alice 1884-

WEBB

Frank 1876-1953
Pearl 1886-
Josie M. 1882-1957
Markers F., Ga. Pvt. CAS Det 23 Regt. Inf.
1/25/1876-6/2/1953

WESTMORELAND

Rev. W. R. 11/7/1858-11/12/1911

WHITE

Annie H. - no dates
Robert F. - no dates
Roxie Ann P. 1868-

WHITFIELD

Sgt. J. P., Co. A 61st Armored Inf. Bn.
12/19/1914-4/1/1945

WIER

Henry T. C. 8/9/1884-6/23/1954
Lizzie R. 1/19/1915--/10/1915
Annie Mae 8/21/1910-10/18/1952
Nina Eckles 5/28/1895-11/24/1943
Clarende E. 1869-1954
Infant son of Henry and Nina 8/16-17/1920
Arlie 2/12/1913
Myrt C. 1877-1948

BETHANY METHODIST CHURCH, Hwy #335, Brockton

WILEY

John 7/5/1910-4/23/1911

WILKES

Infant son of Mr. & Mrs. R. H. 1908
Sarah S. 1860-1945
Myrtis 5/22/1920-5/14/1921
Waymon A. 6/12/1883-10/10/1957
Alline D. 1885-1957
L. Jeff 1861-1927
Charles E. 2/24/1928-3/11/1928
Rosa G. 1890-1963
Valna Pauline, daughter of W. A. & S. C. 9/25/1904-7/9/1914
C. Herbert 12/21/1890-7/10/1959
Radford H. 1885-19
Steven Allen 1963-1/6/1925
Claude T. 1888-1969
George Edwin 9/25/1918-3/10/1920
Daniel Parker 1921-1966
John A., Co. G, 66 Ga. Inf., C. S. A.
Thomas S. 1859-1926
J. Edd 5/16/1892-8/21/1968, Ga. Pvt. Co. L, 12 Inf. WW I
Mary E. 1889-1968
Gerome C. 1908-1954
Audrey F. 11/11/1904-
George S. 1908-1919
Sadie 1911-

WILKS

Charlie D., son of L. J. & S. F. Wilks, 11/15/1881-9/17/1887
Dorris Laconia Wilks 8/1/1926-5/17/1929

WILLIAMSON

Nathan 1877-1965

Caroline F. 3/3/1837 -
G. L. 5/12/1827-5/18/1906
Nancy L., wife of - J., 10/7/18-- -/24/1902
Junius H. 5/19/1861-1/14/----

A. J. 1854-1935

BETHANY METHODIST CHURCH, Hwy #335, Brockton

WILLIAMSON

Josephine Freeman, wife of A. J. 6/7/1857-11/26/1918
married 3/2/1876
Infant of A. J. & Josephine died 3/1882
Infant of A. J. & Josephine died 5/9/1881, aged 9 days

Cranston B. 9/17/1817-2/17/1900
Eliza J. 1/3/1827-3/14/1889

FAITH BAPTIST CHURCH, Hwy 11, Jefferson, Ga., Est. 1952

BISHOP

James W. 5/15/1916-4/18/1966

COLVARD

Eunice A. 1897-

HOWINGTON

Charles P. 1948-1965

MILLS

Infant, Walter B. 1968-1968

TONEY

Ruby W. 1897-
Thurston S. 1886-1956

WARD

Melinda S. 1959-1960

WILLIAMSON

Thomas Ray 1910-
J. David 9/25/1941-6/14/1967
Thomas Ray, Jr. 1934-1959
Charlie R. 6/3/1902-
Nelle B. 1914-
Sallie Mae 8/6/1910

OCONEE CHURCH, HIGHWAY #82 NORTH

ADAMS

James E. 12/28/1850-12/1/1890
Eugenie Waddell, wife of J. E. 10/9/1852-5/26/1932
Sallie R. 2/3/1890-8/10/1905

BABDS

Thomas, son of J. H. & B. H., born and died 2/27/1895

BAILEY

Ralph L. 1/11/1850-1/29/1926
Ella G. 4/19/1861-6/29/1952
Blondean, daughter of L. A. & Ida 2/19/1929-7/5/1930

BARBER

Ellen D. 8/25/1862-8/17/1945
Sara Jane 3/8/1866-10/18/1954
Bessie, wife of T. C. 4/30/1878-3/5/1912
Archie 2/22/1892-2/9/1908
Edwin 9/12/1858-12/24/1943

BARRETT

Susie, wife of G. C., 9/26/1883-1/30/1907

BECK

Charlie 1892-1960
Emma S. 1892-

BENTON

Robert Arnold, son of Mr. & Mrs. R. V., 4/12/1914-12/20/1916

BRADFORD

James Dean 1962-1962

BROCK

Mary P., daughter of H. H. & Sarah, 9/3/1856-3/10/1864
Willie Harrison 3/23/1870-8/23/1872
Eula, daughter of E. S. & O. L. 12/3/1884-7/9/1885
Eulah, daughter of C. A. & M. F. 12/8/1900-3/17/1901
Ora 12/13/1881-1/4/1888
H. H. 5/8/1822-4/23/1908

OCONEE CHURCH, HIGHWAY #82 NORTH

BROCK

Fred S. 11/8/1886-11/30/1957
Bessie, daughter of C. A. & M. F., 12/27/1886-8/1/1901
Essa 8/18/1879-8/29/1879
Sarah, wife of Henry H., 11/22/1826-9/25/1872
Susan F. 10/5/1895
Ralph, son of C. A. & M. F. 9/15/1903-7/15/1905
Benjamin H., son of H. H. & Esther 1/31/1875-8/19/1875

BROOKS

Nancy Susie, wife of W. W., 11/13/1874-10/16/1937
W. W. 11/7/1867-10/2/1949

Nancy Elizabeth, wife of C. T., 2/23/1837-12/23/1915
C. T. 6/8/1847-2/25/1922 married 12/3/1865 Nancy Elizabeth

J. L. 1841-12/11/1919

BROWN

Charles E. 9/22/1957-9/23/1957
Lemuel T. 2/19/1853-9/21/1886
Amanda 11/30/1877-6/29/1885
W. G. 8/28/1924-8/14/1952
Samuel Newton 1878-1932
Flora Patrick 1886-

CAGLE

Mildred 3/23/1938-11/24/1945
Grocer 12/4/1917-11/24/1945
Willard 7/9/1936-11/24/1945
Jnett D. 9/8/1917-11/24/1945
Lilley 1889-1948
W. J. 1881-

CARROLL

Jane 1871-1907
Harvey R. 11/15/1865-4/6/1926
Clyde 1923-
Dell S. 1885-1957
Charles 1927-1941

CARRUTH

Harvey R. 11/15/1865-4/6/1926

OCONEE CHURCH, HIGHWAY #82 NORTH

CARTER

Robert Lee 4/27/1873-10/4/1901
James Zenous 1869-1942
O. G. Washington 7/4/1836-8/3/1889
Nora Tarrant
George Robert, son of Mr. & Mrs. J. Z., 2/23/1917-6/14/1920
John A. 1/29/1859-8/21/1937

CATLETT

Infant son of J. L. & H. H. 3/20/1886
Caroline M. Polk, wife of J. F., 10/8/1834-1/14/1909
Leila B. 1884-1942
Mary Ann Wilson, wife of J. F., 12/5/1822-8/3/1858
Roy P. 1890-1953

CILLILAND

Mary 12/19/1824-10/22/1887

CONNALLY

Mary 6/12/1878-2/7/1949

George W. 1/24/1849-2/14/1910
Martha T. Brock, wife of G. W., 9/5/1834-4/25/1897

CRAIG

Guy William 1887-1968
Ernest E. 8/31/1918-6/28/1920

DANIEL

Hoke L. 8/30/1923-6/26/1949

DARNALL

S. J. 1852-1912
Nalda 1910-1910
Tom B. 1902-1956
Minnie L. 1891-

DAVIS

Charles Edward died 8/2/1940
Emma Mae M. 3/21/1919-4/22/1938

OCONEE CHURCH, HIGHWAY #82 NORTH

DAVIS

Charles E. 7/14/1940-8/29/1940

DODD

Mary Mote 2/8/1853-9/13/1901

DONAHOO

May Sims 1878-1963
Doss P. 1871-1958
Wife of D. P. 1898-1963
R. B. 1894-1897

DOSS

Thomas M. 1856-1925
Minnie 10/1881-
Claude W. died 12/1960, 78 years
India E. 1905-
George M. 1902-1968
Charles Jackson 1/14/1927-12/24/1927

DUNNAHOO

Jimmie, son of J. G. & M. L. 7/27/1890-7/28/1890
Marshall K. 8/23/1873-11/19/1937
Sam E. 3/27/1893-10/21/1909
Thomas N. 10/8/1872-6/22/1937
John J. 12/1/1818-12/9/1892
Lucy W. 8/3/1876-
Newt B. 6/22/1895 - killed in France 10/15/1918
J. H. 1885-1961
Martha Jane Lemaster, born 4/15/1847 married John G. Dunnahoo on 12/10/1868, died 7/6/1911
Sallie M. 9/20/1871-6/22/1951
Eva H. 1890-1952

ECKLES

Mary Ann
John W. D. 7/7/1825-3/14/1898
Elizabeth Clay, wife of J. W., 10/31/1831-5/31/1915

EDWARDS

Ernest G. 1892-1965
Edna W. 1894-

OCONEE CHURCH, HIGHWAY #82 NORTH

ELROD

Jacob Edgar 12/16/1881-12/2/1908
Blondine, wife of W. D., 7/9/1848-5/22/1904
William E. 6/25/1876-3/30/1916
Sarah M. 1875-1957
Mrs. Maud Connally, wife of J. E., 1882-19--
Mary J. Brock, wife of A. N. 7/7/1845-4/2/1916
E. Nat M. 18809-1932

ELLEN

Morgan 7/6y/1913-11/23/1917, 4 years, 4 months, 16 days

EVANS

Thomas A. 2/15/1859-7/27/1938
Geneva A. 3/20/1859-1/5/1937
Alvin E. 9/13/1883-2/9/1964
Eunice D. 11/17/1888-12/28/1962
Floyd C., died 2/1/1902, 44 years, 11 months, 3 days
Nettie J. Stark, wife of F. C., 12/17/1867-6/24/1892
Joel Selman, son of F. C. & Nettie, 3/31/1883-7/1/1888
Benjamin S., son of F. C. & Nettie, 8/29/1896-8/9/1897
Annis 1825-4/18/1900
Nettie 1880-1921
Mary Dasie, daughter of E. L. & F. G., 6/1/1896-6/2/1899

FERGUSON

Gussie C. 10/1/1888
Charles L. 7/27/1883-7/30/1910

FLEMING

Sarah Mitchell 9/16/1881-2/21/1939

GARRETT

Alexander 1885-195-
Gordon E. 5/13/1895-7/24/1965
Cora B. 6/2/1899-
J. Henry 1864-1929

GARRISON

T. C. 1871-1936
Thomas W., 34 Ga. Inf. C. S. A.

OCONEE CHURCH, HIGHWAY #82 NORTH

GARRISON

Mary J., wife of T. W., 10/6/1852-3/1/1901
Thalma Pink 1/23/1906-12/31/1925
Hilda M. 2/24/1939-11/20/1962

GEE

Herman Dannel 5/7/19-- -/4/1942

GIDDENS

Esther, wife of H. C. 7/1/1806-9/31/1880

GRIFFETH

William 9/28/1822-2/22/1906
Julia 11/1/1802-12/14/1880
Amanda Hitchcock, wife of William 3/16/1829-9/23/1870
John 8/23/1800-11/21/1871

HARDY

Alton, son of Mr. & Mrs. C. H. 10/23/1899-1/11/1900
Ruby 10/16/1922-12/14/1922
Charles H. 4/12/1872/4/30/1923
Albert M. 1891-1950
Henry J. 1865-1927
Rosa M. 10/24/1869-9/29/1943
Blanche C. 1898-
Fannie E. 1869-

HARVIE

Claud N. 1884-1958
Mrs. Ethel 1887-1967

HAWKINS

Mattie L. 12/5/1876-12/22/1962

HEAD

Hautelle 1/1/1903-10/9/1925
Elizabeth Highfield, wife of W. F., 6/18/1854-12/6/1912,
Mother of J. C. Head, A. M. Head, Dessie Wilhite, Emma
Porter, W. C. Head, Ella Rogers
Arthur M. 2/17/1877-5/22/1962
W. F. 7/18/1852-5/8/1936

OCONEE CHURCH, HIGHWAY #82 NORTH

HIGHFILL

Nancy, wife of John F. 4/22/1810-3/31/1872
Martha A., daughter of John F. & Nancy 1/6/1840-12/28/1858

HITCHCOCK

Infant daughter of E. T. & S. L. 4/1/1880-4/15/1880

HOLCOMBE

Jackson (no dates)

HOLLAND

J. Tom 12/5/1858-11/24/1936
Nolla 5/30/1850-6/2/1893
J. F. 8/2/1904-2/7/1963
Allen G. 1900-1938
Nancy D. 7/29/1861-8/30/1937
Ethel C. 1902-1965

HOPKINS

Addie Alma 1879-1927
D. A. 7/22/1852-7/27/1894

HUNTER

Lillie, daughter of Minnie T. 2/11/1868-3/11/1920

HUTCHINS

Ethel H., son of N. H. & Ella D. 1/8/1883-5/6/1898
Little Ella, daughter of N. H. & Ella O. 4/10/1890-8/30/1937

JACKSON

Sterling, Co. G, 16 Ga. Inf., C. S. A.
Margie Wallace, wife of C. S. 8/13/1880-1/7/1913

JOHNSON

John M. 1/26/1850-10/23/1906

JONES

Robert T. 1883-1955
Beatrice B. 1887

OCONEE CHURCH, HIGHWAY #82 NORTH

KELL

M. P. 1/28/1861-3/30/1902

LANGSTON

Clombus N. 3/16/1868-11/13/1923
Eliza G. 10/14/1869-2/17/1962

LORD

Gladys, daughter of J. E. & E. A. 1/12/1894-1/3/1899

LOWE

Charles R. 1959-1961

LOWERY

Thomas E. Jr. 1/20/1959-9/1959
Randall Kenneth 2/20/1966-4/24/1966

MADDOX

J. Arthur 8/10/1871-8/24/1900

MANGUM

Docia D. 1889-
Hoyt J., son of Mansel & Docia 6/28/1908-4/1/1911

MARLER

John E. 8/4/1842-6/11/1921
W. Mansel 1885-1860

MARTIN

George Hampton 12/29/1880-7/11/1944
J. Lee 6/26/1873-8/28/1922
Emma G. 5/5/1883-8/12/1943
Dennie, wife of R. R., 2/5/1888-4/12/1923
Myrtle L. 2/4/1884-9/21/1958
Julia Fannie 3/21/1853-5/7/1939
William C. 7/28/1878-8/18/1905
Cleo Evans, wife of G. H. 10/3/1893-1/1/1917

OCONEE CHURCH, HIGHWAY #82 NORTH

MATHIS

A. W. 1850-1925
Mrs. Callie died 11/16/1966, aged 77
Maggie M. 1873-1932
Laura E. 11/6/1887-9/27/1939
Lou C. 1868-1952

MATTHEWS

Birtie Miriam, dau. of Mr. & Mrs. J. W. 10/4/1902-12/2/1903

MERK

Claude H. 12/13/1888-1/18/1965
Alva G. 6/16/1902-
Infant daughter of J. W. & M. E. born and died 8/10/1882
Mary E., wife of J. W. 9/20/1845-11/27/1906
E. Jurell 12/3/1902
Marcia T. 6/1/1873-5/29/1880
D. S. 4/26/1902-5/8/1902
E. Hoyt 12/3/1896-3/7/1963
Starky H. 6/12/1876-5/28/1880
Dilmus L. 10/16/1869-7/1/1905
John Wesley 2/8/1843-7/2/1920 Pvt Co. G, 16th Regt Ga. Vol. inf. 1861-1862

MILLER

Carrie E. 5/1/1876-1/29/1952

MITCHELL

Cynthia S. 1855-1939
Charlie R. 5/18/1886
Fannie G. 11/12/1879-5/22/1922
Dora 1874-1950
Vassie, wife of G. L. 6/19/1879-1/11/1906
Alice R. 10/17/1886-9/12/1952
John James, Co. E, 5 Ga. Mil. C. S. A.

MORRIS

Betty Ann, dau of Mr. & Mrs. Glen 12/15/1934-2/21/1935
John H. 3/5/1884
Ellis, dau of Mr. & Mrs. Wayne 2/2/1935

OCONEE CHURCH, HIGHWAY #82 NORTH

MOTES

Martha, daughter of C. G. & Lula 8/11/1898-8/16/1899
Thomas T. Madison died 4/12/1941, aged 64 years

NALLEY

Annie Frances, daughter of Mr. & Mrs. B. H. 5/15/1830

NICHOLSON

Wilma Lilly 1919-1936
Etta S. 1899-1956
T. S. 1/10/1882-4/10/1939
Morgan R. 1923-1947
Alma L. 1939
John Otis 1919-1960
Henry F. 1898-1956
J. R. 6/1/1878-6/20/1928

NIX

Walter 1902-
Gladys 1908-

NORRIS

Joseph 1883-1952

NORVILLE

Clevia W. 10/22/1870-5/15/1941

NUNN

Fannie Evans, wife of A. T. 4/9/1859-2/12/1884
Elijah G., son of C. G. & Mollie 10/22/1876-6/8/1879
Betty H. 2/26/1864-10/31/1934
Eunice C. 1891-
Louise, little daughter of Mr. & Mrs. Sandy 4/11/1919-5/23/1919
Mary Arlisa, daughter of Mr. & Mrs. S. J. 4/25/1919
Mollie Evans, wife of C. C. Nunn 11/8/1852-6/30/1890
Mattie A. 1874-1951
Clay, son of R. C. & E. S. 12/25/1892-3/30/1893
Louie, son of C. G. & Mollie 10/2/1878-11/8/1878
Crofford C. 5/15/1848-4/29/1912
Sammie J. 1889-1967
Bennie, son of R. C. & E. S. 6/21/1888-8/4/1888
Elijah G. 10/19/1817-5/15/1885

OCONEE CHURCH, HIGHWAY #82 NORTH

NUNN

Martha Ann 3/28/1827-12/31/1917

ODUM

John Thomas 7/3/1872-10/26/1933

PANTHER

W. W. 5/1903-8/15/1963

PARKER

Mrs. Mollie died 12/1966, 62 years, 5 months, 11 days

PATRICK

Coly, son of Mr. & Mrs. J. B. 7/17/1886-11/13/1893
Emma Brock, wife of T. W. Patrick 8/30/1840-5/7/1914

PERRY

Helen T. 1884-
James J. 1853-1943
Newton H. 1877-1944
Sarah G. 1857-
P. O., Co. C, 4 Ga. Reserves, C. S. A.

PHILLIPS

Miss H. (no dates)

PICKRELL

Benjamin F. 6/8/1827-2/24/1910
Lucy W. 10/25/1827-3/24/1904

PINION

James G. 1916-1940
George W. 1893-1954
Alice C. 1894-
Jim (no dates)
Joyce C. 1946-1946
Linda (no dates)
Webster C. 1930-1948

OCONEE CHURCH, HIGHWAY #82 NORTH

PORTER

Robert B. 1868-1897
Roy M., son of C. M. & C. G. 7/27/1888-6/6/1900
Ralph, son of L. O. & Maude 10/23/1906-6/2/1908
Harold Crawford, son of G. C. & Annie 6/7/1918-6/14/1918

PRUITT

Lucy G. 12/10/1829-5/3/1907
Mandy 1865-1936
W. A. 3/20/1852-4/14/1921
J. W. 11/15/1827-7/7/1888

ROBERTS

Elizabeth 9/18/1838-8/24/1900

SAILERS

Frances Chandler 2/24/1827-6/16/1902

SANDERS

Bessie E. 7/9/1893-

SEABOLT

Lillie A. 1875-1956
Rudolph, son of Mr. & Mrs. J. W. 6/18/1905-10/16/1907
Infant daughter of F. H. & N. A.
Dexter Lee, son of J. W. & Lillie 7/16/1912-4/15/1930

SEARS

Olevia, daughter of T. W. & Mary Garrison, wife of
W. R. Sears 1/11/1881-9/2/1905
Infant daughter of Mr. & Mrs. W. R.

SHORT

Woodie 1907-
Ola D. 1888-1961

SIMS

Joe died 1884
Myrtle died 1883
Mrs. Joe died 1883

OCONEE CHURCH, HIGHWAY #82 NORTH

SMITH

Pearl, twin daughter of J. F. & Viola 1/24/1923-4/5/1923

SOSEBEE

Louise 1/8/1922-11/25/1926
Infant of Mr. & Mrs. M. B. born and died 10/4/1918

STANDRIDGE

John M. 1/1/1846-7/30/1922

STOCKTON

Minnie 1866-1883
John Oscar, son of Mr. & Mrs. J. O. 1897-1899
Mrs. J. W. died 1905
Hulda died 1860
Carlton Patrick, son of Mr. & Ms. J. O. 1884-1885
Fannie, wife of B. B. 6/13/1846-12/21/1901
Arline died 1860
James W. died 1883

STONE

Mamie B. 1/7/1891-12/30/1919

STOVER

Grady (S. F. C.) 8/20/1918-1/25/1955, Ga SFC 309 Field Hosp. WW II

SWAIN

Charles H. 12/2/1943-7/9/1960
Infant daughter of Mr. & Mrs. Walter C.
Annie L. 1906-1967
Infant son of Mr. & Mrs. Walter C.
Hazel 3/18/1928-3/17/1929
Infant daughter of Mr. & Mrs. Walter C.
Walter C. 1905-

TANNER

Joyce E. 1889-1963

OCONEE CHURCH, HIGHWAY #82 NORTH

THOMPSON

Annie Mae, daughter of Charlie & Pearlie
Vernard, son of Charlie & Pearlie

THORNTON

W. A. 11/29/1860-8/4/1905
Sarah E. 3/13/1832-6/2/1904

THURMON

Mary A. C. V. Sailers 7/19/1862-12/16/1917
Little Ruth, daughter of J. B. & C. V. 4/15/1899-8/30/1901
J. B., Jr. 5/1/1901-1/19/1935
John B., Sr. 10/19/1856-9/19/1836
Infant daughter of J. B. & C. V. 8/10/1904-8/12/1904
Mollie W. 6/14/1872-6/24/1967

TOLBERT

Annie Pauline, daughter of Mr. & Mrs. E. M. 1/29/1927

TONEY

Milton G. 1852-1931
Mary E. 1851-1936

TURNER

Mattie, wife of P. W. 3/12/1865-7/25/1884
Fannie E. 4/14/1851
Charles H. 11/12/1847-10/3/1907

VANDIVER

Gertrude 2/26/1884-7/1/1886
J. H. 3/10/1815-11/1/1873
F. Dillard 12/2/1871-8/11/1958
E. Foshia 7/21/1871-2/18/1940
Sgt. Cecil L. 1/25/1924, Radio Gunner on B-25 Bomber, was shot down at Arahata Point in Northern Kuriles 7/12/1945
Hattie 5/6/1830-8/12/1893
George C., Co., D., 16 Ga. Cavalry C. S. A. 12/29/1845-5/3/1927
William H. 1896-1945
Vivian L., daughter of Mr. & Mrs. Arthur 8/25/1917-6/22/1920
Hettie 8/1886-5/5/1928
C. L. 5/1/1812-8/18/1882
Emaline 9/26/1842-3/9/1883, wife of G. C.

OCONEE CHURCH, HIGHWAY #82 NORTH

VANDIVER

Williard T. 1899-
Arthur 1893-
Eula S. 1895-
Jacob Warren 3/16/1847-3/21/1916, 11th Ga. Regt. Co. G.
Octavia L. 11/22/1849-3/5/1927

VOYLES

Infant son of W. G. & M. B. 9/3/1906-9/10/1906

WADDELL

Franklin 2/17/1835-6/9/1919
Lottie Bell 4/3/1912-9/27/1912
Sophronia Elrod, wife of Frank, 2/8/1844-6/9/1908
Gordon Hushel 9/16/1901-1/3/1902
Patrick died 9/2/1904, 72 years
Eliza, wife of Patrick, 3/9/1829-5/9/1911

WALLACE

Sarah A. 6/24/1854-8/9/1942
O. F. 12/3/1849-2/27/1906

WHEELER

Baby boy 1969-1969
Ida D. 1884-
Dan J. 1882-

WHITE

Sallie L. Bailey 1/1/1824-6/1/1890 married Jesse White
Lillie, infant of G. W. & N. A. 4/8/1888-4/26/1888
Robert B. 4/16/1867-10/30/1890
Tandy, infant of G. W. & N. A. 3/12/1883-1/309/1885
Jesse died 5/12/1896, aged 72 years
N. A., wife of G. W., born 87/29/1856, married 4/15/1880, died 2/26/1895
Jessie died 5/12/1896, aged 72 years
Hoyt, Ga., Cpl., US Army, WWI 9/19/1890-2/3/1954
Eula May 11/21/1880-7/27/1897
Mattie 4/28/1888-5/11/1891
James J. 3/4/1890-2/25/1926
William F. 6/26/1852-3/16/1904
Anna G. 3/29/1891-7/13/1941
Eugenia 3/18/1877-8/19/1947

OCONEE CHURCH, HIGHWAY #82 NORTH

WHITE

W. E. 10/22/1872-1/20/1956
Martha E., wife of W. F. 1/4/1856-7/2/1897

WHITLOCK

Janice M. 6/28/1957-11/9/1957
Guy Jr. 5/15/1932-5/11/1968
William 1/24/1935-

WHITMIRE

Mildred Nunn 3/28/1918-3/21/1926
Ola C. 1874-
Otis 4/24/1892-5/22/1938
Lee F. 1860-1941
Laura Dell, daughter of L. F. & O. C. 7/25/1904-7/9/1906
Kate M. 1900-1969
Sarah Caroline 1/15/1863-6/15/1899

WIER

James B. 1/22/1878-5/16/1939
Bessie M. 3/24/1901-12/13/1949

WILEY

James D. 1867-1944
Susan S. 1868-1934

WILHITE

S. T. 12/19/1849-10/4/1903
Mary E., wife of M. G. 5/15/1857-5/26/1885
Blanch, daughter of M. G. & A. A. 2/7/1889-3/4/1902
Clementine 9/6/1850-11/7/1925
Clara Belle, daughter of M. G. & M. E. 5/14/1885-11/26/1885
Mattie L., daughter of S. T. & M. C. 8/14/1869-9/21/1884
W. T., son of M. G. & M. E. 4/20/1879-12/22/1879

WILSON

Minnie L., wife of J. S. 10/16/1876-1/12/1906
Nina S. 1887-1956
Daniel W. 1858-1932
Alice, wife of D. W., 8/4/1866-3/20/1907
Joyce, wife of Morn 3/16/1832-11/22/1890
Alice, wife of D. W. 8/4/1866-3/20/1907

OCONEE CHURCH, HIGHWAY #82 NORTH

WILSON

Lucy Boswell 10/25/1871-10/29/1948
Baby of H. V. & Lucy 7/17/1904-9/18/1904
Harvey Valentine 10/17/1859-5/3/1921

WORLEY

Sarah Cantrell, wife of Thomas G., born 4/24/1838, married 7/31/1859 died 6/30/1916
Infant son of S. R. & M. A. born and died 9/27/1915
Frank, son of S. R. & M. A. 1/7/1918-1/10/1918
Annie Ruth, daughter of S. R. & M. A. 12/15/1927-12/21/1927
Thomas H. 7/24/1895-10/24/1934
Artie S. 9/4/1896-
Sim R. 1/6/1894-6/27/1961
John R. 1870-1953
Hannah L. 1862-1935

WORSHAM

E. A. Giddens, wife of J. L. Worsham 5/29/18493/20/1872

WRIGHT

Edde A. 2/10/1895-6/15/1899

YONGE

Frankie 9/23/1903-2/15/1967
Jack R. 1929-1965

DOSTER FAMILY CEMETERY, HWY #332 EAST AND COUNTY ROAD

ANDERSON

Infant daughter of Mr. & Mrs. J. A. 8/26/1893-8/27/1893
Eliza E., wife of J. A. 9/12/1863-8/25/1903
Lula V. 7/14/1878-3/8/1914

ANGLIN

Myrtle, daughter of H. C. & Dolley 8/16/1906-7/31/1907

BOND

Sarah Frances 5/1/1923-7/31/1917

DOSTER FAMILY CEMETERY, HWY #332 EAST AND COUNTY ROAD

BROOKS

Infant son of W. H. & Mary Jane born and died 4/26/1905
Sammie 11/26/1915-4/29/1917

BUTLER

Fred 12/16/1896-3/25/1915

COOPER

Levie, wife of G. W. 7/27/1882-8/13/1914

DILLARD

John Hansel died 7/1/1917, aged 67 years

DOSTER

E. T. 11/7/1842-5/9/1914
Mrs. E. T. 1/19/1840-12/27/1919

Homer B., son of D. L. & N. G. 9/8/1901-11/20/1909
James 1818-1921
Fannie 11/21/1885-11/7/1886

Infant son of Dr. & Mrs. J. A. born and died 1888
Infant son of Dr. & Mrs. J. A. born and died 1897
Infant son of Dr. & Mrs. J. A. born and died 1887
Dr. J. A. died 10/8/1881, aged 84 years

Lula F. Roberts, wife of J. F. Doster 1871-1940
H. C. 11/30/1844-9/18/1927
Luther P. 1883-1962
E. T., son of Mr. & Mrs. Luther 1925-1927
James 9/14/1872-1/31/1951
Birt, son of J. F. & L. F. 9/29/1907-5/30/1908
Rayfield born and died 11/17/1959
Rhoda P. 6/27/1818-5/1885
Prudence Moore, wife of H. J. Porter 12/11/1832-7/3/1908
Rosela Jane, wife of H. C. 10/4/1849-3/19/1921
C. T., infant son of D. L. & N. C. 8/5/1903-8/8/1921
Lona M. 1887-1965
Virginia, daughter of Mr. & Mrs. R. 3/12/1927-6/29/1928
Mary 8/4/1885-9/10/1925
B. F. 5/15/1822-11/10/1882
Daughter of Mr. & Mrs. T. J. 11/13/1895-6/4/1898
Allen 1908-1908
Evie S. 9/9/1870-5/14/1893

DOSTER FAMILY CEMETERY, HWY #332 EAST AND COUNTY ROAD

DOSTER

Infant of W. P. & J. K.
Infant son of J. F. and L. F. born and died 5/26/1908

EDWARDS

Nancy E., wife of Robert 11/8/1843-6/10/1905

ERVIN

Gaynelle, daughter of J. L. & Mandy 4/6/1917-9/10/1918
Jennie 2/8/1887-3/19/1895

FIELDS

J. T. 11/6/1849-7/31/1917
Mandy F. 6/12/1849-2/15/1915
Columbia, son of W. W. & Linnie 10/16/1895-3/21/1896

FOWLER

Lucy 1878-4/20/1900

HAYES

Mrs. N. F. 5/2/1870-10/20/1906
T. B. (Toof) 8/15/1885-8/18/1925

HENDERSON

Lizzie 10/27/1887-11/7/1888
Marrion 10/10/1893-9/10/1894

IRVIN

Rena, wife of J. N. 10/28/1876-4/19/1914

JENKINS

Clinton D., son of F. N. & M. W. 10/5/1905-1/20/1909

PHILIPS

Bertie L. 1912-
Albert T. 1892-1953
Genie 1883-

DOSTER FAMILY CEMETERY, HWY #332 EAST AND COUNTY ROAD

PHILLIPS

Fred Davis 7/22/1910-6/9/1911
Charlie 7/1/1880-8/3/1946
Thomas 9/2/1847-12/12/1922
Caroline Lyle, wife of Thomas Phillips 2/11/1833-12/8/1909
Robert T. 9/28/1898-9/28/1914
Sallie F., daughter of Mr. & Mrs. Hugh 6/10/1903-9/13/1903
Roxie 3/20/1855-12/12/1934

Ada Doster, wife of A. W. Phillips 1/20/1899-2/18/1921
D. L. P., son of L. W. & Ada 2/7/1921-2/8/1921
Alp, son of L. W. & Ada

Hugh 11/11/1869-10/27/1957
Bessie Lyle, wife of Hugh, 5/2/1872-7/12/1927
Genie Brown, wife of Hugh Phillips 7/23/1875-11/17/1951

Sindy Adell 4/4/1915-6/17/1916
Emily J., wife of ? Phillips 10/30/1882-9/17/1918
Miles 12/25/1853-11/1/1896
Effie 6/15/1920-6/14/1916
Finnie 6/13/1861-2/20/1922, married 1881
Robert Lawson 9/20/1858-1/17/1920

ROBERTS

Martha 1/7/1838-4/15/1918, 80 years, 3 months, 10 days
W. D. 6/1883-11/25/1938
Fred 3/15/1908-1/5/1917

SMITH

Frank 10/10/1907-11/17/1954

TATE

Rawlin S. 6/1918-12/1918
Infant of A. D. & S. P. born and died 8/12/1906

WALDEN

Lonnie W. 8/21/1915-5/17/1917

WALLACE

John H. 1855-1926
Nancy Brewer 1866-1955

DOSTER FAMILY CEMETERY, HWY #332 EAST AND COUNTY ROAD

WALLACE

R. E. 1/16/1902-8/12/1910
Willie 3/31/1907-5/13/1908

PINEY FORK BAPTIST CHURCH, Highway 346, Established 1926

BEASLEY

Murphy 4/5/1900-4/15/1965
Viola 4/7/1903-

CAMP

Carlton died 12/23/1968, aged 5 months

CANTRELL

Sarah Loe died 12/25/1959, aged 37 years

COCHRAN

Willie Ruth 9/26/1925-
Elijah Newton 12/25/1921-12/4/1966

COKER

Amony 10/18/1959-11/4/1949

COOK

Rev. D. C. 1858-2/17/1916

DAMMONS

Claude Jr., Geo. P. F. C. Hq & Svc Co. 95 Eng. WW II
7/15/1923-12/11/1964

DAMONS

Mrs. Goldie died 8/1964, aged 62

DUKE

Dewey died 11/29/1968, aged 60 years
James Arthur 1937-1963

PINEY FORK BAPTIST CHURCH, Highway 346, Established 1926

GILMER

Mrs. Woodie 2/17/1966, aged 72 years

JACKSON

Mrs. Hazie died 3/22/1967, aged 79 years

KIMSEY

C. L. (Duck) 6/23/1911-2/11/1964
Pauline 12/10/1910
Frances Bart 1/1/1968, aged 90 years

KINSEY

William Earl died 7/29/1955, born dead

LANCE

Eugene 1940
Arthur Clayton 8/17/1930-5/26/1948
L. C. 4/17/1907-10/23/1955

MADDOX

Harold died 5/7/1965, aged 37 years

MOON

Miss Frances died 6/8/1957

PARK

Robert D. died 1969

PETTY

Stoy died 8/26/1961 aged 60 years
P. died 1952

PETTYJOHN

Helen died 12/22/1967, aged 78 years

PORTER

Evie O. 1893-1967

PINEY FORK BAPTIST CHURCH, Highway 346, Established 1926

RILEY

Eddie D., Ga. Pvt. 1 Regt. ASF TNG Gen WW II
2/22/1916-11/4/1951

SHIELDS

Luther died 10/11/1967, aged 57 years

STANCIL

Thomas H. 11/29/1962, aged 14

TATE

Artie H. 1/19/1936-4/7/1957

TURK

George 3/21/1869-8/22/1932
Tishie, wife of Henson Sims 5/4/1865-4/5/1918

USHER

Paul died 12/25/1966 aged 17 years

WHITLOCK

Jacob 1879-1932
Jim 6/1/1876-9/6/1931
Lillie C. 1896-19

ACADEMY MISSIONARY BAPTIST CHURCH
(FROM HWY 85 GOING TOWARDS JEFFERSON, TAKE 2ND DIRT ROAD ON THE RIGHT, CROSS TRACTS). EST. 1912

BAIRD

W. H. (Billy) 1929-1963
Susie Blackstock 1890-1967

BLACKSTOCK

J. Carl 10/8/1888-8/18/1949

W. A. 10/10/1856-2/13/1924
Mattie Lee Roverts, wife of W. A. Blackstock, 8/13/1861-2/16/1921

ACADEMY MISSIONARY BAPTIST CHURCH
(FROM HWY 85 GOING TOWARDS JEFFERSON, TAKE 2ND DIRT ROAD ON THE RIGHT, CROSS TRACTS). EST. 1912

BLACKSTOCK

Annette, infant daughter of Mr. & Mrs. A. N. 7/19/1927-7/23/1927
Hubert N. 3/23/1902-9/2/1921
Samantha Luncy 6/21/1864-4/12/1955
Thomas H. 4/28/1852-1/6/1919
Tom B., Georgia Pvt. 157 Depot - 10/5/1958
Pleasant J. 4/22/1859-2/25/1918
Son of J. B. and M. M. 7/26/1890-8/26/1891
Susan Elmine Echols 1/8/1867-1/5/1901, married to P. J. Blackstock 1/8/1885
William Elmer, son of W. A. L. & M. L. 7/29/1895-1896

CHAMBERS

D. C. 12/26/1849-5/28/1911

DANIEL

Infant son of Floria and George 1/6/1943
Infant daughter of Floria and Georgia 1/2/1940

GAINES

Mrs. Willie Mae died 1/2/1960, aged 44

GODFREY

A. B., Co. C Ga. Regt., and wife

HANSON

Lammoth Joe, PFC 143 Inf. 36 Div. WW II 12/1/1923-6/16/1944

HARRISON

James F. 5/3/1856-3/10/1927
Mary Evelyn Roberts, wife of James F., 12/30/1858-10/8/1936

LANGSTON

M. J. 5/13/1822-2/2/1865

MARLER

Aunt Betty

ACADEMY MISSIONARY BAPTIST CHURCH
(FROM HWY 85 GOING TOWARDS JEFFERSON, TAKE 2ND DIRT ROAD ON THE RIGHT, CROSS TRACTS). EST. 1912

MARLOWE

H. C. 1895-19
Susie P. 1907-1968
Betty Sue 4/14/1933-2/11/1934

McDANIEL

Mrs. Frances 1/3/1943, aged 51 years

OLIVER

J. C. died 6/27/1906, aged 78 years
A. N. 10/12/1864-9/14/1908
Mrs. A. N. 1/1872-9/1936
Lula Reynolds 9/20/1871-3/12/1966
Worth 4/24/1890-6/25/1891
Lila B. 11/13/1903-12/27/1903
Theodocie 4/9/1870-4/5/1957
J. Thomas 7/25/1864-3/18/1945
Amanda A., wife of J. B. Roberts, 3/14/1861-11/23/1924
Charles N. 10/29/1866-
Fannie E. 3/17/1871-2/15/1936

PARKER

Charles W. 1934-1935
D. L. 1923-1936

PATRICK

Thomas L. 7/14/1862-4/6/1934
Martha H. 11/30/1865-12/18/1936
L. Estelle 1894-1956

PHARR

John Young 12/16/1854-12/3/1918
Mannie Roberts 7/15/1856-5/18/1934

PINSON

Infant daughter of C. W. 9/27/1910-12/3/1918
Mattie E. 1872-1935
Croff Y. 1866-1937
Kathie Sue 9/27/1910-12/3/1918

ACADEMY MISSIONARY BAPTIST CHURCH
(FROM HWY 85 GOING TOWARDS JEFFERSON, TAKE 2ND DIRT ROAD ON THE RIGHT, CROSS TRACTS). EST. 1912

PINSON

J. N. 8/1832-5/22/1897

PRUITT

C. T. 1904-1951
Bertie Lee 1904-19
Johnny 1944-1936

REYNOLDS

Eula Waddell died 6/1936
Thomas William 9/6/1879-1/28/1962
Arthur William 7/14/1916-1/28/1939

ROBERTS

Ada 1894-1965

D. H. 8/13/1841-2/7/1906
Darenda, wife of D. H., died 1867

Stephen 11/1/1816-5/19/1902
W. W. 4/15/1828-2/4/1887
J. B. 8/13/1861 married 1/6/1881
W. C. 7/3/1848-4/17/1879
Margaret J. 12/12/1836-11/6/1911
Mary A. 11/19/1852-5/24/1928
Mrs. Evie 12/29/1847-4/20/1882
J. R. 4/15/1828-11/30/1890
Arthur William 7/14/1916-1/28/1939

Callie, daughter of J. R. & Nannie 5/18/1875-5/21/1905
Nannie E., wife of James R. died 1/4/1908, aged 65

Edward H. 6/1/1873-3/17/1936
S. C., wife of Aisa 9/21/1855-7/7/1895

SAILORS

Hubert P. 10/7/1911-3/18/1930
E. M. 4/3/1919-4/23/1921
William C., Ga. Pvt. 121 Inf. 31 Div. 9/15/1934
Robert S. 6/16/1873-12/5/1954
Bernice 9/3/1875-12/10/1938

ACADEMY MISSIONARY BAPTIST CHURCH
(FROM HWY 85 GOING TOWARDS JEFFERSON, TAKE 2ND DIRT ROAD ON THE RIGHT, CROSS TRACTS). EST. 1912

SHAW

H. W. 11/28/1874-11/29/1946
W. B. 5/1/1868-3/18/1951
Tom Pinson 3/19/1905-6/2/1909
George W. 1877-19
Mary Evie 1872-1949

SIMS

Alice B. 4/7/1904-7/31/1904
Annie 10/16/1905-7/31/1905

SPRINGER

Millard A. 1883-1963
Infant of Millard died 9/26/1943
Willie died 11/1925, aged 13 years
William P. 1875-1964
Anna A. 1880-1948
Gary Sean 12/27/1967-12/28/1967

THRELKELD

Virginia L. Hanson, wife of G. W. Threlkeld 9/22/1921-12/2/1940

TURNER

Harold Lee 7/10/1910-4/11/1933
Hugh H. 2/23/1873-6/9/1961
Kittie B. 11/25/1890

WALL

Thelma 4/13/1905-1/18/1940
Ola, wife of W. F. White, 2/5/1868-11/23/1902

CENTER GROVE BAPTIST CHURCH, HWY 346. Est. 1857

ANDERSON

Marvin 1907-1956
Cora M. 1917-19
Marvin J. 2/21/1938-6/17/1939

CENTER GROVE BAPTIST CHURCH, HWY 346. Est. 1857

AIKENS

Nettie Louise died 10/9/1962, aged 28

AYERS

Mrs. Mary E. 1884-1967
D. J. 3/1862-1922

BEATY

Frances, daughter of W. D. & M. J. 6/13/1833-3/14/1899
Marler B., son of J. C. & F. L. Batey 2/18/1904-7/4/1905

BENNETT

W. C., son of Mr. & Mrs. M. C. 12/6/1914-2/22/1915

BLACK

Mary E. 11/26/1872-5/2/1938

BOWLES

Frank 6/25/1838-6/3/1917
J. F. 11/25/1865-3/3/1905
Mary 2/27/1833-6/8/1926

BROCK

Lucy A. 4/6/1829-4/5/1883
James A. 2/17/1822-12/5/1903

BROWN

Tillman C. 7/31/1885-11/13/1942
Nell, daughter of T. C. & R. I. 1/4/1910-11/7/1916
Mildred, daughter of T. C. & R. I. 5/11/1914-8/11/1914

Jane I. 1850-1922
Ben C. 1879-1958
Tillman C., Jr. 3/5/1919-6/14/1959
Annie Lou 1886-1963
Uriah L. 1853-1937
Eliza B. 1847-1929
Sarah 11/26/1829-4/5/1899
Marshal S. 1877-1948
O. Belle 1886-19
Mattie Samantha, wife of Rufus C. 2/10/1870-2/19/1907

CENTER GROVE BAPTIST CHURCH, HWY 346. Est. 1857

BROWN

Ernest A., son of J. M. & O. F. 3/4/1886-2/13/1902
D. F. 10/12/1844-1/7/1916. A Confederate Soldier
Evelyn 5/31/1920-4/4/1936

CAIN

Robert M. 1870-1944
Carl, son of Emma 3/4/1901-6/22/1902
Jesse, son of M. S. & Emma 7/3/1885-7/1/1901

CAMPBELL

Cora, wife of E. A. 10/23/1892-3/13/1920
Mary J., wife of W. P. 10/29/1850-12/28/1902
Estella J., daughter of W. D. & M. J. 2/4/1878-8/31/1894

CANUP

Matison M. 1874-1938
Mary A. 1878-19
Edmund D. 2/28/1917-1918
Deamie 9/26/1905-1914
Infant of Mr. & Mrs. M. M. born and died 1907
Ruby G. 2/4/1900-1901
Carl C. 1907-1951
Ozelle H. 1913-
E. A. 7/13/1901-7/21/1937

CARTER

Monteen 1911-1911

CHILDERS

Georgia A. 1867-1899
Joe B., son of D. C. & Nina 4/17/1909-7/26/1909

CLEVELAND

Velma Shubert died 8/12/1946, aged 18 years, daughter of Nonnie J. A.

COKER

Rosie, Infant of W. B. & C. E. 10/10/1905-5/11/1907

CENTER GROVE BAPTIST CHURCH, HWY 346. Est. 1857

COX

Eleanor B. 1922-1948

CROOK

Henry 12/15/1836-12/23/1910
Riley D. Sr. 1881-1954
Hattie Tolbert 1882-1951
Jeanette 1918-1919
Mary Evelyn 1918-1919
Pauline, wife of J. A. 7/17/1871-3/15/1931
James A. 9/16/1868-1/27/1943
Mary E., wife of G. W. 6/2/1843-10/23/1901
G. W. 10/23/1846-5/16/1906
Mattie L. 1866-1950
Carrie M. 1866-19
Comer A. 1884-1956
Belle W. 1887-1906
Earl Whelchel 6/24/1884-12/24/1948
Teddie Lee 12/20/1884
John R., Ga. Sgt. Army Air Forces WW II 6/5/1920-3/28/1958

CULPEPPER

Claude E. 1902-19
Grace J. 1908-1968

DALE

Bobby 7/11/1951-8/1/1951
Phillip 8/27/1960-10/6/1960

DAMOTH

Frank 1868-1933
Jessie B. 1890-

DANIEL

Lula Brown 9/25/1877-4/27/1924
J. T. 2/2/1835-1/2/1916
Sarah 10/28/1840-3/4/1913, aged 73 years

DAY

Edward 1/2/1824-8/26/1907
Susan A. 5/2/1825-2/6/1899

CENTER GROVE BAPTIST CHURCH, HWY 346. Est. 1857

ELROD

Martha 1868-1954
Hoke, son of Pat & Martha, 6/5/1900-3/5/1933

FREEMAN

Hilda Grace 7/22/1922-8/22/1926
Infant of J. H. and N. E. 11/8/1911-1/20/1912
N. E., Mrs., wife of J. H., 4/28/1877-11/9/1911
Rufred, son of Mr. and Mrs. J. L. 3/13/1906-7/19/1909
John H. 3/12/1877-10/12/1940
Harriett E. 1859-1949

GARRETT

Curtis Lawson 2/2/1940-2/14/1940
Methal L. 5/22/19oo1-2/22/1964
Lucy D. 10/12/1908

GREER

Bessie E. 9/26/1884-4/27/1946
H. M., son of S. L. and A. L. 6/20/1880-7/1/1909
S. L. 3/29/1854-2/22/1921
A. O., wife of S. L., 4/18/1852-7/26/1910

GRIFFETH

Ann O. 1858-1933
John W. 1858-1927
Emma L., daughter of J. W. and A. O. 2/18/1887-6/22/1902
Eula A., daughter of J. W. and A. O. 1/18/1882-2/11/1901
Maud, daughter of J. W. and A. O. 8/20/1880-10/26/1899
William B. 10/23/1878-4/18/1897

HAWKINS

Susie E., daughter of J. B. A. and M. E. 2/14/1903

HENDRICKS

John J., Sr. died 2/4/1954

HENDRIX

Roy 3/1/1905-7/7/1905
Grandson of Mr. and Mrs. J. J. ----
Earnest T., son of M. M. and J. J. 9/9/1899-5/24/1908

CENTER GROVE BAPTIST CHURCH, HWY 346. Est. 1857

HIGHFILL

Clara May 6/18/1906-2/13/1919
Frank 8/9/1911-1/10/1930
Harold 8/28/1958, aged 19 years
Claud, son of Mr. and Mrs. J. T. 1/20/1905-7/10/1907
Mahala 4/30/1949-4/9/1926
James Thornton 2/15/1884-7/1/1919
Neva 6/17/1881-10/30/1957
Nancy Jane 2/18/1843, aged 84
J. N. 11/13/1844-11/13/1923

HITCHCOCK

Martha L., wife of John W. 10/5/1831-5/3/1917
Robert E. 7/22/1857-3/31/1941
Sallie L., wife of R. R. 1/12/1853-6/9/1927

HUGHES

Arllie O., husband of Mollie 7/24/1876-9/28/1907

HUTCHINS

William D. 1850-1904
Newton H. 6/21/1852-6/1/1917
Etta T. 1870-1932
George Bryan 12/7/1940

IVEY

Thomas C. 1877-1934
Bannie B. 1892-1961

JACKSON

Ned L., son of M. N. and J. A. 10/20/1928-11/26/1928

JAMES

Rufford Delain 6/24/1894-3/27/1906
Samantha H. 9/26/1848-1/20/1925

JONES

Thearon, son of Roy and Cora 11/18/1917-6/22/1920
Amanda G. 1866-1905

CENTER GROVE BAPTIST CHURCH, HWY 346. Est. 1857

KENT

Walter R. 1889-1934
Pearl Z. 1881-19

LAND

Infant daughter of F. Land 3/1904

LATTY

Stoy A. 3/27/1968, aged 62

LECKIE

Sammy Columbus, son of Mr. and Mrs. W. C. 5/1/1917-7/6/1917
Harrison Newell, son of W. C. and Gussie 7/21/1912-9/19/1915

LEE

W. 10/24/1882
Annie H. 4/29/1887-3/22/1961
Hessie 1/7/1901-11/16/1901

LEMLEY

Katie Bell, daughter of V. C. and M. V. 8/7/1908-9/18/1908
Mrs. Victoria 1888-1964

LOGGINS

J. B. Sr. 9/19/1884-11/27/1958
Infant daughter of Mr. and Mrs. W. R. 6/11/1927
Charleston L. 8/21/1857-12/10/1935
Julitt O. 8/31/1860-8/12/1935
William R., Ga., Pvt. 168 Inf., 42 Div, WW I, 1/9/1892-9/5/1946

LOVEL

Lizzie 4/15/1902

MARION

Ransom O. 1/28/1851-1/9/1925

MARLOW

W. Lee 9/18/1856-12/3/1932
Lovie 4/11/1856-3/9/1931

CENTER GROVE BAPTIST CHURCH, HWY 346. Est. 1857

MARLOW

Delonie D. 1884-1956
Woddie B. 1881-1954
Infant son of W. L. and M. L. 8/31/1883-9/23/1885
Donnie S. 1885-1961
F. F. 9/21/1848-4/10/1903
Lizzie E., wife of R. M., married 11/11/1906, 11/11/1886-6/6/1908
Paul F. 5/12/1940-9/5/1964
Essie L. 6/26/1902-6/16/1959
W. J. 1/31/1849-2/10/1909
Johnnie Claude 5/31/1931-8/23/1953
W. J. 1/31/1849-3/10/1909
Grady W., son of R. M. and Lizzie 1/8/1906-7/28/1908
Sylvey Lee, daughter of W. M. and D. W. 1/21/1909-2/21/1911
Hubert R. 3/6/1898 -
Ransom C. 1/29/1851-19/1925
Martha M. 1/26/1862-8/23/1959
Infant son of Lum 12/13/1900
D. R. 1873-1930
Mannie H. 1878-1962
Richard Dewey, son of D. R. and Maude 10/10/1899-9/12/1901
R. B. 6/3/1839-4/25/1921
Catherine, wife of R. B. 12/27/1831-9/25/1911
Evelyn 5/4/1850-2/12/1925
F. W. 10/8/1842-9/17/1913
Tilithia C., wife of F. "Uncle" W. 5/16/1837-3/16/1903
Levie M., daughter of F. W. and F. G. 3/1/1871-12/5/1907
Irene, daughter of C. E. and D. M. 9/19/1912-11/2/1919
Lizzie, daughter of Mr. and Mrs. T. A. Emmett 11/11/1886-6/6/1908
Louise S., daughter of A. D. and Ollie 4/1/1920-7/20/1930
Lena E., daughter of A. D. and Ollie 11/7/1923-6/25/1924
Edna R., daughter of A. D. and Ollie 7/10/1918-1924
Ada L., wife of A. D. 5/20/1888-6/2/1912
W. H., son of A. D. and Ada 6/28/1912-7/26/1912
Cynthia E. 1896-1925

MARLER

Sarah E., wife of D. P. 5/20/1855-8/14/1933
David P. 11/8/1850-7/24/1918

McINTYRE

Infant
Mattie 1881-1925
C. C. 1869-1949

CENTER GROVE BAPTIST CHURCH, HWY 346. Est. 1857

McLARY

Marsisia 8/8/1884-2/27/1907

MOTE

Will M. 1882-1962

NALLY

Grady 1893-2/6/1957
Harriett Susan, wife of Webb 8/10/1863-11/29/1909

NASH

George O. 1881-1964

NIX

Francis 4/7/1918-12/27/1940
Mary E. 12/31/1848-1/29/1913
John A., son of B. and M. E., 12/31/1881-6/5/1902
M. F. 12/31/1891-8/13/1925

NORRELL

John F. 12/26/1857-12/10/1935
Drusilla 3/18/1866-9/19/1923

NORRIS

Sarah C. 1907-1934
Jessie C. 19o02-1957

PATRICK

Samuel 6/9/1879-12/5/1967

PARSONS

Nettie Louise, daughter of Mr. and Mrs. E. D. 6/1/1913-10/24/1916
Nettie Marler 7/2/1894-7/25/1922

PERRY

Manolia B. 9/20/1909-6/22/1944
W. K. 9/20/1842-5/15/1925
Adelia, wife of W. K., 4/11/1854-5/30/1910

CENTER GROVE BAPTIST CHURCH, HWY 346. Est. 1857

PORTER

Florence M. 1878-1957
Jim 1882-19

RAGAN

Mrs. Lee 1888-1961
Alice C. 2/7/1851-7/24/1948
Infants of Mr. and Mrs. W. L.
John A. 8/20/1855-7/25/1944

REYNOLDS

George C., son of Claude and Minnie 1929-1930
Minnie, daughter of M. M. and J. J. Hendrix 1902-1939
Susie Bryan 6/8/1895-5/24/1925

SEXTON

Rafe. 1/13/1969, age 59

SIMS

Woodie Callie 4/30/1908-12/27/1908

SMITH

Terry Lee, son of G. C. and F. 12/4/1905-1/12/1906
James Henry died 7/12/1961
Mary E., wife of Isaac S. 9/18/1866-9/2/1918
Mary, daughter of William and Lola 9/2/1918-3/27/1921
Annie L., wife of A. C. Dee

SPENCER

Ella J., daughter of William and Sarah A. 9/2/1881-5/6/1909

STOCKTON

Infant daughter of M. M. and J. E. 2/19/1915-2/30/1915
Infant daughter of M. M. and J. E. 1/13/1913-1/15/1913
Infant daughter of M. M. and J. E. 9/26/1908-9/28/1908
Lurline, daughter of M. M. and J. E. 8/20/1906-6/1/1908
Sarah Joe P. 1/31/1931-3/34/1953

STRICKLAND

Sarah A. Marler, wife of Charles Strickland 3/26/1832-9/7/1916

CENTER GROVE BAPTIST CHURCH, HWY 346. Est. 1857

STRINGER

Dewitt S. 6/25/1911-11/21/1924
Oscar D. 1888-1967
Scott 1858-1933
Sarah M. 1860-1935

TEAL

Little Ernest, son of S. F. H. and F. A. 5/25/1905-8/3/1906

TROUT

Nancy Myrt 11/22/1884-9/28/1954

UNDERWOOD

Sarah 5/5/1892-1/2/1929
David P. 3/7/1886-10/21/1959

WARD

Nancy 1869-1911
Infant son of W. L. and Z. A., died 9/27/1896

WATKINS

George T. 2/12/1903
Essie B. 5/14/1906-10/1/1950
Robert A. 1872-1936
Laura C. 1873-19
Infant daughter of C. C. and F. M. 8/7/1916
Sarah Ann, daughter of C. C. and F. M. 1/7/1914-1/7/1914
Fannie Mae 2/31/1893-11/12/1924

WEBB

A. P. Pye 1888-1968
Curtis W. 1916-1947
Faye C. 1915-19

WHELCHEL

Amanda, wife of R. F. 3/19/1857-8/11/1927
R. F. 3/25/1856-9/24/1917
R. J. 6/3/1896-6/11/1906

CENTER GROVE BAPTIST CHURCH, HWY 346. Est. 1857

WHITEHEAD

Mrs. Sallie 5/12/1872-8/23/1931
Hessie Lee 1/7/1901-11/16/1901

WILKERSON

Maggie, daughter of Mr. and Mrs. R. 2/21/1881-11/1/1908

WRIGHT

Marion W. 6/12/1899-10/1/1962
Sarah M., wife of T. N. 5/30/1859-6/2/1907
Thomas, son of T. N. and S. M. 1/9/1879-6/18/1907
Magnolia, daughter of T. N. and S. M. 4/15/1896-7/20/1907
Howard 5/14/1820-6/15/1920
Maggie 12/10/1921-12/13/1921
Ruth Mae 3/12/1938-4/13/1938
C. F. 4/10/1921-6/5/1924
L. A. Nell 12/31/1815-10/1/1926
Ila G. 3/1/1894-6/25/1961
Jim W. 12/5/1887-6/25/1961
Lelar T. 7/21/1897 -
Harve J. Jr. 6/20/1890-9/2/1942
Benjamin L. 8/10/1892-8/19/1962
Noria S. 8/15/1898

YONCE

John R. 6/21/1864-7/28/1944

JACKSON MEMORIAL PARK, Hwy 55 North

ANDERSON

Gartrell W., born 1923

ANDREWS

Margaret S. 1926-1968

BARNET

Lov. Lenaid 1898 -

BARNETT

Emma Lena 1902-1967

JACKSON MEMORIAL PARK, Hwy 55 North

BARRETT

Dub 1925-1962
Lal 1924 -

BONE

Barbara Sue 1951-1965

BORDERS

Hiram J., Ga. Pvt. Co. L., 2nd Regt. Inf., Spanish American War
10/13/1882-11/2/1967
Hiram H. 8/14/1914-2/15/1961

CARLAN

Ira E. Jr. 1930-1968
Maulene M. 1933 -

CHANDLER

Stacie Amela 11/7/1966-11/14/1968

CHEATHAM

Thomas L. 1893-
Allie Ruth 1902-1965
Kathleen Wofford 5/21/1927-10/30/1966

CHESTER

Isaac Thomas 1/20/1945-11/17/1963

COOPER

Hoyt T. 1919-1968
Elizabeth 1923 -

COX

Frances D. 1905-1968
William F. II (Kismet) 1906 -

CRAIG

Myrtie W. 1907-1960

JACKSON MEMORIAL PARK, Hwy 55 North

CRENSHAW

Howard 1908-1965

DAILEY

Tatum L. 1880-1964

DAVIS

Emmie Ima 4/15/1903-3/29/1964

DILLS

Clyde W. 1/27/1903-11/6/1964

EDINS

Charlie L. 1885-1967
Alice L. 1886-1965

EDWARDS

George H. 9/28/1941-5/31/1968

FERGUSON

William P. 1908-1968
Lillie Mae 1913 -

FORD

W. Cosby 1901-1962

GARLEN

Jack M., USS Forrestal, 11/17/1945-7/29/1967

GARRISON

Harwell Lee 1896-1963
Allene E. 1902-
James E. 1901-1964
Robert E. (Bobby) 1956-1966

GIPSON

Verner W. 1896-1964
Dona H. 1898-

JACKSON MEMORIAL PARK, Hwy 55 North

GRIFFIN

Elmer J. 1904-1965

HAMBRICK

Charles E. 7/2/1951-7/9/1967

HANLEY

Tammy Darlene 1966-1966

HARRIS

Pierce 4/22/1939-12/25/1965

HENDERSON

Ulysses S. 1881-1966

HILL

Oliver L. 4/22/1942-5/25/1968
Marie 2/23/1943
George, Ga. TEC 4 US Army, WW II 8/1/1916-9/25/1961

HOSCH

Elmer F. 1902-1967
Agnes H. 1909-

IVESTER

W. Dennis 1928-1967
Katie Lou 1923-

IVEY

Riley A. 1/13/1889-8/27/1968
Annie S. 3/2/1885-

JOHNSTON

Pauline H. 8/10/1902-8/28/1966

JONES

James H. 1917-1969
Dorothy C. 1927-

JACKSON MEMORIAL PARK, Hwy 55 North

JORDAN

Gordon H. 1890-1964
Addie Mae (Coot) 8/13/1907-4/30/1968
Delia P. 1891-
John T. 12/10/1909
Geraldine 12/16/1931-

KING

Allen 1907-
Ola L. 1904

KITCHENS

John B. 1928-1966

LACEY

Barbara Lee 7/4/1948-8/15/1968

LANGFORD

Ralph A.
Ga Tec 5 Co B
38 Armed Inf. BN WW II
7/20/1919-2/18/1961

LANGSTON

Norman D. Sr. 1895-1966
Hoytie S. 1901-

LOGGINS

Hope E. 1903-1966
Christine L. 1910-

LYLE

Luther J. 1890-1967
Elma B. 1902-

MALEY

Guy T. 1890-1966
Sara B. 1892-1960
Barnett G. 1911-1969

JACKSON MEMORIAL PARK, Hwy 55 North

MAULDIN

Lewis C. 9/4/1909-5/31/1966
Ruth S. 2/11/1914

McCOY

George Otis 1936-1968

McDONALD

Ronny O. (Ron) 10/27/1948-11/24/1966

MINISH

A. E. "Tom" 1906-1968
Annie Lou H. 1912-

MORRISON

David P. 1873-1959
Rev. Lester B. 1905-1964

NEW

William L. Jr. 6/12/1930-8/25/1959
Barbara Ann 9/25/1928-9/25/1928

NUTTAL

Robert H. 1887-
Leah 1886-1961

POLTS

Thomas K., Ga T. Sgt., US Air Force 2/6/1933-8/25/1966
J. D. (Jake) Sr. 1/2/1909-9/3/1966

PRITCHETT

Edward 1933-1969

REIDLING

James O. 1936-1968
Thomas D. 1902-
Ola H. 1900-1965
Olcy F. 1904-1968
Mae Bell 1910

JACKSON MEMORIAL PARK, Hwy 55 North

ROACH

J. Nelson 1893-1968

SAILERS

Walter Henry, Ga Cpl Gen Hosp., 19 WW I, 6/29/1895-1/1/1960
Harvey F. 11/7/1898-2/1/1965
W. Lamar 1931-1967
Mae Onie 1932-

SEAGRAVES

J. B. 1903-1966
Bernice 1901-

SHIRLEY

Anna Carol 5/25/1959-8/21/1961

SHORT

Mary A. 1912-1961
Obie 1891-1965
Minnie Lou 1891-1965

SNIPES

Thomas E. 10/1941-1/1966

STANDRIDGE

Mary Helen Lacy 1928-1965

STEWART

Daniel W. 1935-1968

STRICKLAND

Virginia G. 1948-1965

TANNER

George D. died 1964
Jane Davidson 11/1/1934-9/7/1968

JACKSON MEMORIAL PARK, Hwy 55 North

THURMOND

Bertha I. 9/21/1916-10/2/1946
John A. 1882-1953
Woots O.

TUCKER

Milton 1895-1962
Leolane 1898-

WARD

Forrest A. 1901-1968
Annie Mae 1902-

WATERS

Dorothy 12/5/1924-11/18/1962

WILBANKS

Hoke D. 1906-1963
John Sr. 1894
Nettie L. 1900-1966

WILLS

J. Herman 1910-1967
Ola Mae 1913-

WILSON

John B. 1884-1967
Ora K. 1889-

WOOD

Shirley Ann 10/14/1938-9/2/1960

YATES

John Lacy 2/21/1961-12/1/1962

SHORT-MASSEY-WILBANKS FAMILY CEMETERY
Hwy 59, Near Junction of #326, Commerce, Ga

COY

Thomas 2/3/1889-
Hettie L. Moss 1/2/1880-1/25/1945

CRISLER

Jeptha 8/31/1816-3/20/1854
Elizabeth, wife of J. S. 5/20/1819-1/12/1895

EDWARDS

Maggie E. 11/10/1953-12/5/1939
James N. 1866-1950
Mary E. 1873-1943
James T. 2/15/1851-6/19/1931

EVANS

Hoke S. 9/13/1907-8/29/1967
Maryleen 12/5/1913-

FAULKNER

Carl W. 1892-1967

GADDIS

Nancy Wilbanks 1873-1946

HALL

Eliza Ann, wife of W. J. 8/15/1845-7/4/1897
Clifton E., son of W. J. and E. A. 1/6/1831-6/21/1891
Edna L., daughter of W. J. and E. A. 2/17/1890-7/11/1890

HUNTER

D. Glen 1895-1936
Laura W. 1879-1944

MASSEY

James E. 5/13/1824-8/24/1910
Elizabeth 3/11/1829-2/23/1914

SHORT-MASSEY-WILBANKS FAMILY CEMETERY
Hwy 59, Near Junction of #326, Commerce, Ga

McCOY

Roy Ledforfd 11/30/1909-2/20/1943, Reg. USA, Husband of Faye Short, Killed In North Africa

PRICKETT

Rev. A. P. 3/24/1836-11/8/1863

ROBERTS

Mrs. Pearl W. 1891-1966

SCARBOROUGH

Geneva N. 1917-
Elmer A. 1913-1946

SHORT

L. E. 12/22/1840-1916
James H. 5/30/1838-11/11/1908
Etherlinda L. 10/22/1854-4/10/1915
George L. 11/9/1847-7/8/1910
Johnie L. 5/30/1874-5/8/1875
Maudie 6/27/1883-5/17/1883
Infant daughter of Mr. and Mrs. D. G. born and died 9/28/1896
Grace, daughter of Mr. and Mrs. D. G. 7/16/1903-10/2/1903
Jesse Williams 1883-1960

STREETMAN

Toilet, infant son of A. F. and B. L. 4/4/1891-4/14/1891

TURNER

Mitt W. 11/11/1892-
William 7/17/1896-9/5/1945

WILBANKS

John W. 1857-1937
James E. 1849-1931
Eddie, son of J. H. and Josephine 8/26.1893-12/21/1895
Josephine, wife of J. H. 8/25/1859-10/9/1905
Mary Johnson 1851-1891
Edna, daughter of J. H. and Josephine, died 3/28/1892, aged 18
Jeff C. 1884-1957

SHORT-MASSEY-WILBANKS FAMILY CEMETERY
Hwy 59, Near Junction of #326, Commerce, Ga

WILBANKS

J. M. 1880-1967

THYATIRA PRESBYTERIAN CHURCH, HWY 15 NORTH OF JEFFERSON, GA., ESTABLISHED IN 1786

BAILEY

Mary, wife of S. T. 9/12/1836-2/10/1913

BAIRD

Hattie F. 1900-1958

BARNETT

Anna K, 1854-1931
William G. 1854-1912
C. M. 1882-1947
Lillie 1891-1957
Ida 1/19/1874-8/22/1901
Gladys 10/18/1900-3/22/1901
G. D., son of J. H. and P. A. born and died 11/8/1888
W. S., son of J. H. and P. A. 7/6/1878-5/6/1880
Ann B., daughter of J. H. and P. A.
James H. 2/8/1846-2/17/1911, Co. F, 16th Ga. Vol. Cav., C. S. A.
Vennie E. 1875-1961
Sgt. Henry C., Co. C, 18 Ga Inf. C. S. A., 10/8/1843-11/28/1932
Savannah P. 1871-1953
William L. 1879-1957
Son of W. L. and Vannie 4/26/1899-3/24/1900
Claude G. 1884-1958
Clara A. 1892-

BENNETT

Billy, son of Mr. and Mrs. Bill 7/23/1936
Una 12/20/1880-11/9/1948
Thomas Jack 5/27/1869-9/27/1877

BRADBERRY

Fred C. 6/3/1904-8/24/1950

THYATIRA PRESBYTERIAN CHURCH, HWY 15 NORTH OF JEFFERSON, GA., ESTABLISHED IN 1786

BRANYON

Alta May, daughter of J. T. and M. E. 4/27/1883-5/8/1884

BURNS

Thomas D. 8/20/1855-11/16/1885
Ella L. 1/1858-6/21/1886
Sarah L. 1864-1/15/1887
David M. 1860-11/6/1893
Infant daughter of W. J. and Bessie 10/15/1894-10/16/1894
S. H. died 5/2/1857, aged 36 years, 2 months, 27 days
D. M. died 5/12/1857, aged 32 years, 6 months, 21 days
Joseph Brantly, son of J. M. and S. H. 5/26/1865-10/25/1865
Sarah H., wife of J. M. 10/7/1837-9/27/1877
Dr. J. M. 12/12/1833-11/21/1908

DARNELL

Felton Jay, son of D. E. and G. A. 1/9/1915-10/14/1917

DAVIDSON

A. J. 11/15/1841-4/12/1924
Russel Resine 8/5/1847-1/8/1921
Ophelia 1869-1939
Cora 1892-1941
J. Hosea 1880-1964
Charlie Lee 5/15/1866-8/20/1910

FOSTER

Jimmey D. Wight B. 3/3/1926-10/16/1939

GLENN

Perry, son of J. M. and S. N. 7/23/1877-6/22/1885

HARRISON

Margaret, wife of Rev. John 11/4/1789-4/1/1883

HILL

Lawrence Herndon 4/1/1891-6/14/1945 "Carnegie Hero", died attempting to save the life of Samuel B. Corbitt. WW I. In Loving Memory, Brunswick Shipyard Electricians

THYATIRA PRESBYTERIAN CHURCH, HWY 15 NORTH OF JEFFERSON, GA., ESTABLISHED IN 1786

HILL

Anncybill, born Elbert Co., Ga. 11/4/1815, died 6/18/1897
Jennings Bryan 1/7/1897-8/27/1897
Infant daughter of Mr. and Mrs. C. T. born and died 3/1/1907
Edith V., daughter of C. T. and M. V. Hill 6/3/1910-10/20/1910
Henry Hoyt 11/10/1898-3/19/1917
Ollie Belle, daughter of C. T. and M. V. 7/15/1900-1/22/1918
Minnie Viola, wife of C. T. 4/5/1874-12/13/1920
Jewell T., son of Mr. and Mrs. C. T. 1/10/1894-6/18/1918
Charles T. 2/10/1855-10/23/1927

JENNINGS

Mammie 1891-
George 1885-1947

LACKEY

Julia Montino, daughter of W. B. and Lizzie 3/26/1901-6/7/1901

LONG

Miss Annie 12/28/1815-2/18/1893
Mrs. N. C., wife of H. J., died 9/25/1871, aged 34 years, 4 months, 2 days

MAHAFFEY

William H. 4/28/1887-5/29/1925
Lewis N. 9/27/1920-5/4/1943

MALEY

William Henry 1875-1958
Bessie Evans 1881-1965

MAULDIN

Nancy H. 1859-1947
Basiel L. 8/28/1847-3/14/1924
Lester Gibson died 11/6/1965, aged 72 years, 10 months, 19 days

McCURRY

Estell S. 1885 -
Ray 1880-1951

THYATIRA PRESBYTERIAN CHURCH, HWY 15 NORTH OF JEFFERSON, GA., ESTABLISHED IN 1786

PINSON

Dell Pharr 9/12/1905
William Worth 9/9/1895-11/23/1964

PORTER

Lester 6/6/1815-9/25/1953, Ga, USNRF, WW I

POTTS

Jim Henry 1905-1969
J. M. 6/12/1824-6/28/1879
Odell 1907-1951
Ervin D. 1887-1957
Edna M. 1913-
Ernest L. 1881-1967

PRICE

Estella, daughter of Mr. and Mrs. W. W. 7/29/1907

SANDERS

Ann 5/19/1815-4/12/1891

SCOGGINS

Levi Lincoln died 11/16/1964, aged 65 years, 6 months, 18 days

SELF

Mrs. E. H. died 10/10/1933, aged 70

SHARP

Margaret, wife of E. J. 1/10/1829-8/6/1865
E. H. 7/8/1844-4/30/1922

STOREY

Martha R., wife of James A. 9/11/1860-3/3/1903
Infant son of Mr. and Mrs. James A. born 12/18/1887
Hoyt E. 4/11/1898-5/22/1914

THYATIRA PRESBYTERIAN CHURCH, HWY 15 NORTH OF JEFFERSON, GA., ESTABLISHED IN 1786

STORY

Caroline, daughter of Mr. and Mrs. James A. 8/28/1810-10/4/1876
Woodie, daughter of Mr. and Mrs. James A., 7/6/1883-11/22/1886

TOW

William, son of Charlie and Lula 2/17/1919-7/27/1920

TRAMMELL

Ralph, son of O. A. and N. G. 6/5/1902-2/11/1906

TURNER

J. Marion 1/18/1886-
Fannie K. 10/9/1888-7/18/1951
Inese B., daughter of Mr. and Mrs. R. H. 3/9/1917-3/9/1917
Ida Mae, daughter of Mr. and Mrs. R. H., 6 months old
John M. 12/31/1869-2/15/1963
Ida Mae 5/22/1879-6/12/1917

WIGINGTON

Harriet E., wife of E. G. 12/11/1836-8/22/1875

WILHITE

Morgan 1879-1956
Mamie M. 1882-1965

WILSON

Mrs. Caroline 12/27/1828-3/4/1896
Minnie Mae 1894-1958
Mattie Belle 10/18/1903-12/23/1964

YEARWOOD

Clara Barnett 1889-1950
G. E. 1884-1923
Helen 1921-1922
Rachel 1917-1921
Katherine 1919-1920

Cpl. Lancaster B. 11/19/1914-11/28/1950. Enlisted USMC 1939. Served in WW II, Pacific Theatre of Operations, Killed in Action, Korean War, while on patrol duty 11/28/1950

THYATIRA PRESBYTERIAN CHURCH, HWY 15 NORTH OF JEFFERSON, GA., ESTABLISHED IN 1786

YEARWOOD

Avis S. 12/28/1913-10/18/1962

MACEDONIA CONGREGATIONAL CHURCH, HWY #53 NORTH, BRASELTON

ARMISTEAD

Harold W. 5/7/1940-10/1/1940

BECK

Leora A. 10/4/1898
Minnie
Estell, wife of Marrion 6/8/1902-7/2/1936
Annie Bell 4/11/1926
Fred Lee 4/24/1924
J. M. 4/19/1951, 89 years old
Idell H. 8/10/1904-12/31/1966
Mrs. Pearl 1900-1968
Della 1862-8/21/1910

CASH

Hoyt B. 3/2/1929-9/26/1952, Ga., Sgt. Co. K, 7 Inf., 3 Inf. Div. Korea

CHAMBLEE

Maud, daughter of Mr. and Mrs. E. C. S. 5/8/1906-7/31/1906

CHRONIC

Agusta M. 1873-1909
William T. 1873-1952

COOPER

Olive 1920-1921
Dewey, son of J. C. and Lizzie 5/11/1901-7/10/1901
Ruby, daughter of W. T. and Etta 9/30/1907-10/24/1907
Mrs. J. C. 5/12/1968, aged 76 years, 1 month, 4 days
C. P. 12/13/1882-4/6/1921
Herbert, son of C. P. and T. L. 8/18/1917-11/25/1917
Augustus, son of J. C. and Lizzie 3/23/1906-5/27/1906
Infant daughter of W. H. 11/30/1904-12/4/1904
James C. 1856-1913
Ina L. 6/23/1888-11/24/1956

MACEDONIA CONGREGATIONAL CHURCH, HWY #53 NORTH, BRASELTON

COOPER

Mary Lue, daughter of C. P. and T. L. 4/21/1908-9/23/1916
Lizzie, wife of J. C. 10/8/1860-9/14/1910
Jewel, son of J. C. and Myrtie 11/24/1916-9/16/1918

CORY

J. M. 3/14/1930

DAVENPORT

Mary J. Moore 1867-1949
James W. 12/25/1808-4/13/1903
Asbury J. 1860-1928
Montine, daughter of Mr. and Mrs. A. J. 11/16/1892-7/7/1916
Martha J., wife of James 12/26/1818-9/6/1930

DUNCAN

Ammon M. 3/2/1874-4/18/1908
Mrs. S. B., wife of H. H. 6/3/1870-5/13/1917
J. Trammel 1/5/1910
Tom 5/16/1850-4/1/1924
Miss Asler 4/13/1961, aged 58
Naomie 12/8/1908-1/21/1940

EMMETT

Curtis, son of Lily 9/15/1907-1/12/1908

Children of Mr. and Mrs. T. A.:
Uniece 7/14/1895-7/18/1896
Roselee G. 4/20/1883-7/2/1890

FORRESTER

George 7/2/1820-2/3/1954
Guy 3/21/1898-10/21/1938
Pearlie L., wife of George 12/21/1879-12/15/1967

HAINES

Sarah 1865-1932
Joseph Burton 1864-1938
M. P., Husband of S. P., 9/1/1850-3/26/1916
Elizabeth, wife of Matthew, died 12/24/1910, age 79 years
Ella, wife of Joseph B., 1/20/1871-9/30/1905

MACEDONIA CONGREGATIONAL CHURCH, HWY #53 NORTH, BRASELTON

HALL

Augustus G., died 4/29/1948, aged 69 years, 9 months

HOLDER

William W. 5/26/1865-2/21/1920

HOWINGTON

Birdia
J. W.

LINCEFELT

Infant of W. H. and Bessie, 3/20/1918

LOTT

Mary 5/1908-1955
Walter N., Sr. 8/2/1825-1/9/1947
Isaac Fred 10/25/1896-7/9/1924
William L. 3/5/1874-9/16/1938
Lena L. 3/24/1877
Andrew T. 12/21/1848-4/12/1926
Margaret C. 6/1/1832-5/28/1935
Darwin A., son of Mr. and Mrs. J. J., 2/17/1918-3/14/1963
Infant son of Mr. and Mrs. J. P., 5/8/1938
Mrs. Fannie Marlowe, wife of J. T., 8/2/1869-2/22/1914

MADDOX

Julia H. 1895-
Walter G. 1889-1962
Infant son of Mr. and Mrs. W. G.

MASSINGILL

J. A., wife of H. A., 12/3/1860-10/15/1904

PUGH

"In Memoriam, one grave moved in 1957 from Martin Pugh Burial Ground within Buford Dam and Reservoir Project. Erected by Corps of Engineers, U. S. A.
Martin Pugh 2/1
Anna Bell Howington"

MACEDONIA CONGREGATIONAL CHURCH, HWY #53 NORTH, BRASELTON

REEVES

J. D. 1864-1940
Becky 1862-1954

ROBERTS

Arthur 1888-
J. Davis 1860-1911
Mandie E. 1890-1912

THOMAS

Robert H. 4/23/1886-1/23/1919 married Jessie Annie Pear 11/7/1912

Infant son of R. H. and Messie A. Thomas 5/20/1916-5/21/1916

MT. OLIVE BAPTIST CHURCH, JCT. HWY #98, COMMERCE, GA

AYRES

Pearl W. 1906-
W. Holman 1898-1956

BAILEY

W. T. 1/8/1845-2/9/1923
Sara Elizabeth, wife of W. T., 6/2/1847-4/22/1913

BARRETT

Joe B. 9/4/1864-1/10/1930
George Truitt, son of Mr. and Mrs. E. W., 9/25/1924-10/9/1924

BECK

Tim 10/6/1946-10/27/1946
J. T. 5/6/1863-8/9/1927
Phoeba H. 8/6/1872-11/30/1960

BENEFIELD

William E. 9/15/1890
M. Parlee 9/19/1897-10/13/1936
Evelyn Mae 8/19/1919-12/16/1919

MT. OLIVE BAPTIST CHURCH, JCT. HWY #98, COMMERCE, GA

BENTON

W. M. 4/24/1884-2/19/1928

BOYER

James W. 1913-1968

BROWN

Nellie 11/27/1913-4/5/1937
Tishie Marilla 7/19/1876-8/13/1941
Genie G. 5/17/1882-2/5/1919
Infant son of J. N. and Genie, born and died 2/3/1919
Tressie 8/22/1907-5/10/1940
J. Newt 3/11/1871-1/9/1952
Pvt. Toy J., 7/23/1901-8/15/1932, 72nd Bombardment Sqd., Air Corps. Died while in service, Honolulu, Hawaii

CATLETT

Jasper 1856-1950
Martha N. 1862-1955
Ellie Grace 1902-1960
Clarence N. 1903-1960

CHANDLER

Maxie L. 10/7/1882-8/2/1926

CHEEK

Cora S. 1/1/1872 8/2/1951
Henry M. 6/26/1865-5/21/1955

COLE

Hoyt Otis, son of W. C. and E. A., 1/14/1900-2/15/1902

COTTON

Gibb Leroy 7/30/1907-2/7/195t1
Theodosia 3/10/1908

CRANE

Alvin Thomas 4/30/1930-6/6/1930

MT. OLIVE BAPTIST CHURCH, JCT. HWY #98, COMMERCE, GA

DAVISS

Glen 6/20/1911-6/13/1912

EDWARDS

Fannie Parker 6/20/1895
Henry Alvan 4/17/1888-9/13/1966
Austine, daughter of J. Y. and L. D. E., 7/28/1904-8/28/1904
James V., baby of Mr. and Mrs. J. N., 2/2/1909-11/10/1910
Laurie, dau. of J. N. and Mollie E., 1/7/1919-8/21/1920
Ottis Short, son of J. N. and Mollie E., 6/15/1911-9/22/1928
Jonathan Lee, infant son of Mr. and Mrs. D. F., 1/6/1945

EUBANKS

George H. 4/27/1853-4/9/1931
J. B., son of Mr. and Mrs. G. H., 8/7/1916-4/30/1917

FAULKNER

Candler 1885-1957
Mary P. 1887-1920
Lizzie Oliver 1862-1927
William J. 1847-1912
Julie H. 2/26/1872-1/30/1955
George W. 7/4/1877-12/15/1925
Pat S. 5/13/1869-9/19/1956
Minerva Jane 2/1/1847-4/27/1935
Essie P. 4/20/1884-7/13/1961
Eva Lou, dau. of Mr. and Mrs. S. P., 10/6/1924-10/27/1924

FLEMING

Vannah E. 10/6/1879-8/26/1967
Homer H. 7/4/1874-7/7/1950
Thomas M. 6/24/1846-8/6/1910
Ellen M. 7/17/1846-7/29/1938
Mabel 1929-1952

GAILEY

Kittie V. 1877-1957
John T. 1873-1923
Woodie M. 1887-
Claude H. 1884-1960
W. Jackson, son of Mr. and Mrs. W. D., 1/3/1915-6/13/1916
Jeannette, dau. of L. T. and Nettie 2/27/1921-8/29/1929
William P. 1868-1965

MT. OLIVE BAPTIST CHURCH, JCT. HWY #98, COMMERCE, GA

GAILEY

Hattie L. 1874-
Othel G. 1/17/1898-11/14/1966

GOBER

Vira E. 7/17/1883-2/6/1940

GREGORY

Susie C. 1884-1957

GRIFFIN

Infant son of Mr. and Mrs. I. W., born and died 7/10/1940

HENDRICK

Asa C. 12/16/1834-11/27/1922
Nancy B. 7/27/1855-8/23/1936
John H. 5/11/1859-1/5/1939

HENDRICKS

William J. 1874-1960
Ida W. 1877-
Howard, son of Mr. and Mrs. W. J., 1917-1927
Elizabeth Harp and Mae Standridge, sisters
Edna, dau. of Mr. and Mrs. W. J., 3/6/1920-1/5/1948

HOLLIDAY

Faye E. 1892-1958
Dovie Galvin, dau. of C. T. and A. J., 3/3/1883-6/20/1912
Bertha Randall, wife of L. W., 8/2/1888-6/8/1924
Joseph David 1879-1962

HOPKINS

Mellie, wife of W. D., 7/16/1879-9/10/1911
John Clinton 8/20/1906-4/12/1909
C. Howard, son of W. D. and L. M., 3/5/1914-11/7/1916
W. Dennis 1871-1955
M. Lula 1893-1967

JACKSON

Robbie Evelyn 8/1/1925-7/20/1961

MT. OLIVE BAPTIST CHURCH, JCT. HWY #98, COMMERCE, GA

JONES

Julia B. 1883-1960
J. W. 1893-1947

LACY

Edith Carol, dau. of Mr. and Mrs. C. W., 7/13/1948

LOGGINS

Mary E., died 9/8/1902, age 52

LORD

J. E. J. 1862-1933
Easter A. 1867-1941
Sybil, sister, 1908-1921
Gladstone E., son, 12/24/1897-10/13/1957
M. E. 7/29/1839-3/21/1919
W. F. 1/15/1837-10/16/1903
George Grogan 4/7/1879-6/21/1931
Mary Maude 2/28/1886
Florence P. 4/14/1877-6/17/1964
Charlie G. 2/26/1873-9/3/1938
Jack B. 7/23/1902-11/25/1935
Mary H. 4/14/1867-1/11/1933
Fletcher 10/25/1866

McELROY

Lester P. 1/30/1894-11/27/1960
Flora R. 7/8/1907
Infant son of Lester and Flora 2/18/1942

McGINNIS

Frederick Hutcheson, son of Mr. and Mrs. Fred, 5/24/1928-5/24/1928
Mary F. 2/23/1907
J. Reuben 8/12/1900-8/22/1959
Lamartine H. 8/31/1876-6/1/1946
Lowena Ray 6/23/1882-7/2/1956

MALEY

Johnny Lee 8/3/1919-4/30/1921

MT. OLIVE BAPTIST CHURCH, JCT. HWY #98, COMMERCE, GA

MASSEY

Harold 1922-1924
Swep D. 1896-1962
William Curt 4/29/1884-3/10/1958
Herman 4/18/1925-4/19/1925
James A., son of E. R. and Bertha, 1/10/1913-5/21/1914

MOSS

William T. 1882-1955
Delia G. 1888-
F. W. 4/15/1852-4/20/1912
Emma R., dau. of F. W. and E. A. 8/26/1867-5/25/1919
Jack 1924-1944
Laura Frances, dau. of W. T. and E. C., 2/28/1917-12/21/1918

NUNN

Valley L. 1/8/1873-5/25/1919
Minnie E. 1/4/1884
Samuel, infant son of V. L. and Minnie, born and died 9/26/1915
Elizabeth H. Porter, wife of W. T., 6/16/1839-3/13/1914
Drucilla, dau. of G. L. and M. J., 6/10/1890-7/18/1913
Norman R. 1935-1966

OWENSBY

William Gordon 4/24/1882-12/2/1947
Mamie Iola Ray 9/15/1882-2/17/1939

PATTERSON

Lantia V. 4/25/1858
Wister T. 3/27/1846-3/17/1911

POE

Buford, son of Mr. and Mrs. J. F., 1/23/1915-8/24/1916
Mattie Lee C. 4/13/1888-
John Ferd 1/1/1887-6/1/1954

PORTER

Columbus B. 1881-1853
Mollie T. 1886-1943

Marion S. 11/8/1841-6/8/1926

MT. OLIVE BAPTIST CHURCH, JCT. HWY #98, COMMERCE, GA

PURCELL

Nora M. 9/12/1884-6/5/1944
Lam H. 6/29/1879-12/29/1949
R. T. 9/24/1909-4/13/1937
Lavina Kesler 4/10/1849-8/17/1930
Hugh C. 7/8/1887-4/28/191

RAMEY

Marvin J. 7/3/1907-8/20/1968

RANDALL

Mrs. Mary 8/18/1827-9/24/1903

RAY

Samuel Sylvestus 1858-1940
Katie M. 9/10/1902
Hubert J. 8/8/1898-7/6/1960
Lillie Gailey 5/16/1896
S. Gibson 8/29/1892-10/31/1935
Rosa N., dau. of Mr. and Mrs. S. R., 2/9/1884-4/20/1924

REECE

Mamie F. 8/14/1903-2/5/1920

REYNOLDS

Infant of Mr. and Mrs. E. M. 3/6/1905-3/6/1905
Paula Jean 12/18/1942
Edward M. 1885-1966
Minnie V. 1882-1957

SAILERS

Jane S. 8/21/1862-12/29/1943
George W. 10/14/1844-2/2/1922

SHORT

William H. 5/3/1844-4/20/1923
Jane M., wife of William H., 12/23/1847-4/4/1934
Hattie 3/3/1881-3/17/1966
Dovelee B. 8/29/1888-
Lt. William Grief 11/15/1880-3/27/1961, Ga., 1st Lt. Inf., World War I
Joseph D. 6/4/1884-11/10/1963

MT. OLIVE BAPTIST CHURCH, JCT. HWY #98, COMMERCE, GA

SHORT

Clyde 11/23/1897-11/3/1967
V. Alberta 6/1901-3/8/1959
Ethleen, dau. of W. H. and M. J. 7/31/1877-7/15/1919
Martha E. 2/10/1850-7/8/1923, wife of A. F.
A. F. 2/17/1843-3/20/1912
Frank Olin 1/18/1925-9/19/1965
Retha F. 1903-
Keff 1901-1964
Ada Ray 11/4/1874-7/13/1942
Dooly C. 5/4/1872-9/24/1940

SMITH

Lillie FC. 1892-1929
Fletcher 1894-1926

STANRIDGE

Hilda Runa 4/20/1922-1/9/1925, granddaughter of Mr. and Mrs. J. D.
Docia 7/25/1877-6/5/1920
James J. 1/1/1868-4/25/1956
Howard 1905-1952
William C., son of Isaac and Hettie 3/18/1907-3/27/1909
Julia Jarrett, wife of J. A. 2/3/1879-7/10/1915
William Preston, son of J. A. and J. C. 8/19/1903-6/7/1905

STOCKTON

Mary M. 1931-1931
Edward 1932-1932
Edna L. 1933-1935
Mae 1903-1937
W. M. 1898-1950

STONE

Curtis 4/1/1910
Mary Lee 3/31/1907-8/28/1964

STREETMAN

N. C. 3/21/1875-1/30/1939
Larman, son of J. W. and N. C. 4/12/1912-3/11/1913
J. W. 3/6/1866-3/4/1926

MT. OLIVE BAPTIST CHURCH, JCT. HWY #98, COMMERCE, GA

THOMPSON

Robert E., son of Mr. and Mrs. Ford 4/25/1925-8/9/1925
Robert G. 6/23/1924-1/18/1937

VAUGHN

Levonia Catlett, wife of Herman 5/8/1894-9/5/1963
Dosia A. 2/11/1860-9/5/1940
John F. 7/10/1849-2/13/1911
J. Boyd 11/6/1883-5/4/1941, his wife, Mary Lou
Curtis C. 1901-

VOYLES

Florence 10/18/1914
George O., 5/11/1916-1/22/1950, Ga., S. Sgt., 3AAT Bomb GP, World War II

WHITE

Annie 1943

WILBANKS

Ella, wife of W. L. 6/8/1877-6/17/1925
William L. 125/1871-5/27/1940
Lillian, dau. of W. L. and Ella 6/9/1902-10/25/1913
Betty, infant of Mr. and Mrs. Guy 12/22/1934
Huldah N. 1883-0
William M. 1882-1938
Carole 1/28/1943, child of Mr. and Mrs. Broadus Wilbanks
Oliver B. 5/7/1937, child of Mr. and Mrs. Broadus Wilbanks

WILEY

J. W. 1847-

WILLIAMS

Hilda M. 1/31/1909-
Elma H. 6/19/1911-4/14/1964

WOOD
Tyria L. 7/16/1886-1/19/1944
Beulah E. 10/17/1888-2/15/1926
Hoyt D. 2/20/1905-3/25/1925
T. L., Jr. 1/10/1926-1/21/1926
Irial E. 2/2/1923-9/17/1944

JEFFERSON CITY CEMETERY, Jefferson

AARON

Viola 1881-1962
E. 1880-1963
Minnie B. 1880-1947
Thomas
J. (Pink) 1857-1949
Mary Alice 12/2/1861-4/8/1911
Chessie A. 1890-1926
Nettie Lee 1899-1930
Joseph W. 1886-1957
Alma L. 1894-1959

ADAMS

Eldridge Decatur 1/26/1915-6/8/1961

AIKEN

J. Holmer 1891-
Maggie A. 1885-1958
Eliza Thompson 1/7/1872-5/27/1933
Oscar Pierce 3/2/1886-12/9/1947

AKINS

James E. 7/12/1878-4/17/1949
Eloie Mae died 2/2/1952, age 8 months

ALEXANDER

Willie 3/27/1864-10/12/1932
Clarence B. 1904-1953
John Russell, son of J. V. and W. H. 9/20/1884-7/17/1907
John W. 1862-1947
Matthew 1874-1961
Norma M. 1903-1930
Samuel 1903-1959
Emma E. 1901-1963
Pansy 1917
J. B. (Dutch) 1894-1968

ALLAN

Laura D. 1857-1930

JEFFERSON CITY CEMETERY, Jefferson

ALLEN

Marilyn R. 8/11/1924-5/24/1964
Victoria died 2/25/1923, age 68

AMICK

Ben C. 1889-1958

ANDERSON

Guyla 6/28/1903-7/14/1936

ANGLIN

Susan C., wife of H. C. 8/16/1855-7/16/1904

APPLESBY

Robert Travis Sr.
Lynn Cooper 3/23/1931-2/22/1964
Ann Stockton
George Douglas 10/4/1890-10/16/1948
Guss A. Johns 6/9/1870-12/14/1925
Cora W. 8/23/1877-12/7/1900

ARCHER

Jack, Ga. Pvt. SP Training, World War II, 7/4/1919-7/24/1949
Amanda L. 11/4/1851-5/14/1921
Samuel Bell 3/26/1852-9/23/1930
Lula Jarrett 8/19/1878-1/6/1950
Henry M. 7/6/1875-9/14/1919, US Mail Service, RFD #14 Jefferson, Ga.
Lenna Turk 11/11/1876-10/14/1960

ARNOLD

David Kenneth 7/26/1958-10/8/1958

ASKEW

James A. 6/20/1878-5/11/1900

ATTAWAY

Oscar H. 2/22/1909-2/12/1968, Ga. M. Sgt., US Air Force, World War II

JEFFERSON CITY CEMETERY, Jefferson

BAILEY

J. L. Co. A, 23rd GA Regt. State Troops, C. S. A.
Mary A., wife of J. L., born in Elbert Co., Ga 1/14/1837, died 1/1878
Julis E. 1868-1930
Donia H. 1878-
F. M. died 11/2/1924
Gus Wyatt 1913-1917
Minnie W. 1877-1953
Catherine 1907-1918
George W. 1873-1942
George Dewey 1898-1866
T. Stoy 1895-1944

BAKER

Frank, Ga. Pvt. Corps of Mil. Police, World War II, 2/5/1922-8/26/1943
George 6/23/1899-2/7/1907

BALDY

Estell A., wife of J. L. 3/7/1889-7/25/1909

BALES

Emma L. 1904-1963

BARBER

Horace Oscar, son of Mr. and Mrs. D. P. 12/13/1914-7/31/1918
Mrs. Flossie D. 1887-1964
Robert Reese, Jr. 1912-1913
Woodruff 7/27/1961
Harold T. 1914-1936
Ola Stockton
Robert Reese 8/25/1925
Minnie Stockton, wife of D. P. 1891-1922
David Stockton, son of Mr. and Mrs. D. P. 4/16/1911-9/1/1911

BARNETT

Ida Sudderth 8/12/1908-1/25/1952
infant son of Henry Polk and Ida Barnett 2/1/1946
Charley Baxter 5/13/1966, aged 68 years
Charlie Embry 3/29/1873-9/17/1947
Infant son of Henry Polk and Ida Barnett 6/13/1937

JEFFERSON CITY CEMETERY, Jefferson

BARRETT

Laura Bell Roberts 8/4/1901-10/15/1968

BARTON

Emlyn D. 8/28/1908
Julius J. 7/30/1900-9/3/1959

BEASLEY

Georgia Trout died 2/15/1920

BELL

A. J., Co. C., 18th Ga. Regt., C. S. A.
Wilson Cartrell 9/12/1880-10/23/1910
William Lane 2/3/1843-3/28/1843
Mary E. 10/17/1839-5/18/1917
Harry P. 12/3/1860-11/3/1916
H. W. (Rache) 8/11/1881-10/18/1952
Minnie Allan 1881-1949
Cornelia Watson 1842-1926
Joseph M. Storey 1/1/1839-9/4/1895
Andrew Jackson 5/19/1844-2/17/1911
James A. 1898-
Jackson 3/26/1813-6/23/1880
Luella L. 11/1851-2/9/1886
Eula Stockton, wife of H. W. Bell, Jr. 1882-1908
Samuel Jackson 1879-1948
Horatio Webb 1842-1916
Harriet Eliza 9/2/1840-12/28/1922
Laura Cheatham 12/20/1844-12/4/1912
Mattie P. 11/11/1897-9/28/1953
David L. 11/25/1853-2/13/1872
Rebecca 11/28/1817-5/23/1891
Augustus A. 3/6/1849-7/3/1890
Judge H. W., Co. C, 18th Regt., C. S. A.
W. Parks 3/12/1864-3/15/1901
Baby Florrie 3/12/1862-8/25/1862
Willie 8/15/1863-8/22/1863

BENNETT

Thomas Holder 1900-1949, brother
Thomas Jackson 1870-1918, father
Alice Louise 1903-1924, sister
William T. 10/23/1859-10/4/1890

JEFFERSON CITY CEMETERY, Jefferson

BENNETT

Jesse Marie, dau. of J. C. and L. D. 9/4/1894-8/21/1896
Dr. J. C. 1/7/1869-4/19/1934
Thomas, Co. C, 18th Ga. Regt., C. S. A.
Joseph, son of J. C. and L. D. 7/27/1896-8/28/1896
Infant daughter of Dr. Jim 9/23/1892-9/2/1892
Lizzie O. 1/10/1870-8/31/1955
Sam Dean 3/18/1889-6/7/1964
Mattie L. Holder, wife of T. J., 12/4/1873-8/15/1911

BIRD

Robert E. 4/8/1889-4/9/1945
A. Burel 11/2/1904

BLACKSTOCK

Alexander N. 3/26/1882-10/4/1967
Freddie H. 5/16/1896-

BLACKWELL

Henry 1875-1961
Mary L. 1884-1949

BLASINGAME

Lovette M. 1882-1953

BOGGS

John Wesley 12/27/1850-8/10/1923
Harlow Bullock, wife of J. H. 8/24/1863-7/19/1927
Julius H. 4/19/1854-3/26/1932
Addie Hunter 3/31/1859-

BREAZEALS

C. Norman 6/23/1890-12/29/1951

BREWER

Dennis O. 1900-1907
Ruby B. 1903-

JEFFERSON CITY CEMETERY, Jefferson

BROCK

Jason Mays 1900-1963
Lou Dowdy, wife of Charles O. 4/28/1867-3/18/1954
Charles O. 10/23/1857-5/29/1920
Augustin Harrison 11/26/1852-9/15/1928
Sallie Simpkins 11/2/1860-12/25/1928

BROOKS

Walter M. 1899-1969
Edward S. 4/6/1881-3/2/1900
Henry L. 7/18/1870-12/11/1929
Mauddell 2/11/1903-10/7/1942
Dell M. 5/5/1876-9/10/1950
Mary Lila 12/17/1864-3/30/1949
Bessie 12/25/1894-10/7/1927
Annie Lucile, dau. of Mr. and Mrs. A. L. 6/7/1901-7/11/1903
Annolevia, wife of A. F. 8/8/1843-9/23/1898
James L. 12/2/1873-2/27/1945
Andrew L. 9/8/1875-1/1/1955
Thomas M. 12/30/1845-3/8/1930
Adolphus E. 4/15/1835-4/10/1919
Clyde 4/5/1906-3/17/1909
Sarah F. 1807-1877
Clifford N. 1/2/1916-12/22/1956
Lila Mae Levell 1912-1949
E. A. (Pat) 11/20o/1882-3/8/1962

BROWN

Leighton Littleton 12/18/1905-1/28/1912
Elisha H. 5/22/1882-2/18/1927
L. H. 6/20/1915-11/24/1949
Billy Chandler, Ga PPC 17 Inhf. 7 Inf. Div., Korea PH 10/20/1930-7/21/1952
Marion N. 3/10/1896-2/16/1947

BRUCE

William F. 11/22/1897-1/22/1958
Annie E. 3/23/1887-

BRYAN

John Curtis 4/30/1960-12/13/1960

BRYSON

Barbara, infant dau. of Mr. and Mrs. C. B. 11/4/1937

JEFFERSON CITY CEMETERY, Jefferson

BRYSON

Charles L. 11/26/1874-3/13/1942
Infant son of Mr. and Mrs. C. T. 6/26/1910-6/26/1910
Miss Pauline Winifred died 6/6/1966, aged 63 years, 9 months, 8 days
Gertrude E. 1/26/1876-7/24/1937

BURKE

Martha Twitty 11/30/1898-7/6/1945

BUSH

Lucius T. 1/23/1850-12/22/1883
Elizabeth, wife of W. W., 5/22/1828-1/1/1892

CALLAHAN

John 3/7/1807-5/24/1879
Abarilla 7/19/1806-12/3/1891
Linda

CAMPBELL

O. H. 12/1/1852-6/9/1880
A. E. 3/20/1862-3/22/1880

CARITHERS

T. A. 8/4/1900-3/21/1935
Samuel R. 1/11/1868-1/4/1920
Talie 1/13/1876-10/15/1937
Jewel 12/3/1898-10/19/1918
Robert T. 6/11/1823-9/13/1875, aged 52 years, 3 months, 2 days
Sarah P. 8/24/1823-7/22/1918, aged 94 years, 10 months, 29 days

CARPENTER

Lou Ellen, wife of T. C., died 10/13/192, aged 44

CARROLL

Lertrelle S. 1918-1955
Lillie H. 1/9/1900
A. Boyd 9/22/1899-5/20/1964

CARTER

David Augustus, son of Mr. and Mrs. P. A. 1/8/1908-1/10/1908

JEFFERSON CITY CEMETERY, Jefferson

CARTER

John Orr, son of E. E. and Edna 54/27/1915-5/29/1915
T. W. 5/31/1856-12/4/1925
Pratt A. 11/20/1882-5/1/1962
Theron Niblack, son of Pratt and Conie 12/13/1910-3/11/1913
William Henry 12/22/1854-8/20/1923, his wife, Loucinia Porter, 10/30/1858-10/5/1941
Conie N. 5/18/1888-8/9/1965
R. Earl 1887-1959
Billy 7/24/1916-7/6/1942
Elizabeth A., wife of Thomas 3/27/1869-12/26/19

CATLETT

Claude, Ga. Wagoner 123 Fld. Hosp., World War II, 5/18/1893-1/18/1959
Daisy G. 161905

CHILDS

Kitty W. 1889-1964
Martha 3/1/1893-4/6/1934
Lee R. 1889-1957
Curtis E. 8/24/1924-1/1/1952
Edward M. 1893-1953
Marsha 10/21/1956

CLARK

Omce Carroll 9/11/1896-
James Coil 3/14/1889-5/31/1962

COLLIER

Curtis H. 3/26/1889-1/12/1939
Frances V. 12/17/1858-2/21/1941
Benjamin H. 7/29/1856-1/12/1930
William D. 9/23/1924-11/13/1924

COUNCIL

Willie S. 3/5/1884-4/26/1968

CRAIG

Reba Vernell 9/18/1943-11/22/1943
Reba Vernell 9/18/1943-11/22/1943

JEFFERSON CITY CEMETERY, Jefferson

CRAFT

William M. 1883-1940

CRIMMINS

Mary P. 1911-1947

CROWE

Napper 1909-

CRUMLEY

Dickie C. 1877-1957
Esco 1910-1968

CULBERSON

Susan S., wife of R. M. 3/5/1879-6/15/1910
R. M. 1/10/1879-12/8/1941
Mattie Sears, wife of R. M. 10/10/1880-7/20/1950
Edgar 3/28/1913-12/23/1913

CUNNINGHAM

Ansel, Whittons' Co., Tucker's Regt., Revolutionary War

DADISON

Darlene (Dadisman) died 8/2/1966, aed 92 7ears
Bessie (Dadisman) 11.14.1890-12/8/1900

DADISMAN

Doris Josephine 9/5/1920-10/25/1920
S. E. 6/10/1851-4/5/1935
Stiles W. 9/26/1893-1/25/1943
L. M. 12/9/1841-7/26/1919
Howard D. 4/1/1898-3/16/1951

DALTON

Baby Vicky 8/19/1960-11/12/1961

DANIEL

Fay E. 1889-1959
Emma J. Carter 8/11/1860-4/19/1913

JEFFERSON CITY CEMETERY, Jefferson

DANIEL

Claude Y. 18882-1957
Son of C. Y. and F. E., died 5/5/1913

DARLEY

Alma S. 1899-
Harvey J. 1900-1960

DAVENPORT

Joseph Archer died 1/2/1969, aged 48 years, 8 months

DAVIS

Cloub B. 4/25/1898-7/26/1964
Henry W. 3/4/1860-190/13/1914
Mary E., wife of Henry W. 1/28/1852-

DAY

Curtis L. 1948-1949
James R. 1946-1947
Robert Harold Jr., Ga. CPL 19 Inf. 24 Inf. Div. Korea, 8/6/1928-7/31/1950

DICKSON

Mary Elizabeth 1/20/1843-10/9/1923
W. W. 1872-1938
Infant of J. C. and Dollie 1897
Eliza 7/10/1807-7/17/1886
Hattie Potts 1876-1957
Jeptha 4/6/1830-11/22/1884
Miss Ella died 12/9/1968, aged 91 years, 6 months, 22 days
Taylor Jr. 3/14/1943-10/6/1962

DOOLEY

Wilborn Cantrell, son of J. C. and Mattie J., 5/23/1891-12/11/1907, aged 16 years, 6 months, 18 days
James Clifton 10/15/1859-3/3/1927
Martha Jane 6/12/1865-5/25/1955

DOSTER

Judge T. J. 1874-1964 (Thomas J.)
Mattie D. 1879-1959

JEFFERSON CITY CEMETERY, Jefferson

DUKE

Billie, son of B. F. and Vannie 9/8/1901-11/18/1911
William Ralph 7/20/1923-1/4/1957
David H. Sr. 7/31/1888-6/4/1952
Eliza G. died 7/1851, born 1823
Will Henry 9/7/1871-6/18/1915
Hattie Daggett 6/29/1869-1/26/1962

DUNCAN

William H. 3/20/1885-11/4/1961
Minnie Lee 1/30/1892-5/4/1968

DYE

Beth Bennett 6/6/1903-4/17/1933

ECHOLS

Mrs. Mamie R. 1881-1968
J. S. 1871-1939
Ella E., wife of Rev. H. U. died 5/28/1883, aged 24

ELLIS

Mrs. G. W. 11/18/1866-4/30/1917

ELLINGTON

John D. 3/28/1879-5/23/1924, his wife, Jessie Frances Storey, 2/10/1889-11/23/1918

ELROD

Luther F. 11/10/1881-10/26/1944
Cranford Pierce 7/16/1899-11/9/1917

ENGLISH

Ulysses H. 6/1/1883-1/25/1967
Lois M. 9/24/1889-5/16/1966

ESCOE

James Daniel 11/8/1901-1/16/1964
J. D., Jr. (Jimmy) 1921-1923

JEFFERSON CITY CEMETERY, Jefferson

ESPY

Robert 12/28/1795-1829
Sarah G., dau. of H. and M. 4/9/1831-4/16/1870

ETHRIDGE

Ira Washington 6/7/1870-3/12/1945

EVERETT

James C. 5/15/1921-5/20/1956

FARR

Bert Franklin, Pvt. U. S. Army, World War I, 11/5/1889-5/15/1955
Raymond, son of Mr. and Mrs. B. F. 1937-1944

FERGUSON

Dow W. 5/4/1884-11/3/1936
Nelson 12/29/1932
Bell B. 3/7/1887
Callie M. 6/24/1911-1/4/1933
Louisa 10/12/1936

FITE

George Henry 1909-1963

FLANIGAN

Allan J., PFC Med. Dept. World War I, 3/28/1896-9/17/1958
Eva M. 1893-

FLEEMAN

Eliza A. 3/22/1825-1/3/1910
Timothy David, husband of Gail Pritchett Fleeman, father of Timothy, David, Tami, Denine, 1946-1947

FOSTER

Mamie Johnson 2/3/1875-1/22/1956

JEFFERSON CITY CEMETERY, Jefferson

FREEMAN

Eliza A. 3/22/1825-1/3/1910

FROST

A. A. 1876-1957
Ruby E. 1892-19
Alice Guest 4/10/1882-12/22/1927
William P. 1/18/1878-11/29/1949

GIBSON

Cora A. 10/8/1882-9/4/1964
Duke 7/17/1880-10/4/1964

GILBERT

Farris C. 3/31/1917-10/4/1959

GILSTRAP

E. Willie 1913-1966
Addie T. 1884-1963

GLENN

J. H. 10/22/1832-3/17/1897
S. N. 8/7/1844-11/30/1901
Dr. J. M., Echols Artillery, C. S. A.

GOBER

Frances Jane Bell, wife of Fletcher Sanford 8/31/1835-8/17/1893
Fletcher Sanford 4/18/1825-8/9/1862
Henry Jackson, son of Fletcher Sanford and Frances Jane, 1858-9/1858
Fletcher Estell, dau. of Fletcher Sanford and Frances Jane Gober 9/19/1862-6/9/1863
Marcus, son of Fletcher Sanford and Frances Jane 1854-1954

GRIER

Gordon Lee, son of Cleve and Laura 4/13/1925-7/30/1925

GRIFFIN

Patsy 11/13/1948-6/7/1953

JEFFERSON CITY CEMETERY, Jefferson

GRIFFITH

Sara Ann 1936-1938

GRINDLE

Troy Lee, 1 year
Shirley Jean, 3 years
Emma Mae Echols 11 years
Roy John, 29 years old
Liley Mae, 21 years. Buried 11/2/1962

GRIZZLE

Lewis H. Jr. 4/27/1940-2/6/1963

GUNNELLS

Ella Montgomery 3/31/1871-6/4/1951

HALE

Elmer W. 2/19/1878-6/20/1930

HALL

L. C. 1912-
Julia D. 1873-1961

HANCOCK

Sarah Annie 8/22/1856-3/7/1915
Hugh Haroldson 11/19/1849-4/27/1911
Infant of H. H. and S. A.
John B. 9/24/1852-6/24/1943
Thomas Donald 10/9/1911-11/28/1950
Mary O. 1880-1949
R. J., Co. C., Cobbs Legion Cav. C. S. A. (Robert J.), 2/9/1839-7/6/1877
Claud 1881-1942
Harold, son of Mr. and Mrs. Homer 3/4/1907-8/6/19

HANSON

J. Calvin 1868-1957
David W. 1872-1952, Co. L, 1st Regt. , U. S. Artillery
Ada W. 1876-1953
Kathryn R. 1950
Alia S. 1951

JEFFERSON CITY CEMETERY, Jefferson

HARDY

C. D. 2/1/1861-4/12/1943
John W. 1901-1960
Ada Q. 1895
Laura Merritt 2/27/1870-5/15/1923
Clyde B. 1901-1965
C. Edward 1895-1901
Spratlin William H. 1910-1961

HARGRAVE

Evelyn S. 11/26/1921-10/25/1963

HARRISON

Mary Eliza 12/8/1847-9/22/1940
T. P., Co. E, 5th Ga. State Troops, C. S. A.
J. C. 11/26/1852-2/8/1916
Louisa 12/8/1847-12/28/1927
Sarah A. 1860-1923

HARTSFIELD

Ethel Stockton 3/21/---
Rev. Jesse 3/17/1880-3/30/1956

HAWKINS

Ruth M. 6/12/1941-1/24/1955
Martha Elaine, dau. of Fred and Emma

HAYES

Mary R. 1884-1939

HENRY

Annie Dell, dau. of Mr. and Mrs. C. B. 6/29/1905-8/17/1905
Katie Lucile 7/28/1899-7/15/1904

HOARD

Floyd G. 3/11/1927-8/7/1967
Harvey T. 10/5/1913-1/4/1962

JEFFERSON CITY CEMETERY, Jefferson

HOLDER

Thomas Rhodes 1/12/1814-11/29/1895
Thomas R. 12/23/1871-1/22/1896
Martha Angie, wife of Thomas Rhodes 7/14/1841-8/15/1915
Ada M. 8/24/1871-11/6/1959
Infant, Myrtle May, dau. of John and Ada M.
John M. 7/22/1868-1/7/1961
Franklin Pendergrass 1/22/1878-9/11/1946

HOLLIDAY

Robert A., Pvt. Co. 11 Ga. Inf., Spanish American War 9/12/1860-5/11/1953
Maude Pendergrass 4/10/1874-5/10/1943
T. C. 5/26/1898-2/26/1920

HOOPER

Charles F. 1866-1944

HOUSE

Jessie L. 4/16/1904-12/16/1928
John C. 10/10/1872-7/20/1938
Sallie Jennings, wife of J. C., 10/2/1881-10/20/1909

HOWARD

Frances Elizabeth, wife of Wiley Chandler 1/22/1849-12/13/1925

HOWELL

Mary Belle 8/3/1938-5/14/1935
Henry Raymond 7/23/1895-8/27/1953
Robert S. 1856-1930
Anne Randolph and Frances Elizabeth 10/20/1869-6/30/1946
Wiley Chandler, son of Asa Jefferson and Elizabeth (Gilmer)
Glenn 11/23/1838-4/30/1931

HOWINGTON

Pearly M. 1885-1917
Sybil E. 1916-1923

HUFF

J. Herman 9/20/1902
Annie B. 10/11/1904-10/1/1957

JEFFERSON CITY CEMETERY, Jefferson

HUMAN

Henry D. 4/27/1823-7/10/1883
Joseph Daniel 8/1840-1870

HUNTSINGER

Callie Dale 1890-1950

HUNTER

Martha A. 12/26/1822-12/29/1980
Elizabeth Wier 5/29/1848-1/25/1920
John S. born in Camden District, SC 4/4/1810, died in Jackson Co. Ga. 11/26/1879
H. C. 4/9/1848-2/20/1892

IVEY

Larry Lee 9/30/1947-8/30/1953
Ella, infant of A. J. and E. J., 5/6/1895-6/16/1896
Alice Meade 9/7/1917-9/12/1965
Beatrice, wife of Jim, 8/12/1823-8/21/1905

JACKSON

Kate R. 9/13/1872-11/22/1889

JARRETT

L. D. 8/28/1868-8/11/1947
James A. 5/28/1844-11/18/1925

JOHNSON

Ralph Emerson, son of R. D. and M. E. 10/29/1896-2/11/1898
Albert S. 12/3/1894-4/14/1962
Robert David 6/31/1860-10/1/1913
James E. died 4/27/1897, aged 87 years
J. K. born Knox Co., TN 12/8/1843, died 1/9/1930
Allen R. 6/26/1817-11/22/1889
Robert 1881-1851
Richie B. 3/21/1894
Pauline McRee 10/5/1902-6/9/1953
Robert E. 1883-1962
Jeremiah 2/16/1841-3/2/1916
Emily, wife of Allen 3/8/1818-9/6/1889
Robert David 1/31/1860-10/1/1913
Julia 1889-1956

JEFFERSON CITY CEMETERY, Jefferson

JOHNSON

Capt. 12/3/1894-4/14/1962
James E. 10/18/1897-1/30/1918
Margaret W. 11/14/1850-2/11/1934
Jacob K. 4/1/1846-5/18/1891

JONES

Frances Hanson 1911-1965

JORDAN

John T. Jr. 3/5/1912-3/8/1912

KELLY

May H. 1875-1942
Robert Judson, Ga. Pvt. Stu. Army Trng Corps, World War I, 9/5/1899-5/1/1965
A. J. 1831-1906
Sam 1874-1934
Idonia 1852-1936
Peggy Jane 10/20/1940-10/31/1940

KESLER

Stanley 1891-1944
Thurman 1902-1931

KICKS

Walter A. 8/30/1904-6/6/1958

KININGHAM

Joy M. 3/26/1874-4/30/1936
J. L. 4/7/1858-6/6/1929

KINSEY

Rosa Lee 10/27/1910-6/15/1965
Emma A. 8/8/1888-7/16/1964

KITCHENS

J. T. 8/9/1913-3/24/1936
Peggy 7/3/1934-1/2/1935

JEFFERSON CITY CEMETERY, Jefferson

KIZER

Herbert J. W. 1892-1962
Iva F. 1896-

KNOX

Samuel, Lt., Locke's N. C., Regt., 1/1/1747-11/1836

LANCE

Fred R. 1916-1959
Claudine P. 1915-

LANE

B. Morsey, son oc F. E. and M. 8/27/1905-2/21/1904

LANGFORD

Luther A. 1887-1955

LEE

R. 1907-1951

LEDFORD

Alice Johnson 7/31/1903-1/21/1904

LINDSEY

Samuel Middleton, son of James and Jane 6/13/1816-9/6/1852
Jane M. 3/4/1810-4/2/1856
James 7/15/1815-1/1/1865
Mary Caroline 4/6/1814-2/5/1890

LONG

John Anderson 4/17/1905-1/3/1959
Hazel Pittman 5/12/1919-7/23/1960
Robert A. 10/29/1942-8/23/1954
Annie 10/22/1893-2/5/1953
John David 2/19/1824-10/28/1875
Alice Griffeth 7/13/1878-
T. Frank 1902-1944

JEFFERSON CITY CEMETERY, Jefferson

LORD

John H. 7/10/1875-11/1/1957
Helen R. 10/29/1882-2/8/1964
Emory S. 12/15/1882-12/26/1928
Lavina P. 3/23/1840-2/28/1915
John H. 7/10/1875 11/1/1957
James W. 3/21/1840-4/11/1927
Helen R. 10/29/1882-2/8/1864

LYNN

Sarah Elizabeth, dau. of Mr. and Mrs. G. W., 6/2/1932-1/11/1933
PFC Weldon G. died 2/17/1967, aged 19 years

MABRY

Eva Leila Carithers 4/2/1846-3/11/1887
Mary Alice 9/16/1869-7/11/1886, daughter

MADDOX

Edd 1855-1931
Olive M. 1877-1854

MAHAFFEY

Lurlie 3/20/1886-12/18/1917
James H. L. 9/19/1874-11/17/1896
Evie C. 4/2/1851-6/15/1930
J. A. B. 4/9/1843-7/3/1919

MALOOK

Jessie Freeman, wife of Edd Maddox 11/5/1863-1/10/1908

MANUS

Estelle H. 1896-
Rome J. 1891-1956

MARLOW

Neeby Donald 4/10/1937-2/27/1965

MARTIN

William James 7/5/1859-12/25/1910
George 1908-1942

JEFFERSON CITY CEMETERY, Jefferson

MARTIN

Tiney 12/15/1957-3/29/1966, "A Loving Pet"
R. B. 1916-1963
Alvin, Ga. Pvt. US Marine Corp., World War I 1/16/1895-11/15/1954
Azzylee 1916-
Clara Williamson 1886-1961
Weyman Jarrett 1884
Dedicated to the memory of our son and brother, Joseph Garland Martin born 9/25/1913. Gave his life in the service of his country on Bourgainville Island 9/28/1944. 182 Inf. Am. Div. Army

MASSEY

Milo H. born Washington Co., Ga. ordained a Baptist Minister 1/2/1896-12/1/1958
Kate Roberts born Jackson Co., Ga. 8/22/1879-1967, married 1/15/1929

MATTHEWS

Alyce H., wife of Paul B. 5/13/1881-8/12/1906

MAULDIN

Ora A. 10/3/1854-1/6/1908
James G. 5/8/1850-12/29/1925
James 10/1/1830-4/17/1900
Coleman 1885-1950
Azilee Ray 1890-1963
Allen D. 1882-1953
Ola H. 1894-

MAXWELL

R. B. 1857-1945
Mamie Christian, wife of R. B. 1875-1921

McCLURE

Wayne W. 12/21/1934-4/17/1957
Rennie D. 8/21/1952-8/24/1952

McCOY

Susan C. 1843-1912
John C. 1838-1896

Children of John C. and Susan C: Wilmath A. 1858-1902; James B. 1862-1890; Minnie 1865-1888; John 1873-1922; Mannie H. 1874-1903; Montine 1875-1885;

JEFFERSON CITY CEMETERY, Jefferson

McCOY

Alexander F. 1879-1887; Eva E. 1886-1919; Malissa Adeline 1856-193--; James Benjamin 1862-1890

McDONAL

Jerry E. 10/3/1939-3/20/1947

McDOUGALD

R. J., Jr., son of Mr. and Mrs. R. L. 7/4/1911-1/7/1928
R. L. 2/25/1876-1/7/1928
Tina, wife of R. L. 10/21/1868

McELHANNON

T. A. 5/11/1846-11/26/1915
Ida 9/1/1870-5/29/1960
Mary Lee 1881-1927
John Emory 1876-1964
James E. 1919-1968
S. E. 9/4/1849-1/7/1928
Johnie H. 1924-
Thomas Asbury 5/11/1846-11/26/1915, 17th Ga. Regt. Co. K, C. S. A.

McGARITY

Pearl
Father 10/22/1846-4/20/1918
Mother 10/22/1852-6/4/1912

McMULLAN

Ethel J. 12/31/1906-10/14/1965
James L. 5/2/1905

McREE

William Jefferson 1863-1956
Beulah B. 1879-1960
Lula Pittman 1866-1947
Arthur H. 1871-1962

MERCIER

May Zelma 1899-1968

JEFFERSON CITY CEMETERY, Jefferson

MIDDLEBROOKS

Lucille N. 12/4/1915
Ila Roberts 9/10/1879-8/3/1945
Herman T. 6/13/1876-11/15/1960
Thomas P. 10/2/1911-8/31/1965

MITCHELL

Alice, wife of C. T. 2/27/1867-7/29/1900

MOBLEY

Jacqueline 12/14/1929-9/28/1941
H. Lewis 4/12/1901-1/27/1950
Mildred, dau. of Mr. and Mrs. H. J. 11/30/1904-6/26/1905
Louise Pendergrass, wife of H. L. 4/6/18880-10/24/1935
Henry Isham 5/1/1870-6/18/1952

MOON

Lonnie B. 11/13/1887-8/17/1954
Emma 1863-1948
M. G. 1865-1949

MOORE

A. Hal 3/24/1887-8/6/1958
R. D. 7/16/1850-1/12/1926
Lilliam B. 5/14/1886
Calderwood Harrison 10/10/1858-5/22/1937
Sarah Ethel 10/19/1880-12/27/1960
Letitia Sander 1857-1943
Alva Appleby, wife of R. D. 4/10/1893-6/22/1938
Milliard Fillmore 1854-1934

MONTGOMERY

Thomas E. 10/2/1873
Carrie Deupree, wife of C. L. 12/19/1852-9/27/1902
Walter C. 11/4/1882-1/27/1929

MORRISON

Miss Minnie Head 1877-1959
Christian Ann 12/13/1850-12/20/1917
Leary Fillmore 1890-1964

JEFFERSON CITY CEMETERY, Jefferson

MOSLEY

Infant twins (daughters) of H. L. and L. P. born and died 7/28/1902

NABERS

M. D. L. 11/12/1830-7/11/1845

NIBLACK

Virgil Augustus 1857-1950
Alice Hardy 1866-1934

NICHOLSON

Juanita 4/18/1919-11/15/1920

NIX

Andrew J. 1900-1932
Rosana A. 1912-1966

NUNN

Dora H. 1888-1964
William H. 1881-1966

ORR

Fannie G. 4/19/1855-4/25/1939
John J. 1/9/1853-8/11/1912

PATRICK

Gladys H. 7/20/1891
Josephine S. 9/8/1861-5/17/1945
John Henry, Ga and Sgt. 321 Dept. Repr. Sq. AAT World War II
11/9/1904-10/24/1964
Miles J., Co. G. 16 Ga. Inf., C. S. A.
Lizzie Carter, wife of Lonnie 4/7/1884-5/12/1920
Noble M. 12/17/1894-2/4/1967
Mary M. 1834-1916
John B. 10/23/1856-11/27/1940

PENDERGEASS

N. N. 3/4/1851-11/7/1903
Wesley 6/5/1872-7/29/1899
Alva Nathaniel P. 11/13/1916-9/18/1942

JEFFERSON CITY CEMETERY, Jefferson

PENDERGRASS

Harold, infant son of Mr. and Mrs. Alva W. 9/10/1928
Ned Nixon 3/30/1886-5/5/1947
Phillip Trout 12/6/1888-10/2/1960
Mrs. N. N. 5/9/1855-2/15/1927
Mrs. Nellie E., nee Miss Nellie E. Egerton born in Franklin
Co., N. C. 6/6/1860 married Dr. J. B. Pendergrass 3/3/1887, 8/5/1889
James E. Jr. 4/1/1893-1/21/1919
William Lane 5/22/1901-4/18/1917
Thomas Nathaniel, son of Dr. and Mrs. J. B. 3/21/1899-11/30/1907
Joseph 1908-1951
Worth H. 1887-1940
Daughter of N. M. and S. B. 12/11/1882-4/6/1885
Dr. James Bascomb 1851-1927
Franklin L. 1855-1925
Martha Elizabeth, dau. of Dr. and Mrs. J. B. 10/11/1903-12/9/1907
Mattie Dell Heath 1870-1964
Mary Lou 1863-1939

PERRY

Charlotte S. 1899-1954

PETTYJOHN

E. H. 11/15/1839-3/28/1915
James E., son of J. J. and E. H. 8/3/1874-4/29/1907

PIKE

Lucy A. 7/5/1843-
W. I., Co. D. 16th Ga. Cav.
W. I. 1/17/1842-5/26/1907
Henry 1870-1872
Jefferson D. 7/4/1861-3/27/1926

PINSON

Ina Lindsay 1878-1931
Charlie W. 1872-1946
W. A. 5/14/1830-3/25/1907
Mattie O. 9/23/1842-11/2/1925
Ina Lindsay 1878-1931
Charlie W. 1871-1946

PIRKLE

Claude 1885-1926

JEFFERSON CITY CEMETERY, Jefferson

PIRKLE

Robert N. 1880-1944
Pearl A. 1888-1953
Dr. Edward L. 1898-1964

PORTER

Robert L. 1884-1952
Mary W. 1889-
Samuel Asbury 7/25/1840-11/2/1915, 52nd Ga. Regt. Co. A
Lenard 1/9/1916-7/29/1918

POTTER

Dilmus 1869-1930
Nora Gilbert 1870-1950

PRUITT

William C. 5/2/1871-4/12/1956
Celia M. 9/17/1870-1/19/1938
Lee Roy 6/28/1889-12/6/1913

PURCELL

Harold L. 4/28/1918-5/17/1962

RANDOLPH

Joshua H. 8/12/1877-2/29/1879
Cornelia Moon, wife of H. J.
James E. 10/31/1837-4/21/1905
Elizabeth C. 12/11/1838-2/7/1905
Fannie May 5/6/1872-6/15/1880

ROBERTS

Mattie Bell 3/12/1878-7/29/1968
Frank 10/28/1873-1/3/1906

ROSS

Capt. T. L., Co. Ga. 16th Ga. Regt. C. S. A. 12/6/1825-9/10/1920
Charles, son of T. L. and E. C. 1/12/1861-2/14/1885
Lucy Whitehead, wife of John N. 3/13/1866-5/15/1921
Elenor Caroline 3/3/1835-5/31/1904
John N. 11/7/1855-4/9/1928
Tommie, infant son of J. N. and Lucy, died 7/4/1885, aged 5 months

JEFFERSON CITY CEMETERY, Jefferson

PITTMAN

May McRee 8/24/1866-8/15/1966
Amy J., wofe of N. 4/6/1836-10/5/1905
Mordecia Monroe 10/13/1828-3/3/1896

SAILORS

Y. Z. 1909
Christine L. 1914-1966

SAMPLES

Raymond Jr. 1/23/1968
Ishmael DeWitte 3/19/1915-12/18/1961
Mary D. 1920-
R. W. 1/31/1882-1/31/1948
Mrs. R. W. 9/29/1884-10/12/1937
R. M. 1918-1952

SATTERFIELD

Tonia S. 1896-1963
Royce H., Ga S/Sgt. 3566, Fld. Maint. Sq. AF, World War II,
BSM 11/29/1920-2/29/1960
Royce David 7/7/1951-7/12/1951
Jeffrey D. 11/10/1953-11/13/1953

SCOTT

Jack Shelnutt died 10/28/1967, 58 years, 6 months, 3 days

SEAY

W. J. 8/30/1890-3/22/1911

SHERARD

Cornelia 5/8/1840-6/8/1919
S. W., Co. F, 24th S. C. Regt., C. S. A.

SHIELDS

Ella 8/18/1872-12/24/1952
Emma 12/20/1857-11/3/1930
Emanuel Scott 7/19/1855-8/29/1935

JEFFERSON CITY CEMETERY, Jefferson

SHOCKLEY

Cynthia 5/1/1890-7/17/1947

SHROPSHIRE

Lucius A. 1905-1948

SHUMAKE

Emory Gordon Sr. 6/26/1905-7/18/1959
Laura Lee 8/10/1873-11/2/1963
Emma W. 1/28/1870-9/5/1965

SIKES

Lillian Lorane 5/26/1933-11/7/1936
John Bell 1855-1927
George E. 1892-1966

SILMAN

Jane Yearwood 11/4/1882-10/28/1946
Capt. J. B., Co. C, 18th Ga. Regt., S. C. S.
Kathleen Couch 1/25/1910-5/11/1947
Henry M. 10/27/1869-11/4/1927
Robert Ralph 6/19/1909-11/16/1944
James B. 1/25/1836-2/8/1890
Robert Ralph 6/19/1909-11/16/1944

SIMMONS

Carroll J., dau. of Mr. and Mrs. W. P. 11/9/1940-11/11/1952

SIMPSON

Talmadge Brock 10/1/1886-10/30/1887

SMALLWOOD

Mattie 5/17/1884-
John H. (Jake) 9/11/1911-9/5/1951
Youle F., dau. of Jack and Ruby 10/10/1921-7/24/1922
Newt 1878-10/1931
J. L. 8/29/1914-9/11/1923
Loy 11/6/1912-11/11/1967
Lizzie 9/18/1863-10/22/1931
Wilton M., son of Jack and Ruby 6/14/1926-10/7/1926
W. E. 3/10/1882-8/1/1935

JEFFERSON CITY CEMETERY, Jefferson

SMALLWOOD

Agnes M. 10/19/1909-
Mellie 9/30/1898-10/5/1933

SMITH

Walter C. 1877-1924
Clark Howell, son of C. P. and J. A. 6/4/1901-2/19/1902
George Erwin 5/12/1873-6/21/1951
Arnold Randolph, son of Mr. and Mrs. W. H. 7/23/1902-6/11/1904
J. Chester 1884-1954
Walter C. 1877-1924
Ora Dyaman 3/10/1875-10/9/1946
Myra Thompson, wife of William H. 5/23/1870-4/16/1938
Donald Brooks Jr., son of Mr. and Mrs. D. B. 4/15/1927-12/8/1930
Dr. S. J. 9/12/1862-9/17/1926
William Henry 10/20/1864-11/11/1944

SOLOMON

Jake 1869-1951

SOSEBEE

Mattie Hulsey 1890-1919
Cora E. McGee 1885-1957

SPRATLIN

William T. 1936-1960

STANDRIDGE

Isaac B. 1909-1962

STANLEY

G. W., Co. Ga 16th Ga. Calvery C. S. A.

STARK

D. M., Co. K, 3rd Ga. Regt., C. S. A.

STATON

Frank Christopher 6/1/1889-10/20/1968
Lizzie Segars 1/31/1896

JEFFERSON CITY CEMETERY, Jefferson

STATON

Thomas C. 1925-1962

STEPHENS

Pvt. Crawford 1928-1945, killed in service
Lindsey S. 4/27/1931-4/30/1955

STOCKTON

John Oscar 1854-1934
Leila B. 1874-1966
Mary Patrick 1861-1947
James W. 1873-1933
Infant son of Mr. and Mrs. J. W. 3/5/1911-5/24/1911

STOREY

Calvin T. 3/10/1848-10/12/1939
Hugh H. 1878-1967
Martha M. 9/8/1854-2/8/1941
William Jackson 10/5/1909-2/5/1950
Dell McRee 1897-1930

STOVALL

James Thomas, M. D. 3/20/1906-1/19/1957

STOVER

David Gordon 5/11/1888-6/23/1968
Leila Emmett 8/24/1896

STRICKLAND

James E. 1848-1913
Arlie C. 1892-
Infant dau. of Guy and Arlie 1/6/1931
Nancy E. 1853-1942
Guy 1889-
James H., son of Gus and Arlie 11/26/1916-12/28/1916
John W., 1st Lt., US Army 1918-1944

SULLIVAN

Janell, dau. of J. P. and Pearl 1/22/1926-2/5/1926
Earnestine, dau. of J. P. and Pearl 11/20/1923-1/13/1924
James E., son of J. P. and Pearl 9/8/1922-11/7/1922

JEFFERSON CITY CEMETERY, Jefferson

SYKES

Reba B. 1906-1932

TALMADGE

Leta Montgomery 2/13/1876-4/30/1962

TATUM

William O. 1889-1954
Hubert 1917-1943
Minnie S. 1894-
Hoyt J. Ga PFC, World War II, 7/5/1921-7/17/1965

TAYLOR

Donnie Clyde born and died 9/16/1941
Mary Lee 2/4/1880-2/7/1944
Grady W. 4/12/1918-10/1/1941
Milledge 6/24/1878-7/1/1951

THOMPSON

Milton, Co. G, 16th Ga. Regt.
E. M., Co. G, 16th Ga. Regt., C. S. A.
Francisa 3/3/1830-3/30/1851
William S. 1843-1921

TILEER

Tommie Lou 7/14/1911-6/3/1949

TOLBERT

James D. 1918-1958
Ruby L. 1909-
James W. 1868-1956
Charlie A. 1905-
Eula T. 1913
Emma W. 1878-

TRIBBE

Susie Thompson, wife of J. E. 10/28/1876-9/20/1918

TROUT

Laura L. 12/8/1831-12/12/1893

JEFFERSON CITY CEMETERY, Jefferson

TROUT

Florida B. 1/22/1829-11/16/1894

TURNER

John Collier 10/4/1867-5/4/1959
Clyde Hancock 7/1/1884-11/22/1964
J. A. 2/6/1875-5/29/1948
Jennie Ann 2/4/1877-4/17/1962
Ila Eurene 11/11/1900-10/11/1923

TURPIN

Earnest Jack died 8/26/1965, age 38, 7 months, 9 days

TWITTY

Jasper Newton 10/27/1852-4/20/1912
Mary Carithers 12/26/1861-7/10/1910

VANDIVER

Claudia C. 5/23/1889-5/16/1963
Foster M. 1/13/1881-1969
Randy Lee 10/6/1953-7/27/1955

VARNUM

George W. 5/13/1882-
Deana 1/7/1884-6/27/1962
Alvin D. 7/8/1911-1/7/1957

VENABLE

James Leslie 12/15/1848-6/5/1911
Alice Pittman 11/25/1857-8/11/1937
John A. 2/10/1843-10/5/1909
Oscar E., son of J. A. and S. E. 3/19/1880-7/26/1894
Sarah E., wife of John A. 10/13/1840

VENERABLE

Lottie Wade 8/9/1902
Okie Long
5/6/1894-2/28/1961
Okie L., Ga. Pvt. 47th Inf., World War I
Okie, In Memory of S/Sgt. Okie Venerable, Jr. who gave his
life in service of his country in North India 9/8/1944. At rest somewhere in N. India

JEFFERSON CITY CEMETERY, Jefferson

VOYLES

Lessie P. 3/27/1893-4/28/1945

WALL

Edna W. 12/31/1883
Richard H. 5/27/1880-3/20/1966
David Olin 1918-1920

WARD

Jerry Melton died 12/12/1941, aged 1 year

WATSON

Martha J. 9/30/1834-1/25/1893
William Anderson 11/9/1838-3/1/1889
Samuel Alexander 8/3/1876-6/15/1877
Mary Elizabeth 1/1/1849-9/6/1917
Harrie A. 9/26/1810-7/24/1880
Gussie Long 2/2/1871-5/11/1878
Callie Eloise 9/22/1875-11/2/1949

WEBB

W. L. 8/20/1837
W. L. 2/22/1837-4/4/1893
T. W. 12/15/1861-9/16/1901
Olah W. 12/18/1874-12/5/1912

WEIR

Fred B. 2/23/1894-3/22/1920
Della C. 3/10/1896-
Maud, wife of T. W. 12/23/1866-9/20/1888
Alice May Jackson, wife of T. W. Webb 7/23/1872-
T. W. 12/15/1861-9/16/1901
William J. 1882-1966
Jessie A. 8/2/1880-12/18/1951
John Gordon 10/4/1840-10/30/1923

WESTMORELAND

George W. 7/4/1892-12/6/1961

JEFFERSON CITY CEMETERY, Jefferson

WHEELER

M. L. 1877-1949

WHELCHEL

Hattie B. 6/17/1888-11/22/1960
Julis B. 6/13/1914-11/10/1955
Robert Eugene 10/17/1873-5/4/1918
Coyle B. 4/23/1879-4/30/1953
Nedy U., dau. of R. E. and L. P. 5/10/1904-10/9/1904
James H. 2/22/1916-4/12/1941
Ned C., son of R. E. and Lucy 1/29/1908-4/6/1908

WHITE

Lois Elizabeth 5/7/1923-1/30/1929, age 5 years
Sarah A. 1833-1907

WHITEHEAD

Jerry Ann 11/30/1943-1/15/1944
W. O. (Pete) 1873-1956

WHITMAN

Lorena J. Callahan, wife of David 8/26/1831-1/25/1855, erected by son, John B. Whitman

WHITMIRE

Eddie Omer Sr. 1907-1936
Sophie 1858-1920
Beulah W., wife of T. E. 1879-1961

WILBANKS

Patricia 1934-1940
Ora W. 1/19/1910
Jackie 1943-1965
Roxie Mae 1886-1947
Jackie 1943-1963
Henry W. 11/18/1909-9/12/1966
Billy J., Ga. F N USNR 3/24/1932-6/25/1958
Patricia 1934-1940
Kathryn J. 1932

JEFFERSON CITY CEMETERY, Jefferson

WILHITE

Infant dau. of S. V. and Myrtle 5/25/1913
M. G. 1851-1920
Jean Moran 1890-1954
Angeline Doss 1851-1920
J. C. 1882-1922
Doss T. Sr. 11/27/1886-3/14/1952

WILKES

Lowery Grant 1/2/1943-3/25/1944

WILLIAM

Willis, Co. C, 18 Ga Regt., C. S. A.

WILLIAMSON

J. L. Jr. 10/26/1918-10/29/1918

WILLS

James A. 1865-1922
Clara M. 1869-1952
J. E., son of J. A. and Clara M. 1900-1936
Laura C. 1867-1909
Florence, dau. of Mr. and Mrs. W. C. 11/4/1878-4/23/1905
Mary Lou 1/29/1881-3/25/1961
William Crofford 5/19/1849-3/13/1921
Frances Olivia Holliday 7/21/1857-1/5/1937

WILSON

Fred C. Gurley 7/15/1892-10/12/1946
Martha C. 8/23/1808-9/4/1880
Catherine H. 5/6/1810-12/18/1879
G. J. N., Co. E, 34th Ga. Regt., C. S. A.
Arthur C. 1874-1948
Robert R. 1913-1964
Paul F. Sr. 6/4/1902-1/30/1948
Addie C. 1881-1958
Lottie R.
Samuel Wright 1870-1947
Angeline E. 1891-1958
Nancy E. 1852-1941
Sallie Dickson 1874-1939
Guy 1886-

JEFFERSON CITY CEMETERY, Jefferson

WINBURN

Mrs. A. A., wife of William, 10/16/1821 Banks Co., Ga., d. 6/17/1891
William 9/21/1806 in York Co., S. C., died 9/8/1886

WITT

David. In memory of David Witt, a native of State of Virginia, born 1/15/1772, departed this life 4/15/1835. For more than 30 years prior to his death, he had been a resident of this country, during which time he won to a large degree the confidence of his fellow citizsens, his life of just and honorable conduct in his private transactions and by a firm, independent and patriotic career as a public man. Often called upon to represent this county in the State Legislature and was chosen to preside over the Representative branch in the discharge of the important duties of every station, he displayed a sagacity and sound judgment, which linked to an unbending integrity rendered him public benefactor in the character of a public servant.

Ann Oliva, wife of William
Infant child of Ann Olivia Middleton Witt born 2/16/1844
Nancy, wife of David, died 6/23/1861

WOOD

J. A. 11/6/1881-11/23/1900
Fletcher 9/28/1882-1907
Mary A., wife of J. A. 11/6/1861-11/28/1900

WOODALL

Walter Gene 8/10/1958-12/12/1958

WORLEY

Mellie P. 1905-
Tom D. 1907-1957

WORSHAM

Elizabeth Evilene 12/13/1817-6/5/1899
W. A. 12/4/1877-6/11/1907

WRIGHT

Mamie Sudderth 7/30/1876-1/14/1901

JEFFERSON CITY CEMETERY, Jefferson

YANCEY

Bonnie Carter 1906-1967

YARBROUGH

Luther J. 4/7/1889-10/25/1967
Cora C. 4/13/1891-12/11/1961

WALNUT FORK BAPTIST CHURCH, HWY #60, JUNCTION I-85 NORTH, ESTABLISHED 1802

ARMSTRONG

L. M., wife of J. T. 6/3/1867-3/27/1905

ATTAWAY

J. F. 5/10/1844-10/26/1861
J. D. 9/14/1855-11/13/1855

BAILEY

James L. 8/26/1856-6/29/1901
Nancy Adline, wife of James L., 1/31/1861-3/8/1905, married 7/17/1881

BAIRD

Jessie 1884-1928
Mary Lou 1914-1928
Colie A., wife of Paul 1914-1952

BANKS

Infant dau. of Mr. and Mrs. Z. Z. 11/20/1942
Zeanos Z. 5/6/1910-7/2/1966
Hannah W. 10/1/1913-
Wade Hampton 6/7/1886-10/31/1910
Ollie H. 1897-
Azalee 2/12/1894
William J. 4/19/1851-5/24/1913
Lottie Corine, infant dau. of J. A. and Ollie 12/1/1914-2/3/1915
J. Abner 1895-1961
W. Alex 4/20/1882
Ruby 7/21/1914
Lottie Bell, dau. of J. A. and Ollie 9/18/1918-3/29/1929
Susan E. 2/7/1854-5/27/1913

WALNUT FORK BAPTIST CHURCH, HWY #60, JUNCTION I-85 NORTH, ESTABLISHED 1802

BANKS

William Hamlin, infant son of W. A. and Asilee 6/20/1919-6/25/1919
Warren B. 7/13/1861-9/2/1943
Eva T. 8/19/1867-7/20/1951

BATCHELOR

Nancy M. 7/6/1848-8/28/1915
Mattie A. 10/25/1845-6/23/1905 married 12/21/1866
Jessie Ruth 5/2/1903-6/13/1927
Lela 2/7/1871-8/18/1911
George W. 11/16/1846-11/14/1928
Lillie Evans 4/29/1875-7/29/1949

BERRYMAN

May born and died 2/23/1936
Martha J. 1/12/1851-10/5/1934
Luther J. 1872-1945
Harrison 10/22/1846-6/11/1924
Charles T. 3/1/1882-6/19/1945
Martha Jo 4/18/1944-4/1944

BLACKWELL

John C., son of J. S. and L. H. 7/31/1909-9/17/1909

BOHANNON

Martha A. Simmons 4/6/1841-9/13/1933

BOWLES

Elizabeth, wife of C. R. 3/17/1842-9/9/1905
Cicero 3/9/1832-3/11/1907
Zine May, dau. of J. J. and May 10/3/1909-9/5/1910
Elizabeth, wife of A. 12/13/1830-5/2/1904

BRASELTON

Jacob, born N. C. 3/17/1785, died 11/17/1819, Revolutionary War Soldier
Mrs. Mary died 3/2/1856, aged 69
Margret B. 4/6/1850-11/23/1850, aged 7 months, 17 days

WALNUT FORK BAPTIST CHURCH, HWY #60, JUNCTION I-85 NORTH, ESTABLISHED 1802

BRIDGES

Mary Rebecca, wife of L. C. 4/29/1850-2/15/1883
Eula M. 1/1/1887-
Roy W., son of J. R. and M. R. 8/4/1901-6/10/1902
T. W. 7/9/1859-6/9/1929
J. Ernest 7/1/1881-6/13/1927
Nancy A. 2/28/1866-11/18/1952
Georgia M., dau. of T. W. and N. A. 10/1/1885-9/18/1900

BROOKS

D. M. 4/10/1844-8/11/1922
Nancy 9/28/1845-8/16/1929

BROOKSHIRE

J. D. 7/4/1861-9/2/1925
Elizabeth 1869-1952
Rebeckie J. Poston, wife of J. D. 3/4/1864-
George L. 1864-1930
Ellen, wife of R. W. Barton, dau. of Mr. and Mrs. C. L. Brookshire, 5/21/1891-10/7/1918

BRYANT

Andy, son of W. B. and M. J. 6/8/1907-6/13/1907
Waldo, son of W. B. and M. J., 1/8/1909-6/8/1909
James W. 1923-1945

CAMPBELL

Herbert Gewel 2/5/1913-3/8/1913
Lola Estell 4/3/1902-4/8/1902

CANTREL

Charlie J. 7/31/1864-10/8/1927
Ralph Junious 9/13/1922-6/23/1923
Nancy J. 7/18/1874-2/18/1957

CARTER

Infant of Martha and William born and died 8/28/1899

WALNUT FORK BAPTIST CHURCH, HWY #60, JUNCTION I-85 NORTH, ESTABLISHED 1802

CASH

Phillip Bruce, son of Mr. and Mrs. Larry born and died 9/30/1963
Parilee E. 2/8/1866-4/29/1940
Infant dau. of Mr. and Mrs. Ralph M. born 9/18/1939

CLARK

Linnie, wife of J. N. 5/10/1882-5/8/1908
E. D., son of J. N. and Linnie 3/10/1902-6/4/1902
Moses, husband of Carrie 12/5/1825-5/18/1874

COOPER

Charles Curtis, son of Mr. and Mrs. Charlie 11/12/1926-12/2/1926

CROOK

Etta E. 9/8/1885

CRUCE

Infant son of Mr. and Mrs. J. W. Bose born and died 10/18/1912
Polly 8/7/1845-8/5/1931
J. W. (Bose) 3/9/1872-11/5/1941
Paul H. 8/21/1899-5/31/1964
J. M. 8/8/1853-1/31/1924
Mattie A. Batchelor born 10/25/1845 married 12/21/1866 W. T. Cruce, died 6/23/1905
Sam M. 9/25/1870-1/25/1939
Jewell R. 5/20/1899-
Alvin 12/28/1968, aged 66 years, 7 months
Dovie E. Roberts 1/22/1879-3/21/1930

DANIEL

Artimisa V. 12/4/1827-12/8/1896

DAVIS

H. 1/3/1851-10/1862
W. T., son of C. L. and S. A. 1857-1861
Jane, dau. of C. L. and S. A. 8/27/1857-1871

DICKERSON

A. J. 1/3/1836-1/18/1913
William A. 1890-

WALNUT FORK BAPTIST CHURCH, HWY #60, JUNCTION I-85 NORTH, ESTABLISHED 1802

DICKERSON

Molly C. 1888-1959
Mildred 10/16/1922-5/11/1929

DOSTER

Dwight Raymond, infant son of Mr. and Mrs. Dea, born and died 5/13/1962
Gladys 4/24/1914-4/27/1914
Nancy S. 10/18/1894-5/1/1914
Raymon R. 3/1/1899-3/28/1968

EDWARDS

Mary J., wife of J. R. 3/29/1856-2/3/1900
W. V. 1852-1941
Guy Norman, son of Eutaw B. and Rosa H. 3/25/1909-9/26/1909
Mary N. 4/23/1881-9/10/1902
Mark A. 8/6/1843-7/4/1919
J. P. and M. J. 5/15/1893-10/11/1893
Mary M. 4/23/1881-9/10/1902
J. R. 4/28/1854-12/3/1918
Mrs. Mary A., wife of M. A., 12/30/1844-5/19/1911
W. M. 1853-1914
PFC Durward R. 4/11/1922-3/28/1945, 1st Cavalry

EKINS

Mrs. Ethel Blackwell died 1/11/1963, aged 66

EVANS

Charlie F. 1872-1942
Floyd J. 8/29/1883-6/5/1937
Royce M. 7/14/1918-
John G. 1873-1909
Jutson B. 1880-1944
Maudie Agnes, dau. of A. and S. A. 9/8/1887-9/12/1897
Rev. William T. 1891-1935
Lula J. 2/27/1887-9/29/1949
Lucile D. 2/5/1923-2/10/1960
Sarah Anne 4/23/1852-11/7/1918
James H., husband of Fannie, 2/9/1880-4/14/1909, son of Andrew and Sarah Evans
Mayrelle B. 1892-1966
Harriett Dorota, dau. of A. and S. A. 9/28/1884-9/10/1897
N. Hattie 1874-

WALNUT FORK BAPTIST CHURCH, HWY #60, JUNCTION I-85 NORTH, ESTABLISHED 1802

EVANS

Virginia P. 11/1/1926-
Roy, son of F. L. and Lula 4/1/1910-8/10/1910
Andrew 2/12/1847-7/4/1922
Martha 10/5/1869-11/29/1932

FAULKNER

John L. 10/21/1877-10/25/1962
Rebecca O. 1/14/1883-

FEAGINS

Dollie B. 1896-1945

FIELDS

Mrs. Carrie

GARRETT

Eunice Simmons 9/24/1898-1/16/1929

GARRISON

Rev. Samuel R. 12/3/1827-10/28/1892

GEARIN

Louise F. 1925-1954, wife of R. Boyd

GREGORY

Charles D. 6/7/1850-1/12/1937
A. W. 3/2/1883-8/28/1958
Martha Jane, dau. of G. D. and M. E. 1/8/1879-3/13/1898
Louise M. (sister) 1874-1961
Elizabeth, wife of C. D. 1852-1926
Grover C. (brother) 1887-1963

GRIER

Jessie 5/5/1906-10/22/1930
Hattie 7/12/1876-3/23/1935
Richard 5/19/1874-8/5/1963

WALNUT FORK BAPTIST CHURCH, HWY #60, JUNCTION I-85 NORTH, ESTABLISHED 1802

GRUCE

Ophelia, wife of M. M. 7/22/1879-2/15/1899
William J. 1868-1944
Myrtle Muhulda, dau. of M. B. and M. M. 4/8/1886-11/30/1898
Jensie P., wife of Peter 8/12/1828-6/26/1900
Jessie L. 1878-1962
Elijah M., son of M. B. and N. B. 12/18/1882-11/15/1898

GUNTER

Billy J. 1936-1966
Brenda Carol, died 12/6/1962, 5 days
Lester, infant son of J. E. and Martha 10/13/1916-9/20/1917
Annette E. 1938-

HALL

William B. 9/25/1884-8/20/1929
Ruth 1908-1951
David 1911-1935
Bartow 6/21/1936-10/10/1938

HARWELL

Clarnie, son of J. H. 11/22/1888-9/11/1892

HAYES

Edmond Wiley 4/3/1926-12/22/1953
Wiley 1887-
Mamie 1891-

HEALAN

Mary E. 12/1/1864-4/16/1938
Curtis W., infant son of Mr. and Mrs. J. F. born and died 10/23/1913
Arminda Missouri, dau. of C. F. and A. L. 12/12/1883-6/30/1913
James Hume, son of Mr. and Mrs. J. W. 12/13/1926
J. L. 12/16/1861-1/31/1911
Arminda L. 1851-1933
J. Wilburn 4/15/1892
Joseph F. 11/20/1884-3/5/1931
C. F. (Lum) 1849-1923
Annie Myrtle 3/30/1892-5/24/1954

WALNUT FORK BAPTIST CHURCH, HWY #60, JUNCTION I-85 NORTH, ESTABLISHED 1802

HOSCH

Janice Gale, infant dau. of Mr. and Mrs. W. C., born and died 5/12/1947

HOWINGTON

Ola, wife of R. J. 5/23/1876-8/31/1900

HUDSON

Minnie 1874-1948

HULSEY

Eunice Arietta, dau. of Mr. and Mrs. R. A. 9/26/1909-12/4/1911
Estell Morgan, wife of R. A. 5/3/1881-6/16/1935

HUMPHRUS

Mrs. J. V., wife of R. C. 7/4/1864-10/21/1905

HUTSON

Stephen G. 7/11/1852-9/19/1892

IRVIN

J. O. 9/23/1848-9/14/1913
Lucindia 4/11/1837-5/2/1888
J. F. 11/13/1821-1861
E. A. 10/16/1831-5/6/1911
Samson born 1/30/1878

IVEY

Cora A., wife of Homer J. 7/11/1897-
Loyd 6/17/1917-5/21/1921
Homer J. 5/27/1895-3/1/1935

JONES

Dorothy Loudell, dau. of Mr. and Mrs. C. A. 4/4/1928-8/5/1939
Lula D. 1885-
W. Perry 1883-1951

JUSTUS

George W. 5/24/1959, Ga. Pvt. Base Hosp. 124

WALNUT FORK BAPTIST CHURCH, HWY #60, JUNCTION I-85 NORTH, ESTABLISHED 1802

JUSTUS

Georgia Ruth 6/29/1931-1/10/1933

KINNEY

Norma M. 1883-1994
Jane Enerkube 1.26.1864-5/22/1942
Virgil A. 2/23/1892-11/13/1961
George Washington 6/21/1861-5/24/1951
Alma B. 7/21/1896-4/19/1957
Estelle Maddox, wife of Elmer L. 6/18/1911-5/24/1941
Polly Ann born and died 7/13/1917
George Ann 1839-1884
Martha F., wife of H. H. 10/13/1879-3/1/1916

LANDERS

H. C., son of W. W. 1/6/1918-5/3/1919

LEE

Infant dau. of Floyd and Lilly, aged 1 month, 18 days
Curtis E. 4/13/1945-9/13/1966
Mrs. Zelar Wilson died 9/1960
Floyd 10/3/1889-11/18/1965
Lilli 5/12/1894-

MADDOX

Elizabeth 4/11/1839-11/20/1914
T. S. 6/29/1867-9/18/1936
James L. 4/1864-12/8/1929
Annie D. 12/10/1890-
Ina T. 1884-1946
Lula Frances 10/24/1871-10/11/1936
Charley C. 9/10/1871-8/15/1897
Infant girl of L. C. and L. F. 12/22/1902-1/1/1903
Infant son of L. C. and L. F., Sebe, born 12/25/1890
Elizabeth Areleane 3/6/1839-11/28/1912
Madelyn 3/11/1912-4/28/1913
N. L. 5/20/1828-2/30/1904
India, wife of Harrison 2/26/1867-1/24/1904
Martha E., wife of James L. 11/13/1867-4/20/1927
A. Jackson 1875-1953
Lenard C. 4/22/1869-11/19/1934
J. W. 7/10/1835-6/12/1899
Infant boy of L. C. and L. F. 12/20/1901-12/22/1901

WALNUT FORK BAPTIST CHURCH, HWY #60, JUNCTION I-85 NORTH, ESTABLISHED 1802

MADDOX

Infant of Mr. and Mrs. Charley died 6/6/1896
Martha Adeline 4/11/1833-3/16/1913
Beretha Bell, dau of Jack and Ina 4/14/1905-4/28/1905
Mrs. T. S. 5/2/1873-7/9/1940
Lovie Lee 7/25/1896
Bertha Mae, dau., of Mr. and Mrs. T. S., 1/9/1902-1/21/1918, aged 1t years, 12 days
H. R. 1861-1933
W. H. (Burster) 10/16/1890-2/24/1966
L. C. 8/2/1904-1/26/1958
Infants of Mr. and Mrs. J. H.
Mary 8/1/1841-12/18/1921
Seaborn M. 11/29/1866-7/16/1890
Infant of Mr. and Mrs. Charley 5/11/1897-5/18/1897
Hoyt M. 8/19/1916-8/21/1917
Clayborn D. 10/11/1786-2/11/1846
Mary 12/28/1798-10/21/1875
Herbert H. 3/22/1898-11/26/1925
David Claude 2/2/1892-5/27/1963
James H. 1880-1953
Maude T. 1887-

MANUS

Mrs. Ann 1/8/1870-1/12/1935
Pearl 5/17/1905-6/29/1921
John W. Jr. 6/13/1907-9/6/1933
Mrs. J. W. 1/1/1872-3/2/1932
J. Hubert 8/22/1892-1/14/1929
Jewell T. 2/2/1900-11/14/1932

MARLOW

William M. 1871-1954
Lizzie A. 1887-1957
Mose S. E. 1918-1960

MARTIN

Mendell 1916-1956
Julia 1917-

MATTHEWS

Pollie McEver 7/21/1872-1/8/1942
J. M. 7/13/1866-11/3/1928

WALNUT FORK BAPTIST CHURCH, HWY #60, JUNCTION I-85 NORTH, ESTABLISHED 1802

McEVER

Charlie, son of J. A. and N. J. 8/27/1907-2/5/1909
Rev. B. E. 9/7/1884-7/2/1965
Robert A., son of J. H. and E. C. 5/8/1882-8/24/1932
Miron, son of Mr. and Mrs. J. A. 7/14/1920-7/15/1920
N. J. Batchelor, wife of J. A. 7/16/1888-5/14/1935
Lula E., dau. of J. H. and E. C. 11/7/1883-2/16/1884
Infant son of Mr. and Mrs. J. A., born and died 8/15/1927

McNEAL

William A. 9/13/1852-8/29/1927
Jurell 1923-1925
Elizabeth 8/10/1873-4/26/1956
Voy Jeanette 1909-
Rev. B. E. 9/7/1884-7/2/1965
Bessie H. 8/8/1890-7/14/1955
Nancy 11/30/1823-3/19/1912
J. A. 1/26/1882-9/29/1927
Maggie R. 1889-
William Hoyt died 8/15/1968, 52 years, 1 month, 10 days
Cora 4/9/1889-
3 sons of Mr. and Mrs. Jack: Willie, Didlard, J. D. May
T. M. (Bus) 1895-
John T. 2/10/1867-5/17/1951
D. S. Jr. 1902-1951
Lula E., dau of J. H. and E. C. 11/7/1883-2/16/1884
Infant son of Mr. and Mrs. J. A. born and died 8/15/1927
William 10/12/1821-4/16/1896

MORRIS

John D. 1880-1924
Susan E. 1880-

MURPHY

Martha E. 1848-1929
Lucy, wife of J. M. 12/26/1831-12/14/1905
Polly Ann 1877-1937
Martha A., wife of Terrell 8/22/1841-6/2/1883
Ula Mae 9/1/1907-6/8/1908
J. M. 3/7/1829-1/14/1908
Raborn Lee 1877-1960
William J. 1832-1933
Lily Mae 5/9/1915-5/9/1915

WALNUT FORK BAPTIST CHURCH, HWY #60, JUNCTION I-85 NORTH, ESTABLISHED 1802

MURPHY

Annie Mae 1913-1922
T. 1/2/1887-11/7/1932

NEWBERRY

Ada M. 8/28/1877-10/12/1923

OLIVER

Armineda T. 11/25/1861-10/23/1947
Mary Ann 5/4/1881-10/25/1939
Henry J. 1/10/1856-6/19/1932
Delphia 2/12/1885-8/21/1941
Laura 11/16/1882-6/10/1917

PALMER

Randall K. 1/22/1968-1/24/1968

PAYNE

Eunice P., wife of J. L. 9/25/1890-5/27/1917

PERDUE

Carl 7/24/1892-1/7/1921

PHILLIPS

Lula Mathews, wife of Russell 12/30/1900-8/17/1920
Onie 1876-1961
Minnie Lee 4/24/1876-1/1/1900
Mary E., wife of Augustus 11/29/1858-3/12/1909
Martha Elizabeth, wife of Augustus, 3/20/1847-2/9/1919
Augustus 11/25/1849-4/23/1923
Donald E., son of Mr. and Mrs. Edward
Myron Russell born and died 8/16/1920
J. Robert 1874-1943

PIERCE

Early 1888-
Peark K. 1887-1965

WALNUT FORK BAPTIST CHURCH, HWY #60, JUNCTION I-85 NORTH, ESTABLISHED 1802

PITTMAN

Lowell J. 9/10/1941-10/22/1964

REDDICK

Robert E. Lee 11/23/1909-9/17/1948

REYNOLDS

Ava 1891-1928
Bennie Donald, infant son of Mr. and Mrs. Ernest 1/18/1930-3/31/1930
Dave A. 1854-1939
Hattie S. 6/14/1876-8/13/1956
Larry J., infant of C. H. 4/13/1860-3/29/1895
Estelle S. 11/29/1905-5/26/1967
Johnnie 12/28/1886-
Jane S. 1862-1936
William H. 7/6/1874-9/12/1896
G. W. 1/25/1876-11/3/1920
James D. 12/13/1872-3/17/1907
Ernest C. 5/29/1904-
Aby Myrtle 1/22/1888-5/27/1957
Lena M., dau. of D. A. and N. J. 3/14/1886-3/21/1890
Mary M., wife of A. J.
Rev. Andrew Jackson 8/4/1842-2/9/1900

RIEVES

T. J. 4/14/1843-2/15/1896

RICHARDSON

J. W. 8/10/1855-4/13/1994
M. Lula, dau. of J. W. and S. F. 12/14/1884-10/1/1889
E. Clyde 1897-
Clarence 6/18/1894-2/21/1948
Sarah Frances 7/18/1864-10/4/1921
David R. 3/15/1862-3/14/1932
E. C. 2/1940
Margie H. 1891-1954
Clara Mae 1/9/1897
Johnnie, son of J. W. and S. F. 12/7/1889-6/8/1891
Augusta K. 3/16/1865-
Margie R. 1902-1967
Marshall H. 1890-1953
Julian L. (Foxie) 1920-1945

WALNUT FORK BAPTIST CHURCH, HWY #60, JUNCTION I-85 NORTH, ESTABLISHED 1802

SAILORS

Henry M. 1875-1918

SAULS

Malitt 8/31/1832-8/18/1915
G. W. 12/10/1831-6/26/1877

SAYLORS

Parina H. 9/23/1854-3/24/1904

SHAW

Betty A. 1873-1946
H. Foster 1873-1926

SIMMONS

Laura J. 1871-1943
William P. 1870-1919

SIMS

W. S. (Bill)
1891-1963
Matilda C. 5/23/1836-6/4/1885

SKELTON

J. B. 1/1854-6/1878
George W. 2/15/1883-3/15/1885
J. M. 12/21/1886-
Martha Ellen 2/26/1874-12/22/1938

STANCIL

Mrs. J. H. (Mollie) died 12/29/1962, aged 86
H. 1884-1945
Eli 5/27/1836-6/15/1899
Ila Mae, dau. of J. H. and Mollie 3/4/1903-6/12/1917
Mrs. N. E., wife of Eli 11/10/1845-4/30/1928
Tirza Loucile, dau. of J. H. and Mollie 1/2/1915-8/6/1915
Malvin 7/6/1903-9/5/1903
Junius A., son of J. H. and Mollie 12/12/1899-7/5/1917

WALNUT FORK BAPTIST CHURCH, HWY #60, JUNCTION I-85 NORTH, ESTABLISHED 1802

SIKES

Carrie E. 5/12/1877-6/6/1914
Mary Ruth 6/1914-7/1914

SMITH

John C. 4/7/1834-12/10/1867
Margaret F. 10/25/1842-

STARGIL

Mary E., dau. of A. T. and M. M. 4/10/1874-3/29/1910
Mary, wife of A. T. 5/10/1852-5/4/1909
A. T. 1/17/1849-1/5/1919

STEWART

Infants of Mr. and Mrs. D. O.
George H. 5/10/1813-12/10/1867
Sarah A. 5/18/1813-1/10/1893

STRANGE

Ora May 8/17/1903-8/31/1904
Martha E., wife of W. N. 11/15/1855-3/18/1898
Octavia Dunahoo, wife of W. N. 3/1/1869-3/18/1932
J. R., son of W. N. and M. E. 6/27/1882-7/2/1906
W. N. 1/24/1845-2/12/1924

TANNER

Otis 11/10/1900-1/20/1969
Billy George, son of Mr. and Mrs. Otis 5/30/1940-3/28/1941

TAYLOR

Dau. of C. B. and Z. O. 4/26/1912

THURMOND

Rosie B. 2/4/1899-
J. M. 1/10/1853-11/20/1893

TIMBS

Chesley died 3/1885, about 70 years

WALNUT FORK BAPTIST CHURCH, HWY #60, JUNCTION I-85 NORTH, ESTABLISHED 1802

WADE

Emma May, dau. of Marion and Elizabeth S. 7/22/1908-3/9/1909

WALL

Robert D. 8/16/1852-4/17/1886

WARD

William died 8/31/1922, aged 76
Candler 1/1/1883-3/24/1948
Bertha 2/19/1887-7/28/1965

WATKINS

Wayne 1938-1938
Rodney 1942-1942
Ronnie 1942-1942

WEATHERFORD

Clara 8/11/1894-7/29/1930
Earley 11/23/1886-5/4/1965

WOOD

Charlton N. 1868-1926
E. 1821-1876

WRIGHT

Barbara C. 6/20/1925-7/2/1965

YEARWOOD

Oscar, son of A. T. and S. J. 8/29/1882-1/13/1891
Sarah J., wife of A. T. 3/2/1887-5/10/1892
Ida E. 11/2/1873-6/8/1888
B. F. 8/11/1863-8/15/1863
Mrs. Eli 5/24/1808-3/1/1858
A. T. 3/7/1830-8/16/1885, Joined the Church 1850, Ordained a Deacon 1855

THE FIRST METHODIST CHURCH, COOLEY AVENUE, Jefferson

MARTIN

William D., born on Stone Horse Creek in Hanover County, Virginia, on the 18th day of January 1771, and died on the 21st of March 1851

MOUNTAIN CREEK BAPTIST CHURCH, NEAR TALMO, GA. AND HWY #129 SOUTH

ADDINGTON

Bennie G., son of J. P. and Fannie 11/15/1887-10/8/1914

ALEXANDER

Annie Mae 1922-1947

BEATY

Paul Randolph, Ga. Pvt, 124 Cav., Repl Trg. Bn, World War II, 12/10/1928-2/5/1949
Pearl, dau. of Mr. and Mrs. J. S. 4/17/1900-9/2/1906
J. B. (Bud) 1890-
Lenie Joe 1/7/1917-7/1/1918
Victoria, wife of J. S. 7/15/1868-7/25/1908
J. S. 8/6/1854-2/8/1929
Henry G., son of Mr. and Mrs. J. S. 2/14/1908-6/25/1908
Eva C. 1890-

BACHELOR

Elizabeth 2/13/1834-4/13/1914

BARRETT

Lawrence died 7/7/1956, 8 months
William died 9/1955, 6 years

BOND

Mrs. L. J. 5/11/1859-4/5/1917

BORDERS

Fannie O., wife of S. L. 2/24/1844-7/27/1915
Ella E., wife of A. V. 10/2/1882-8/18/1903
S. L. 1/20/1842-10/25/1911
Joseph D., son of S. L. and F. O. 9/26/1883-10/24/1883

MOUNTAIN CREEK BAPTIST CHURCH, NEAR TALMO, GA. AND HWY #129 SOUTH

BOWLES

Infant of J. B. and Agnes 11/20/1927
Sarah E. 1862-1940
Nathan M. 1858-1945

BRIDGES

Ann 6/22/1859-5/2/1933
Mary Lee, dau. of J. D. and M. C. 8/1/1896-9/2/1896
Nettie May 5/7/1894-4/19/1909
Ethel Gertrude, dau. of J. D. and M. C. 3/5/1889-10/1/1890
W. H., Jr. 10/7/1853-9/12/1914
William Fred, son of J. D. and M. C. 2/7/1892-10/26/1906
Martha A. 4/15/1824-2/22/1892

BROOKS

Ina Bell 8/3/1899-7/14/1901
Howell 4/26/1913-12/10/1914

BRUMBALOW

Martin 1/1/1857-2/1/1906
Earley, son of Mrs. and Martin
Susan 2/19/1855-7/24/1920

BRYANT

Thelma 1/13/1901-1/24/1904
Paria F. 2/28/1865-12/26/1931
Mrs. E. M. C., dau. of S. L. and F. O. Borders 7/15/1876-10/14/1903

CAYLOR

Nancy 8/15/1866-7/12/1911

CAMPBELL

Mandy, wife of W. H. 7/22/1854-2/20/1900
W. H. 5/9/1845-10/7/1916

COOPER

Thomas Wiley 4/18/1941-5/12/1941
W. Earl 2/24/1948-1/1/19

MOUNTAIN CREEK BAPTIST CHURCH, NEAR TALMO, GA. AND HWY #129 SOUTH

CROSS

Ethel 1/24/1915-5/6/1917
Elizabeth S. 12/28/1878-5/6/1953

DAVIS

John Henry 1869-1950
Ola Pethel 1881-1914

DAY

Margret G., wife of G. T. 3/3/1851-8/3/1910

ETHRIDGE

Thomas A. 10/10/1819-3/31/1900

FIELDS

Ella, wife of Thomas 10/12/1858-11/3/1909
Thomas 4/15/18609-5/27/1911
Cora, wife of J. A. 1/16/1890-9/21/1915

GADDIS

Sallie 1/4/1896-11/6/1911
Mrs. Pearlie Mae Rider died 11/6/1964, aged 67 years, 6 months, 5 days

GEE

Golda Braskalou, wife of J. W. 11/3/1893-6/1/1916
J. M. 3/20/1857-2/9/1931
Berdie Pethel 1885-1959
Lillie R. 1892-1925
Lollie 1872-1958
Harold L. 7/18/1913-7/28/1961
Pam 4/24/1956-10/13/1963
Elizabeth 5/4/1856-5/28/1937
Myrtie M. 1877-1951
W. F. 1893-1934
J. H. 1872-1943
George W., son of M. T. and M. R. 8/28/1907-1/16/1908
Baby Girl died 11/5/1953
Frank, infant baby of Mr. and Mrs. J. W. 1/18/1906-8/12/1908
E. L. 1859-1937
Nancy L. 1861-1929

MOUNTAIN CREEK BAPTIST CHURCH, NEAR TALMO, GA. AND HWY #129 SOUTH

GEE

W. H. 12/3/1884-10/24/1936
Joe Lee 1869-1947
Bonnie Fay died 8/22/1843, 5 months
Buddy Jr. 1936-1936
Bonnie Lou 8/2/1917-1/21/-----
A. J. Sr. 1867-1945
Callie 1870-1950
Infant girl died 1964

HALL

Pauline D. 12/27/1890-8/14/1963
Henry H. 7/5/1878-3/23/1940

HARDY

Ida L., dau. of F. M. and M. A. 10/29/1886-8/9/1893

HAWKINS

Infant son of Mr. and Mrs. R. A. 9/25/1923-9/28/1923

HAYES

Thedosia, dau. of J. M. and P. N. 6/19/1892-12/18/1895
Tommie, son of A. L. and Bell 8/13/1905-8/25/1905
James W. 1880-1939
D. C. 3/13/1857-10/4/1920
Luther Glenn 11/2/1904-3/5/1905

HEAD

Bertha, dau. of Mr. and Mrs. L. J. 9/198/1910

HIGGINS

Rev. S. P. 12/20/1851-6/6/1939
Lacy 10/15/1819-3/9/1901
Angile 11/14/1812-6/19/1898
Chastine C., wife of Rev. S. P. 2/1/1863-8/30/1938

HILL

Archie F. 12/20/1902-2/18/1951

MOUNTAIN CREEK BAPTIST CHURCH, NEAR TALMO, GA. AND HWY #129 SOUTH

HOLLAND

Arch 12/1/1874

IVEY

Pollie J., dau. of Mr. and Mrs. E. G. 5/4/1939-7/24/1939

JOHNSON

William 8/1/1840-5/30/1923
Minnie died 10/5/1919, aged 60 years

KINNEY

Thomas Norman, son of Mr. and Mrs. W. J. 1/14/1897-9/24/1898
Claude 3/1886-6/1967
W. J. and wife
Junions M., son of T. M. and W. F. 8/29/1884-5/5/1885
Sarah Frances, dau. of Mr. and Mrs. J. H. 8/1/1922-2/7/1923
Willie M. 5/6/1891-3/21/1964
Thomas M. 9/1/1862-1/17/1925
Thomas 5/26/1830-2/19/1901
James M. 2/28/1874-11/27/1940
W. Garner 12/13/1888-2/3/1946
Willie F. 1/28/1866-11/4/1940
Martha J., wife of Thomas 8/25/1836-12/2/1901
Lula 12/24/1879

LACKEY

Hannah F. died 8/5/1888
Andrew died 1/29/1910

LANGSTON

John

LYLE

Hester J. 1867-1950
I. H. 1842-1922
Mary J., wife of I. H. 10/4/1864-4/21/1909

MARTIN

Beulah May married to S. W. Martin on 3/4/1912, born 11/17/1894, died 2/15/1917

MOUNTAIN CREEK BAPTIST CHURCH, NEAR TALMO, GA. AND HWY #129 SOUTH

MARTIN

Infant of S. W. and Bealah born 3/30/1914
Samuel Walter, Ga. T. Sgt. Army Medical Service,
World War I and II, 4/29/1891-11/7/1963

MATHIS

Ina
Mary L. 2/25/1854-2/1/1942
M. G., son of B. H. and Belle 5/10/1909-7/15/1910

MOORE

John W. 1874-1906

MORGAN

Pauline, dau. of Mr. and Mrs. J. E. 11/9/1908-1/5/1909

MURPHY

Floella 9/21/1933-10/28/1933
Lycurgus G. 1860-1910
Zemily G. 4/17/1850-2/24/1930
Infant of D. E. and M. E. died 12/5/1907
Franklin D. 1/14/1932-5/2/1932
Clyde 2/12/1898-7/2/1898
Fred 9/28/1906-6/19/1909
Eliza S. 1896-1962
Idea E., wife of L. G. 8/187/1869-9/9/1909
A. J. 10/28/1845-4/4/1902
Jerry W. 1881-1960
Clyde, son of G. T. and E. L. 2/11/1898-7/2/1898
Janette 1/19/1909-9/23/1909
Charles Terrell 8/15/1870-5/9/1953
William P. 1890-
Julia Mae 5/8/1926-11/1935, mother Este
Minnie Mae G. 1889-1925
Gartrell, infant of F. T. and E. L. 12/12/1907-6/19/1909
Fred 9/28/1906-6/19/1909
Emma Love 4/29/1874-1/30/1911
Andrew E. 2/16/1878-1/21/1954
Nora Foster 2/24/1887-7/23/1964
Natalie 8/17/1919-2/25/1921, dau. of Andrew E. and Nora
Neola 4/10/1916-10/8/1919, dau. of Andrew E. and Nora

MOUNTAIN CREEK BAPTIST CHURCH, NEAR TALMO, GA. AND HWY #129 SOUTH

PETHEL

Grace 1908-1945
Fred 1907-
Gannie J. 2/4/1886-11/8/1959
Edgar J. 9/21/1878-12/9/1918

REED

Rose H. 1906-
T. Gilford 1900-1954

RICHARDSON

Charlie 9/9/1883-
Charlie Herbert, son of Mr. and Mrs. C. C. 3/21/1918-7/1/1920
Ola 6/2/1835-10/5/1944

SELF

Roy Ernest, son of D. T. and Eva 4/23/1919-10/22/1919

SHAW

Children of Mr. and Mrs. Boyd Shaw:
Hubert 1912-1913
Herbert 1912-1918
Rache 1916-1918
Sarah A., wife of J.P. 10/7/1844-7/1/1916
J. P. 4/16/1847-5/14/1921

SIMMONS

Woodie 10/19/1913-1/22/1915
Albert C. 1881-1958
Annie Mae 1893-
J. Anderson 1854-1893
Northern 1890-1964
Emma Mozelle, dau. of H. G. and Nina 6/14/1912-4/8/1914
Harriett Eviline (Whitmire) 1/6/1826-7/5/1899
Winford, son of H. G. and Nina 1/4/1916-1/5/1916
Bashia S. 1880-1907
Belle B. 1890-
Ellen, Miss 1888-1968
Rachel Y. 11/10/1834-12/9/1905
Truman T. 1886-1968

MOUNTAIN CREEK BAPTIST CHURCH, NEAR TALMO, GA. AND HWY #129 SOUTH

SIMPSON

William N., Ga. Pvt. HQ Co` 162 Inf. 41 Div. World War I, 2/26/1894-10/23/1963
Kate, dau. of Wm. N. and Fletcher 4/7/1930-11/23/1933

SMITH

Hoke, son of Claud and Pearl 2/24/1910-9/28/1911
Johnnie Louise 3/19/1947-9/18/1963
Pearl C. 2/22/1891-3/20/1968
Benjamin C. 11/12/1882-12/14/1948

SOSEBEE

J. B. 8/13/1904-11/11/1905
Ralph Lee 1922-1955
Richard T., Ga. TEC 5 Guard DET 1918, SCU World War I 7/16/1916-7/4/1964

STANRIDGE

James H. 2/10/1872-6/14/1955
Dozier 1/3/1903-11/28/1915
Dillard, son of J. H. and E. T. 12/8/1889-10/27/1905
J. P. 1/17/1910-5/23/1916
Ella T. 11/27/1878-7/1966

STEWART

James B. 1858-1921
Eliza 1854-1911

TANNER

Elizabeth 12/9/1838-2/9/1921
Bunyon born July, died 12/31/1923

TATE

Thomas R. 2/19/1878-5/26/1947
Julia E. 5/26/1888-

THOMAS

Rosie E. 9/23/1863-5/30/1922
Onie Bridges, wife of J. E. 2/6/1886-4/16/1922
Sarah 1834-6/26/1923
Norris Emory 3/26/1921 5/25/1922
William 2/3/1860-9/21/1925

MOUNTAIN CREEK BAPTIST CHURCH, NEAR TALMO, GA. AND HWY #129 SOUTH

TIMBS

Elizabeth 9/4/1906, age about 90 years

TURNER

F. Marion, husband of Clara L. 11/13/1863-2/10/1909

WATERS

Larry Harrison 1/19/1939-1/30/1939

WATSON

Johnny 1932-1946
Robert 1/22/1894-10/1/1918
Louise 1941-1951
Billy Ray 6/24/1948-11/7/1962
Hannah H. died 12/25/1925 aged 66 years

WHITMIRE

Ludie Frank, son of T. E. and Beulah 4/16/1910-5/26/1910
Myrtie J., wife of T. E., died 12/9/1896, aged 20 years
T. E. 8/9/1873-10/11/1910

WILLIAMS

Cora May, dau. of Joe and Callie 7/29/1907-2/12/1908
George T. 1/7/1879-12/3/1911
Clarence, son of J. S. and M. C. 5/4/1905-9/18/1909

WOOD

Lavina Whitmire Bowles, wife of W. P. 1/10/1837-5/30/1914
W. P. 11/9/1818-2/2/1899
Fannie Epsy 1846-1898
Walter Mitchell 1882-1902
Ellen B., wife of R. C., 8/22/1880-2/24/1906
J. W. 4/2/1848-4/26/1907

YOPP

Minnie O. Morgan 6/5/1884-10/23/1935
Georgiana 11/8/1886-9/2/1903
Joseph E. 11/3/1883-6/12/1885
Mattie, wife of S. D. 8/6/1882-11/3/1909
Martha J. 8/13/1852-6/28/1919

MOUNTAIN CREEK BAPTIST CHURCH, NEAR TALMO, GA. AND HWY #129 SOUTH

YOPP

Infant 8/10/1888
Velmer 1/30/1910-10/22/1911
Samuel D. 11/24/1879-1/13/1966
James E. 4/20/1858-1/27/1888

COMMERCE CITY CEMETERY, Jackson

ADAMS

Lettie R. 5/3/1884
Bonner C. 12/28/1880-

ADDERHOLT

Ida 6/10/1891-10/7/1894
Attice died 7/10/1925
Francis Himer 6/5/1863-12/27/1938

ADERHOLD

Wortie E. 3/12/1888-5/12/1963

AKINS

Mollie S. 6/2/1889-1/20/1964
John S. 6/10/1862-1/30/1941

ALLAN

Little May, dau. of I. G. and L. L. 5/16/1886-12/31/1886

ALEXANDER

Alice M. 1869-1949
C. C. 9/15/1847-4/22/1913, 11th Ga. Cav., C. S. A. 1861-65
Dorothy Montgomery 9/16/1915-12/9/1962

ALLEN

Sarah L. 1884-
Ira C. 9/10/1886-3/10/1956
Lillie, wife of H. C. 11/12/1900-3/12/1931
Maymie A. 4/24/1832-1/29/1905
Lumpin, son of T. and Ed 1888-1891
Ella C. 1906-1947

COMMERCE CITY CEMETERY, Jackson

ALLEN

Jack C. 1906-
Dudley O. 11/20/1909-4/15/1940
Harvey L. 7/18/1875-4/4/1936
Georgia 1/6/1872-11/30/1933
Harvey 1/4/1872-10/11/1944
Robert (Bob) 12/13/1913-8/24/1948
Infant of Mr. and Mrs. V. T. 5/6/1870-11/25/1951
Wilma J. Green 5/20/1901-6/8/1962
William E. 3/25/1874-4/15/1961

APPLEBY

Alvin C. 1852-1932
Henry M. 1882-1960
Mary M. 1860-1949

ARMOUR

Mary Carlan 4/30/1870-11//25/1951

ASBELLE

Albert M., Ga. CPL Btry C, 36 Field Arty World War I, 6/1/1896-6/20/1963

BAGWELL

Amory Donald, son of Joseph H. and Sallie M. 10/30/1957
Sallie M. 1921-
Joseph H. 1918-

BAIER

J. H. 5/29/1853-9/1/1900

BAILEY

Lilla O. 3/29/1874-6/20/1958
Samuel E. 5/20/1848-4/21/1925
Mary E. 5/26/1848-7/2/1914

BAKER

Susie W. 1865-1943

BARBER

R. T. 12/27/1863-10/24/1892

COMMERCE CITY CEMETERY, Jackson

BARBER

Augusta C. 6/28/1878-7/14/1968
Littleton 1821-1899
Billy 1940-1945
Mary 1829-1906
William L. 1871-1945
Clifford D. 3/8/1880-1/19/1919
Susan K. 1878-1961
Alfred 1889-1961
Earl P. 1880-1938
Eliza Nunn 1861-1942
W. L. 12/6/1856-9/27/1922
Clinton E. 11/10/1874-11/25/1938
Sarah, wife of Charles T. 1/5t/1853-4/18/1922
Charles T. 7/14/1852-5/20/1905

BARDEN

William Edna, dau. of Mr. and Mrs. W. J. 4/12/1915-10/5/1916
Annie Belle 1920-1925

BARNES

Ruthie 1882-1969
Sybil T. 1919-
William A. 1899-1953
Robert W. 1945-1946

BARNETT

Cynthia Thomas, wife of W. B. 1/27/1868-3/7/1915
Lula D. 1876-1952
Grace 1889-1892
John D. 1864-1922
Harriett 1887-
Harold G., Ga Pct. 320 Field Arty 82 Div. 7/7/1943
John Paul 1906-1958

BARRETT

Lunda Sue 5/28/1947-6/2/1947

BARRON

Marvin 6/1/1896-6/13/1966
Ora I. 6/29/1903-
Glenda Martnelia 6/28/1943-3/18/1955

COMMERCE CITY CEMETERY, Jackson

BATES

Guilford 7/27/1892-10/17/1897

BAUGH

D. D. 10/5/1852-5/17/1922
Martha J. 10/17/1851-10/21/1925

BAXTER

Jerry 1957
Brenda Carol, dau. of Mr. and Mrs. J. B. 9/1/1945

BECK

Erastus H. 1904-1966
Robert Stiner 5/30/1935-5/14/1966
John Clyde Jr. 2/29/1964-9/24/1964

BEENE

Bess B. 8/18/1890-3/2/1963

BELLAMY

R. Caroline 5/15/1852-4/5/1929
A. Newt 8/18/1850-4/25/1925

BENNETT

A. C. 1884-1950

BENTON

H. Theo 1875-1949
B. Jack 1879-1953
Mary Sander 1878-1947
Willie B. 12/4/1898-3/9/1966
Nannie R. 4/15/1908-
Delilah C. 1886-1955
William Jackson 10/14/1928-11/2/1959
Maggie I. 5/27/1878-10/18/1963
Viola Holland, wife of O. S. 6/26/1904-3/23/1946
Claud Byron 4/6/1879-11/22/1910
Milton A. 1/18/1851-3/23/1935
Emma W. Culbertson, wife of Milton A. Benton 9/1/1855-5/17/1923
Clarence E. 1891-1946
Florence Ayers 3/20/1878-4/19/1950

COMMERCE CITY CEMETERY, Jackson

BENTON

Clyde G. 1900-1954
Eleanor 12/25/1890-
Walter W. 1/8/1902-5/16/1931
Eudora G. 3/29/1862-10/29/1934
Albert M. 7/2/1855-12/20/1930

BERNETT

Tommie Lee 12/28/1942-1/31/1949

BERRONG

Willie W. 1893-1956
Emma B. 1895-
1st Lt. Wildon Hoyle, Co. C, 109 Inf. Regt. R, Killed in Action in Saint Lo France 4/18/1920-8/7/1944

BISHOP

Harry Oscar 12/1/1874-8/1/1954

BLACK

Leo G. 8/22/1902
Nozell L. 3/7/1911
Henry T. 9/11/1883-12/7/1956
Ida M. 9/5/1877-7/17/1935
Eddie D. 7/27/1876-11/22/1937
Rebecca J. 1922-
Harold To. 1920-1958
Robert Lee 10/4/1883-9/7/1948
Clara Dale 8/24/1886-6/21/1913

BLUME

Adam A. 1/23/1892-7/23/1946
Elaine 12/16/1923-8/23/1925

BODDIE

Assie Power 5/26/1886-1/17/1956

BOHANNON

Berry S. 2nd Lt. Co. A 52 Ga. Inf. 1835, C. S. A.- 1925
Ida 12/4/1861-10/14/1945
Eliza O. 9/11/1843-4/2/1928

COMMERCE CITY CEMETERY, Jackson

BOLTON

Gene Lanetta 6/27/1946-1/12/1951
Nancy Dawn 10/20/1944-10/26/1944
Hattie 1882-1961
D. Pat 1874-1948
Ellis B. 1900-1952
Annie G. 1904-
Joe E. 1888-
Myrtle M. 1888-1948
Texas Embry 12/30/1902-4/16/1947
Charlie M. 1901-1965
Reba L. 1901-

BONE

W. Grady 1902-
Agnesw E. 1900-
William K. 9/11/1875-1/9/1935
Abi S. 10/26/1876
G. W. 1893-1952

BORDERS

Thomas L. 4/14/1895-12/22/1945
Regis A., Tech Sgt, US Army Air Corps born 7/21/1921
Lost at Sea to the Line of Duty 9/15/1943

BOYD

Marie A., dau. of E. W. and Bertha L. 3/23/1906-4/19/1908
Ben T., son of B. W. and Ertha L. 11/30/1904-11/9/1909
Bertha Little born in Carnesville, Ga, 7/20/1879, died Newnan, Ga. 2/17/1954
Benjamin W. born Mt. Carmel, S. C.l 4/29/1872, died Union Point, Ga. 9/9/1947

BRADBERRY

Arthur 5/19/1898-8/28/1966

BRASELTON

Almeh H. 3/7/1886-12/26/1948

BRAY

Harvey F. 1877-1949

COMMERCE CITY CEMETERY, Jackson

BREWER

Donald W. 3/24/1932-7/13/1953
Weldon O. 1908-1963
Holman 1882-1923
Dollie J. 1888-1963

BROCK

Leila . 3/18/1875-7/14/1954
Elias G. 5/23/1874-2/20/1946
J. Iasure 1903-
Barbara B. 1903-
Clifford W. 2/26/1820-2/21/1967
Bernice T. 11/25/1922
Jimmie, son of Mr. and Mrs. J. F. 6/27/1922-1/16/1923
James F. 9/25/1895-8/18/1943

BROOKS

William M., husband of Modena 11/21/1858-11/18/1903
Modena W. 7/30/1863-4/16/1942

BROOKSHIRE

Margie N. 12/26/1923
George T. 1/23/1921-8/17/1967

BROOME
Pearl 5/9/1884-4/27/1962

BROWN

Lanora H. 1888-1965
Sam Kenneth 2/13/1943-7/20/1943
Infant dau. of Mr. and Mrs. J. H. 4/17/1954
Infant dau. of Mr. and Mrs. J. H. 9/19/1966

BRYANT

C. H. 1884-1935

BURGERS

Lawton J. 9/25/1862-12/24/1945
Lettie Bird 11/11/1862-8/17/1937
Beatrice, dau. of Mr. and Mrs. L. J. 5/25/1895-10/2/1897

COMMERCE CITY CEMETERY, Jackson

BURNETT

Willie Mae 1879-1969
John W. 1881-1954

BURNS

Emma Powel 8/1/1872-6/11/1949
Buford A. 1/29/1955-
Susan E. 1/8/1861-7/12/1921, wife of Buford A.
Sallie C. 1861-1954

BURRUSS

Agnes D. 3/15/1879-3/12/1916
J. B., Jr. 1/28/1906-5/15/1960

BYERS

Wellington born Albemarle Co., VA 3/10/1825-4/22/1895

BYRD

Evelyn 1918-1932
Andrew J. 1863-1928
Lula L. 1867-1934
Alton L. 1903-1952
Hassie Byrd Edwards 5/2/1896-9/4/1944

CAMP

B. L. 7/13/1873-1/13/1913

CAMPBELL
Gipsond 9/9/1857-11/7/1889
Eunice B. 5/3/1886-12/5/1941

CARLTON

Harrison A. 10/16/1878-9/27/1945
Bealer Augustus, son of Mr. and Mrs. H. A. 7/22/1918-2/28/1919

CARRINGTON

Mattie Mae 5/7/1879-6/30/1968
William David 12/24/1849-1/10/1913
Hal C. 8/13/1882-1/10/1913
Amanda Paralee 3/22/1850-10/25/1938
Mattie Herring 87/19/1883-2/18/1954

COMMERCE CITY CEMETERY, Jackson

CARSON

A. Clarence 1870-1939
Bert A. 1871-1960
George L. 11/10/1860-4/20/1910
Laurinda M. 12/10/1863-1/29/1941
George L. Sr. 8/23/1844-12/16/1929
Curtis C. 1900-1961
David H. 12/1/1856-10/29/1909
Georgia Westbrook 11/12/1849-12/3/1900
Charles Maxey, son of J. M. and Lizzie, 11/30/1898-6/20/1899
Hortense 8/3/1896-12/12/1901
George L., Sgt. Co. E J6 BN CA Partisan Rangers, C. S. A.
Mattie Holley 10/12/1859-2/8/1922
Bessie Love, dau. of D. U. and M. C. 12/7/1883-8/29/1884

CARTER

Dock S. 2/13/1891-1/25/1950

CASTELAW

Pauline White 10/26/1887-4/2/1943
Dr. G. O. 1/17/1885-1/23/1949

CHANDLER

Eunice J. 12/7/1909-2/18/1963
Grace H.
Herbert 11/28/1873-10/13/1912
Mattie Ingram 6/2/1876-6/29/1949
Winford T. 1907-1967
Mary Irene 1916-
Rupert Clarence, son of J. M. and M. J. 1/1/1897-5/29/1878
J. Edgar, son of J. M. and M. J. 1866-1884
J. M., husband of M. J. Farmer 7/26/1845-1/2/1883

CHILDS

Roy S., Ga PFC Co. L 381 Inf. Regt. World War II, BSM-PH 6/29/1920-1/11/1963
Lucy 3/6/1878-8/4/1931
Dolia S. 1903-
Dewey W. 1904-1960
Sam H. 1882-1962
Carrie L. 1885-1967
Jesse C. 1880-1961
Rufus, son of E. D. and Stella 10/11/1924-10/18/1935
M. Fannie 1886-1942
W. E. 5/5/1901-9/4/1932

COMMERCE CITY CEMETERY, Jackson

CHRISTIAN

Burdette, son of Ida 1887-1889
Burrell, son of J. L. and Ida 4/5/1889-11/11/1889

CLEGHOEN

Claud 7/9/1886-5/13/1951

CLEMENT

Kathleen, wife of George C. 11/2/1885-10/14/1969

COCHRAN

Henry 1898-1956
Sue 1901-

COFFEE

Lucy Helen, dau. of Mr. and Mrs. E. H. 1/30/1920-2/20/1924

COKER

Thomas Clyde 11/20/1952

COLE

William C.
Cecil W.
James Owen 3/13/1895-9/22/1961
Soleda B. 6/21/1899-
Luther N. 1/15/1893-9/16/1963
A. Elie J. 8/17/1872
Theodore, son of T. and L. J. born 9/25/1892

COLEMAN

Mary L. died 1/1/1908
D. A. 11/12/1848-7/10/1930
F. A. 4/21/1838-11/30/1917
Carlton died 8/29/1893

COLLINS

Rev. George H. 1873-
Clemmie B. 1883-1951

COMMERCE CITY CEMETERY, Jackson

COLLUM

Infant dau. of Guy and E. R., born and died 3/11/1909

CONN

Thomas F. Jr. 4/29/1941-10/16/1957

COOPER

John Hightower 1884-1953
Lamar Jackson 1897-1965
Margaret S. 1895-1964
Charles K. 1890-1926

COTRELL

Infant son of Mr. and Mrs. A. R. 4/30/1944

COUCH

Angie Marie 1965-1965

COWART

George E. 8/24/1923-3/3/1935
Tommie M. 10/2/1951-6/13/1952

COWLES

Mrs. C. M. 8/20/1864-5/27/1924

COX

Walter M. 4/24/1895-5/6/1936

CRAWFORD

Janie Lou 2/24/1902-6/18/1959
J. Ben 3/30/1874-11/9/1953
Mary Lena 5/7/1879-9/24/1940
Joseph B. 7/17/1907-10/7/1950

CROCKER

Neadie R. 2/27/1888-11/19/1959
Fred J. 7/2/1883-4/1/1934
Guy G. 1902-1942
Charles C. "Doc" 12/11/1889-12/17/1958

COMMERCE CITY CEMETERY, Jackson

CROCKER

Mary Joe 1/19/1931-12/4/1938
J. P. 6/4/1913-
Ethel M. 9/2/1914-3/12/1968
A/1 C, Alan D. 2/21/1945-11/11/1968
Clora Duckett 2/20/1893-
William E. 4/4/1886-3/25/1955
Herman Young 5/11/1908-12/4/1965
Winett Elizabeth, dau. of W. E. and Clora 11/1/1922-3/6/1924
Hazel Jenett, dau. of W. E. and Clora 3/25/1921-2/21/1924
Curtis C. 10/16/1928-1/13/1929
Darald J. 5/16/1949-7/24/1968

CROW

Alice Vinson, wife of John H. 3/17/1860-10/8/1939
Ernest Bartow 8/1/1882-8/7/1955
E. B. Jr. 6/28/1926-7/18/1926
Mary Janice 1/13/1956-2/21/1957

CROWE

H. Luther 1905-1965
Emma Dalton 9/4/1876-8/20/1945
Asbury Stephen 4/6/1867-1/15/1947

CRUMLEY

Oeda B. 6/7/1884
D. Hershel 11/27/1883-10/14/1965

DALE

Eugenia H. 6/17/1841-9/1/1916
John M. 7/18/1872-10/30/1922
Harry Coil 1/6/1856-8/10/1954
Lena Ruth 11/11/1862-10/25/1944
William A. 3/14/1836-12/8/1924
Samuel G. 6/16/1843-4/30/1915
Ann Phillips, wife of S. G. 9/22/1862-4/7/1910

DALTON

Loy, son of S. J. and Icie Dalton 6/30/1911-11/21/1912
M. C. 6/21/1844-104/1924
J. T. 11/5/1848-3/28/1925

COMMERCE CITY CEMETERY, Jackson

DANIELS

Mildre Mill
Harlan H. 1911-1967

DAVES

Charles J. 10/25/1929-9/6/1946
Priscilla Wofford 11/19/1897-7/26/1961

DAVIS

Lillian Lorene 10/7/1909-2/20/1910
Verne Luther 7/29/1898-11/25/1958
W. Potts 12/8/1909-5/9/1950
Bertha P. 5/9/1873-8/13/1950
J. Carlton 1890-1935
Luther L. 5/27/1873-8/13/1950

DEADWYLER
Kyle T., dau. of William T. and Almeda J. Thurmond 12/28/1876-8/22/1927
Clyde, son of Valentine H. and Harriet A. 10/23/1876-7/4/1895
Harriet A. Wilhite, wife of V. H. 4/20/1831-11/22/1912
Albert Bartow 2/24/1862-6/2/1936
Dora Carson 8/1/1868-12/5/1946
Valentine H. 1/29/1828-10/28/1886
Dr. V. H., Co. A, 11th Ga. Cav. 1861-1865
William V., son of Valentine and Harriet A. 4/1/1852-4/21/1876
Theressa Miller, dau. of Valentine & Harriet 5/15/1847-11/14/1905
J. P. 11/20/1849-5/19/1914
Cornelia C. Montgomery, wife of Joseph P. 9/1/1853-7/10/1911

DELL

Byrum C. 1898-1960

DILL

Wilburn, son of E. C. and Hilda
Seaborn E., Ga. Cpl. 82, Chemical Mortar Bn., World War II, 8/30/1926-2/9/1952

DILLS

John S. 1869-1943
Fannie L. 1873-

DIXON

Loyle G. 1894-1965

COMMERCE CITY CEMETERY, Jackson

DOWDY

Dwayne D. Sr. 3/13/1900-4/6/1936
Estelle W. 1901-1967

DUCKETT

William D. 1887-
Pearl C. 1892-1961

DUNCAN

Columbus A. 1880-1960
Mary Frances 1926-1944
Olen 2/13/1890-9/2/1890
Minnie B. 5/1/1872-10/30/1941
Olivia Power 11/11/1856-5/3/1890
Henry H. 4/27/1851-9/1/1929

DUNSON

J. Owen 2/24/1879-7/17/105-
Eula E. 3/6/1876-4/23/1944
Sallie Rogers 8/14/1871-11/24/1941
Lamontine Odell, son of L. J. and M. R. 11/11/1887-6/10/1888

DURHAM

Grace S. 1892-1952
Bonner M. 1891-1937
Columbus A. 1880-1960

DURST

Fred E. 1871-1943
Florence Jackson (Dolly) 12/18/1897-9/21/1964

DYER

Barbara Lee, dau. of Mr. and Mrs. J. P. 9/21/1935-9/20/1936

ECKLES

Coleman, Ga. Pvt US Army, World War I 11/25/1897-12/4/1956
William F., Pvt. 152 Depot Brig., World War I,12/12/1893-1/22/1955
Henry C. 8/24/1891-11/11/1934
Cecilia 10/2/1904-4/4/1924
Joel Henry 1/5/1862-2/17/1921
Martha Clevia Shankle, wife of J. H. 1/8/1870-9/12/1915

COMMERCE CITY CEMETERY, Jackson

ECKLES

R. A. 12/21/1848-6/2/1903

EDWARDS

Farris 1904-1936
Orlena M. 1882-1962
Samuel N. 1879-1937
William S., Co. B 15 Ga. Inf., C. S. A.
Easterly C., Ga. Sgt. 517 SVC Bn Engr. Corps, World War I, 12/17/1893-12/
John E. 6/1/1876-11/21/1943
Hattie Hix 8/29/1883-7/7/1955
Arthur E. 9/15/1911-12/19/1936
Frank Rudolph, son of A. E. and Ruth 4/17/1930-5/1/1934
Farris 1904-1936
Orlena M. 1882-1962
Samuel N. 1879-1937

EIDSON

R. S., Co. K, 8th Ga. Regt. Inf. 1861-1865, 11/17/1839-11/14/1909
Elizabeth Bowling 9/8/1846-

ELLIOTT
Alma Watson 10/3/1884-3/16/1926
Samuel J. 3/18/1861-
Caroline Justice, wife of Samuel J. 6/9/1865-2/6/1929
C. M. 5/6/1884-5/6/1940

ELROD

Jesse B. 3/21/1889-3/8/1946

EMBRICK

Richard 1889-1960
Fannie 1890-
Brenda Carole 2/19/1949-3/26/1949
Annie M. 9/3/1918-5/19/1967
Robert L. 9/29/1922

EMBRY

James T. 12/6/1865-1/2/1948
Emma C. 9/21/1873-6/23/1945

COMMERCE CITY CEMETERY, Jackson

EVANS

S/Sgt. Harin O. 2/19/1920-6/24/1944
Allie 7/1/1897
Atha 9/1/1894-2/20/1953
Guss A. 1881-1945
Laura H. 1884-1958
Ruby B. 1904-1939
Roy 1896-1957
Lillie 1897-
Infant son of Mr. & Mrs. J. T. 10/3/1948
Clarence H. 4/22/1905-
Ella S. 4/26/1910-11/1/1962
Garnette, dau. of Mr. and Mrs. S. C. 8/12/1952
Samuel Philip 1963-1969

FARABEE

L. J. 4/6/1862-4/29/1907
W. C., Co. E, 4th Ga. Regt. Mil. (1861-1865) 6/15/1818-4/7/1903
Luther B. 1872-1947
Mauder M. 1879-1959
Roxanna Drusilla 10/171854-5/17/1922
Josie Belle, dau. of L. B. and M. B. 8/2/1904-12/8/1905

FARMER

Mary Chandler 4/6/1842-1/12/1927, wife of J. M.

FAULKNER

John P. 9/18/19801-6/8/1951
Mary Alice 5/29/1926-7/5/1944
John P. 9/18/1901-6/8/1951

FILLINGIM

Mary W. Eckles 11/3/1885
Lonnie F., Ga. Cpt B, 10 Inf. 7/11/1880-8/1/1959

FINCH

Laura E. 1859-1899
John F. 1842-1905, Co. E, 16th Ga. Batt. 18651-654
Mrs. William G. 1894-1947
William Turner 7/9/1920

COMMERCE CITY CEMETERY, Jackson

FOWLER

Paul B. 1916-1964
Ruby M. 1917-
Ward Timothy 2/19/1946-11/24/1946

FRADY

Laura Hart 6/22/1873-11/6/1963

FREDERICK

George W. 1859-1938

GARNER

Tony N., infant son of Sammie and Thomas 1/14/1962

GARRISON

William Don 7/7/1948-11/24/1966

GIBSON

Lonnie 4/14/1869-11/13/1925
Nancy Garrison, wife of Lonnie, 10/23/1867-

GILLISPIE

Charles William III 1938-1941
Charles W. 1884-1960

GILMAN

Mildred P. 1916-1962

GLAZNER

Kathleen Sharp 5/2/1896-8/10/1920

GOBER

Thomas H. 4/21/1841-4/12/1905, Co. G, 43rd Ga. Reft. Inf. (1861-1865)
James Thomas 1874-1942
Gertrude Glosson 1880-
Willie 1871-1896
Amanda Owen 1845-1940
Infant dau. of H. D. and Maggie, born and died 3/30/1905
W. Alden, son of R. B. and Maggie 12/24/1908-3/7/1909

COMMERCE CITY CEMETERY, Jackson

GOBER

Eulah, dau. of W. J. and Claris died 5/25/1903
Clarrisa, wife of W. J. 4/17/1845-1/18/19816
William J., Co. Ga. 10th Ga. Batt. Cav. 1861-1865, 9/17/1844-2/9/1917
John M. 8/25/1868-3/15/1944
Allie S. 10/12/1872-
Lora I. 1906-
Delona 1908-1957
Marvin 1875-1941
Levi H. 1836-1962

GOODIN

Annie Belle Hudson, wife of C. A. 4/20/1883-8/28/1919

GOSITT
Bud 1870-1961

GOSS

William Robert 4/19/1819-6/16/1886
Elizabeth Ann 4/10/1821-7/298/1877
William Judson 5/18/1841-1/10/1898
Louise Parolee 4/29/1851-8/22/1896
Jessie Helen, dau. of W. J. and L. P. 6/25/1872-5/23/1875

GREEN

Beulah Peeler, wife of W. E. 2/19/1879-4/4/1947
Grace 6/29/1899-7/24/1943
Roy, son of W. E. and Beulah 5/16/1897-5/17/1898
Paul J. 7/30/1953-9/25/1955
James R. 1881-1961
Daisey P. 1888-1865

GREGORY

Harley 4/19/1906-7/7/1967

GUEST

Ida Cleo, dau. of Ira. and Nealie 1/1/1901-7/17/1907
Lettie Jane, dau. of W. O. and C. T. 1904-1905
Dossie 1913-1915
Dellar W. 1879-1919
Thomas 1919-1919
E. H. 1859-1934
C. B. 1857-1932

COMMERCE CITY CEMETERY, Jackson

GURLEY

Walter M. 10/11/1875-12/27/1934

GULLY

Lou C. 9/26/1891-5/14/1965

GUNNELS

J. H. 6/10/1839-3/15/1913, 10th Ala. Regt. 1861-65
Cora 11/9/1847-2/29/1924

GUNTER

Het Carson 2/8/1886-12/31/1960

HAGGARD

Mrs. E. S. A., wife of W. L. 10/87/1859-5/23/1931
J. B. 7/2/1858-11/30/1914
Genie 11/24/1861-6/18/1925
Rosa 9/26/1884-7/1/1959
Arthur 6/13/1887-4/3/1946
Oscar J., Ga. PFC 317 Inf. World War II 5/23/1916-12/3/1965
Vernen 1934-
Annie C. 1987-

HALL

Boston 9/26/1895

HAMAKER

Frank
John
Katherine

HANCOCK

Infant daughter of Mr. And Mrs. Jack 2/12/1948

HANLEY

John P. 1884-1954

HARBER

William Y. 9/30/1878-4/9/1946

COMMERCE CITY CEMETERY, Jackson

HARBER

William Y. 930/1878-4/90/1946
Mittie Wright 7/30/1878-5/17/1962
Infant son of W. T. and L. A. died Jan 1888, age 1 month
Lucy W. 1851-1930
Lucy Henley 12/23/1887-8/20/1935
Homer R. 2/14/1881-5/12/1965

HARDEN

W. T., Co. B, 1st Ga. Inf. State Troops 1861-65, 3/28/1846-3/22/1902
William Preston II, M. D., 2/7/1866-11/11/1918
Ada Pruitt 7/13/1861-8/18/1950
William Preston III 4/19/1893-3/5/1955
Mary Adair, wife of William Preston III, 11/15/1903-5/29/1952
W. T., Co. B, 1st Ga. Inf. State Troops, 1861-1865, 3/28/1846-3/22/1902
T. Colquitt, Jr. 7/29/1894-9/28/1940 "the eldest son"
Thomas Colquitt 2/7/1870-8/21/1958
Mildred Barber 12/1/1867-11/11/1917
Lawrence G. 6/14/1899-8/22/1917
Joseph E. 12/14/1901-7/28/1953

HARDMAN

Leona Wright Nelms 11/7/1874-8/1/1961
R. Clayton 8/10/1912-7/16/1950
Van Payne 11/24/1866-3/7/1932
R. L. 9/1/1860-10/24/1927
W. B., M. D. 3/31/1865-10/28/1918
Ida Murrah Shankle, wife of W. B. 7/3/1870-9/16/1911
Infant 11/8/1904
Infant son of Mr. And Mrs. L. G. 1/24/1936
Emma Griffin 12/10/1881-12/27/1853, wife of Lamartine Griffin Hardman
Lamartine Griffin, M. D. 4/14/1856-2/28/1937, Governor of Georgia (1922-1931)
Nora O'Neal 10/11/1894-3/3/1936
Elic Jackson 4/28/1888-11/1/1960
John Barnett 10/8/1873-11/18/1938
Nancy Trotter, wife of John Barnett

HARGNEWOOD

Willie B., son of B. S. 10/28/1892-4/8/1896

HARDY

Clifford J. 3/30/1918-12/26/1945
A. Smith 1898-1963
Anna N. 1903-

COMMERCE CITY CEMETERY, Jackson

HARMON

Francis C. 1890-1963

HARRIS

Abb Dorsey 10/5/1876-7/13/1954
Robert Lafayette M. D. 1858-1927
Frances Barber, wife of Robert Lafayette
1862-1935
Jesse Newton 10/29/1882-11/12/1959
Jesse N., Jr. son of Mr. And Mrs. Jesse N. 1/10/1922-1/13/1922
Mary Cleghorn, wife of J. W. 12/18/1876-12/6/1929
J. W. 8/21/1870-4/27/1940
Tina, wife of A. J. 4/30/1845-11/30/1927
Andrew J., Co. E, 34 Div. Inf., C. S. A.
Hubbard Isaac 1890-1946
Ruby Dunson
Emma Elizabeth 3/6/1861-7/25/1936
Isaac Franklin 8/19/1851-11/10/1926

HARRISON

William W. died 8/12/1916
Mary Frances died 10/22/1926
Marion Barber 11/7/1884-7/20/1913

HARTLEY

William D. 5/18/1883-8/17/1967
Annie B. 5/18/1886-9/21/1966

HAULBROOK

George Frank Jr., son of G. F. and Lovie 4/9/1930-4/18/1930

HAWKS

H. Cal 9/3/1884-3/6/1952
Eldridge 1873-1917
Obie 10/22/1871-4/10/1916
Albert W. 1896-1954
Jessie M. 1896-
Cynthia Buckett, wife of R. H. 7/16/1866-1906
Robert H. 7/6/1858-2/21/---
Floyd, son of R. H. and C. E. 4/16/1892-1/22/1894

COMMERCE CITY CEMETERY, Jackson

HAYES

Robert H. 11/1/1947-2/3/1962

HAYNES

Etta 9/15/1884-3/15/1949
Claudee E. 1886-1963
Mary P. 1886-1963
Emory lee 1931-1963
Martha Ann, dau. of R. L. and L. M., age 6 months
Robert L. 1875-1948
Ettie C. 1876-1940
Mildred, dau. of R. L. and Ettie 7/31/1920-9/14/1921
Emory Lee 1931-1963
Martha Ann, dau. of R. L. and L. M., age 6 months
Robert L. 1875-1948
Ettie C. 1876-1940
Mildred, dau. of R. L. and Ettie 7/31/1920-9/14/1921
Ernest 12/10/1948

HEAD

Susan, wife of G. W. 3/18/1876-1/12/1907, infant buried with her
Minnie Lee, wife of G. W. 1887-1931
Infant dau. of Lee and Bernice 11/18/1938

HENRY

Lovic B. 8/3/1883-10/4/1928
Cleta A. 12/28/1890-1/20/1966
Fannie E. 7/1/1912

HENSLEY

Ray 3/13/1910-11/24/1967
Allie 10/22/1909-

HERBERT

Vera B. 1907-1959
James E. 1904-

HERRING

Hoyt, Ga. Pvt. 157 Dep. Brig. World War I,1/9/1889-5/29/1946

COMMERCE CITY CEMETERY, Jackson

HIGHTOWER

Beulah 1866-1930
Charles W. 1858-1922
Henry Linton 1901-1938
John Z. 1829-1909, Co. B., 5th Regt. Ga. Vols. 1861-1865

HINES

Jesse

HIX

Bertha O. 12/18/1892-1/25/1967
John R. 3/13/1888-5/17/1943
Infant dau. of I. R. and M. L.
Mattie R. Vandiver, wife of L. R. 3/14/1862-8/19/1901
Ruby J. 2/18/1904-9/20/1962
John F. 7/28/1893-
Raymond L. 5/11/1943-2/14/1969
Jean C. 12/22/1941-
H. Beemon 1897-
Maurine W. 1903-
Grace T. 1912-1964

HOGAN

Nell May 5/17/1913-11/11/1913

HOGWOOD

Robert F. 4/6/1900-10/16/1954
Annie E. 10/20/1907-

HOLBROOK

Alice 7/27/1888-12/24/1909
Howell P. Jr., M. D. 12/28/1923-1/14/1956

HOLLAND

Elizabeth E. 1902-
Norris R. 1897-1943

HOLLIFIELD

Esther M. 1871-1955

COMMERCE CITY CEMETERY, Jackson

HOOD

Adelia 2/14/1878-10/3/1959
Estelle 9/11/1869-7/22/1947
Ben 9/30/1875-12/28/1946
Eza, wife of John 5/3/1875-3/14/1904
John 5/12/1872-2/10/1956
Christiana Maley 5/27/1892-1/21/1950
William Talmage, Sr. 9/8/1884-4/5/1965
Frances Suddath 8/11/1889-11/22/1920
Olin Sharkle 6/18/1916-5/14/1919
John 5/12/1872-2/10/1956
Eza, wife of John 5/3/1875-3/14/1904
Adelia 2/14/1878-10/3/1959
Istelle 9/11/1869-7/22/1947
Ben 9/30/1875-12/28/1946
Samuel 4/1/1909-9/12/1961
Clement Jefferson, son of Mr. And Mrs. Samuel, 8/12/1933-3/19/1935
Infant daughter of Mr. And Mrs. Samuel, born and died 3/8/1939
Alice Owen, wife of C. W. 9/9/1872-2/25/1958
Willie Clement, son of C. J. and Nora 12/28/1885-1/31/1886
Nora Hardman, wife o f C. J. 7/25/1863-10/9/1887
Addie, wife of C. J., died 8/4/1895, aged 29 years, 1 day
Clement Dobbs 4/16/1894-5/17/1896
Melissa, wife of C. W. 12/16/1836-1/4/1896
C. W. 2/27/1827-1/3/1910, Co. A., Col. Dorroughs, State Cav.1861-65
Grace Goss 3/1/1877-7/19/1948
Clement Jefferson 3/29/1861-6/9/1943
George C. 1884-1965

HOPE

Claude Durham 7/13/1918-8/21/1931
Ollie Durham 6/22/1890-11/28/1964
James Claude 7/11/1889-10/4/1946

HOSCH

Ralph W. 1905-1961
Ellis 1900-
Russel F. 1876-1938
Mattie E. 1877-1967

HOWENSKY

Otis 1907-1968

COMMERCE CITY CEMETERY, Jackson

HUBBARD

Eudie P. 1854-1918
F. Marion 1848-1934

HUDSON

Infant dau. of J. A. and H. J. 12/27/1891-1/28/1892
J. N. 1/30/1853-2/20/1911
Ella 10/20/1860-10/15/1915
Julius Fred 3/22/1897-10/14/1939
Capt. James P. 4/27/1819-3/6/1893, Co. E, 4th Ga. Regt. Mil. 1861-65
Sarah Jane, wife of J. P. 11/10/1829-10/21/1890
James Thomas, son of T. P. 4/6/1870-6/20/1918
Thomas P. 2/24/1845-7/8/1915, Confederate Veteran enlisted 1/1862 Story's Co. BG 43rd Vol. Inf.
Mattie A., nee Wood 4/5/1842-4/8/1920
Julius C., son of T. P. and M. A. 11/4/1872-12/27/1889
James Thomas, son of T. P. 4/6/1870-6/20/1918
Thomas P. 2/24/1845-7/8/1915, Confederate Veteran enlisted 1/1862, Story's Co. BG, 43rd Vol. Inf.

HUGHES

Nellie Mae 1886-1951
John H. 11/25/1877-8/26/1957
John Dennis 6/14/1925-11/15/1952

HUNT

Janerio Toccoa 9/25/1863-1/2/1939

INGRAHAM

Rufus 1/25/1874-/25/1875

INGRAM

Ezekiah H. Jr. 5/26/1872-10/14/1952
Dora Wilson 4/26/1872-1/14/1948
J. W. 12/31/1904-11/1/1949
Joanne, daughter of Mr. And Mrs. A. G. 1/23/1943-9/17/1943
E. H. 8/29/1836-3/5/1913, 34th Ga. Regt. Inf. 1861-1865
I.H., wife of E. H.

COMMERCE CITY CEMETERY, Jackson

JACKSON

Lois H. 10/30/1918-4/3/1962
Ernest W. 1884-1967
Carl Haynie 11/3/1878-10/20/1953
Fred 1900-1955
Bertha L. 1899-1956
William Pirkle 9/23/1895-4/30/1941
Leary M. 6/28/1904
Savannah Christian, wife of William P., 10/14/1861-3/4/1950
Horace Green 7/26/1900-9/3/1952
Sidney W. 1873-1955
Nellie 1881-1955
S. Wise 1844-1927, Cobbs Legion, C. S. A.
Lou Haynie 1845-1933

JAMES

J. 1913-1942
Robert, son of S. B. and Begar 9/4/1932-5/6/1963
Harvey A. 1889-1957
Martha W. 1893-

JOHNSON

Young Joseph Sr. 10/28/1875-7/1/1960
Virginia T. 8/11/1877-

JONES

Dorothy S. 1922-1959
Julia Ann, daughter of Mr. And Mrs. W. H. 12/16/1953-12/30/1953
Decatur B. 7/14/1884-12/1/1947
Angie Belle Cape 4/7/1888-1/30/1946
Mary E. 9/10/1915-
John Lewis 7/10/1914-9/7/1967
W. (Hub) 1887-1958
Lula M. 1902-
Ed
Mrs. Leary Baugh

JORDAN

Mattie O., wife of W. W. 10/27/1852-12/11/1903
Robert, Son of W. W. and M. O. 4/19/1876-6/6/1893
Sarah 12/11/1813-1/23/1897

COMMERCE CITY CEMETERY, Jackson

KEITH

Clarence C. 1896-1958
Lola W. 1896-
Lauren Harris
Cicero Harris 3/10/1890-10/23/1961

KELLUM

Ambra Rogers 1/23/1922-5/21/1960

KEY

T. Erasmus 1850-1917
M. Elizabeth 1855-1925

KING

Mary E. 4/9/1868-7/27/1945
John C. 1/13/1859-12/23/1946

KINSEY

Louise Rees born Llangollen Wales 5/19/1863, died 11/26/1938

KINZ

James C. 1901-65
Ethel W. 1910-

LAMB

Bessie Smith 10/2/1913-12/13/1960

LANDRUM

T. Clarence 1893-
Alma R. 1897-1957
Infant son of Mr. and Mrs. Gartrell 10/12/1929
Gartrell Riley 6/27/1905-9/23/1948
Alma Minish

LANGFORD

Mary S. 1904-
Clyde 1898-

COMMERCE CITY CEMETERY, Jackson

LANGSTON

Albert C. 6/14/1875-1/21/1951
Gladys R. 12/12/1904-

LEACH

Bessie Orpha 6/20/1886-5/16/1962

LEACHMAN

Mattie 1890-
Willie 11/5/1885-6/18/1949
Gertrude 1924-1966

LEWIS

Mildred B. 1906-1962
Baby Richard Lee died 6/27/1954, son of Mr. And Mrs. T. S.

LINDERMAN

Infant daughter and son of Mr. And Mrs. J. H.
John F. 1892-1963
Lola P. 1883-
Jack Hampton 1/30/1887-10/3/1938
Ora Hudson 9/5/1892-
Dewitte 1881-1949
Ella F. 1878-1956

LITTLE

Infant son of Mr. and Mrs. H. P. 8/6/1929-8/7/1929
Howell Park 6/25/1899-1/16/1948
Lois, daughter of Claud and Cora Q.
Frank Quillian 1900-1935
Claude 1873-1955
Cora Quillian 7/19/1876-5/6/1961

LOCKMAN

Howard 1916-1955

LORD

W. French 6/21/1910-3/13/1945
Verner Gwynell 1925-968
James W., son of Bolen and Clementine 5/14/1872-11/10/1953
Clyde V. 1896-1957

COMMERCE CITY CEMETERY, Jackson

LORD

Ina I. 1900-
Charlie W. 4/24/1874-5/22/1956
Maggie H. 11/27/1874-5/22/1956
Jesse L. 12/21/1870-
Nelia Vaughn 10/15/1871-4/18/1943
June Charlotte, daughter of J. M. and W. N. 6/2/1933-7/15/1934
Charlotte Jane, daughter of Mr. and Mrs. Gerald W. 6/7/1950-2/1/1952
Gwynell 1925-1968
Mack (N. G.) Jr. 9/22/1911-8/21/1956
Lois E. 3/9/1919-
Hewlett Ellis, Ga. Amm.2c US Navy WW II 9/21/1923-6/14/1947
Luther 1884-1955
Mary H. 1884-1963
Jessie M. 1920-1943 "Lost in north Atlantic"

LOVE

Mary 1897-1948

LOVIN

Nancy A., wife of W. P. 8/22/1862-1914
Johnie Elizabeth 1/18/1922-2/14/1924

LUTHIE

Charles E. 5/29/1907-9/29/1963
William M. 1890-1949
Jessie M.
George C. 9/24/1885-7/12/1930
Minnie P. 12/31/1886-1/18/1968
R. Ellis 1897-1918
Eva Collins, wife of W. H. 1863-1922
William Henry 1864-1933

MADDOX

J. Cecil 1899-1962
Ruby E. 1905-
Emory Anthony 5/9/1909-11/14/1968
Ralph E. 1909-1938
Wilma L. 1915-

MAHAFFEE

J. F. 6/14/1850-11/13/1904
Helm, daughter of M. T. and Lois 2/9/1906-2/21/1907

COMMERCE CITY CEMETERY, Jackson

MANDERS

James J. 5/8/1916-4/22/1968
Mary C. 9/23/1920-

MANGUM

Ellie Mae 6/11/1900-
Henry W. 9/8/1896-
Kathrin 1918-1919
Darell D. 1936-1942

MANLEY

Candis S. 3/22/1830-11/29/1913

MARLOW

H. Henry Jr. 10/29/1946-6/11/1965
Christina 11/23/1917
Edward James born London, England 1867, died 1951
Jane Margaret born Oxford, England 1881

MARONY

Ellen, wife of W. B. 5/5/1885-
Z. B. 1/12/1872-10/12/1912

MARTIN

PFC William L., Ga. US Marine Corp. 8/28/1946-12/17/1966
Dorothy Lanell 11/4/1944-12/6/1945
Marion, son of Lee and Mary born and died 5/6/1930
Augusta Harber 10/2/1881-
Gabriel Pierce 1/17/1874-7/14/1955
Reed W. 12/6/1906-
Joe Sharp 10/1/1907-2/5/1968
Doyle
Margaret D. 1916-1954

MASON

Infant son of Rucker and Emmie 8/24/1915

MASSEY

J. C. 1921-1957
Tommie A. 1918-

COMMERCE CITY CEMETERY, Jackson

MASSEY

J. W. 8/17/1863-
Ellen O. 4/29/1867-4/6/1915
Ruby C. 2/10/1903-6/20/1921
Nela Chandler 9/24/1874-7/24/1968
Madison Thomas 11/10/1866-8/27/1923
Onie 1882-1966
Claud 1882-1947

MATTHEWS

Richard Earl 9/15/1902-7/1/1950
Nina Lou 1/16/1906-
Ada 1881-1959

MATHEWS

Mary 3/12/1852-6/1/1920
R. F. 1847-1910
W. J., Co. B, 1st Ga. Regt., 1861-65

MAXWELL

Jim A. 1879-1954
Emma J. 1890-

McCLURE

Grady H., Ga. Pvt. US Army 10/3/1897-2/5/1936
Winnie B. 1878-1937
William H. 1862-1927

McCONNELL

Noel 1894-1952
Melissa Hood 1898-1960
William Felton 3/30/1858-11/27/1934
Katharine Adams, wife of W. F. 7/7/1867-10/2/1949

McCOY

William P. 1916-1960

McDONALD

Kathryn 5/12/1908-3/15/1950
Grace M. 1908-1966

COMMERCE CITY CEMETERY, Jackson

McDUFFIE

William Penn 6/5/1908-5/28/1949

McENTIRE

Edith, daughter of J. C. and Selina 11/23/1881-8/21/1909
W. E. 11/19/1889-10/13/1957
Vesta 1915-
Paul 1914-1961

McEVER

Memph M. 1912-1948
Marguerite S. 1917-1968
Jake W. 1883-1949
Carrie L. 1887-1956

McGALLIART

Robert P. 1868-1925
Florence P. 1868-1938

McGINNIS

Richey J. 1918-1956
Lillie R. 6/13/1880-3/7/1954
E. Young 9/3/1878-11/25/1947
Susan, daughter of Mr. and Mrs. G. D. 2/11/1951

McGUIRE

Oliver, Ga. Cpl. 14 Inf. Korea PH 8/19/1931-3/2/1952

McPHAIL

Lizzie Pilsbury Ward, wife of Rev. J. D. 7/29/1869-6/26/1930

McWOOD

Dane 1886-1957

MEALOR

Lillian Ann, daughter of Mr. and Mrs. T. C. 4/14/1936

COMMERCE CITY CEMETERY, Jackson

MEDLEY

Henry B. 1887-1955
Louis Lord 1886-1955
Myrtle, daughter of J. E. and H. J. 2/15/1906-7/26/1907
Eulous G. 12/12/1883-4/4/1964
George W. 1/12/1880-1/29/1963
Gertrude 7/17/1902-9/13/1903
Billy Lee 3/19/1924-3/19/1924
Frank Henry 10/11/1906-4/20/1957

MEEKS

Nellie Anglin, daughter of N. L. and M. S. 1903

MERCIER

B. F. 2/19/1833-5/13/1907
Susie E., wife of B. F., 6/21/1832-5/6/1907
Ethel G. 1898-1940
Obed B. 1893-
A. Louise 1923-

MINISH

Walter N. 12/12/1903-9/10/1966
Ella H. 7/25/1881-10/11/1956
Edna Louise 2/17/1911-4/20/1937
Joe B. 12/15/1896-7/13/1942
Robert L. 4/18/1899-2/1/1965
Bonnie Lavorne 3/30/1965-5/22/1968
Milton H. 1882-1964
Terry W. 10/12/1948-12/9/1956
Rita B. 6/25/1926-12/9/1956
Dwayne A. 1/16/1956-12/9/1956

MITCHELL

Frank Elijah 2/27/1895-1/10/1940
Maud Coleman 2/1/1893-5/12/1966

MIZE

Leila Ritchie 1/15/1879-9/5/1958
Charles Allen 8/24/1873-10/27/1940
Theron N. 6/24/1889-10/13/1957
William S. 9/17/1856-11/13/1920
Ella Neal 11/22/1856-11/6/1913
Samuel A. 1870-1943

COMMERCE CITY CEMETERY, Jackson

MIZE

Louise T. 1886-1944

MONTGOMERY

Lizzie Harber 8/27/1887-10/28/1959
Claude 10/4/1875-6/9/1956
Elizabeth Griffeth 10/25/1844-1/15/1923
Mattie Lillian 2/16/1870-7/31/1922
Ruby Ritchie 12/20/1880-3/11/1967
John Oliver 7/31/1872-5/6/1945

MOODY

Pamela L. 4/29/1957
Murwyn M. 5/10/1914
H. Art 10/9/1910-8/26/1967

MOORE

Thomas A. 11/11/1878-7/29/1954
Hattie E. 7/29/1880-12/26/1951
George F. 1871-1928
Heppie B. 1872-1964

MORGAN

James R., son of Mr. and Mrs. J. P. 5/9/1853-6/1/1953
Thomas J. 1866-1949
Maybelle H. 1898-

MORRISON

Jessie J. 1873-1943
Alice C. 1872-1949

MULLINS

Blanche V. 1906-1942

NELMS

Lydia Elbert, daughter of L. B. and V. L. 1/23/1909-3/11/1909
Leonidas 1857-1915
Harriet L. 1860-1946
Mary Hamaker
Charles H. 9/7/1881-11/17/1949
Francis M. D. 3/31/1871-2/16/1922

COMMERCE CITY CEMETERY, Jackson

NICHOLSON

Howard E. 1924-1949

NIMMONS

Waymon A. 1886-1957
Ammer A. 1889-

NIX

Infant son of Mr. and Mrs. J. Nelson 9/7/1941
Infant son of Mr. and Mrs. Dillard M. 4/7/1921
Cora Lee Bland, wife of L. M. 12/26/1901-4/1/1946
Lloyd M. 12/13/1901-2/11/1952
Hymer L., son of D. M. and F. J. 1/3/1881-9/24/1882
Claud, son of D. M. and P. J. 6/10/1886-9/25/1888
Richard M. 6/25/1905-1/4/1959
Mary Gray, infant daughter of Mr. and Mrs. Richard 6/12/1936-7/12/1936

NUNN

Crawford M. 1900-1959
Jim T. 1897-
Ezra B. 1894-1962
Thomas J. 3/22/1866-8/16/1939
Hattie 10/14/1873-9/18/1962

O'CONOR

Minnie S. 1890-1908

O'REAR

Charles W. 10/7/1896-12/11/1963

OLSEN

Elizabeth Smith 1/7/1909-6/20/1961

OTT

Mary Elizabeth, infant daughter of Mr. and Mrs. Kenneth W., Sr. 11/28/1963

OWEN

Mary Elizabeth 4/1/1920-4/11/1920

COMMERCE CITY CEMETERY, Jackson

OWENSBY

Hattie B. 11/18/1894-
Roscoe H. 9/7/1895-2/21/1969
Charles W. 12/4/1953-4/13/1957

PAGE

Mildred R. 1922-
Clarence A. (Tater) 1920-1956, Ga. S. Sgt. USA WW II,
Am & 5 OLL 10/13/1920-5/23/1956
Howard H. 12/16/1897-11/12/1937, Ga Pvt. 9 Inf. 2 Div.
Lou Willie 1/10/1895-

PALMER

James F. died 7/25/1933
Pearl Barber, wife of James F. died 3/15/1936

PARNELL

Charity L. 6/10/1861-12/7/1914
Rupis N., son of Charity

PARTAIN

Sara Q. 9/24/1937-
Charles O. 6/1/1938-12/13/1961

PARTRAM

Joseph A. 1877-1955
Savannah P. 1878-

PATTON

J. Tolbert, wife of T. D. 6/1/1872-12/1/1895

PAUL

H. C. 1869-1947
Nancy 1873-1940
Hinton G. 1/17/1910-7/12/1966

PAYNE

Ethel 10/29/1876-2/17/1945
L. E. 8/6/1833-10/27/1908

COMMERCE CITY CEMETERY, Jackson

PEELER

Ruth, daughter of C. E. and B. M. 2/26/1906-/14/1907
William Henry born Commerce, Ga. 5/1/1881, died Polk Co., N. C. 5/17/1936
Mrs. Ettie Williams 4/29/1886-8/6/1924
Noel Clifford 12/24/1886-10/24/1918
Margaret W. 3/15/1857-1/30/1946
Henry died 9/26/1893, 46 years

PEEPLES

Edna A. 12/8/1894-9/8/1956

PENDERGRASS

Rev. W. T. 1883-
Bessie 1894-1949

PERRY

N. H. 1907-49
Ruth L. 1909-

PHILLIPS

Maud S. 1890-1965
Ella T. 1888-1941
Grover 12/25/1899-2/21/1935
Baby Latimer 1923-4
Johnnie L. 11/30/1900-5/26/1966
Flora S. 5/7/1903
Rev. C. P. 1882-1955
Martha 1882-
Estell G. 1911-1950
Sara 6/16/1925-3/19/1942
Lewis 2/14/1894
Minnie 3/21/1896-12/10/1940

PICKENS

Walter R. 4/19/1889-8/24/1957
Lillie E. 2/25/1885-12/16/1962

PITTMAN

W. Kenneth 3/31/1927-12/19/1965
Alfus R. 10/13/1900-12/16/1951
Clarence W. 8/21/1909-
Clarence C. 6/4/1912-

COMMERCE CITY CEMETERY, Jackson

PITTMAN

Clarence E. 1874-1957
Frances B. 1876-
Oliver 1885-1886
Ulee 1892-
Pamelia Hilley 1858-1945
Pleasant Owen 1851-1928
Wilmer Owen 1897-1948
Lillian Augusta 1890-1964

PORTER

Emma Head, wife of Carlton Floyd, 11/24/1881-6/28/1937

POWELL

James Horace 1859-1926
Celia Carnes 1869-
James Clyde 1909-1964

POWER

Annie Williford 3/2/1854-10/5/1909
W. B. 5/18/1848-12/30/1904, Co. K, 13 Ga. Regt. 1861-65

POWERS

Ella Josephine Wood, wife of W. B., 2/24/1862-7/29/1912

PRICKE

Olin Hester, son of J. H. and P. R. 9/1/1907-9/2/1907

PRUITT

Larry E. 1948-1967
John J. 1883-1951
Nezzie M. 1890-
Eula Ethel 1/1/1881-6/30/1958
Dock Harvey 7/31/1879-8/9/1956

PUGH

Corrie L., daughter of John and Lizzie, 12/3/1925-4/18/1930
Carrol, son of John and Lizzie 2/3/1925-10/27/1935

COMMERCE CITY CEMETERY, Jackson

PURCELL

John H. 1875-1965
Elvira F. 1884-1955
W. Odell 4/29/1902-
Elbertice 1/20/1909-6/21/1967

PURDY

Etta B. 1890-1965
C. Haskell 1885-1966
Albert Haskell, Fla. CMM USNR WW II 3/6/1913-4/14/1958

QUILLIAN

Kasiah Malissa Meadors, wife of Rev. Fletcher Quillian 11/20/1827-11/30/1900
Clarissa, daughter of T. F. and S. N. born and died 6/1/1904
Clarissa Dean 1846-1901
William Anthony 1846-1913, Co. E. 11th Ga. Cav., 1861-65
Robert T. 1871-1929
Sadie C. 1868-1947
Thomas F. 1869-1939
Ophelia 1849-1932
Mary C. 1858-1925
Joseph A. 1856-1948

RAGSDALE

Nannie Emma Lord, daughter of Leonard and Margaret Ragsdale, 1/4/1879-4/12/1931

RAMSEY

Millard C. 8/26/1856-8/2/1928
Susan E. 12/19/1858-3/15/1936
Will N. 1883-
Mattie Lee 1888-1961
Howard D. 1917-1966

RAY

Rev. Martin 1888-1957
Eula Estelle 1895-

REDMON

Joe 1882-1964
Mandy Baker 1882-1950
Richard Bud 7/5/1866-8/15/1928
Leila 1922

COMMERCE CITY CEMETERY, Jackson

REDMON

John 1928
Elice S. 1887-1959
Bessie S. 1898-
Betty Gene, daughter of Mr. and Mrs. Wiley 6/4/1934-6/5/1934
G. Wiley 7/11/1892-2/10/1969
Lenear B. 8/12/1897-
Infant son of J. R. and L. 9/16/1916-10/22/1916
John Richard
Lonie 1910-1967
George, son of J. O. and H. J. 10/26/1910-12/13/1914

REED

Moses Wesley 1888-1956
Flora L. Nelms 1893-

REIDLING

Beatrice G. 1931-1962

RHODES

J. R. 1861-1865 C. S. A.
Mary J. 7/9/1822-4/11/1916
James M. 9/25/1819-2/11/1905
Julian G. 3/6/1892-6/11/1951
Leila C. 1/11/1894-
Dozier B. 11/7/1915-3/5/1942

RICE

Homer Hoot, son of W. B. and Nelle 8/27/1905-5/11/1907
Infant son of W. B. and Nelle 12/28/1909-2/8/1910
Nelle Harber, wife of W. B. 12/27/1882-9/13/1922
William Brannon 6/5/1879-11/18/1949
George T. 1876-1964
Claudia C. 1874-1958
Marion H. 7/31/1884-5/21/1920
Allen P. Sr. 10/30/1870-3/31/1941
Pearl Power 10/4/1874-5/6/1908
Allen P. Jr. 11/19/1902-7/26/1948
John G. 1875-1953
Ola H. 1889-1965

RICHEY

Lola Benton, daughter of M. A. and E. W. 2/28/1885-7/1/1915

COMMERCE CITY CEMETERY, Jackson

RICHEY

Otis Samuel 8/16/1884-12/9/1939
Evelyn P. 4/19/1915-7/13/1915
Son of J. S. and Lola 2/18/1902-2/18/1903
Bessie May, daughter of James R. and H. M. 1/16/1901-6/23/1901
Sarah born 11/10/1842, aged 49 years
James R. 7/6/1870-12/7/1903
Henry T. 1/24/1926
Annie T. 4/2/1920
Mary Ruth Allen 12/24/1920-10/13/1945
Infant son of J. O. and C. O. 1/9/1910-1/10/1910
John Olin 5/7/1975-2/8/1930
Cordelia Lord 1/3/1883-6/6/1941
Pearl 4/30/1880-7/2/1938
William T. 11/28/1874-12/29/1875
Garner R., son of J. S. P. and L. F. died 2/9/1900, aged 22 years, 2 months
Lou Eaton, wife of L. S. 3/6/1839-7/16/1906
J. S. P. 9/12/1833-12/3/1903
Merdelle H. 11/4/1901-6/29/1922
Charlie H. 1945-1959
Charlie B. 1908-1955

RICHARDSON

David L. 5/12/1889-4/27/1953

RITCHIE

Frank Telford 2/9/1884-12/20/1937
Susie Evans 8/10/1887-6/25/1956
Georgia Usry, wife of Thomas Evans Ritchie, died 10/14/1942

ROACH

Randall 1946-1946
Marion Fay 1945-1945

ROBERTS

Major C. 11/22/1868-10/7/1961

ROBINSON

Amanda E. 1882-1920

ROGERS

Marion Irene, wife of Dr. A. A. 5/21/1898-1/9/1967

COMMERCE CITY CEMETERY, Jackson

ROGERS

Martha Elizabeth O'Kelly, wife of James T. Rogers 4/23/1843-7/27/1912
James T. 2/26/1841-2/8/1912

ROY

Henry L. 1900-1956
Lilliam P. 1905-

RUSSELL

Stiles 1893-1967

RYLEE

E. J. 6/10/1833-3/30/1897, Co. E, 18th Ga. Batt. Cav. 1861-65
Wilkie 3/28/1889-8/24/1964
Elizabeth, wife of E. J. 6/27/1838-5/6/1914

SAILERS

George W. 12/20/1884-2/15/1944
Obe O. 7/23/1890-10/13/1933
Laurie Ingram, wife of Obe O. 9/4/1890-
W. Carl 2/17/1894-12/2/1968
Carrie Lay 5/10/1888-11/8/1954
Joe 1886-1960
Ethel P. 1893-1965
Deloney 1/8/1837-8/7/1921

SANDERS

Lastus M. D. 1874-1947
Mary Bennett 1879-1915
Ruth Denham 1912-1964 "A dedicated teacher"
D. Gwinn 2/21/1864-9/26/1883
T. Poullain 7/29/1875-6/13/1878
Turner H., Ga. Pvt. Inf. 34 Div. 8/14/1922
Plumer S. 1890-1936
Ada B. 1868-1951
Howard, Ga. Pvt. 121 Inf. WW I, 7/4/1893-1/28/1931
M. Tharpe 1879-1954
Eliza Barnett 6/21/1838-1/7/1913
Donald J. 9/9/1820-9/21/1887
James B., son of Mr. and Mrs. R. L. 4/8/1915-4/11/1915
Robert L. 9/17/1873-7/3/1961
George W. 12/20/1884-2/15/1944

COMMERCE CITY CEMETERY, Jackson

SAXON

Mary G. 7/10/1894-3/5/1953
Grady W. 6/23/1893-2/17/1945
Infant son of Mr. and Mrs. H. E. 8/16/1935
Lewis 12/8/1862-9/8/1928
Mary S. 4/15/1871-9/29/1937
Maybell J. 10/9/1932-12/24/1933
Willie M. 1888-1948
Rena G. 1895-1956

SCOGGINS

Emma Greer 8/8/1910-8/3/1965
C. M. 2/20/1876-2/22/1946
Harriet Arminda 1/18/1848-1/26/1924
J. H. 3/26/1848-9/2/1928
Claud 9/20/1872-10/18/1902
John Jr. 9/5/1900-11/14/1913
Mary E. 6/13/1868-2/27/1936

SEAGRAVES

Berr A. 1891-1955
Iva F. 1895-
Claude 1896-1956
Nezzie W. 1895-

SEARS

Arthur G. 4/1/1930-
M. Evelyn 12/27/1931-3/3/169

SELLARS

Emma Brady 9/14/1882-7/23/1951

SERODING

Ruth B. 1905-
Norbert R. 1900-1941
Eugenia M. 11/6/1861-2/12/1951

SEYMOUR

Charlie T. 1883-1955
Francis O. 1889-1958
Malcolm H. 1913-1962
Louise C. 1923-

COMMERCE CITY CEMETERY, Jackson

SEYMOUR

Glenn Rondol 1/1/1934-2/28/1937
Claud F., son of C. T. and C. F. 5/8/1918-1/15/1938

SHANKLE

Lovic P. 1876-1948
Andrew Marvin 7/20/1874-5/6/1944
Pearl Bush 10/11/1876-11/22/1949
Nana Johnson, wife of Olin E. 7/20/1891-3/19/1960
Olin E. 8/11/1880-3/31/1929

SHANNON

John F. 5/22/1855-7/12/1928

SHARP

Nelly N. 1864-1942
Esther Lee, wife of Dr. L. H. 4/17/1865-8/25/1901
Clara Mae 1897-1958
B. B. 10/31/1872-5/25/1959
Infant son of Dr. and Mrs. L. J. born and died 1/3/1904
Ifant daughter of Dr. and Mrs. L. J. 12/25/1918-12/26/1918
L. J., M. D. 2/10/1862-7/6/1926
Pauline S. 5/6/1883-4/21/1963
Anna 1867-1942

SHELL

Willie McCurdy, wife of Henry Hilliard Shell 2/25/1876-10/4/1927
Henry Hilliard 11/24/1864-12/28/1951

SHEPHERD

Rosalie Smith, wife of J. W. Shepherd 7/3/1873-5/7/1891

SHEPPARD

Rosena Maret 3/21/1894-4/23/1943
Margaret Shankle 12/1/1871-12/31/1927
William Daniel 3/11/1866-1/31/1938
Infant son of J. J. and Iva 1/8/1908-2/1/1908

SHIELDS

Annie Mae 11/9/1904-2/24/1949
John W. 1/27/1880-2/14/1961

COMMERCE CITY CEMETERY, Jackson

SHORE

Tempy B. 11/7/1859-11/12/1929
T. H. 8/27/1849-2/24/1918
Salome Hunt 3/8/1902-4/10/1937
Luther C. 6/10/1890-8/22/1958
M. E. 9/27/1850-10/13/1880
Cander 2/15/1871-7/15/1886
Odell 1897-1954

SICOLS

Infant daughter of Lener born and died 1906

SILMAN

James Paul 10/6/1923

SIMS

Jeanett H. 10/13/1914
Paul H. 10/6/1914-8/16/1955

SLATER

J. A. 1860-1925
Earlie T. 1963-1942

SMALLWOOD

Thomas P. 1890-1964
Drucilla G. 1890-
Roy D. 2/25/1912-4/24/1962
Odessa V. 9/14/1912-
Elisha Litt 7/21/1880-1/24/1941
Roxie T. 10/22/1882-1/13/1947
John T. 4/22/1888-6/6/1930
James D. 6/6/1893-11/15/1962
Minnie B. 5/9/1893-
Grady 12/15/1921-11/13/1937
Susan Elizabeth 5/13/1927-11/16/1936
Debra Ann born and died 2/7/1957
Willie Pearle, daughter of E. L. and R. A. 4/8/1908-12/18/1908
T. N. 6/2/1853-4/26/1914
Martha E. 5/1/1849-7/5/1932
Lucius Littleton 12/15/1924-4/11/1925
Ada Belle 9/9/1924-9/17/1936
Lou 9/2/1883-12/31/1930

COMMERCE CITY CEMETERY, Jackson

SMALLWOOD

Luke L. 1900-1960
Ethel E. 1903-1967

SMITH

Jessie L. 5/18/1854-2/4/1926
Cornelia Thurmond, wife of Jessie L. 2/13/1852-2/14/1934
Lamb B. 10/2/1874-7/14/1903
Jeptha A. 1/9/1877-9/22/1917
Icie Cornelia 1882-1934
Otis 3/20/1895-2/28/1968
Nezzie R. 1/9/1896-
Hazel J. 1/25/1917-12/6/1968
Annie L. 4/20/1884-5/2/1957
Elizabeth 3/19/1889-1/31/1964
Martha M. 7/21/1857-4/27/1926
Henry M. 11/1/1853-7/22/1925
Margie E., daughter of H. M. and M. M. 11/8/1896-3/27/1952
Emma Walton 12/25/1862-1/25/1947
R. L. J. 12/21/1864-1/14/1935
William Floyd, son of W. G. and Rosa 9/1/1907-12/22/1917
W. Gordon 7/28/1887-11/24/1931
Rosa B. 4/20/1889-
Selwyn J. 1905-1947
Zuline T. 1907-
Harry Lee, son of M. O. and Emma 3/13/1890-6/6/1891
Annie Mae 12/28/1893-5/4/1957
Carl E. 1899-1962
Lee V.
William L. 1891-1952
Mary B. 1894-
William G. 1884-1960
Lena S. 1866-
Lucy F. 9/6/1865-9/25/1907
F. A. 10/2/1858-
Allen 11/27/1893-11/2/1918
Asa L. 1879-
Etta W. 1878-
Florene James 1880-1968
John W. 1882-1925
Hollis 12/16/1909
Julia W. 12/10/1913
Bobby 3/18/1935-5/3/1965
Sally 2/19/1936-
Lucile G. 1913-1948

COMMERCE CITY CEMETERY, Jackson

SNIPES

Hoyt Allen 10/9/1927-10/16/1943
Parker 7/5/1867-12/13/1947
Fannie G. 6/10/1868-9/12/1946

SORRELLS

Carrie 12/17/1878-11/9/1961
Wyley 4/26/1875-8/14/1941

SORROW

Lila L. 1899-1968
Mrs. J. H. 8/25/1904-7/9/1941
Samuel Carlos 12/2/1886-8/30/1968
Lonnie M. 7/28/1894-12/6/1944
Rilla I. 1/20/1895-6/29/1962
Sgt. W. O. 1920-1944 (Killed in Germany 11/17/1944)
James V. 10/23/1925-5/23/1963
Harber D. 1892-
Olia S. 1896-1956
Castellaw B.
Sidney L. 4/20/1929-4/12/1966

SOSEBEE

Nancy, wife of E. H. 12/13/1861-1/3/1912

STAGNER

Susie B. 1911-1954

STANDRIDGE

Leona M. 1903-1953
Luke 1900-1951
Alice and Dallas, infants of Mr. and Mrs. J. B.
Jessie P. 1907-
Clyde Joe 1904-1947
Hettie R. 6/17/1874-4/5/1942
Riley 5/11/1897-12/20/1945
Ruby C. F., daughter of Mr. and Mrs. D. M. Lord, wife of Victor Standridge 6/12/1916-11/11/1940

STAPLER

Hoyt 9/8/1885-12/15/1890
W. T. 1851-1926
Harriet B. 1851-1935

COMMERCE CITY CEMETERY, Jackson

STAPLER

Robert B. 1882-1944

STARK

Kathrine 1/27/1920-1/28/1920
Thelma 1/20/1905-10/22/1940
Clara F. 12/27/1888-1/17/1958
Weldon F. 8/15/1882-12/16/1939
Cicero D. 10/15/1854-1/29/1925
Susan 10/1/1859-4/4/1947
Aldine, daughter of G. D. and S. L. 12/3/1895-12/18/1895
Infant son of Hope and Evelyn 10/4/1927-10/6/1926
Arabella Brown, wife of William Weldon Stark, 4/9/1871-2/18/1939
William Weldon 9/17/1864-12/12/1949
Grade Elizabeth, daughter of Mr. and Mrs. W. W. 11/24/1899-1/11/1900
Infant son of Mr. and Mrs. W. W. 7/30/1894
Lula Helen, daughter of Mr. and Mrs. W. W. 12/23/1889-1/26/1890

STEADMAN

John B. 1/10/1897-1/18/1969
Rosa L. 6/30/1908-

STEELE

Roy R. 11/17/1896-1/1/1927
Sarah B. 11/3/1867-6/27/1944

STEPHENS

George Garner, son of J. E. and Addie 11/29/1900-8/19/1901

STEPHENSON

Tom B. 1894-1945
Willie O. 1914-1969
Baby Joan 9/8/1958-5/1/1961
Hattie R. 1900-1969
Jim U. 12/1/1870-
Lula J. C., wife of Jim U. 5/27/1872-12/4/1936

STEVENSON

Jessie Merle 2/22/1887-4/18/1918

COMMERCE CITY CEMETERY, Jackson

STEWART

Mamie L. 1890-
Amanda C. 1865-1941

STOVALL

Albert B. 1910-1910

STOWE

Willis M. 1874-1937
Susan H. 1882-1956
H. DeWitt 8/2/1911-3/9/1964
Grace B. 6/19/1911-

STRICKLAND

Permelia Farabee 7/27/1859-7/12/1951
William H. 1880-1965
Emily H. 1890-
Brant W. 1918-1958, Ga. Tec 5 SVC Btry 93 Armed Fa Bn WW II
Wilbern 1904-1942

SULLIVAN

Martha M. 1899-
James W. 1865-1929

SWINDLE

Hoyce M. 1/31/1930-1/24/1939

SYRAN

Thomas J. 1888-1961
Carlbel H. 1894-
Infant son of Mr. and Mrs. T. J. 7/31/1926

TALLENT

Edward D. 11/3/1884-5/14/1960
Agnes L. 3/10/1915-

TATE

Irvin M. 8/2/1896-5/20/1967
Lucy S. 10/3/1897
Ineze 12/30/1907-6/13/1939

COMMERCE CITY CEMETERY, Jackson

TENCH

Margaret Lois 1915-1949
Fannie Annabell Hicks, daughter of Mr. and Mrs. M. B. Tench 1908-1933
Mack B. 1877-1951
Celia H. 1890-
Clyde 8/24/1914-5/15/1916
Bular Mae 6/22/1920-2/2/1924
Guy 7/10/1911-12/5/1965
J. B. 12/12/1904-9/18/1906

THOMAS

Susan Lockhart, wife of J. W. 7/8/1853-4/29/1906
A. Paul 9/21/1907-5/6/1944
Bashie M. 8/3/1884-5/15/1946
Susan 10/22/1892-10/20/1958

THREATT

Odell G. 1888-1941

THURMOND

Delyon Elwanda, daughter of Y. L. and L. E. 2/23/1930-11/7/1936
Rhodes, infant of Alvin and Jessie 2/18/1901-4/2/1901
Jessie Rhodes, wife of Alvin H. 11/2/1870-3/23/1930
Alvin H. 11/25/1872-2/19/1958
Frank 8/10/1893-2/26/1968

TOLBERT

Martha, wife of H. H. 1/1/1872-9/27/1896
William T. 3/20/1897
Allis H. 5/4/1897-8/23/1966

TOOKE

Charlton Clinton 3/20/1889-2/141963 "Minister of the Gospel for 50 years"

TOUCHSTONE

Thomas B. 1/8/1908-11/15/1951

TRAWICK

Paul B. 1888-1944
Paul B. 1927-1955

COMMERCE CITY CEMETERY, Jackson

TRUITT

Nathan Wylie 11/23/1833-4/13/1892
Susan Virginia Barbara, wife of Nathan Wylie Truitt 1/6/1853-2/11/1932
E. W., Co. Ga. 22nd Miss. Regt. Inf. 1861-65

TUCKER

Mary F. 1916-1942

TUGGLE

Milissia A. 10/20/1857-11/10/1916
J. L. 1857-1930

TURNER

Infant of Calhoun and Mary
Mary, wife of Calhoun, died 3/30/1901, aged 32 years
Carrie Gober 1880-1912

TURPIN

James H. 11/29/1871-

VAUGHN

Keith 1898-1950
Infant daughters of Mr. and Mrs. Emory 2/22/1931

VENABLE

Eula M.
John J. 1913-1964
Grover C. 1888-
Easter M. 1882-1937

VERNER

John Clark 12/28/1882-6/29/1964 "Physician-Surgeon"

WADDELL

Agnes 7/25/1936-3/1/1952
Marion B. 1885-1963
Lillie C. 1892

COMMERCE CITY CEMETERY, Jackson

WADE

Erastus C. 1879-1963
Mittie C. 1879-1962

WAGES

Lucille P. 1907-1950

WAGNON

W. B. 3/14/1862-7/21/1899
Leila 2/7/1869-4/6/1943

WALDROP

Cora R.
H. Eugene 3/15/1934-7/9/1960
Guynita S. 4/29/1934

WALDROUP

Sam W. 1877-1962

WALKER

Charles M. Jr. 11/2/1827-6/28/1899
Naomie Smallwood, wife of W. D. 4/27/1882-4/14/1929
Marvin 10/11/1901-1/4/1946
Grace L. 8/4/1910-

WALL

William C., Ga. Pvt. 39 Co. 157 Depot Brig. WW I, 10/2/1890-3/14/1958

WANDECK

Sammie, son of Mr. and Mrs. James 12/24/1943-12/25/1943
James 12/21/1917-4/30/1966

WARD

Arthur I. 11/19/1897-3/11/1936
Emma L. 9/15/1903-7/5/1737
Roscoe 3/2/1902-8/23/1967
Lillie Mae 3/17/1905-
Clifford Clay 8/2/1891-10/6/1938
Mamie L. 1895-
Eddie C. 1878-1948

COMMERCE CITY CEMETERY, Jackson

WARDLAW

Dairo Resta, son of Mr. and Mrs. L. G. 7/11/1915-10/26/1916
Walter M., son of B. F. and A. J. 5/14/1880-1/15/1909
William Franklin 3/28/1938
Esther Lucille 1/12/1904-8/23/1966
Mary R. 8/12/1904-8/23/1966
Mary R. 8/12/1873-2/1/1938
Rufus Franklin 11/26/1874-4/9/1957
Benjamin Franklin 4/15/1908-12/21/1964
Benjamin F. 12/7/1847-10/26/1903
Amanda J. 8/10/1848-3/30/1933
Corrie Estell, daughter of B. F. and A. J. 7/10/1870-6/29/1896
Jason C. Jr. 12/3/1890-4/9/1891
Jason C. 3/1/1858-2/12/1891
Anna D. 8/30/1860-2/8/1891
Sarah A. Howard 1830-1889
Jesse Calvert 1823-1885, South Carolina Pvt. Co. E 16 Regt., S. C. Inf. Confederate States Army 12/26/1825-3/29/1885

WATERS

Urcy 2/17/1914-10/3/1916
Carson C. 1906-
Willie Mae R. 1911-1968

WATSON

Elijah B. 10/13/1857-7/30/1935
Laura Owen 2/28/1864-10/4/1951
J. David 1852-1913
Zilla C. 1854-1909

WEBB

Annie Lord 4/3/1920-8/12/1941
George W. 8/18/1880-10/17/1955
Pearl E. 7/26/1883-1/19/1937
Vella 1888-1888
Cymenthia L. 1895-1896
Americus S. 1856-1909
Martha L. 1861-1933
Martha Susan Allen, wife of W. M. Webb 7/28/1838-11/15/1914
W. M. 1/12/1841-5/18/1900
William Albert 2/1/1875-3/22/1919
Perry E. 9/17/1906

COMMERCE CITY CEMETERY, Jackson

WELLS

Wesley L. 12/22/1906-5/10/1967

WEST

Susie Bishop 8/17/1866-3/8/1954

WESTMORLAND

George 1902-
Henry 1902-
Ida B. 1884-1966
B. Clyde 1882-1957

WHEELER

Minnie 1884-1955
W. J. 1868-1952

WHITE

J. W. Jr. 1931-
Sara B. 1930-1952
Marvin 1884-1947
Alice T. 1890-
Agnes Hood 7/16/1901-4/24/1951
Mae Parker 1888-
John Wesley 1884-1942
Infant son of Mr. and Mrs. R. J. 10/26/1947

WHITEHEAD

Margaret E. 4/7/1849-12/22/1930
William T. 12/21/1865-10/26/1942
Mary Holland 7/12/1876-4/15/1949
Elijah D. died 3/31/1895
Annie, wife o f E. D. 1/26/1838-2/18/1892
George Bee, son of E. D. and R. A. 1/1/1864-6/27/1882
Baby John, son of J. G. and Eva 5/13/1900-7/14/1900
Berner, son of E. D. and Emma 9/5/1898-12/11/1899

WHITFIELD

Janet E. 11/24/1945-1/16/1966
Michael B., infant son of Mr. and Mrs. Boyd 8/7/1947
Grover C. 7/7/1892-12/1/1946
Lavender P. 12/25/1898-

COMMERCE CITY CEMETERY, Jackson

WHITLOW

Vera Pauline 1899-1957
William A. 1877-1955
Julia McKie 1875-1943

WILBANKS

Grady O. 1896-1969
Ida E. 1876-1954
Laura Wilson 12/10/1892-10/9/1939
Aubrey W. 10/1/1904-2/27/1947
Isaac 9/3/1846-3/22/1891

WILDER

Sharon, daughter of Mr. and Mrs. H. W. 5/25/1953-5/29/1953

WILHITE

Myra 4/5/1883-11/13/1955

WILKES

Lorenzo D. 3/26/1888-
Fannie I. 4/13/1888-8/14/1962

WILLIAMS

Hattie, daughter of G. T. and B. P. 3/11/1897-10/16/1899
J. Billy 8/4/1922-4/2/1939
Lillie C. 6/21/1896-2/26/1948
Emma 8/8/1878- - /18/1964
Henry Eugene 10/11/1878-4/20/1938
Billy 8/4/1922-4/2/1939
Lonnie L. Jr. 1902-1954
A. B. Dawson, son of Mr. and Mrs. E. B. 2/1/1922-2/2/1922
Joyce, daughter of Mr. and Mrs. E. B. 5/14/1923-5/20/1923
H. Odell 1904-1952
J. D. 1906-1955

WILLIAMSON

Woodson Lafayette 11/19/1857-8/30/1942
Ethleen 6/18/1858-5/17/1942
Fred H. 9/2/1882-
Ethel T. 1/19/1884-11/10/1963
W. Donald 7/1/1895-
Violet M. 7/14/1901-8/1/1968

COMMERCE CITY CEMETERY, Jackson

WILLIAMSON

Hazel Lee, daughter of V. M. and Dillie 1/1924-1929

WISE

Jessie Mae, daughter of F. W. and B. S. 7/20/1902-7/9/1904

WOFFORD

Cynthia Jill, daughter of Mr. and Mrs. J. W. 8/12/1949
Daniel Lamar 1/14/1948-5/31/1948
Infant son of Mr. and Mrs. Hugh M. 6/4/1944

WOOD

Omer Odell 5/15/1886-3/25/1943
Dr. D. C. 8/1/1860-3/18/1894
Ethleen T. 1875-1957
Ida, daughter of J. N. and S. A. 6/6/1874-5/27/1876
Jasper Lee 8/24/1868-4/27/1899
James K. 1892-1951
Odie G. 1900-
Charles O. 1893-1944
Aretha E. 1891-
Barbara, daughter of Mr. and Mrs. C. O. 6/5/1931-6/10/1931
Caleb Mack 10/2/1849-2/17/1936
Pelina Loggins 1/8/1856-3/27/1922
Cary 5/8/1873-3/15/1920
Edna Moody 1881-1950
Emory Speer 1876-1957
Infant of Mr. and Mrs. J. P. 9/9/1878-9/11/1878
Fannie, daughter of Mr. and Mrs. J. P. 6/11/1875-6/7/1888
Jesse P., Co. G, 16 Ga. Batt. 1861-65, 3/14/1837-5/10/1911
Eveline 4/2/1847-7/23/1923
Jasper Newton 12/11/1834-1/20/1914, Co. G. 1st Ga. Batt. Cav. 1861-1865

WOODALL

Ronald E. 1940-1968

WRIGHT

W. H. 11/29/1849-7/17/1911
Sue T., daughter of William and Almeda J. Thurmond 2/28/1881-10/19/1928
James W. 1913-1939

COMMERCE CITY CEMETERY, Jackson

WORLEY

Charlie 9/17/1963-12/10/1964

WILLIFORD

Henry Oscar 1861-1943
Carrie Head, wife of Henry Oscar

WILSON

Harold W.
Tallulah H. 1887-1948

YARBROUGH

Thomas N. Jr., Ga. S1 USNR WW II, 8/22/1921-2/16/1957
Alma R. 1909-1957
Thomas U. 1921-1957
Blanch H. 1926-
Jimmy D. 7/31/1952-1/17/1969

LIBERTY CHURCH

ASH

Billy Ray 1936-1959

AUSTIN

Mary Bessie 6/25/1897-10/25/1918

BEAM

Infant of Mr. and Mrs. Alfred 5/15/1915-5/16/1915
Annie E.
James 1888-
S. M. 1883-1948

BROCK

Marshall G. 4/20/1896-11/30/1961
Woodie B. 8/7/1905-
W. Larence 8/22/1862-12/27/1925
Nora T. 11/18/1869-7/18/1946
Julie Reed 6/12/1882-10/30/1918
Oma Estella, daughter of Mr. and Mrs. W. L. 8/12/1914-8/28/1916
Elizabeth 7/21/1831-3/22/1915
Arnold A. 1886-1949

LIBERTY CHURCH

BROCK

Parilee H. 1888-1949
J. T. (Jim) 1888-1959
Roy, son of Mr. and Mrs. J. T. 7/8/1914-5/17/1928
Miron H. 5/8/1930-1/8/1931

BURR

Victoria Wood 7/14/1967-7/14/1967

CARTER

Ethel died 12/25/1932 3 months
Ray died 8/17/1948 5 months, 6 days
Grady died 4/19/1946 1 year, 4 months, 31 days

CASH

Annie H. 1882-
Noah J. 1880-1961

CLARK

Selma C. 1902-
Lamar W. 1908-1962

CLEVELAND

Alfred P. 12/25/1863-5/28/1948
Mina G. 8/24/1877-3/26/1934
Leeonia Bell 6/9/1908-1/14/1927

CRONIC

Dr. F. Maier, Radiologist, 7/19/1921-1/20/1968
Mattie Lee
Jesse A.
Minnie H. 10/1/1877-
Lewis V. 10/13/1871-6/5/1954
J. Allen 1/16/1904-2/0/1916
W. B. 1862-1909
Josie S. 1872-1965
David Eli 2/14/1872-6/1/1948 "brother"
Anna Mae 3/1/1876-10/28/1924 "sister"
Billy M. 7/15/1943-7/4/1967
Arah L. 1907
John H. 1905-1953
Frankie Lynn 9/9/1964-9/9/1964

LIBERTY CHURCH

CRONIC

Jasper P. died 9/29/1967, aged 96
Odom F., Ga. T. Sgt. US Air Force, Korea, 7/2/1931-9/5/1966
Worley 1893-1951
Elvira 3/8/1872-8/26/1958
Warren W. 2/6/1866-5/20/1936

DAVIS

Lou B. 1878-1954
John W. 1873-1956

DUNCAN

Edwin and Elvin (twins) 1912-1912
Emory S. 1877-1949
Ella Roberts 1885-1967

FREEMAN

Thomas A. 1881-1946
Lula Bell 1889-
Loyce, daughter of T. A. and Lula 7/7/1911-1/19/1912
Eueric, infant of J. B. and Ethel Mae, born and died 4/11/1923
Ethel Mae W. 9/29/1900-2/17/1957
James Bascom 6/14/1902

GABLE

Nettie A. 1882-1953

GILLILAND

Gladis 1/3/1909-8/25/1911
Martha Brock, wife of L. S. Gilliland 3/17/1859-6/15/1912
L. S. 1855-1939
Ethel 4/20/1910-8/23/1916
Loy 12/5/1930-12/16/1930
Minnie A. 5/29/1885
Lake O. 3/17/1884-1/10/1935
Canzadie 1/28/1917-10/17/1917
Ola Mae 7/8/1909-8/13/1935
Jesse M. 9/15/1892
Corrie M. 1/16/1890
Marie 5/15/1935

LIBERTY CHURCH

GILMORE

Milton Johnson 3/2/1947-3/3/1947

HOLLAND

John H. 1854-1921

HOSCH

Gertrude Agnes, wife of P. A. 4/5/1895-11/22/1927

HOWINGTON

Ralph J. 1923-1959
John 8/10 1909-5/27/1966
Sarah C. 12/11/1916

HUDGINS

Ilah Murphy 9/25/1895
Wyatt Bevily 3/7/1885-12/28/1960
Virginia Lee 2/6/1924-7/17/1926
Beverly Jane 12/23/1919-4/24/1921

HULSEY

Ada Virginia 1859-1947
Jefferson I. 1853-1940
Thomas Wynn, son of J. I. And A. V. died 2/2/1911, 20 years
Alma Mae 6/12/1912-8/31/1913
Ralph 12/2/1913-6/13/1916
Dora C. 1888-1934
J. Paul Sr. 1884-1961
Lummie M. 1898-

HUNTER

J. J. 12/17/1843-10/1/1913

KILGORE

Myrtie H. 5/30/1896-8/15/1968
Marvin T. 11/1/1890-5/5/1964

KNIPHFER

Infant of C. F. and Miranda born and died 3/26/1910

LIBERTY CHURCH

KYTE

James Nelson 1946-1968
Margrett M. 1936-1968

LEE

Hannah 1880-1952
Henry 1883-

LITTLE

Fannie S. 1877-
J. Tom 1875-1948
Annie 1/14/1881-1/11/1931
Gracie 7/12/1914-2/25/1918
William Howard 10/19/1909-10/13/1913

MADDOX

Jannie Mae 1/25/1898-12/6/1921
Harrison T. 9/13/1888-3/28/1955
Hester R. 6/5/1890
Talmadge C. 2/24/1917-1/4/1944
Fronie, daughter of T. T. and H. E. 3/12/1910-8/10/1913

McDANIEL

Elizabeth 2/1/1856-4/22/1944
James A. 7/6/1855-3/5/1934

McDONALD

Charles Tate 3/23/1875-10/2/1961
Pattie, wife of C. T. 1/5/1865-9/7/1926
Sherry Ann 12/18/1952

PARKS

Buck Leo Howard 7/8/1906-3/27/1941

PEPPERS

Winnell 1/22/1941-1/26/1941

RAINEY

Wilma Wylene 4/25/1938-6/13/1938

LIBERTY CHURCH

REDDICK

Alvin Jeff 11/12/1948-4/2/1952

ROBERTS

Grace 1925-1927
Vada Skelton 1898-1930
Rhoda 11/11/1886-12/7/1925
Frances 4/30/1861-1/22/1927
Desma M. 1911-
Alvin E. 1900-1967
Esther D. 1900-195
Early U. 1894-1962
Hubert Jefferson born in Gwinnett Co. 12/13/19011 died 9/23/1946
Effie Jane 6/16/1875-12/12/1955

ROE

Loyce S. 3/9/1912-8/13/1967

SKELTON

Estelle Roberts married to J. H. Shelton 10/11/1889-11/10/1912

SMITH

A.N. 11/13/1842-12/26/1917
Zora T. 1883-1950
Clyde S. 1886-
Lizzie 5/6/1875-11/7/1966
Gus 5/11/1883-12/25/1920

SPEALMAN

Mae Etta McDaniel 8/9/1878-3/13/1956

TANNER

Ruby Dean 1911-1941
Roy 1904-

THOMAS

J. Luther 1/28/1886-5/26/1966
Pearl W. 5/10/1892

LIBERTY CHURCH

TIMMS

Dukie? 1914-
Edd 1909-1961
Tracie Runa 4/8/1967

TITSHAW

Mary 4/16/1823-1/12/1883
John 2/6/1802-4/1/1892

WOOD

Hoyt C. 1903-
Thelma M. 1910-1949
Howard 11/20/1896-12/25/1950
Lula Cronic 7/29/1868-1/2/1933
Lou E. 11/7/1866-4/3/1949

WORLEY

Arizona 3/20/1895-12/12/1937

HARMONY CHRISTIAN CHURCH, COMMERCE

ANDERSON

Mary Wheeler 8/11/1880-3/24/1958
John Walter 5/15/1875-3/24/1958

BENTON

James 1930-1939

BROWN

Freddie H. 2/25/1915-5/1/1960

BRYAN

William P. 2/19/1896-2/23/1948
Elzie A. 3/7/1900-

BUTLER

Reba Lee 1901-1961
Claudine 10/20/1942-12/17/1958

HARMONY CHRISTIAN CHURCH, COMMERCE

CATLETT

Miram David 11/14/1833-10/14/1913
Louise 1921-1923
William L. died 11/19/1948 aged 49

DALTON

Leonard 5/8/1917-5/16/1917
Imojan and Francis 3/7/1915
R. Ernester, daughter of Mr. And Mrs. L. N. 4/2/1908-4/8/1908
L. Nands 1880-1955
Lula H. 1887-1959

DARNELL

Leila 5/2/1869-2/13/1931
J. C. 5/2/1872-5/25/1937
William W. 9/18/1903-7/15/1934

DAVIS

Sarah J. 11/3/1841-1/17/1913

DIXON

R. Hubard 1892-
Ellie H. 1895-

DODD

Maedy M. 11/9/1838-10/30/1934

DUNCAN

Infant son o f Mr. And Mrs. A. O. 1/8/1952-1/22/1952

DUNSON

George W. 6/18/1832-4/3/1909

ELSESSER

Nettie J. 1/15/1891-7/20/1925

EVANS

O. D. 4/21/1919-4/19/1921
Mrs. Martha C. 5/21/1845-11/23/1921

HARMONY CHRISTIAN CHURCH, COMMERCE

EVANS

W. C. 11/21/1845-5/9/1931
H. Monroe 6/2/1876-12/18/1937
Pearl E. 1/1/1880-2/8/1943
Emma C. 9/12/1890-10/24/1938
Rubin O. 9/19/1926-11/25/1956
Diamond T. 3/23/1886-2/18/1954
Mary M. 7/26/1897-1/1/1934
Wilda 9/17/1918-9/8/1934

HAMMOND

Franklin, son of Mr. And Mrs. E. E. 6/27/1905-3/14/1924
Edwin E. 12/3/1879-6/13/1938
Lenora B. Wilson, wife of E. E. Hammond, 11/24/1881-5/8/1961

HENRY

Andrew Lafayette 1/1/1843-7/21/1813
Eliza A. Keith, wife of A. L. Henry 7/7/1834-11/27/1912
Joseph Patrick 1/13/1880-4/21/1882
Mrs. Permelia 11/10/1822-6/14/1903 married James R. Henry 10/1/1939
Johnnie P. 7/13/1876-10/7/1887
W. Milton 3/1/1855-6/18/1913
Amanda C. 9/2/1849-5/10/1921

HILLAND

Mary Frances 5/10/1850-12/4/1939

HOOD

Infant born and died 12/24/1900
J. V. 9/8/1907-10/23/1907
Infant born and died 1/26/1905
Rachel M. 1845-1892
James L. 1841-1923
James W. 12/9/1870-4/4/1941
Mattie H. 1/25/1875-12/10/1961
Children of Mr. And Mrs. J. L. Hood
Farrer, daughter of C. W. and M. L. Hood 8/7/1901-11/7/1902
Lewis O., baby of Mr. And Mrs. C. W. Hood 1/19/1910-11/4/1910
Nettie Lorene Smith, wife of V. F. Hood 9/14/1906-6/11/1941
Bob L. 5/10/1877-5/27/1945
Woodrow, son of Mr. And Mrs. C. W. 7/3/1916-8/16/1936
C. Wilburn 3/17/1881-6/9/1953
Eula M. 10/10/1904-5/10/1944
Luther M. 2/16/1900-5/4/1961

HARMONY CHRISTIAN CHURCH, COMMERCE

HOWELL

Donald 12/19/1935-4/18/1957

HUGHES

Loda Dunson 1868-1937
Joseph 1864-1950

IVEY

Winifred Jr., son of Mr. And Mrs. W. W. 7/28/1935
Betty Jean 10/30/1932-7/11/1934

JACKSON

Addie Lou 5/28/1878-11/8/1904
Claude E. 1878-1968
Willie S. 1886-1946
Laurie 1910-1911

JONES

Roy F. 1/10/1898-11/29/1966
Marie T. 4/17/1911-

KEANUM

Jeannie Marie 3/6/1964-1/29/1966

KEITH

Infant son of Mr. And Mrs. Clarence 1918
Nellie May 1898-1917
Rachel Angeline 1848-1905
Marvin C. 1875-1904
Emely B. 1876-1960

KING

Geneva 9/30/1916-4/1/1923
Eva, daughter of Mr. And Mrs. H. J. 4/24/1913-6/22/1913
Ruby 6/19/1922-1/30/1923
Daniel E. 2/23/1885-8/24/1953
Sallie N. 8/27/1883-
Trelle 3/10/1924-11/25/1932
Sarah 3/4/1922-11/25/1932

HARMONY CHRISTIAN CHURCH, COMMERCE

LANDRUM

Infant son of T. C. and Alma born and died 6/24/1920
Dorie E., daughter of E. D. and Winnie born and died 2/26/1927
Riley 4/10/1861-8/14/1907
Ardellag, wife of G. R. 6/10/1868-11/19/1905

LANGSTON

Geneva 1914-1922
Oscar B. 1893-1947
Obe L. 9/18/1897-3/6/1962
Eunice E. 12/8/1899
Lucy E. 7/10/1844-1/13/1906
Gertrude 11/14/1877-8/31/1919
Robert Livingston 1869-1937
Rosa Lee 1865-1937

LENDERMAN

Robert D., Ga. PFC Motor Ambulance Co. WW I, 7/24/1887-12/19/19-
Ora H. 3/20/1902-11/5/1960

LOGGINS

Ida 1865-1940
Luther, Ga. Pvt. 101 Inf. 26 Div. 3/9/1920

MILFORD

W. Brantly 1891-1965
Florence W. 1886-1965

MORRIS

David Tillman, son of Mr. And Mrs. R. V. 12/8/1935-12/6/1936

MURRAY

Lucy B. 8/23/1879-1/9/1943
William J. 2/9/1875-4/21/1949
Mamie 11/25/1899-10/11/1911

NEW

James M. 5/12/1866-6/26/1944
Eugenia T. 1021858-2/21/1942

HARMONY CHRISTIAN CHURCH, COMMERCE

NICHOLSON

Thomas F. 3/2/1882-12/25/1959
Pearl R. 8/2/1884-2/29/1944

NUNN

Joseph O. 10/31/1882-2/21/1965
Mary Janne D. 1863-1950
George L. 1860-1948
Charles Patrick, son of J. M. and E. T. 6/12/1892-7/22/1892
Robert M. 10/30/1875-2/17/1935
Folia D. 3/9/1880-10/8/1931
Reuben C. 12/28/1845-6/9/1925
Elizabeth S. 5/16/1850-10/20/1936
William 7/11/1877-11/2/1954
Martha A. 2/6/1875-8/6/1958

O'KELLEY

Thomas Randolph 9/4/1931-2/12/1935

PACE

Sidney J. 2/2/1940
Mary Jane, daughter of Mr. And Mrs. J. H. 6/20/1946

PARKER

Jessie

PITTS

Jessie J. 3/18/1818-5/10/1895
Angeline 2/1844-10/26/1920
Jessie O. 3/18/1887-5/27/1947

PORTER

Cora Irin, daughter of M. S. and M. T. 1/5/1897-1/22/1898
Earl O. 1906-1941
Henry Eugene, son of Mr. And Mrs. Boyd 8/10/1924-7/3/1926

PUGH

Ollie L. 1911-
Betty Corene, daughter of Ollie 12/19/1937-8/2/1939

HARMONY CHRISTIAN CHURCH, COMMERCE

PURCELL

Corene 10/27/1890-6/7/1912
Mildred 6/6/1912-11/7/1912
Vivian H. 7/18/1915-
Odis S. 11/6/1904-6/28/1948
Bessie L. Hughes, wife of O. S. Purcell 5/14/1903-3/3/1940

ROBERTS

J. Rainey 1889-1957
Exie S. 1891-1967
James E. 4/21/1916-10/24/1936

SAILORS

Nancy, wife of J. M. 5/2/1835-8/27/1913
J. Lou 8/6/1870-1/16/1942
Cordelia D. 10/3/1872-3/27/1949
Jack 1/14/1909-6/23/1923
Young 9/26/1904-10/28/1920
John W. 2/28/1861-1/22/1943
Tallulah G. Short, wife of John W. Sailers 6/22/1867=8/31/1928
W. C., Jr., son of Mr. And Mrs. W. C. 5/20/1917-3/7/1925

SHANKLE

William 1/24/1880-11/21/1922
Minnie B. 8/8/1879-2/3/1944

SMITH

B. Paul 1898-1967
Dora E. 1907-
Mittie G. 1/26/1931-8/10/1931
Andrew T. 9/29/1891-11/26/1949
Ruby, wife of J. L. 11/11/1910-9/14/1939
Bobby 11/17/1936-8/24/1939
A.J. 9/9/1855-3/3/1922
Lula A., wife of A. J. 11/12/1867-12/27/1925

SNIPES

Ray 4/15/1939
Wilma C. 8/26/1938

STEPHENSON

Kathleen W. 1911-1965

HARMONY CHRISTIAN CHURCH, COMMERCE

TANNER

Carrie Jane Love, wife of L. P. Tanner 4/2/1895-9/17/1917

THURMOND

W. M. 12/8/1859-1/11/1941
Mattie C. 10/29/1865-3/1/1948

TUCKER

Vera E., wife of W. A. Jr. 6/14/1914-11/15/1936
Virginia, daughter of Mr. And Mrs. W. A., 11/4/1926-5/2/1928
Julia V., wife of W. A. 9/27/1888-11/14/1928
William A. 12/15/1882-12/2/1941
Homer Allen 1/4/1909-7/18/1963
Merle Ginn born 8/7/1910 married Homer Allen Tucker 8/5/1931

VAUGHN

Martha J., wife of Z. 1847-187-
Boyd Carey, son of W. Z. and Martha J. 4/29/1881-3/1/1897

VERNON

Mrs. Nettie E. 1872-1965
James T. 1866-1949

VICKERY

Ruth W. 12/25/1907-10/14/1932
Jack, son of Herman and Ruth 6/9/1929-11/19/1929
Grover W. 3/12/1888-3/27/1934
James V. 10/20/1926-6/8/1943

VOYLES

Erastus M. 1885-1966
Laura S. 1889-

WADE

John 1897-1962

WELLS

Larkie Etta 11/27/1878-6/10/1950

HARMONY CHRISTIAN CHURCH, COMMERCE

WHEELER

Infant sons of Mr. And Mrs. Claude 4/19/1918-10/19/1923
Charlena 6/4/1918-10/3/1919
Little Horatio, son of H. W. and M. A. 11/25/1896-6/24/1899
Horatio W. 8/19/1856-5/1/1934
Martha Ann 7/29/1862-2/6/1940

WILSON

Sanford 10/4/1854-6/23/1921
Mary Elizabeth 6/27/1858-9/23/1922
Mary Lanier 12/24/1922-11/25/1939
Dewey H. 9/2/1898-11/25/1932
George Noble 2/25/1926-11/25/1932
Woodrow 4/4/1913-3/13/1914
James Weldon 11/9/1906-2/11/1907
J. B. 2/3/1915-6/9/1916
Infant of Mr. And Mrs. W. L. 12/20/1892-1/9/1897
Johnnie 7/22/1889-11/9/1946
Leila L. 7/3/1895-
Olin, son of G. S. and R. B. 1/7/1914-5/22/1915
Grover 1892-1948
Ruby C. 1895-
Willie 1/10/1866-3/4/1930
Martha A. 3/2/1872-8/19/1950
Leila L. 9/3/1895-
Johnie 7/22/1889-11/9/1946
Rosa Leo, daughter of Mr. And Mrs. W. W. 4/27/1908-8/6/1914
Betty Jo 5/3/1940-7/24/1940
Willie W. 10/10/1887-
Minnie T. 9/13/1886-6/8/1936
Ethel R. 7/27/1899-10/19/1964
Infants of G. C. and Ninie
Lillie Brown, wife of C. C. Wilson 6/23/1865-8/17/1904
Allie J., son of C. C. and Lillie B. 9/29/1899-10/13/1918
Crawford C. 8/1/1857-2/22/1927
A.Grady 8/31/1906-5/24/1944
Olline M. 1895-
Allen D. 1882-1957
Eunice V. 1885-1920
Emma Lou 8/5/1859-1/5/1940
George N. 1/7/1857-4/4/1938

WOOD

Mildred, daughter of J. C. and Sallie Wood 7/25/1965-2/19/1907

HARMONY CHRISTIAN CHURCH, COMMERCE

YARBROUGH

Arthur C. 1887-1944
Mollie P. 1883-1957

STAPELER CEMETERY, NICHOLSON

ANDERSON

Flavys 2/9/1893-6/10/1894

ANTHONY

Bertha, daughter of A. M. and Annie 5/22/1891-5/1/1896

COLEMAN

Thomas W. 3/21/1888-2/13/1900
James Samuel, son of Claude and Vassie 2/1915-6/1916
Claude T. 8/10/1889-3/25/1959
Samuel A. 3/19/1860-12/10/1900
John Franklin 9/27/1855-3/1/1894
Ella Stapler 5/17/1862-4/22/1942
Thomas W., son of S. A. and M. L. died 2/13/1900, age 11 years, 10 months, 23 days
Samuel A. died 12/10/1900, aged 40 years, 6 months, 21 days

CROWE

Thelma, daughter of Mr. And Mrs. W. H. 1898-1899, 10 months
Ora, wife of W. 12/18/1874-6/1/1918

DAILEY

Thelma, daughter of N. E. and E. S. 4/25/1907-11/7/1919
Infant son of Mr. And Mrs. N. E. 8/27/1924-8/30/1924
Nesby Edgar 10/2/1878-3/11/1944
Eula Coleman 3/15/1882-12/15/1967

DUNCAN

John L., Ga. Pvt. Engrs 82 Div. 1/31/1934

FLEEMAN

Charles Edward 5/26/1884-11/6/1947
Nezzie Eliza 5/16/1890-11/18/1936
Pauline, daughter of W. H. and Dora 11/18/1903-4/1/1904
Addie May, daughter of C. S. and Mattie 6/22/1891-8/12/1898
Charlie S. 5/22/1845-3/8/1907

STAPELER CEMETERY, NICHOLSON

FREEMAN

Bonie Viola 1894-1941
Mamie 1888-1942

McMURRY

Flora 1895-1953

MURRAY

Horace E., Ga. PFC 41 AMD Inf. 2 Am Dv WW II 6/31/1921-6/13/1944
Robert Lett 4/14/1879-7/4/1949
William T. Sr. 11/27/1818-11/22/1892
W. Columbus 1877-1919
Eula 1885-1956
W. T. Jr. 6/10/1849-7/7/1923
Elizabeth Potts, wife of W. T. Murray, Jr. 1/22/1852-12/14/1905

MURRY

L. B. 1888-1961
Mary Belle 1883-1937
Cleo Ofus 1881-1935
Emeline, wife of W. T. 7/17/1824-6/17/1900

MASSEY

Jessie M., wife of J. H. 4/8/1885-1/2/1919
E. A., wife of J. W. 1/29/1839-9/13/1895
J. W. 5/9/1845-1/14/1933
Agnes Freeman 6/25/1861-7/10/1949
Mae Potts, wife of R. N. Massey, 3/17/1888-1/25/1908

POTTS

Lou E. Murray, wife of A. W. Potts 4/30/1851-5/11/1910
J. T. died 6/26/1927 aged 48

STAPELER

L. A., daughter of Thomas and Katharine 11/26/1818-2/11/1876
Katharine Hale, wife of Thomas Stapeler 2/28/1798-8/17/1810
Thomas 10/29/1786-7/8/1888

STAPLER

John M., Co. C, 43 Ga. Inf. C. S. A.

STAPELER CEMETERY, NICHOLSON

STAPLER

Timothy T. 10/30/1860-3/28/1929
Floyd 3/15/1876-6/16/1962
Infant son of Mr. And Mrs. T. T. 10/16/1911-10/18/1911
Myrtie 9/18/1869-4/15/1956
Robbie A. 5/4/1898-5/5/1898
Joseph Archibald 1867-1943
Margaret Edmondson 1875-1952
Leonora E., wife of D. T. and T. A. 12/19/1873-2/17/1944
John O. 1/18/1865-7/1/1929
Susannah M. 9/21/1833-4/23/1870
Thomas J. 1/22/1827-11/23/1913
Frances A. Jennings, wife of T. J. Stapler 12/5/1837-7/9/1906

WALLACE

James O. 5/22/1886-10/14/1962
Johnnie C. 1/9/1894-

WALKER

Lenora 3/14/1886-6/3/1949

WHITEHEAD

William H. 11/12/1899-2/8/1954
Walter T. 10/29/1870-1/26/1939
Hautie, wife of W. T. 11/9/1874-5/9/1905

NIEMNO CHURCH, Center

BERRY

John N. died 8/1952, aged 76

BILLUPS

Anna Gates 1870-1947

BROWN

Joe died 1969
Robert died 8/4/1968

CRADDOCK

Sarah 1965

NIEMNO CHURCH, Center

DEADWYLER

Lewis 1864-1943
Mamie E. 1888-1914
John H., Ga. Pvt. US Army World War I, 1889-1962
Josephine 1866-1944

DUPREE

Mrs. George 1/18/1956, aged 65

FORD

Jane Anita 7/18/--

GATES

Betty 5/12/1923, aged 50
Charley 8/16/1937, aged 72

GOSS

Patricia Faye, daughter of Luther and Virginia 5/15/1967-8/8/1967

HARRIS

Mr. Willie 10/10/1900-3/21/1945

HECTOR

Mrs. Jessie 9/25/1902-11/15/1960
Westley 10/7/1961
Julia Thomas 5/12/1884-9/27/1958
William T. 4/19/1966-6/28/1966

HOWARD

Katie Ann 1913-1955

IRELAND

Nancy 1/8/1954, aged 59

JOHNSON

Baby Wanda J.
Charlie 1921-1967

NIEMNO CHURCH, Center

JONES

Eliza R. aged 97 years
Arrie, wife of W. J. Jones 3/26/1861-1/9/1927

LANDRUM

Cordelia 1877-1958

LUMPKIN

John 10/4/1959-1966

McKINLEY

Nathan 10/25/1914-1/2/1962

NORRIS

James Jr. 1925-1969

OWENS
Floyd 1/1937

PATTON

Jack 1/17/1953

PITTMAN

Etrich Sr., Ga. Pvt. US Army WW I 11/7/1890-6/14/1949

SEEGARS

Otis 1881-1964

SHARPE

Momme
J. W.
J. W.
Mae\Sara
Anne Lou 9/22/1945
Jack

STEVENS

Anna, wife of Homer 1896-1961

NIEMNO CHURCH, Center

TAYLOR

Laurence, Ga. Pvt. US Army 4/13/1903

WILLIAMS

Charlie 6/16/1958, age 30

MT. HARMONY CHURCH, CENTER

ERDMAR

Mary Adelaide 11/18/1881-9/20/1962

FARMER

Rupert T. 8/24/1898-2/25/1963
Alton Ray 9/8/1907-12/10/1967
Joe Omar, C. P. H. M. U. S. N. retd, 6/2/1901-5/5/1966

HAWKES

Ellis 2/24/1878-8/26/1936

BETHANY CHURCH ROAD, Nicholson

DOWDY

Mary E. 1/19/1941-4/15/1941
Paul, son of R. M. and M. L. 5/8/1895-8/29/1907
F. D. 12/5/1872-6/28/1948
F. W. M. 11/25/1823-5/4/1902
Robert M. 12/4/1849-6/20/1923
Little Charlie, son of F. M. and M. L. 3/19/1892-5/30/1897
Mattie 1/19/1875-11/5/1901

HAYNIE

Infant son of C. G. and K. G. died 4/16/1902

DIRT ROAD, Nicholson

GODFREY

John H. 1909-1933
Mattie I. 1875-1955
John 1875-1909

DIRT ROAD, Nicholson

SCOGGINS

Elma C. 4/29/1911-1/4/1967
J. M. 1876-1939
Mark W. 1914-1935

SMITH

Joe B. 3/10/1883-7/14/1947

WATKINS

Roy 1907-1950

ESTEES-WHITEHEAD FAMILY CEMETERY, Nicholson

ARCHER

Dave A. 12/31/1882-10/2/1949
Carrie S. 4/30/1887-7/27/1952

BANKS

James 1833-1917
Victoria 1846-1897
Edgar 1874-1917

COILE

J. R. 2/19/1862-1/11/1926

ESTES

Eliza Jane 6/10/1835-12/1/1911
Jane 4/6/1842-1918
James Anderson 11/13/1829-10/13/1902
J. W. 1825-4/12/1894
Marcus C. 4/15/1869-12/26/1950
Thomas G., son of John W. and S. E. 1/15/1822-4/22/1900

HARRIS

Jane Vickie 6/21/1872-6/22/1930
John R. 4/16/1849-9/18/1922
Martha E., wife of J. R. 11/25/1850-9/20/1921
Essie Lenora 10/6/1874-12/17/1925

ESTEES-WHITEHEAD FAMILY CEMETERY, Nicholson

JONES

Phoebe B. 12/24/1837-6/15/1896

KESLER

Martha, daughter of Mr. And Mrs. J. B. 1943-1943

McNAIR

Ruby Irene Page, wife of William Green McNair 3/25/1894-5/10/1918

MOON

Annie E. 1898-1969

MURRAY

David D., Pvt. Co. F 25 8 C. Inf. C. S. A. 3/1/1844-11/28/1912

OWENSBY

Ruth 1918-1968

PACE

George R. 1866-1949
Effie B. 1870-1914

PAGE

Mary A., wife o f A. S. 9/1/1866-11/3/1914

PITTMAN

Susie, wife of H. H. 8/30/1847-9/25/1898

STANRIDGE

Mamie B. 1882-1966

WHITEHEAD

Mrs. Fannie P. 7/27/1839-10/18/1900
Claude C. 1902-1949
Jimmie 1917
Leala S. 12/4/1877-3/17/1948
Willie 1898
Eugene 1/28/1873-3/2/1930

ESTEES-WHITEHEAD FAMILY CEMETERY, Nicholson

WHITEHEAD

May 1895-1896

WOOD

Alice B. 1878-1953
Hester B. 1843-1929
Sam 1849-1936

FAMILY CEMETERY, Center

ARNOLD

Mary B. 1862-9/16/1896

BAILEY

Samuel Wesley 4/28/1841-8/20/1912
Lou Stone 8/29/1862-3/3/1921

BARNET

R. C. 2/28/1880-6/15/1901

CASH

Baby
Eldred G. 2/2/1833-3/17/1937
Marion L. 6/6/1931-1/1/1832
America P. 11/16/1805-8/24/1872, first wife of John Sr. Married 7/25/1827
John Sr. 1/4/1846
S. Adelaide, wife of Dr. N. 7/18/1847-6/19/1902
Madeleine Elizabeth 7/6/1875-12/8/1885

COLEMAN

Riley W. 1897-1969

LOVERN

Estelle Stone 1886-1967

MATTHEWS

Alice B. 6/7/1865-10/14/1888

FAMILY CEMETERY, Center

PIKE

Estelle C. 3/2/1873-4/24/1962
Montine, wife of J. D. and E. A. 6/9/1901-7/31/1898
Estelle Adelaide, daughter of J. D. and Estelle 5/15/1903-8/24/1924

PUCKETT

Albert Floren 4/8/1883-12/27/1941

STONE

Infant o f E. A. and E. B. 4/14/1908-6/25/1908
Infant of J. A. and Annie died 9/15/1887
Eunice L. 1911-1912
Alton Luther 1874-1924
Margie R. 1898-1899
Nilda, infant of E. A. and E. B. 11/2/1905-12/15/1905
John R. 6/12/1830-6/16/1887
Marvin A. 2/22/1887-8/25/1960
Jim E. 1906-1906
Gwyn, daughter of E. A. and E. B. 3/7/1897-11/19/1899
Mary G. 3/17/1840-12/11/1903

THORNTON

J. Mark 1882-1934
Jessie H. 4/21/1855-11/23/1932
J. Glover 1/22/1880-3/23/1915
Jessie M. 1880-1952
Eugenia, wife of Mark 5/25/1878-9/22/1905
Ira G. 8/29/1853-2/23/1923

WALKER

Usuler A.
Martha A. 7/2/1904, age 63 years

WILKES

M. Josephine 12/2/1861-6/3/1914
Benjamin A. 2/3/1856-4/28/1932
Murley Mae, daughter of J. O. and A. L. 11/26/1904-2/9/1905
Ellison 4/7/1894-8/28/1901

ANTIOCH BAPTIST CHURCH, CENTER, Established 1799

BALES

Ferrell 4/27/1907-3/17/1965
Lilliebell 1901
Ellis J. 1891-1961
Judy Ann 1962-1963
Lem 1881-1966
John Henry 1911-1961
Mrs. Lizzie C. 1891-1960

BARNETT

David W. 3/1/1827-10/21/1898
Osborn 8/22/1883-6/23/1965
Maud E. 2/14/1887-10/23/1962
Ritchie, son of Mr. And Mrs. Jimmie 6/15/1959
Onia K. 12/15/1915-3/24/1946
Augustus T. 1908-1969
Chester A. 7/19/1913-

BLALOCK

J. B. 1855-1918
Johnnie J., son of J. B. and Mary 10/2/1901-8/30/1909

COLEMAN

Augustus A., Co. C, 4 Ga. Reserves C. S. A.

COLLINS

R. A. 7/17/1872-2/10/1905

FARMER

Willie E. 1893-
Martha E., wife of H. D. 9/3/1847-8/26/1887
Mattie, daughter of H. C. and M. E. 8/1884-9/1887
Thomas 4/30/1862-8/27/1942
Oza M. 1893-1951
Evie M. 3/27/1867-1/28/1931
Henry G. 11/13/1840-7/29/1913

FIELDS

SP 4th Herman T. 1949-1969

ANTIOCH BAPTIST CHURCH, CENTER, Established 1799

FITZGERALD

Wayne, son of Mr. And Mrs. C. W. 11/11/1962-1/25/1963

FOWLER

William H. 5/10/1834-12/8/1917
Lizzie B. 7/12/1832-

GARY

John C. 12/25/1871-7/14/1924
Annie Maude, wife of John C. 12/6/1874-9/7/1905
Viola Maud, daughter of J. C. and Annie M. born 7/21/1898, infant
Three infant children of J. C. and Annie M. Gary died 8/3/1903

HARRISON

W. D. 9/10/1836-2/7/1909

JARRETT

W. H. 1857-1927
Abrila 1/10/1818-11/1/1889
Whitson died 7/3/1885, age 85
W. N. 1851-1934
Sallie, wife of W. H. 8/30/1865-7/9/1920
Mollie 9/11/1862-4/25/1895
Bell 1848-1908
Addie 4/23/1845-8/6/1866

KESLER

Kenneth Wayne, infant son of Bethel T. and Annie Mae 11/12/1950
Thomas Martin 4/12/1884-11/20/1939
Emma Lou 5/12/1890-

MASSEY

Lizzie, wife of J. W. 1/14/1839-8/15/1912
W. R. 2/11/1843-9/17/1909

MATTHEWS

Carol Sue 11/4/1949-1/14/1967
Milton Edward, son of Mr. And Mrs. Robert 4/14/1938-4/19/1938

ANTIOCH BAPTIST CHURCH, CENTER, Established 1799

MATHEWS

Homer Milton 1876-1943
Ashby, wife of Mr. And Mrs. M. H. 4/6/1916-8/11/1935
Homer L. 1919-1920
Anzy M. 1912-1914
Lillie Mae 1886-1958
John T. 1917-1917

MERCER

Bertha G. 6/5/1895-4/13/1920
Sidney, son o f Mr. And Mrs. William
O'Neal W. 9/16/1914-8/20/1933

MILLER

John H. 1918-1919
Fannie E. 1890-1955
Jim R. 1885-1965

PAGE

Lillia, wife of W. H. 5/11/1864-5/11/1923

SANDERS

Ida P. 2/2/1872-6/7/1959
Lenard C. 1911-
James Willie 9/24/1938-8/2/1959
Billy 9/11/1941-4/20/1942
Ralph 1/20/1950

SMITH

William D. 6/28/1793-10/9/1860
Anza 9/9/1799-10/3/1862

WALKER

Emma Martin 1888-1963
Samuel A. 1/27/1852-2/27/1929
Lonnie M. 8/15/1883-12/21/1957
John B. 2/8/1894-5/2/1958
Zack F. 1880-1951
Cynthia A. Austin 6/20/1853-11/7/1918

DAMRON CEMETERY, Arcade

DAMRON

Harriet 5/13/1889, age 81
Mrs. Mattie died 8/4/--- age 88
Uriah 65 years
Edward C. 1943-1950
C. M. 7/27/1846-10/25/1912
Shirley Eleen died 6/18/1938, age 8 months

HOLLIDAY FAMILY CEMETERY, Arcade

HOLLIDAY

Infant son of F. M. and A. M. 2/28/1859-3/23/1859
F. M. 11/16/1825-3/23/1880
Artimirre M. 8/4/1829-8/8/187-

MIZPAH PRESBYTERIAN CHURCH, near Center

ALEXANDER

Crawford
Joseph E. 5/2/1858-8/10/1934
Louisa O. 6/14/1869-10/10/1934
Callie J. 1878-1933
William T. 1852-1924
Lillian M. 1905
Louise Ann, daughter of J. and N. E. 1843-1904
Emily Wier married to John Alexander 10/26/1840, 2/19/1920-5/16/1903
Herty E. 1897-1957
Thomas P. 1892-1951
S. P. 11/19/1854-7/1/1923
Rachael C., wife of S. P. 1/15/1859 married S. P. Alexander 11/9/1876
Mrs. Lucinda 9/18/1812-7/23/1884 married 5/3/1832

ALLGOOD

Alice died 5/23/1911, age 26

ARCHER

Zebulon 1878-1889
James W. 1848-1929
Nancy Emily, wife of James W. 1848-1926
Dewitt 1872-1973
William Milton, son of Sam and A. J. 6/17/1878-5/1/1889
Robert L. 12/25/1865-7/20/1943
Mary Allie 8/29/1873-5/9/1931
John Hubert, son of G. T. 4/4/1899-7/10/1900

MIZPAH PRESBYTERIAN CHURCH, near Center

ARNOLD

W. D. 9/1858-3/1909
Alice K. 9/1863-8/1914

BAILEY

R. Smith 5/18/1904-6/18/1909

BARRETT

Lula Spencer 3/28/1903-7/13/1930

BEAVERS

James Louis 12/23/1899-12/20/1919
Pearl Huff 10/2/1899
Robert Nelson, son of James and Pearl 4/3/1941

BORDERS

Eugene H. 1861-1936
Elizabeth Wilhite 3/26/1823-4/15/1900

BYRD

John 4/1/1895-8/30/1895

CARTLEDGE

Rev. John L. 6/29/1828-12/30/1910

CHANDLER

Calvin C. 1879-1932

CHATHAM

Mary Lizza Cartledge, wife of W. G. Chatham 6/6/1866-7/5/1909
W. G. 10/31/1844-4/22/1921

CHEATHAM

G. H. 12/3/1860-6/22/1901
Aaron, son of D. H. and A. G. 9/2/1895-9/16/1899
Philip, son of G. H. and A. G. 10/18/1882-5/10/1892

MIZPAH PRESBYTERIAN CHURCH, near Center

COFER

Wanda Maxine 9/16/1950-9/22/1950

COMPTON

Charley D. 5/1924-10/1961

CROW

Annie L., wife of J. N. 3/18/1850-1/5/1884
J. N. 6/28/1858-10/4/1915

DANIEL

Nettie C., wife of J. F. 12/24/1869-12/11/1891
J. Foster 8/11/1845-8/11/1896

DEAVOURS

Grady Hardy 7/27/1890-11/6/1911

DOTTERY

John W. 6/19/1848-11/9/1912

FIELDS

Precilla 11/7/1841-1/10/1898
Thomas J. 11/9/1840-8/8/1913
Lula 1870-1930
Ruby, wife of E. C. 9/3/1890-7/17/--
Joseph E., son of E. C. and Gladys F. born and died 9/9/1925
Gladys F., wife of E. C. 3/14/1902-8/24/1926
Robert O. 7/26/1875-1/17/1931
Lonnie, Ga. BM 2 US Navy WW II 5/18/1918-4/11/1961
Emma Ophelia 10/20/1876-2/25/1950
John F. 5/16/1867-9/1/1937
Harry L. 1/22/1895-8/31/1967
Jennie 6/2/1928-6/20/--

FLEMING

Mrs. Sara Monica died 7/27/1969 aged 72, 9 months, 29 days

FOX

Elizabeth 12/31/1872-5/3/1925

MIZPAH PRESBYTERIAN CHURCH, near Center

FREEMAN

Henry Harrison 9/28/1853-4/17/1936
James Frances 6/7/1865-3/9/1955

GARRINGTON

M. G. 12/8/1818-11/11/1887
Mary, wife of M. G. 10/4/1823-5/30/1912

GARRISON

Sara Walton 1909-1930

GIBSON

Mary 5/8/1836-11/3/1901

GOBER

Infant son of G. W. and S. D. born and died 4/16/1906
Infant son of G. W. and S. D. 6/25/1905-6/26/1905

HARDY

Lulah A. married J. W. Hardy Jr. 4/5/1873, 5/5/1889-9/26/1893
Mrs. M. G., wife o f Charles F. 7/22/1819-8/12/1891
Artimus G. 9/2/1856-12/23/1905
Mary Jane 3/29/1882-2/26/1964
Albert Sidney Sr. 2/2/1884-8/4/1944
Nancy C., wife of S. H. 1/4/1829-3/13/1905
Harry P., son of Mr. And Mrs. J. W. 12/31/1908-4/20/1925
Julia A. Kenney 9/20/1843-10/21/1886
Susan M., daughter of Charles F. 8/8/1836-6/27/1911 married James H. Moore
Mamie E.1870-1942
Joseph W. Jr. 1862-1929
Julia B. 7/9/1922-3/9/1882
Infant son of Mr. And Mrs. J. W. Sr. 8/18/1881-10/7/1881
Charles F. 12/14/1808-8/8/1882
John G. 10/1/1926-3/3/1969
Staff Sgt. Edward M. 4/29/1916-9/8/1944
Samuel H. 11/28/1832-2/24/1910, C. S. A.
Joseph H., son of S. W. and S. E. 9/1897-1899
Samuel W. married Fannie Dottery 12/25/1894, 8/9/1873-9/11/1903

IVERSON

Jarvel
Daisy 1880-1885

MIZPAH PRESBYTERIAN CHURCH, near Center

IVERSON

Alfred 1899-1929
Frances 1896-1939

KITTLE

Cornelius F. 12/28/1876-8/25/1956
Fannie M. 8/30/1877-2/18/1960
R. 3/14/1871-11/24/1904
R. 3/14/1871-11/24/1904

LENRY

Roy, son of Jim and Beulah 4/12/1901-10/29/1901

MARTIN

Elizabeth T. 9/23/1856-6/16/1917
Max Hilda Jess 5/4/1878-2/19/1962
Hettie Inez Williamson 12/12/1892-10/5/19-
W. D. 11/12/1885-7/13/19-

MATTHEWS

Frances 1921-1909

McCLESKEY

James W. 3/11/1808-5/16/1893 married to Lou Wier 3/11/1835
Lucretia 2/19/1815-4/17/1907

McGINTY

Mary Alexander, wife of Will

MERK

Alice Alexander Cheatham Roberts

MORRIS

Rabun Gilmore 3/1/1857-8/1/1936

PARNELL

Junus L., son of G. R. and C. born 1884, infant
Julia E., daughter of E. P. and M. 3/3/1881-3/17/1896

MIZPAH PRESBYTERIAN CHURCH, near Center

PINSON

Mary born and died 8/27/1916

RICH

Carrie E., wife of Dr. W. W. 4/9/1841-10/23/1909
Dr. W. W. 2/26/1844-8/6/1823
Edna E., daughter of W. W. and C. E. 12/30/1877-4/12/18-
Cordelia F., wife of Dr. W. W. 11/5/1846-7/15/1878

RITCH

Jewell V., son of J. E. and Ella 6/13/1892-5/8/1892

ROYAL

Irene 10/29/1903-11/27/19-

SHIFLETT

Claude 1898-1941
Alexander, infant 1938

SMITH

Charlie Emery 11/25/1878-8/3/1942
John L. 1848-1917
Julia Hardy 1853-1925
Willie Rich 1893-1958
Robert Lee 7/11/1871-3/9/1932
Flora Hardy 8/22/1878-12/24/1953

SPENCER

John Tillman 9/12/1907-10/1/1928
Thomas J., son of W. M. and S. C. 12/26/1875-10/26/1895
Claude W., son of William and S. C. 3/16/1885-1/6/1894
William W., son of W. M. and S. C. 5/14/1882-12/27/1893
Sallie G. and W. M. 8/28/1850-1/10/1894
Robert J. 3/18/1880-9/15/1929
William M. 2/15/1851-1/10/1931
Odie I. 5/6/1879-
Finley B. 5/17/1901-3/25/1964

STOCKTON

Runa W. 1902-
Miller 1900-1944

MIZPAH PRESBYTERIAN CHURCH, near Center

WALTERS

Oscar, son of C. O. and S. F. 3/21/1895-7/14/1896

WIER

Mrs. Sarah J., wife of Robert W. 11/29/1828-2/21/1910
Wesley 1876-1928
Elizabeth Wilhite 6/4/1818-4/8/1898
James 5/12/1816-1888
Samuel D. 4/15/1847-1/9/1921
Lamissie, wife of Samuel D. 10/20/1850-2/2/1918
Ida Pinson 8/5/1897-9/20/1966
Charlie Reese 10/20/1887-

WILLIAMSON

Floy Juanita 1/22/1928-2/5/1928
George Earl, son of M. G. and M. M. 5/12/1897-9/11/1900
Robbie T., son of M. G. and M. M. 1/1/1902-3/22/1905
James G. 3/22/1827-7/24/1903
Frances A. 11/23/1833-7/30/1922
Talmage, son of C. F. and Floy 4/5/1907-5/6/1907
Jamie Polk 1906-1908
Hilda Marie, daughter of Mr. And Mrs. J. P. 10/10/1904-9/29/1905
M. Glenn 4/9/1867-12/30/1944
Bertram C. 10/19/1899-7/4/1957
Mattie M. A. 1/18/1873-5/24/1909
Julius Donald 1891-1958
Hettie C. 1873-1956
Julius P. 1865-1940

YARBROUGH

Owen, son of R. D. and L. G. 6/10/1900-7/19/1901
Lemon, son of R. D. and L. G. 8/22/1898-7/21/1901
Henry D., son of R. D. and L. G. 5/22/1902-9/7/1910
R. D. 4/15/1866-4/15/1923
Lottie Caroline 11/12/1880-2/25/1951
Bessie Moena, daughter of C. D. and Marie 5/30/1905-11/4;1905
Ernest, son of C. D. and Marie 2/7/1908-3/3/1914

ARNOLD FAMILY CEMETERY, MIZPAH CHURCH ROAD, near Center

ARNOLD

R. C. 3/27/1847-6/5/1912
Annie Daughtry, wife of R. C. 10/28/1866-11/10/1936
Martha J. Gaines, wife of J. E. 7/13/1858-5/13/1884
Washington 1/16/1816-11/16/1898
Robert D. 10/30/1904-2/9/1905
Caroline Bowels 10/28/1828-3/19/1901
Ingamar born and died 1916

BOWELS

Levina Smith 12/5/1796-6/10/1881

SUMMER HILL CHURCH (NEGRO), Arcade

BARNETT

Jake died 1965
Berry, Ga. CPl. 15 Trans Corps. 5/23/1942

COX

Baby died 8/3/1965

DERRICOTTE

William died 1/23/1900

JOHNSON

Ed, Ga. Pvt. 304 Serv. Regt. 11/10/1938

KENNEDY

Jane, wife of Dan, died 12/18/1916, aged 71 years

LAY

Mrs. Beulah died 1968

LESLER

Mrs. Rosie 5/8/1967

LITTLE

Henry died 1967

SUMMER HILL CHURCH (NEGRO), Arcade

MADDOX

Minnie Wilson 3/29/1865-3/2/1951

MAXEY

Cora died 10/11/1969, aged 52

PAGGETT

Mattie, wife of Jake died 8/11/1930, age 67 years
Jake 12/25/1859-12/2/1952

POLLARD

Mrs. Maydia Juanita Bell

RANDOLPH

Ann died 9/21/1956, aged 14

SHACKELFORD

Mr. Dessie 12/19/198 aged 55 years

STEWARD

David died 2/8/1925, aged 94 7ears

STEWART

Rev. Carlton 1892-1954

TAYLOR

Joe Henry, Ga. CPL Co. B 490 Port Bn TC WW II 7/22/1914-12/16/1963

WILSON

Andrew 5/12/1879-6/2/1929
Mrs. Rosa died 11/12/1957
George died 1/4/1962
Deacon Andrew 2/5/1909-8/1/1965
Dea John died 2/8/1936
Miss Fannie G. 8/17/1872-1/12/1969

SUMMER HILL CHURCH (NEGRO), Arcade

WOODS

Mrs. Charlotte Ethel Jane Wilson 4/30/1882-4/1/1962

MT. TABOR BAPTIST CHURCH, HWY 330 WEST at Barrow County Line (Establishe 1923)

ALLEY

Tilden Hamlin

DOOLEY

Fred Leslie 10/1/1897-9/22/1965, Ga. Pvt. 38 Co. 157 Depot Brig. WW II
Pauline J. 1909-

DUNAGAN

Ezekiel J. 3/11/1889
Ada S. 6/14/1877-9/14/--

HILL

Reba Joe 7/13/1839-12/7/1941

KENNEDY

Baby died 5/14/1957

MARTIN

Lenard P. 9/15/1933-4/3/1961

McDONALD

Jessie E. 1900-
Ella 1894-1966
Joan 3/30/1940-5/16/1951

PERRY

M. P. 2/4/1935-4/13/1951
W. Carse 8/22/1905-1/26/1967
Eula D. 10/10/1905-4/11/1968

SEAGRAVES

William Hoyl 7/28/1901-3/9/1967
Mary Sallie 8/27/1897

MT. TABOR BAPTIST CHURCH, HWY 330 WEST at Barrow County Line (Established 1923)

THOMAS

Columbus 1902-1963
Clara D. 1910-

WAGES

Irmine M. 1897-
Jessie F. 1892-1968
William Andrew 6/30/1889-1/8/1953
Suzy Thomas 12/1/1893-7/9/1965
June E. 1886-1963
Maud Z. 1886-1968
Ellis B. 6/26/1895-4/1/1961

NEW HOPE A. M. E. CHURCH, HWY 53, Hoschton

BLAKELY

Edward, son of J. F. and Sadie 6/9/1907-7/9/1907
Tinner A., wife of Daniel, 11/12/1856-8/12/1897
Autry 8/15/1896-1/29/1931
Abe 1851-2/2/1919
Floyd 12/13/1902-12/20/1964
Dan Calup 10/10/1891-11/9/1952
Daniel 5/19/1854-1/31/1908
Darlene 12/25/1909-12/1/---
Mrs. Odessa Kilson 1/1909-3/12/1969
Willie (Jake) 1932-1956

CAMP

Mrs. Bessie died 3/25/1950, aged 45

CARRINGTON

Arthur died 12/30/1936, aged 50 years

COLLINS

Henry died 1950
Levy

COOPER

John Millsap 7/4/1879-9/19/1950

NEW HOPE A. M. E. CHURCH, HWY 53, Hoschton

FINCH

Willie B., GA APL US Marine, WW II

GORDON

Mrs. May died 8/1954

HAYWOOD

James H. died 2/21/1962

HILL

Ray, Ga. PFC

HOSCH

Joanna 1878-1941
Ciceroe 1862-1923

HUGHEY

Royce, GA CPL 84 CMC Co. WW II, 9/1/1915-2/12/1948
Howard 11/1948, aged 36, 2 months, 10 days

MOON

Griggs M. 12/25/1819-10/9/1883
Macon A. 12/1/1969, aged 85 years
Mary 1827-5/30/1901
Calvin E. 1/19/1902-2/19/1964
Donald, GA SP 3 Signal Corps,USAR,9/21/1933-11/3/1963
W. P. 11/19/1891-

MORRISON

Mrs. Emma died 3/19/1949

PAYNE

Flora M. died 7/21/1950

RILEY

Mrs. Mattie 12/11/1875-9/8/1904

NEW HOPE A. M. E. CHURCH, HWY 53, Hoschton

SCRUGG

Ruby Dora Joan died 8/25/1951

SELLERS

Louoll Harris O'Neal

SEWELL

Monroe, Ga. Pvt. Co. H, 1 Res. TNG Bn WW I, 4/16/1888-6/25/1955

SMITH

Buell 1888-1943
Evie 6/29/1897-12/22/1952

WILBORN

Nelie died 1915

WILBURN

Offie Blakely 5/8/1868-12/28/1952
Elex died 12/27/1953

WITT

Bell, wife of Joe, aged 35 years

FAMILY CEMETERY, Center

BARBER

Genevieve 1875-1963
W. Greensby 1864-1939
Rev. W. 1865-1933

BOGGS

Julianne C. 9/8/1834-4/4/1926

BOWEN

Mary L. 1834-1895

FAMILY CEMETERY, Center

BROWN

John T. 1862-1933
Julia Barber 1862-1939

CASH

Mathew 9/12/1944-8/1/1958
John A. 8/4/1913-7/4/---

JARRETT

William Henry 1870-1932
Roy E. 1903-1950
Paul 5/24/1902-7/13/1968
Foster Lee 1897-1962

MURRAY

Hattie Mozelle Jarrett 2/12/1896-2/3/1966

SHARP

W. T. 7/9/1821-6/5/1889
C. H. D. 3/10/1868-9/9/---

WELCH

Eugenia 1/10/1861-9/3/1891
Baby

CROOKED CREEK BAPTIST CHURCH, near Arcade

BENTLEY

Miss Nancy died 1915
J. C. died 1932
Mrs. Died 3/1920

BINGHAM

Edward 1931-1933

BIRD

T. L., son of J. N. and M. J. 5/24/1872-7/2/1890

CROOKED CREEK BAPTIST CHURCH, near Arcade

BLALOCK

Mary Ella, daughter of Mrs. And Mrs. F. A. 5/29/1910-5/3/1918

CARDIDEN

Mrs. Stella M. died 11/26/1949, aged 71 years

CARLISLE

William C., son of M. and Tiny 10/2/1897-9/10/1910

CHANDLER

Tresvan M. 2/16/1820-1/21/1864

CHEEK

Mary Maggie 9/16/1903-7/1/1951

COUCH

Lettie Bales 11/21/1878-4/4/1957

COX

John Thomas 9/24/1871-1/24/1941
Luther
Sarah Kass Anglin 12/25/1871-10/1/1946
Bennie Arthur 10/18/1937-6/1/1958

DAILEY

Palestine B. 12/28/1877-
Filmore, son of Mr. And Mrs. H. J. 4/17/1924-11/26/1925
James F. 7/31/1850-12/22/1939

ELROD

Robert H. 1845-1915
Margaret E. 1851-1917
Evie A. 1874-1888
Willie G. 1884-1884

HARDY

Martha S. Lee, daughter of S. H. and N. C. 8/17/1860-9/25/1861

CROOKED CREEK BAPTIST CHURCH, near Arcade

KENT

William C., Co. F, 13 Ga. Inf., C. S. A.

LANKFORD

W. T. 4/16/1873-8/10/1900

MASSEY

Rufus N. 8/25/1871
Pearl W. 1/15/1882-5/26/1952
Mildred Ruth, daughter of R. N. and Pearl 3/10/1919-9/20/1919

MAYFIELD

Mrs. Lillie 1897-1969

McDANIEL

Lester 5/8/1912-12/11/1920

McGINTY

Henry E. 1874-1952
Julia L. Moore, wife of J. A., 2/9/1889-9/11/1914
John A. 1884-1957

MILLER

James 4/30/1877-1/30/1853

MOORE

John S. 1881-1940
Emma 1884-
Millie Freeman, wife of G. W. 2/14/1854-10/14/1894
Donald Roy 4/1/1954-8/24/1966
George W. 1845-1930
N. Ross, son of G. W. and Millie 8/9/1883-4/4/1906

OLIVER

Eugene B. 12/20/1868-10/28/1918

PUCKETT

Juday Malinda 6/26/1953-3/17/1962

CROOKED CREEK BAPTIST CHURCH, near Arcade

SMITH

Infant Eulla
Theodocia Victoria Dill 5/12/1872-10/25/1912

STREETMAN

Robert B. 1903-
Allie M. 1908-1860

WALLS

Delmus W. 1880-1960

WALTON

Lizzie M. 12/10/1849-3/27/1912

WHELCHEL

Edward Darwin 2/2/1889-10/15/1939
Martha Kelton 11/4/1848-6/17/1923
Martha Elizabeth Huff 3/13/1874-12/12/1956
Infant son of L. E. and S. N. born and died 8/27/1906
Mattie Lee, wife of H. 12/6/1876-5/24/1908

WILLIAMS

Emma L. 1875-1941
Jim E. 1870-1940
John K. 1905-1952

WILLIAMSON

Oscar, son of W. B. and L. M. 5/5/1900-12/1/1900
Nathaniel J. 6/11/1844-4/6/1906
A.G. (Sporty) 1884-1967

WINGFIELD

Levi 1874-1923

BETHLEHEM CHURCH, Hoschton

ANDERSON

Ida Wiley, wife of W. D. 7/15/1869-3/24/1925
Devilland 10/5/1878-8/12/1915
James C. 2/28/1832-9/26/1908
Mary Catheryne 3/5/1840-3/27/1940

ATTAWAY

Joseph A., wife of H. 1/3/1858-10/17-

BLALOCK

Joe Lindon 5/4/1860-8/31/1917
Mary Alice 3/17/1862-3/30/1907

BOGGS

Junius M. 12/11/1912-2/2/1968
Emma H. 1883-1858
Charlie 1885-1957
Johnnie W. 1922-1969

CLACK

Daniel L. 4/29/1905-8/4/1905

COOK

W. A., son of W. S. and R. E. 6/7/1884-4/12/1903

CRONIC

William R. 9/2/1833-12/10/1901
Simeon H. 9/2/1833-12/10/1901
Jane, wife of S. H. 12/21/1834-7/9/1898
Russell, son of S. H. and Mrs. Jane 12/8/1863-9/9/1864
June 1782-3/6/1864
William R. 6/2/1891-7/21/----
John A., son of S. H. and Mrs. Jane 4/10/1859-11/21/1882

DALTON

Eliza W. 7/12/1880-9/21/1968
Sudie Belle, daughter of J. C. and Eliza 1/18/1901-3/21/1901
Jacob C. 10/7/1877011/24/1912

BETHLEHEM CHURCH, Hoschton

DANIEL

3 infants of J. A. and M. E.

DELANE

Philirxiro, N. S., born in Columbia, S. C. 12/8/1842, died Jackson County, Georgia 8/24/1879

FAMBROUGH

Martin C. 1859-1913
Walker B. 1868-1948

GUNNIN

Lizzie Ophelia, daughter of J. L. M. and M. F. 4/13/1879-6/27/1896
G. E., infant, died 7/16/1882, age 8 months
Arthur Jr. 1918-1924
Walker Edwin, son of A. L. and M. R. 10/24-1916-6/8/1918

HARDY

Sarah E. 5/5/1852-1/2/1901
Lester Rufus, Ga. PFC 23 Inf. 2 Inf. Div. Korea 7/9/1932-1/1/1951
Clifford W., Ga PFC 121 Inf., 8 Inf. Div. WW II 1/22/1916-7/11/1944
William (Doe) 1877-1942
Azzalee 1891-1951
Ethel A. 2/17/1899-12/20/1900

HAYES

Henry M. 1853-1929
Mattie E. 1854-1936

HOLLAND

John Harvey 1/24/1823-11/6/1922

HOLMAN

Vera C. 1884-
David M. 1874-1947

HULSEY

Sabra A., wife of N. H. 3/28/1859-7/3/1923
John O. 12/21/1874-10/19/1936
Nathan H. 7/13/1855-7/30/1941

BETHLEHEM CHURCH, Hoschton

KILGORE

Jod E. 8/29/1867-10/30/1949
Nevada F. 3/4/1870-1/27/1950

MANUS

James M. died 2/13/1953, aged 75 years

MATHEWS

Willie, infant of J. N. and Carrie 8/8/1858
Jessie, daughter of J. N. and Carrie, 10/8/1881-1/11/1886
Monteen 1/28/1888-9/7/1896
Martha 10/18/1911-3/28/---
Eva, daughter of J. B. and M. J. 3/8/1882-8/3/1889
Huiett, son of J. B. and M. J. 9/26/1893-5/3/1889
Martha Jane, 10/18/1911-3/28/---
Martha S. 9/14/1836-9/25/1909
Lewis 3/25/1833-4/1/1916

MAYNARD

James 8/16/1855-5/20/---

PIKE

Margaret, wife of W. S. 1827-11/14/1904
W. S. 2/12/1824-6/7/1894

PIRKLE

P. P. 11/11/1849-8/30/1892
Jane Smith 5/6/1851-8/30/1931
Green H. 8/23/1880-11/11/1909

POPE

Lillia 4/18/1836-10/10/1910

ROBERTS

John S. 4/6/1880-1/13/1899
Infant daughter of D. C. and M. F. died 9/1/1892

RUTHERFORD

Miss Elizabeth Ann 12/25/1841-1/16/1892
Rev. William B. 2/12/1810-1/24/1893

BETHLEHEM CHURCH, Hoschton

RUTHERFORD

Mrs. Anna 5/20/1869-10/17/1888

SELL

B. Elmer 10/11/1885-9/9/1886

SMITH

Mattie J., wife of W. M. 11/23/1853-3/12/1895
Martha, wife of David 6/5/1812-8/11/1907
David 2/18/1808-11/18/1896

STEWART

Parks 12/3/1845-2/4/1903
Myrtle Belle, daughter of S. C. and Annie Lou 7/4/1897-9/30/1897
Rosa Telula, wife of David W. 9/20/1856-12/20/1931
David 11/9/1853-2/9/189-
David Oscar, son of D. W. and R. T. 3/27/1879, died ?

TALLENT

Mary L. 3/9/1851-4/19/1912
Mark A. 6/21/1877-12/18/1941

WILEY

Margaret S., wife of S. G. 11/15/1838-10/12/1890
S. G. 7/4/1824-7/28/1911
Robert Lee 5/1/1866-11/23/1944
Margaret, wife of Robert Lee 8/12/1862-3/8/---
Omer Lee, son of R. L. and Maggie 8/13/1890-10/12/1890
Robert Cobb, son of R. L. and Maggie 7/9/1905-4/10/1906
Ethel Orem 9/30/1892-4/12/1893
Mary E. 1858-1936
Joseph E. 1861-1932
Edna, daughter of J. E. and M. E. 11/9/1881-11/14/1882
Clara 3/11/1894-4/30/1894
Ola 5/7/1896-5/10/---
Mary E., wife of J. D. 8/2/1842-8/22/1915
John D., husband of Mary E. 5/2/1836-11/5/1907

SELL FAMILY CEMETERY, near Hoschton, off HWY 53 South, Center Church Road

FLEEMAN

Cora Sell 1878-1956

JORDAN

Stephen Bandy
Elijah
Margaret E. Stephens

SELL

L. Frank 1862-1948
Angie M. 1873-1968
James 11/19/1814-8/30/1900
Celia, wife of James 6/7/1820-1/16/1919
Lucious C. 6/24/1845-10/31/1861
Sarah L. 11/4/1849-

POPLAR SPRINGS CHURCH, Arcade

ARKINS

Delonia 10/14/1918
Nellie Haynes 5/18/1948

BARNETT

Edward 6/17/1966

BRONNER

Alice 5/12/1963, age 54

CRAFT

Annie died 5/1/19--, age 55

DIE

Willie 1898-1960

DOWDY

Hosea 11/2/1880-1/5/1898
N. E. 1/15/1886-5/1/1886
Julia C. 1/9/1879-4/9/1879
Effie 5/20/1882-6/6/---

POPLAR SPRINGS CHURCH, Arcade

DYE

Coleman died 1/7/1927, age 72 years
Jesse L. PFC 726 AAA S;b/ Cpc/ WW OO 3231918-10/5/---

GAINES

Frances died 5/17/1908, age 63

GARWELL

Jim died 9/10/1965

GRIFFITH

Wiley died 10/12/1940, age 76

HADLEY

Lt. Ga. Co. B 402 Res. Labor Bn WMC WW I 2/6/1902-1/26/1961

HARRIS

Sharon died 9/17/1969

HAYES

Emma 4/8/1911, age 36 years

HAYNES

Bailey 5/8/1910, died age 78
Eliza died 11/24/1914, age 65 years
Adam C., TEC 4-837 Engr. Bn WW II 2/22/1914-9/2/19-
Robert, Ga. Mech. Co. D. 24 Infantry WW I 5/4/1885-11/20/1958

HOPKINS

Hazel 6/3/1937-3/28/1965

HOWARD

Luke

JACKSON

Hershel died 6/10/1956, age 76
Albert 12/7/1870-12/30/1912

POPLAR SPRINGS CHURCH, Arcade

JENNING

Alfred 1881-1960

JORDAN

Annielee 1/9/1916-9/19/----
Earnest 2/12/1948, age 53 years
Jodie 12/16/1911
Jimmie died 10/14/1963 age 67
Joseph 9/25/1954, age 21 years

LESTER

Fannie, wife of S. M. died 10/11/1898, age 65
Lamb 1892-1960

MACK

Mrs. Martha died 11/17/1947, age 64 years, 8 months, 9 days
Henry 2/17/1878-10/24/1918
Pvt. Lewis E. died 9/25/1945, aged 39 years, 6 months, 17 days

MAYFIELD

Eula D. 4/9/1963, age 68 years

McCLESKEY

Cora Mack 1876-1932
Lucile 1902-1918

NEAL

Wingfield died 9/23/1939 age 67

PATMAN

Willie, Pvt. US Army 4/13/1941

PHILLIPS

Greg, Ga. Pvt. 5/6/193-
M. Frank died 1/29/1947 aged 26 years
James H. 8/23/1886
Lula H. 5/22/1888-6/10/1957

POPLAR SPRINGS CHURCH, Arcade

PORTER

Melvin 11/16/1963, age 56

RAKESTRAW

Stella 11/25/1892-9/15/1908
Hannah
Anna L., wife of O. L. 2/12/1865-10/27/1903

SELLERS

Mr. J. died 2/20/1951

STADLEY

Little L. T. died 6/5/1953, 6 days

THOMAS

Willie T. 10/21/1901
Belinda R. died 9/17/1961

WATSON

John Henry 3/19/1923

WILEY

Lee died 3/17/1936, age 53

JUSTICE-VENABLE FAMILY CEMETERY

BROOKS

W. H. 4/10/1870-3/9/1941

FLANIGAN

Susan M. 5/14/1828-1/11/1904
Allen M. 10/21/1863-10/2/1909
Effie 11/9/1870-6/1/1945

JUSTICE

Mary 2/26/1834-10/10/1907
Allen was born 8/1/1795 and died 11/17/1858
Susan 6/13/1795-11/10/1881
John Gillam 11/1/1820-9/22/--

JUSTICE-VENABLE FAMILY CEMETERY

VENABLE

Sara F. 3/28/1852-10/31/1925
Daniel H. 12/20/1951-3/18/1915
Martha A. 1/13/1824-6/11/1867
Mattie 1/1/1876-4/17/19-
A.L. 3/19/1849-10/3/1901
Mollie, wife of A. L. 6/26/1853-1940
Alma Ruth, daughter of A. L. and M. E. 10/10/1893-2/2/1934

WALLIS

John J. 1837-1914
Sarah G. 1863-1916
Virginia V. 1847-1887

BELMONT BAPTIST CHURCH, HWY 346

CARLYLE

James Horace, Ga GM 3 US Navy korea 10/19/1932-4/29/1955

CLARK

Ruby B. 7/26/1900-
Addie T. 12/21/1871-8/25/1948
William M. 1/29/1860-4/27/1954
Wilbur C. 8/28/1889-1/22---

COLLINS

Otto 5/6/1918-8/6/1962
Edith D. 4/15/1928

DENNIS

J. 1/14/1952-8/6/---
Marie A. 4/24/1950-8/6/1962

DURHAM

Alma U. 6/23/1889
Columbus 11/2/1876-12/31/1961

EDMONDS

Florence S. 12/18/1879-1/20/1961

BELMONT BAPTIST CHURCH, HWY 346

FOSTER

Roy C. 10/31/1902-9/4/1967
Fannie S. 10/16/1905

GABLE

J. L. 1870-1952
Emma 1887-

GOSS

Florence 1912-1965

HALL

Wilburn J. 1917-1944
Mildred H.

HAYES

Belle 1888-
Alvin 1881-1942
Aaron, Ga. M/Sgt Btry 4919 AFA BN WW II 7/22/1907-5/21/1962

HUDGINS

Calena Bryan 5/26/1926-4/3/1961

LANCASTER

James Walter 11/6/1881
J. J. 3/9/1906-9/4/1966
Lena Braselton 11/6/1893-9/25/1963
Rev. T. W. 8/16/1886-9/26/1918

MARTIN

Egbert A. 1943-1964 Ga. AIC USAF
Otis E. 1918
Nettie Mae 1920

NEAL

Infant Jennie Lee 2/22/1961
Sarah Jo 8/1936-8/1968

BELMONT BAPTIST CHURCH, HWY 346

RICHARDSON

Henry C. 1892-
Lena W. 1893-1955

SMITH

Lewis W. 1857-1944
Homer L. 1892-1965
Melinda Jane 1859-1943
Alice R. 1898
Alford H. 9/11/1906
Roberta 7/9/1914

STANDRIDGE

Henry G. 1894-1968
Clara M. 1891-1961

WILLIAMS

Mattie L. 3/10/1884-1/9/1967

EBENEZER CHURCH CEMETERY, near Arcade

ABB

J. 1884-1900

ALLEN

Annie Lou 1895-
Martha M. 1852-7/20/1908
Walter Lee 1886-1940
Clanelia A., wife of C. P. 12/6/1872-12/31/1891
Donald, son of Hoke S. 8/2/1935-1/29/1936
Robert Lee 1876-1931
Tinnie M. 1884-
Gladys J. 1/25/1945-6/12/1952

ANDERSON

Infant daughter of Mr. And Mrs. Dewey 11/13/1933
Johnnie, son of B. D. and N. J. 2/22/1875-7/27/1895

BERRYMAN

Jo Nell 11/6/1906-5/26/1963
Cornelia E. Jr. 6/29/1907-

EBENEZER CHURCH CEMETERY, near Arcade

BLACK

Mary Wood, daughter of A. H. died 12/26/1882
Mrs. A. H. 6/8/1816-9/19/1891
A.H. 6/13/1811-9/20/1837

BREWER

Lillie Belle 9/25/1891-3/26/1964
Elich Tom 3/20/1872-5/11/1955
Mannie Mae

CAIN

Martha, wife of James 6/2/1870-8/12/1912

CHANDLER

John Walter 3/8/1873-5/15/1936
Mrs. J. M. (Aunt Sissy) 7/8/1856-9/22/1956
J. M. 10/6/1858-2/7/19-

COCHRAN

Nathan M. 8/24/1829-10/29/1917

COLLIER

B. Gregory, son of Frank and Ettie 6/16/1916-7/31/1916
Andrew W. Franklin 5/22/1885-10/19/1918
Ettie Gregory 10/25/1882-6/20/1916

COOPER

Ira Britt 1903-1942
Willie Mae 1901-1933

CROW

Fannie Elizabeth, wife of Dr. W. H. 2/29/1872-1/7/1907

DOSTER

Allen C., Ga. PVT 30 Inf. 3 Div. 7/24/1918
W. B. 8/6/1880-12/26/1935
James R. 11/3/1850-1/25/1931
Marcus J. 3/11/1883-9/2/1921
Nance 12/15/1849-4/1/----

EBENEZER CHURCH CEMETERY, near Arcade

DOSTER

Lucy Allen 1876-1956
Julia Dot 1/30/1880-6/24/1929
John E. 1872-1930

DUNIGAP

Jessie, daughter of Mr. and Mrs. A. L. 6/26/1906

ELEY

Carrie M. 4/5/1835-12/2/1916
J. P. 10/11/1827-1/25/1892

ELROD

Bonnell, daughter of Mr. and Mrs. H. I. 8/15/1903-11/15/1909
Laura E. 1883-1966
James Terrell 8/4/1908-5/12/1968
Ruth Jacks 6/8/1910-
Judge H. 1881-1939

FIELDS

Emma, wife of J. W. 1/15/1861-3/3/1903

FILE

George W., son of Mr. and Mrs. A. J. 1/15/1902-1/17/1902
Nancy Gamlin, wife of Solomon 11/21/1858-6/29/1909

FINCH

Annie H. 12/20/1910-
Roy C. 12/7/1905-5/7/1968
Charles S. 1872-1949
Susie W. 1876-1958

FITE

Willie M. 1/25/1882-1/21/1919
Alice Armstrong, wife of A. J. 2/19/1862-10/11/1920

FLEEMAN

Mamie (Mother) 1885-
Lucile (daughter) 1925-1942
B. F. (Father) 1884-1961

EBENEZER CHURCH CEMETERY, near Arcade

FULCHER

Emily Lula Wright, wife of J. F. 10/1/1877-
Jodie F. 8/30/1873-12/6/1912
J. Lillian, daughter of Mr. And Mrs. J. F. 5/5/1893-3/31/1904
Ida, wife of J. F. 10/14/1876-2/19/1902
Maggie 1881-1925
Leb 1897-1956
Susie W. 1876-1958
Roy S., son of Mr. And Mrs. J. L. 11/4/1907-1/3/1909

GARNER

Jessie F. 1891-1952
Thomas O. 1854-1917
Thomas A. 1886-1968
J. Frank 1866-1931
Sarah B. 1845-1927

GARRETT

Jewel Allen, daughter of G. D. and Millie 3/5/1912-11/3/1912
Jewel G., son of Mr. and Mrs. J. L. 1/25/1904-3/25/1904

GASAWAY

Sumler Jewel, son of Mr. And Mrs. J. C. 3/11/1918-3/13/1926
J. C. 8/8/1870-8/22/1925
Lizzie R. 3/21/1872-11/7/1955
Johnnie, daughter of J. C. and M. E. 5/18/1911-2/14/1913

GARNER

S. E., wife of J. M. 6/10/1831-1/17/1908
J. M. 10/27/1826-7/12/1892

GINN

Elizie May 3/11/1909-3/30/1909
Emma, wife of J. R. 2/25/1886-3/17/1913

GREGORY

John L. 1861-1940
Sudie R. 1867-1945
Myrtle, daughter of J. L. and S. E. 8/31/1886-5/20/1901

EBENEZER CHURCH CEMETERY, near Arcade

HAMMOND

Elmer M. 11/10/1900-3/2/1954

HAYES

Odessa, daughter of E. L. and Dora 12/1/1911-5/29/1917
Ada, wife of W. R. 7/14/1886-6/22/1908
James
Florence
Omie, daughter of W. W. and Mary 3/4/1897-7/26/1912
Sarah Wilmer, daughter of B. W. and S. L. 8/6/1909-12/29/1909

HEALAN

Tyson D., son of Mr. and Mrs. J. M. 5/11/1907-4/17/1911

HENDERSON

Mollie Jane 1857-1950
M. G. 1854-1943

HILL

Emma 10/5/1859-
Henry T. 3/24/1869-7/24/1919

HOWARD

Lloyd E., Ga. PFC US Army WW II 4/2/1926-1/24/19-

HUFF

George M. 10/15/1865-10/26/1947

JACKS

C. S. 9/1/1846-11/10/1926
Janie 1/18/1847-4/27/---

JENKINS

Georgia, wife of E. N. 10/26/1857-6/8/1906

JOHNSON

Willner V., daughter of J. R. and Mary 3/12/1905-3/23/1907
Martha Jane 1844-1938
Mary Wood, wife of J. R. 1/24/1881-4/18/1911

EBENEZER CHURCH CEMETERY, near Arcade

JOHNSON

Julia E., daughter of Mr. And Mrs. J. M. 8/16/1889
James Monroe 1840-1916

KESLER

Fannie 1/15/1836-
Lam H. 5/7/1888-10/17/19--

KILGORE

Nancy M. 12/1/1885-
Harve W. 10/11/1880-10/13/1942
Mint M. 1/11/1855-8/9/1924
Solomon H. 5/3/1854-4/19/1930

LITTLEFIELD

G. B. 7/11/1863-5/29/1916
Robert A., Ga. Wagoner 7 Inf. 3 Div. 11/13/1955

LYLE

C. W. 9/1/1846-3/22/1921
Malinda, wife of W. C., nee Malinda Seymour, born in Spartanburg, South Carolina 7/19/1823, died 6/3/1896
Caroline C. 1947-1916
Jesse B. 1841-1935
James Henry 6/8/1869-6/17/1962
Lula Wall 1/19/1872-11/2/1940
Louise, infant daughter of J. H. and L. W. 8/3/1904-10/4/1904
John B. 10/29/1816-11/15/1895
Anna 12/15/1873-6/10/1930
G. W. 9/1/1846-9/30/1911
Mary E. 2/5/1849-6/20/1938
Willie A. 12/24/1851-5/31/1923
Little Guy, son of Mr. and Mrs. R. H. 11/15/1910-9/14/1912

LYLES

Elizabeth, wife of J. B. 3/2/1823-8/23/1901

McCAIN

Washington W. 1880-1926
Claudie E. 1880-
Jessie Henry 3/10/1909-2/4/1961
Louise Waddell 1/15/1911

EBENEZER CHURCH CEMETERY, near Arcade

McDONALD

Mae 1895-1949
Walter A., Ga. Pvt Co. C, 330 Inf. 83 Div. WW I 11/2/1896-12/8/1964

McGUIRE

Mattie 1882-1967
William F. 1880-1949
Charles J. 1917-1931
Dorris V. 1920-1920

MARLOW

William H. 5/24/1927-1/12/1938
William M. 1889-1941
Susan 1891-

MATHIS

Nettie Belle 1886-
Bartow Hale 1884-1963
Guy Thomas, Ga PFC 3860 Service Comd Unit WW II 4/10/1913-4/7/1946

MONTGOMERY

Katy 1/25/1853-4/21/1939
Infant son of Mr. and Mrs. B. T. 4/20/1905-4/23/1905
Infant son of Mr. and Mrs. B. T. born and died 7/13/1906
John 9/29/1839-6/20/1914

MOON

Frances died 12/12/1939 (?)
McEVER

Emeline 1845-1916
John A. 1813-1892
Nancy 1815-1876

NICKELSON

Infant of ? 1895
Annie N., wife of B. B. 12/29/1869-3/26/1901
Dock S. 2/20/1865-10/20/1945
John A. 10/14/1901-5/27/1924

EBENEZER CHURCH CEMETERY, near Arcade

NIX

Dovie Hammons 1/1/1896-9/8/1927

POTTER

Pinkie 2/28/1874-3/23/1930
Jack, son of Mr. and Mrs. J. W. 1/19/1927-7/30/1929
Ralph Brightwell 11/17/1899-8/27/1931
John H. 11/1/1861-11/5/1950
Trudie Lee Berryman 12/27/1899-
J. W. 1888-1948
Lottie 1/16/1916-9/28/19-
Lillie M. 1891-
Martha E. 5/10/1836-7/12/1885
Thomas Richard 1864-1937
G. P., son of G. W. and L. C. 2/26/1897-5/22/1900
Lucious W., son of G. W. and L. L. 10/1/1895-2/15/1895
Hattie Jack 1874-1948
Nancy 10/12/1901-2/16/1912

RICKELS

John 9/19/1840-9/27/1911
Sarah E. 7/20/1842-2/27/1916
Ruby Lee, infant of B. P. and Lora

ROBERTS

Leila H. 5/8/1877-1/22/1966
Worth, son of W. C. and E. L. 5/28/1905-2/17/1908
Louella, wife of J. W. 1/28/1850-1/7/1933
W. C. died 5/15/1931
Lucile, daughter of W. C. and E. L. 6/6/1894-7/15/1896
J. W. 10/18/1844-1/9/1920
J. W. Jr. 1932-1934
W. F. 1909-1910
Emma F. 1882-1955

SATTERFIELD

Infant son of Mr. and Mrs. H. W. 1913

SMITH

F. C. 7/22/1855-2/22/1939
Nancy L. 9/15/1865-1/19/1927
James W. 10/26/1901-1/14/1961
Stephen Lester 1876-1962

EBENEZER CHURCH CEMETERY, near Arcade

SMITH

Lula 9/6/1887 1/27/1947
Elizabeth 1/2/1834-12/26/1910

STEPP

Eliza Caroline 7/16/1837-10/31/1907
J. W. 4/27/1862-5/27/1911
Dora A. 7/10/1873-8/5/19--

TERRY

Rufus 1878-1965
Annie Dotson died 1/30/1959, age 62

THOMPSON

Jasper L. 1849-7/27/1900
Dr. James A. 9/22/1848-5/26/1907
Tibbie A. 10/7/1906-5/17/1908
Jacob D. 1/16/1866-1/2/1927
Mary L. 3/7/1844-6/3/1905
John 8/17/1845-7/6/19
Phoebe L. 10/3/1874-10/30/1906
Americus 4/24/1868-12/12/1907

VENABLE

Kate 5/29/1885-7/10/1948
Herman C. 2/21/1885-8/27/1953
Elmer J. 1880-1950
Maggie 1877-1966
Allen L. 1/5/1908-2/3/1968
Sadie M. 3/31/1905-

WADDELL

Wendy 1/22/1964-12/27/1964
Bobbie Scott 2/8/1937-5/17/1938
George E. 3/17/1866-3/24/1950

WEATHERLY

Georgia D. 1890-
John S. 1879-1942
Rhoda Elizabeth 11/26/1843-12/27/1923
John Stanford 4/14/1838-4/28/1903

EBENEZER CHURCH CEMETERY, near Arcade

WHITEHEAD

Mildred 6/15/1864-4/21/1905
G. N. 12/26/1848-11/23/1932

WOOD

J. T. 6/4/1849-3/30/1917
Laura Lumpkin, wife of J. T., 4/25/1847-12/27/1922

OLDHAM-WAGES FAMILY CEMTERY, Off Hwy 330 South, Arcade

ANGLIN

Sarah E. 7/30/1868-7/8/1918

CHEELY

Winnie 11/10/1849-4/3/1904
G. M. 5/3/1842-3/11/1901

NICHOLSON

Baby 1922-1922
Cam C. 1877-1942
Lula W. 1883-
Mrs. S. C. 5/17/1887-7/25/19-

OLDHAM

Cynthia 12/21/1856-11/11/1917
John M. 5/22/1861-8/15/1894
Augusta 3/30/1865-3/21/1939
A.J. 3/24/1853-12/29/1924
Mary 11/15/1822-9/2/1881
Wildey, daughter of A. J. and C.G. 2/1/1892-11/1/1893
J. Weldon 10/31/1878-3/15/1957
Sarah Lu Tiller 10/19/1877-10/31/1942

WAGES

James B., Ga. PVT 116 Co. CAC 3/31/1876-8/1/1948
Mattie F. 10/31/1888-8/9/1958
Jasper I. 2/28/1858-5/21/1927
Susan M. 1/5/1859-11/28/1932
William S. 4/22/1879-3/24/1880
E. G. 5/26/1874-11/20/1953
Elzy J. 4/28/1854-8/5/1910
Andrew 8/15/1802-8/13/1898

OLDHAM-WAGES FAMILY CEMTERY, Off Hwy 330 South, Arcade

WAGES

Wayman, son of Mr. and Mrs. E. G. 5/6/1912-10/25/1927
S. C. 8/19/1849-2/7/1925
Steven 4/13/1889-7/21/1889
Mary A. 1/30/1842-7/22/1890
Brooks B. 9/1/1893-4/1/1906
Nannie 12/6/1884-6/28/1937

WAITS

John F. died 5/31/1941

CENTER METHODIST CHURCH, Hoschton

ALLEN

Grover C. 1906-1957
Mae B. 1906-
Infant daughters of Mr. and Mrs. Harold D:
Betty Jane 2/26/1958-2/27/1958
Barbara Jean 2/26/1958-2/28/1958

CLARK

Little Royce Freeman, son of Mr. and Mrs. E. H. 2/8/1926-2/8/1927

DUNAGIN

Carl E. 8/18/1900-6/3/1932

EVANS

C. Robert 1856-1931
Eliza Ann 1862-1940

GITTENS

Pearl P. 1896-
Adolphus 1882-1938
Minnie 1883-1923

HARBIN

William Terry died 3/26/1965
Robert Jr. 9/24/1931-3/22/1932

CENTER METHODIST CHURCH, Hoschton

HAYES

Master James Brent died 12/24/1966, 3 months
Janice Lynn 1/28/1963-1/20/1964
Sarah Jean died 9/24/1964, 9 months

JARRETT

Jeffie J. 3/30/1897-
Alma 7/29/1920-12/3/1933
Kate 2/8/1899-9/23/1958

MARSINGILL

Corine 8/29/1922-12/11/1935
Mary H. 1883-1936
H. Alonzo 1886-1924
Patricia 1937-1937
Ralph 1/6/1914-1/20/1936
Dewey E. 8/19/1900-11/23/1968

MOSELEY

John N. 9/26/1861-11/3/1929
Manteline Bailey 3/31/1863-4/9/1928

PORTER

Ruth Sonia 12/1/1928-3/20/1929
Homer Ralph 3/20/1931-5/13/1922

REYNOLDS

William E. 4/20/1893-11/11/1956
Minnie L. 4/2/1895-1/23/1960

SHIRLEY

Edward W. died 4/8/1968, aged 63

SWEATMAN

Savannah E. 10/29/1870-1/4/1926
Robert M., Ga. Tec 4 Engineers WW II 12/5/1895-1/24/1963

WALL

William Calvin, son of Mr. and Mrs. C. C. 9/23/1958-9/23/1958

CENTER METHODIST CHURCH, Hoschton

WATSON

Minor H. 1891-1958
Ella C. 1889-

WEHUNT

Farris H. 1911-1960
Lois G. 1914-
Lula M. 1903-1958

MAXIE HILL CHURCH, Arcade

ADKINS

Mrs. Oudie 1894-1965

BORDERS

Rosa L. died 10/22/1962
B. died 10/4/1912

BROWN

M. B. 5/15/1886-1/17/1912

BUTLER

James 6/24/1962
Mrs. Dora died 1/16/1965
Virginia 1928-1946

CHANDLER

Mandy died 5/18/1940, age 105
Wheeler 3/30/1962

COBB

Alina T. 1900-1931
Harold, son of Mr. and Mrs. Homer 1925

DAMON

Patricia died 8/1/1966, aged 1 year

MAXIE HILL CHURCH, Arcade

DUKE

Pross 1879-1939
Matthew 1914-1930

DUKES

Lula V. 1880-1965
C. S. 1906-1955

GREEN

Samuel M., Co. H. (sunk)

HALE

Emory, Ga. Pvt 41 Co. 157 Depot Brig. WW I, 2/3/1894-9/12/1954

HARRIS

Frank 1915-1955

HARRISON

Annie Lee died 12/29/1939, 23 years, 9 months, 21 days

JACKSON

Olan died 3/17/1968, 74 years

JOHNSON

Mr. Robert D. (sunk)

KILPATRICK

Mrs. Olivia 7/25/1908-3/20/1945

LESTER

Lillie D. 1911-1958
Ola M. 1909-1936

MOM

Mr. Rufus 11/2/1959

MAXIE HILL CHURCH, Arcade

POOLE

Baby died 2/16/1956, 1 month, 29 days

RILEY

Mrs. Margie 1880-1960
John died 2/24/1962, aged 82

SHEPHERD

Grace died 3/22/1949

SHIELDS

Mrs. James (sunk)
Jewiel 1904-1968
Victoria died 4/24/1939 age 53 years
Lula 1874-1917
B. S. 1878-1946
Lazunia 1910-1919

SIMS

Nathan passed 1946

STORY

Morgan, Co. 1 Wis. Cav.

TREADWELL

Mrs. Essie Mae died 8/13/1965, age 37

WILLIAMSON

Junie 6/8/1900-12/24/1929

YOUNG

Lottrell Chandler 4/26/1927-5/31/1965

ATTICA CHURCH, Arcade

AMMONS

John Berditt 2/23/1918-7/31/1959
John B. 3/7/1873-12/30/1947
Emma L. 12/1/1877-9/23/1952

ANGLIN

Stacy Leila 8/8/1872-4/19/1939

ARCHER

James C. Sr., Pvt. HQ Trp 3 Army Corps WW II 10/10/1892-11/3/1952
James C. Jr. 5/1/1931-12/22/1938
Robert Y. born and died 9/6/1928

BELL

Clara Geraldine 5/20/1941-5/3/1958

BELLAMY

John Billy 1937-1953
J. Richard 1940-1941

BROCK

Clara 6/20/1883-8/5/1929
C. A. O'Neal 2/25/1855-12/26/1931
Mary F. Catlett 8/29/1861-5/18/1947

CAPES

Ottice Lowe 1916-1951
Joseph B. 1918-

CARITHERS

James G. 1877-1949
Laura 1880-
Virginia 1843-1929
William A. 1843-1922
Jennie 1903-1918

CARNEY

Arlena 2/1/1908-8/7/1918, daughter of Gordon and Etta
Katie, daughter of Mr. and Mrs. C. G. 4/22/1931-8/24/1935

331

ATTICA CHURCH, Arcade

CEARLEY

Martin 1/9/1919-6/5/1939
Mamie Lee 9/1/1916-10/8/1919
C. C. 7/21/1871-9/24/1941

COOPER

Infant son of Mr. and Mrs. M. M. 10/23/1942

DELLINGER

Nancy Lowe 7/14/1871-10/2/1930
Jessie Lee 1/19/1884-3/24/1948
Cora J. Parham 10/31/1895

DOCKERY

Elmer, son of Mr. and Mrs. J. W. 2/16/1923-12/22/1914

FLEMING

William Adcas 1891-1966
Johnnie E. 1891-1962
Giles L. 10/19/1863-3/25/1937
Sara F. 3/15/1863-5/21/1957
D. Jewell, son of Mr. and Mrs. C. L. 7/13/1901-4/6/1927

FOWLER

J. C. 2/14/1912-5/22/1922
Roy 9/1/1917-12/11/1917
Clifford W. 10/10/1897-11/1/1965
Nettie F. 3/14/1892-
Willis F. 1919-1970

FULLER

Dock J. 1910-1969
Thomas S. 1869-1953
Malissa R. 1871-1934
Lilly May 1893-1939

GORDON

Thomas L. Jr. 1898-1950
Jerry Eugene 4/16/1941-8/20/1966

ATTICA CHURCH, Arcade

HALE

Allen 9/5/1884-5/29/1962
Alice 4/9/1887-
Jack 5/12/1921-3/7/1923
Hoyt 8/28/1912-9/25/1915
George Glenn 1/11/1894-

HAWKINS

Charles W. 1885-1949

HEAD

Lon J. 4/3/1874-9/1/1949
Mary L. 1/10/1909

HORNE

Effie N. 1893-1952

IRVINE

J. A. 8/21/1874-5/30/1932, son of Mrs. S. J.
Mrs. S. J. 11/21/1839-11/6/1929

LOGAN

Rev. John F. 11/10/1862-10/19/1912
Elvina R. 1/11/1866-8/17/1958
Mattie P. 9/19/1883-11/1/1961
Jessie C. 1887-1963
Henry Asco 7/14/1868-9/10/1959
Winnie, daughter of Mr. And Mrs. B. M. 4/13/1914-4/15/1915
Minnie Parham 11/13/1876-2/17/1958
Infant son of Mr. And Mrs. F. M. 11/1/1935
Mellie Arminda 4/29/1872-7/13/1936
William R. 4/22/1866-2/20/1939
Benjamin M. 6/15/1879-10/26/1949

LOWE

Marion L. 1873-1957
Winfred M. 1/21/1902-8/12/1964
Mary W. 12/19/1902-
Doris Nell 12/30/1934-1/8/1935
M. L. Jr. 7/23/1921-12/9/1938
Georgia Parham 1878-1928

ATTICA CHURCH, Arcade

MARTIN

David B. 1899-1967

MASHBURN

B. G. 7/25/1873-4/18/1940
Bettie Jean
Ruth
J. Clifton 5/5/1915-12/3/1928
Edgar William 10/19/1902-
Fannie B. 1/17/1918-6/24/1921
Althia J., wife of B. J. 7/27/1876-7/19/1922
Edna Burr 11/15/1904-12/12/1953

MORGAN

Linda 1875-
Nancy M. 1874-1958
L. M. 1875-1951

NUNNALLY

Nancy G. 1896-1967

PARHAM

Mary A. 2/2/1890-
W. L. 9/1/1847-7/9/1920
Mrs. D. A., wife of W. L. 3/24/1843-8/4/1916
Frank S. 5/21/1889-3/6/1951
Jimmie, son of Mr. And Mrs. J. C. 6/10/1927-10/22/1931
Emily J. 1867-
John H. Neal 1855-1947
Reed D. 1909-
H. Ralph 7/19/1912-6/13/1941
James Thomas 1888-1940
Thomas Jefferson 9/13/1860-6/18/1939
Maude S. 1915-1951
Thelma L. 1/2/1921-

PAYNE

Martha J. 9/29/1853-12/23/1925
J. D. 10/22/1851-2/11/1927

PRUITT

T. C., son of Mr. And Mrs. C. A. 7/20/1917-5/29/1919

ATTICA CHURCH, Arcade

PRUITT

Hartley Paraham 5/23/1888-4/4/1950

RATLIFF

Myrtle 6/5/1912-8/27/1948

REED

Logan, son of Rev. and Mrs. W. H. 6/10/1932-1/15/1933

ROBINSON

Samuel Ernest 6/7/1951-7/27/1951

SEBOLT

May 1887-1956
John H. 1865-1957

SMITH

Susie Ester 6/21/1897-

SOSEBEE

1/15/1885-5/8/1923

STEPHENS

Alexander 11/5/1883-12/24/1968
Canon 2/1/1854-9/3/1931
Cleo Weathers 1/6/1892-7/9/1964

VENABLE

Thomas W. 11/29/1908-12/4/1967
Sumnie R., Ga. PFC US Army WW II 9/23/1924-5/20/1966
Jean W., Ga. SGT 3440 Area SVC WW II 6/20/1929-7/26/1953

WALKER

Jesse Y. 4/22/1860-4/10/1924
Jesse Young Jr. W. O. 2nd Marine Division, WW II, Korean War 9/30/1909-6/11/1967
Eula Roba 11/19/1903-7/24/1958
Sallie Z. 1/20/1868-1/4/1959
Ernest M. 1/24/1892-12/13/1934
Frank Lee 22-1893-10/9/1918, WW I, Serial 2924386 M. T. Co., 496

ATTICA CHURCH, Arcade

WHELESS

W. H. 10/23/1886-11/5/1962
Fannie L. 10/5/1882
Paul Darel 9/7/1941-12/23/1949

WHITEHEAD

Bessie Archer, wife of E. B. 8/1/1861-

WOOD

Lassie Mae Lowe, wife of J. N. 10/11/1898-2/22/1942
Raymond A. 5/12/1946-7/29/1964
Thomas N. 1872-1953
Nancy N. 1876-1961
Johnnie Ray, infant son of Mr. And Mrs. J. N. 10/14/1935-10/20/1935

LEBANON METHODIST CHURCH, Arcade, Off Hwy 82 South (Established 1835)

AUTRY

H. K. 9/7/1849-12/29/1905
Martha Ann 8/25/1850-9/18/1905

BETTS

Ira E. 8/14/1814-7/30/1896
Ellis B. 1870-1945
Georgia 1864-1942

BOND

William H. 1946-1965

BOYD

Nellie B. 7/21/1877-6/10/1906
H. Oscar 1871-1935
Mollie E. 2/12/1876-1/29/1901
James 1/24/1901-5/21/1901
Effie 9/26/1881-5/21/1901

CHEELY

W. H. and wife, Cynthia

LEBANON METHODIST CHURCH, Arcade, Off Hwy 82 South (Established 1835)

COLDMAN

Sallie F. 12/30/1830-11/27/1913

COLLINS

Janet G. 8/13/1947-9/28/1947

DAVIS

Thomas P. 1/29/1882-10/1/1962
Zopporah H. 10/28/1888

FROST

Emory Carter, son of W. P. and M. A. 12/28/1906-1/9/1912
William Clifford, son of W. P. and M. A. 8/13/1900-

FULCHER

John B. 12/1886-12/6/1920
Marg L. 3/1882-1/5/1938
Pearl, wife of G. C. 6/17/1888-2/18/1919

GINN

Alfred T. died 4/30/1968, age 60, 10 months, 23 days

GUEST

Alice F., daughter of T. R. and S. M. 10/11/1904-7/2/1905

HAYES

Phoney C. 1867-
M. Elie 1861-1943

HOLLIDAY

Key 4/19/1892-7/23/1969
Alice 3/13/1883-11/17/1935
Claud E., Ga. PFC Mtr Trans Corps WW I 1/31/1888-2/7/1967
Ruth 3/13/1888-11/19/1962
Crie Dell, Ga. Pvt. Co. K, 161 Inf. WW I 10/19/1889-4/7/1957
Sophire, wife of R. W. 1853-8/11/1912
Nancy E., wife of John M. 6/8/1854-8/2/1919
John Martin 7/30/1852-1/14/1928

LEBANON METHODIST CHURCH, Arcade, Off Hwy 82 South (Established 1835)

HOLLIDAY

Claudia Wills 5/30/1861-12/25/1923
Charles Franklin 6/29/1857-6/26/1960
G. W. 11/15/1884-6/15/1957
Angie Maudin 4/30/1887
Infant of W. J. and T. G. 7/1/1897
Imagine G., wife of W. D. 2/25/1867-5/15/1881
George Co. 1, 16 BM Ga. Cav. C. S. A., 1st Sgt.
Infant of C. P. and C. R. born and died 9/30/189—
Mary Louise Strickland 6/13/1827-1/4/1860
Sarah Sterling 9/18/1829-3/5/1896
Pop, dau. Of J. M. and N. E. 10/26/1879-1/17/1881
Pauline, daughter of W. D. and I. G. 3/25/1891-8/15/1892

HUNTER

Virginia Bell 1924-1928
Moriah H. 1/13/1858-3/29/1939
Fannie M. 1902-1961
Hubert D., Ga. PFC Medical Dept. WW I, 1/2/1895-2/1/1945
Sam William 7/11/1900-3/23/1944
Robert J. 6/1/1858-8/10/1932
Stark

JOHNSON

C. W. 1907-1958
James E. 5/10/1871-9/3/1935
Cora J. 9/12/1880
Joe C. 10/4/1937-3/18/1962
George 6/20/1878-8/17/1956

JONES

Pat Kessler, son of Dod and Louise W., 5/31/1945-10/11/1964

KESLER

Bob D. 1876-1919
Lula 1877-1964

LYLE

Mary Elizabeth Holliday 5/29/1853-3/14/1883

LEBANON METHODIST CHURCH, Arcade, Off Hwy 82 South (Established 1835)

MARTIN

D. Ben 11/4/1882-3/27/1958
Julia B., daughter of E. B. and E. T. 4/15/1881-11/25/1890
Artie A., daughter of Levi and N. G. 7/24/1857-2/17/1887
Emma T. 6/21/1855-9/6/1942
John, infant son of Mr. and Mrs. Byrd, 8/11/1945
Levi 4/14/1813-1/23/1893
Elisha B. 11/27/1852-6/5/1935
Elisha Byrd, Ga Pvt. Co. B, 1 Development Bn WW I, 11/29/1892-6/13/1966
Emma T. 6/21/1855-9/6/1942
Octavie I, daughter of Levi and N. G., 11/9/1856-9/14/1884
Nellie G., wife of Levi, 7/31/1819-9/1/1885
Artie A., daughter of Levi and N. G., 7/24/1857-2/17/1887

PENDERGRASS

W. 9/18/1870-1/26/1891
W. B. 8/13/1859-7/3/1890
Hillard 10/10/1887-2/23/1945

POWELL

Mrs. Lula H. 1881-1960
Oliver Lonzo 1847-1952

ROGERS

Henry Jewel 6/10/1894-5/27/1908

TONEY

Dora Holliday 4/28/1878-12/22/1940

WALL

W. J. 11/1861-11/1891
Nancy E., wife of W. M., 12/8/1844-6/5/1906

WHITEHEAD

Robert H. 10/18/1877-12/31/1931
R. A. 1877-1931

WILLS

Edna Wood 7/5/1886-
Jim 7/4/1886-3/2/1948

UNNAMED NEGRO CHURCH CEMETERY, Arcade, Jackson Church School Road

ANDERSON, Trealle died 1960

GARDNER, George 10/21/1958, age 78

GRESHAM

Dearon G. 2/25/1893-6/7/1966
Sylvia E. Dolan 1958-1959

JACKS, Susie, daughter of E. L. and D. A. 4/13/1905-4/17/1905

JENNINGS

Mrs. Nora 1898-1950

JOHNSON

Ora Ruth died 11/13/1965, aged 65 years
Walter D., Ga. Pvt F Res. Labor BN WMC WW I 9/13/1893-11/17/1943

LESTER

Mary G. 1916-1960

SMITH

Minnie 8/3/1880-12/31/1964
Willie, son of J. and A. 12/24/1874-9/24/1905
Idea 6/3/1886-10/3/1955
Martha, wife of Hark died 1/4/1906, age 72 years
Eliza, wife of Ransom died 1/26/1926
Ransom 9/1842-2/13/1926

THOMAS

Vassie died 5/2/1962
Prince 10/8/1860
Dea Clifford (Sark)
George C., Ga. PFC 841 Ga. Trans Co. WW I 5/21/1893-8/4/1961
Estell 1/10/1914-4/1914

TYRON

Art 1949-1967

WAIR

William 1867-6/4/1944

UNNAMED NEGRO CHURCH CEMETERY, Arcade, Jackson Church School Road

WAIR

Annett, wife of William 9/1876-5/2/1942

WASHINGTON

Alice Smith 7/15/1893-4/5/1964
John 1889-1907
Little Teresa R. died 1965, 3 months

GUM SPRINGS BAPTIST CHURCH, G. M. D. 248, United Cities Gas Co. Road, off Hwy 124 East, near Braselton

BROOK

Linda died 5/12/1958, 1 year, 4 months, 6 days
Brenda 8/19/1953, 5 months

BROOKS

William M. 1867-5/1948
Infant Herbert died 6/24/1954, age 10 months, 28 days
Sarah L. 1883-1957

HILL

Lemento M. 10/3/1899-7/22/1959
Frank D. 2/8/1961, age 31

LYLE

A.J.1870-1947

RANDOLPH

Fletcher Jr. died 6/8/1969 aged 27 years

REDSTONE CHURCH, HWY 129, Arcade

ARNOLD

Henry W. 7/21/1921-11/19/1961
James 1921-1938
Dorothy L. 1/9/1932-
John W. Sr. 5/3/1886-3/14/1961
Albert 1889-1960
Lilla Mae 12/11/1886-12/6/1960

REDSTONE CHURCH, HWY 129, Arcade

ARNOLD

Mazie 1892-1941

ARCHER

Carolina E. 3/6/1859-12/17/1936
Edward A. 1863-1926

BROWN

Charles L., Illinois T. Sgt 106 Signal Co. WW II, 7/20/1915-1/30/1965

BUTLER

Judith A. 7/28/1855-2/19/1920
Infant son of John T. 1923
Zach T. 11/2/1849-6/26/1922

COOPER

Oswell P. 3/19/1874-6/16/1947
Sarah E. 11/29/1879-1/31/1961

DAMRON

Charley A. 1874-1958
Minty Ann 1882-1955

DEAVOURS

William H. 5/2/1855-11/23/1951
J. Frances 10/7/1868-1/31/1961

GIBSON

Paul G. 2/8/1899-8/28/1963
Artemus G. 5/5/1876-9/21/1966
Mary D. 8/25/1878-8/14/1956

HARDY

Emma A. 1/17/1866-2/25/1947
Lois B. 1888-1955
Fred J. 1889-1931
S. H. 4/14/1866-10/26/1926
Annie S. 5/10/1909-10/10/1963
Hoke S. 5/23/1907-12/16/1955

REDSTONE CHURCH, HWY 129, Arcade

HOUSE

Ionia J. 1912-1965

JENKINS

J. Wesley 1873-1958
Emma H., wife of J. Wesley 1873-1969

MILLER

Addie L. 1886-1956
Robert M. 11/14/1914-11/10/1952, SFC Medical Dept. WW II
Jane M. 4/3/1921-
Joe C. 1880-

MIZE

Rupert E. 9/24/1905-9/16/1929

OLIVER

Doris 11/7/1922-12/10/----
Nell Ford 7/9/1904-2/22/1966
Charlie H. 9/15/1895-11/13/1919
Maud M. 8/21/1895-1/30/1947
Gladys Smith 7/9/1905
Helen A. born and died 1/31/1931

PARR

Michael H. 5/9/1969-5/10/1969

REEVES

Sharon Wesley 7/25/1938-9/30/1960

ROBINSON

Sallie Walden 1876-1940
Homer 1896-1934
James Henry 1874-1946

SAILERS

Jacqueline W. 8/27/1924-4/12/1941

REDSTONE CHURCH, HWY 129, Arcade

SEGARS

Ada N. 5/2/1889-6/18/1946
John J. 5/15/1882-10/6/1957
Ray 1/5/1888-12/23/1933
Simon A. and Georgia A.
Thomas Leon 10/31/1920-7/17/1924
Olive Florian 4/30/1925-4/30/1925

STEWART

John M. born 1900 married 4/2/1927
Belle W. 1893-1960

THURMOND

Cohen E. 4/22/1925-3/2/1953
Annie Mae 7/3/1897-9/11/1968

WALTON

Henry F. 3/2/1880-11/3/1967
Irene A. 5/3/1885-3/17/1968
Annie Grace, daughter of Mr. and Mrs. H. F. 1/23/1916-3/11/1920

WELCHEL

Ned H. 1909-
Esther A. 1913-1950

WIER

J. Frank 4/11/1881-9/21/1936

WILLIAMSON

Robert O. 4/3/1870-7/30/1953
Jennie H. 9/26/1881-4/12/1954
F. Hoyt 1/1/1905-3/5/1938
Anna Belle 10/26/1890-10/21/1954
Junius S. 10/4/1886-3/24/1947

END

AARON
Alma L. 144
Chessie A. 144
Clarence M. 66
E. 144
J. (Pink) 144
Joseph W. 144
Lenard C. 66
Lonie J. 66
Mack C. 66
Mamie F. 66
Mary Alice 144
Maude F. 66
Mazie A. 66
Minnie B. 144
Nettie Lee 144
Thomas 144
Viola 144
William M. 66
Willie M. 66

ABB
J. 316

ABBOTT
James Robert III 12

ADAIR
A. E. 30
Alice E. 30
Annie Sue 30
H. B. 30
Henry B. 30

ADAMS
Alton 1
Ammar B. 31
Bessie M. 1
Bonner C. 205
Caroline 30
J. A. 1
J. Parks 30
Carrie 31
Clinton 31
Eldridge Decatur 144
Eugenie Waddell wife of J. E. 80
J. Summie 31
J. T. Jr. 30
J. T. 30
James E. 80
Jesse Curtis 1

ADAMS continued
Joseph 30
Julia Ann 1
Lettie R. 205
Mary A. 30
Mattie A. 31
Mollie 31
Myra Lenora 1
Osmers Jackson 1
Parker 31
Rose Preston 1
Sallie R. 80
Susie Effie 1
W. O. 1
Marilyn R. 145
Victoria 145

ADDERHOLT
Attice 205
Francis Himer 205
Ida 205

ADDINGTON
Bennie G. 196
Fannie 196
J. P. 196

ADERHOLD
Wortie E. 205

ADKINS
Jay 43
Oudie 328

AIKEN
Eliza Thompson 144
J. Holmer 144
Maggie A. 144
Oscar Pierce 144

AIKENS
Nettie Louise 106

AKINS
Eloie Mae 144
James E. 144
John S. 205
Mollie S. 205

ALEXANDER
Alice M. 205
Annie Mae 196
C. C. 205
Callie J. 289
Clarence B. 144
Crawford 289
Dorothy Montgomery 205
Ella Freeman 31
Emily Wier 289
Emma E. 144
Gazelle 12
Herty E. 289
J. 289
J. B. (Dutch) 144
J. V. 144
Jack 31
James R. 12
Joe W. 31
John 289
John Russell 144
John W. 144
Joseph E. 289
Lillian M. 289
Louisa O. 289
Louise Ann 289
Martha E. 31
Matthew 144
Norma M. 144
Lucinda 289
N. E. 289
Pansy 144
Rachael C. 289
Russel 31
S. P. 289
Samuel 144
Thomas P. 289
W. H.144
William T. 289
Willie 144

ALLAN
I.G. 205
L. L. 205
Laura D. 144
May 205

ALLEN
A. E. 1
Alberta Elsse 1
Alice E. 1

ALLEN continued
Annie Lou 316
Arpad Alvan 1
Barbara Jean 326
Betty Jane 326
C. P. 316
Carlton Columbus 43
Clanelia A. 316
Donald 316
Dudley O. 206
Ed 205
Eliza Skelton 43
Ella C. 205
Georgia 206
Gladys J. 316
Grover C. 326
H. C. 205
Harold D. 326
Harvey 206
Harvey L. 206
Hoke S. 316
Ira C. 205
Isabelle C. 1
Jack C. 206
L. C. Dr. 1
Lillie 205
Lumpin 205
Mae B. 326
Martha M. 316
Maymie A. 205
Myron B. M. D. 1
Robert (Bob) 206
Robert Lee 316
Sarah L. 205
T. 205
Tinnie M. 316
V. T. 206
Virginia R. 1
Walter Lee 316
William E. 206
Wilma J. Green 206

ALLGOOD
Alice 289

ALLEY
Tilden Hamlin 298

AMICK
Ben C. 145

AMMONS
Emma L. 331
John B. 331
John Berditt 331

ANDERSON
Allen 1
Annie J. 31
B. D. 316
Cora M. 106
D. B. 57
David W. 12
Denie 1
Devilland 306
Dewey 316
Eliza E. 96
Flavys 276
Gartrell W. 117
George E. 12
Golden A. 12
Guyla 145
Ida Wiley 306
J. A. 96
Ja. A. 43
Jack 43
James C. 306
John Walter 267
Johnnie 316
Lizzie C. 55
Lula V. 96
M. A. 57
Maggie 55
Martha A. 12
Marvin 106
Marvin J. 106
Mary Catheryne 306
Mary Wheeler 267
Maude A. 1
N. J. 316
Nancy 55
O. L. 55
Sarah F. 31
Thomas B. 12
Trealle 340
W. D. 12306

ANDREWS
Margaret S. 117

ANGLIN
Clarence 43
Darline S. 31
Dolley 97
H. C. 97145
James R. 31
M. D. 31
Mary B. 31
Mellie 43
Myrtle 97
Ophelia 43
Susan C. 145
W. H. 31
Willie H. 31
Stacy Leila 331
Sarah E. 325

ANTHONY
A. 276
Annie 276
Bertha 276
Mack C. 66
Mae J. 66

APPLEBY
Alvin C. 206
Henry M. 206
Mary M. 206

APPLESBY
Ann Stockton 145
Cora W. 145
George Douglas 145
Guss A. Johns 145
Lynn Cooper 145
Robert Travis Sr .145

ARCHER
A. J. 289
Amanda L. 145
Carolina E. 342
Carrie S. 282
Dave A. 282
Dewitt 289
Edward A. 342
G. T. 289
Henry M. 145
Jack 145
James C. Jr. 331
James C. Sr. 331
James W. 289

ARCHER continued
James W. 289
John Hubert 289
Lenna Turk 145
Lula Jarrett 145
Mary Allie 289
Nancy Emily 289
Robert L. 289
Robert Y. 331
Sam 289
Samuel Bell 145
William Milton 289
Zebulon 289

ARKINS
Delonia 310
Nellie Haynes 310

ARMISTEAD
Harold W. 132

ARMOUR
Mary Carlan 206

ARMSTRONG
J. T. 180
L. M. 180
Martin 31

ARNOLD
Albert 341
Alice K. 290
Annie Daughtry 296
Caroline Bowels 296
David Kenneth 145
Dorothy L. 341
Henry W. 341
Ingamar 296
J. E. 296
James 341
John W. Sr. 341
Lena 1
Lilla Mae 341
M. B. 1
Martha J. Gaines 296
Mary B. 283
Mazie 342
N. J. 1.
Nancy J. 1
R. C. 296
Robert D. 296

ARNOLD continued
W. D.
Washington 296

ARTHUR
Cleo 57
M. C. 57
Rosa 57
Rosa Da. 57

ASBELLE
Albert M. 206

ASH
Billy Ray 261

ASKEW
James A. 145

ATTAWAY
H. 306
J. D. 180
J. F. 180
Joseph A. 306
Oscar H. 145

AUSTIN
Mary Bessie 261

AUTRY
H. K. 336
Martha Ann 336

AYERS
D. J. 106
Mary E. 106

AYRES
Pearl W. 135
W. Holman 135

BABDS
B. H. 80
J. H. 80
Thomas 80

BACHELOR
Elizabeth 196

BAGWELL
Amory Donald 206
Joseph H. 206
Sallie M. 206

BAIER
J. H. 206

BAILES
Harold C. Jr. 1

BAILEY
A.T. 13
Blondean 80
Catherine 146
Donia H. 145
Ella G. 80
F. M. 146
F.T. 13
Frank T. 13
George Dewey 146
George W. 146
Gus Wyatt 146
Ida 80
J. L. 146
Julis E. 146
L. A. 80
Lilla O. 206
Lizzie J. 13
Lou Stone 284
Mary 127
Mary A. 146
Mary E. 206
Minnie W. 146
R. Smith 290
Ralph L. 80
S. T. 127
Samuel E. 206
Samuel Wesley 284
Sara Elizabeth 135
T. Stoy 146
W. T. 135

BAIRD
Alberta 12
Almeta 12
Annie 12
Arthur Belle 12
Arthur H. 12
Caroline S. 12
Clarence 12
BAIRD continued
Colie A. 180
Eliza Caroline 1
Evaline 1
F. E. 1213
Frances R. 13
Fred H. 12
Hattie F. 127
Henry F. 12
Ida 12
J. S. 1213
J. W. S.12
Jack Quillian 13
Jack Wayne 12
James M. 13
James Rev. 1
Jesse 12
Jessie 180
Joe Wilborn 12
John A. 1
John O. 13
Joseph Samuel 12
Julia Carolyn 12
Lucy 12
Mary Ann 13
Mary Lou 180
Minnie 12
Nancy Duck 12
Nelia T. 13
Paul 180
R. M.12
Ritta C. 12
S. B. 13
Sallie R. 13
Samuel B. 13
Susie Blackstock 102
Tenie H. 1
W. Billie 12
W. H. (Billy) 102

BAKER
Frank 146
George 146
Susie W. 206

BALDY
Estell A. 146
J. L. 146

BALES
Ellis J. 286
Emma L. 146
Ferrell 286
John Henry 286
Judy Ann 286
Lem 286
Lilliebell 286
Lizzie C. 286

BALEY
Almar 31

BANKS
Asilee 181
Azalee 180
Darrell Edge P. F. C. 43
Edgar 282
Ella E. 31
Eva T. 181
Hannah W. 180
Hester V. 31
J. A. 180
J. Abner 180
James 282
Kateria Ann 43
Lottie Bell 180
Lottie Corine 180
Ollie H. 180
Ruby 180
Susan E. 180

Victoria 282
W. A. 181
W. Alex 180
Wade Hampton 180
Warren B. 181
William Hamlin 181
William J. 180
Z. Z. 180
Zeanos Z. 180

BANNER
Shella Jeane 44

BARBER
Archie 80
Alfred 207
Augusta C. 207
Bessie 80
Billy 207
Charles T. 207
BARBER continued
Clifford D. 207
Clinton E. 207
D. P. 146
David Stockton 146
Earl P. 207
Edwin 80
Eliza Nunn 207
Ellen D. 80
Flossie D. 146
Genevieve 301
Harold T. 146
Horace Oscar 146
Littleton 207
Mary 207
Minnie Stockton 146.
Ola Stockton 146
R. T. 206
Robert Reese 146
Robert Reese Jr. 146
Sara Jane 80
Sarah 207
Susan K. 207
T. C. 80
W. 301
W. Greensby 301
W. L. 207
William L. 207
Woodruff 146

BARDEN
Annie Belle 207
Nida D. 66
W. J. 207
William Edn 207

BARNES
Robert W. 207
Ruthie 207
Sybil T. 207
William A. 207

BARNET
Lov. Lenaid 117
R. C. 284

BARNETT
Ann B. 127
Anna K. 127

350

Augustus T. 286
Berry 296
BARNETT continued
Bunie M. 57
C. M. 127
Charley Baxter 146
Charlie Embry 146
Chester A. 286
Clara A. 127
Claude G. 127
Cynthia Thomas 207
David W. 286
Edward 310
Eloise T. 66
Emma Lena 117
Ernest 57
G. D. 127
Gladys 127
Jake 296
Jimmie 286
Maud E. 286
Onia K. 286
Osborn 286
Ritchie 286
Grace 207
Harold G. 207
Harriett 207
Henry C. 127
Henry Polk 146
Ida 127
Ida Sudderth 146
J. H. 66 127
James H. 127
John D. 207
John Paul 207
John W. 57
Lillie 127
Lula D. 207
M. P. 13
Mary 13
Omie M. 13
P. A. 127
Savannah P. 127
Vannie 127
Vennie E. 127
W. Andy 13
W. B. 207
W. L. 127
W. S. 127
William G. 127
William L. 127

BARRETT
Dub 118
E. W. 135
Fred R. 57
G. C. 80
George Truitt 135
Joe B. 135
Lal 118
Laura Bell Roberts 147
Lawrence 196
Lillie M. 57
Lunda Sue 207
Susie 80
William 196
Willie A. 57
Lula Spencer 290

BARRON
Glenda Martnelia 207
Marvin 207
Ora I. 207

BARRY
Diane 43
Thomas 43

BARTON
Emlyn D. 147
Julius J. 147
R. W. 182

BATCHELOR
George W. 181
Jessie Ruth 181
Lela 181
Lillie Evans 181
Mattie A. 181
Nancy M. 181

BATES
Guilford 208

BAUGH
D. D. 208
Martha J. 208

BAXTER
Brenda Carol 208
J. B. 208

Jerry 208

BEAM
Alfred 261
Annie E. 261
James 261
S. M. 261

BEASLEY
Georgia Trout 147
Murphy 100
Viola 100

BEATY
Eva C. 196
F. L. 107
Frances 107
Henry G. 196
J. B. (Bud) 196
J. C. 107
J. S. 196
Lenie Joe 196
M. J. 107
Marler B. 107
Paul Randolph 196
Pearl 196
Victoria 196
W. D. 107

BEAVERS
James 290
James Louis 290
Pearl 290
Pearl Huff 290
Robert Nelson 290

BECK
Annie Bell 132
Betty Jean 57
Charlie 80
Cordile 57
Della 132
Emma S. 80
Erastus H. 208
Estell 132
Fred Lee 132
G. M. 57
Harold L. 57
Idell H. 132
J. M. 132
J. T. 135

BECK continued
John 57
John Clyde Jr. 208
Leora A. 132
Manda Aarzela 57
Marrion 132
Minnie 132
Pearl 132
Phoeba H. 135
Robert 57 57
Robert Stiner 208
Ruby E. 57
Tim 135

BEENE
Bess B. 208

BELGER
John Henry Belger 2

BELL
A. J. Co. C. 147
Andrew Jackson 147
Augustus A. 147
C. 2
Clara Geraldine 331
Cline 2
Cornelia Watson 147
David L. 147
Eddie 13
Elise Mae 13
Eula Stockton 147
F. Cicero 13
Florrie 147
H. W. (Rache) 147
H. W. Jr. 147
Harriet Eliza 147
Harry P. 147
Horatio Webb 147
Jackson 147
James A. 147
James F. 2
Joseph M. Storey 147
Judge H. W. 147
Mae C. 13
Laura Cheatham 147
Luella L. 147
Martha M. 13
Mary E. 147
Mattie P. 147
Minnie Allan 147

BELL continued
Nicholas A. 2
Pearl 13
Rebecca 147
Samuel Jackson 147
Trumon O. 13
W. Parks 147
William Lane 147
Willie 147
Wilson Cartrell 147

BELLAMY
A. Newt 208
J. Richard 331
John Billy 331
R. Caroline 208

BENEFIELD
Evelyn Mae 135
M. Parlee 135
William E. 135

BENNETT
A. C. 208
Agnes 57
Alice Louise 147
Bill 127
Billy 127
C. L. 57
DeWitt 66
Effie 66
Howell 66
J. C. 148
J. W. 66
Jesse Marie 148
Jim 148
Joseph 148
L. D. 148
Lizzie O. 148
M. C. 107
Mattie L. Holder 148
Sam Dean 148
Sammie Bascumb 66
T. J. 148
Thomas 148
Thomas Holder 147
Thomas Jack 127
Thomas Jackson 147
Una 127
W. C. 107
William T. 147

BENTLEY
J. C. 302
Nancy 302

BENTON
Albert M. 209
Alice M. 58
B. Jack 208
Barbara 58
Clarence E. 208
Claud Byron 208
Clyde G. 209
D. D. 58
Delilah C. 208
Dell Blackstock 58
Eleanor 209
Emma W. Culbertson 208
Estelle H. 58
Eudora G. 209
Florence Ayers 208
H. Theo 208
Harold L. 58
J. P. 58
J. P. Jr. 58
J. Pope 58
James 267
James Edwin 58
L. D. 58
Lorenzo D. 58
Myrtle M. 58
Maggie I. 208
Mary Sander 208
Milton A. 208
Nannie R. 208
O. S. 208
R. J. 58
R. V. 80
Robert Arnold 80
T. W. 58
Viola Holland 208
W. M. 136
Walter W. 209
William Jackson 208
Willie B. 208
Willie L. 58

BERNETT
Tommie Lee 209

BERRONG
Emma B. 209
Willie W. 209

BERRY
John N. 278
W. 55

BERRYMAN
Charles T. 181
Cornelia E. Jr. 316
Harrison 181
Jo Nell 316
Luther J. 181
Martha J. 181
Martha Jo 181
May 181

BETTS
Ellis B. 336
Georgia 336
Ira E. 336

BINGHAM
Edward 302

BILLUPS
Anna Gates 278

BIRD
A. Burel 148
J. N. 302
M. J. 302
Robert E. 148
T. L. 302

BIRT
Billy 44

BISHOP
Harry Oscar 209
James W. 79

BLACK
A.H. 317
Clara Dale 209
Eddie D. 209
Harold To. 209
Henry T. 209
Ida M. 209
Leo G. 209

BLACK continued
Mary E. 107
Mary Wood 317
Nozell L. 209
Rebecca J. 209
Robert Lee 209

BLACKMON
Myrtle M. Elder 32

BLACKSTOCK
A. N. 103
Alexander N. 148
Annette 103
Freddie H. 148
Hubert N. 103
J. B. 103
J. Carl 102
M. L. 103
M. M. 103
Mattie Lee Roberts 102
P. J. 103
Pleasant J. 103
Samantha Luncy 103
Susan Elmine Echols 103
Thomas H. 103
Tom B. 103
W. A. 102
William Elmer 103

BLACKWELL
Henry 148
J. S. 181
John C. 181
L. H. 181
Mary L. 148

BLAKELY
Abe 299
Autry 299
Dan Calup 299
Daniel 299
Darlene 299
Edward 299
Floyd 299
J. F. 299
Odessa Kilson 299
Sadie 299
Tinner A. 299
Willie (Jake) 299

BLALOCK
F. A. 303
J. B. 286
Joe Lindon 306
John Bascom 2
Johnnie J. 286
Mary 286
Mary Alice 306
Mary Ella 303
Melissa Maynard 2

BLANKENSHIP
Donnie 32
Ruth A. 13

BLASINGAME
Lovette M. 148

BLUME
Adam A. 209
Elaine 209

BODDIE
Assie Power 209

BOGGS
Addie Hunter 148
Charlie 306
Emma H. 306
Harlow Bullock 148
J. H. 66
John Wesley 148
Johnnie W. 306
Julianne C. 301
Julius H. 148
Junius M. 306
Lona Ellen 66
M. A. 66
Ola May 66
S. H. 66
W. P. 66

BOHANNON
Berry S. 209
Eliza O. 209
Ida 209
Martha A. Simmons 181

BOLTON
Annie G. 210
Charlie M. 210
D. Pat 210
Ellis B. 210
Gene Lanetta 210
Hattie 210
Joe E. 210
Myrtle M. 210
Nancy Dawn 210
Reba L. 210
Texas Embry 210

BOND
L. J. 196
Mary A. 14
Sarah Frances 96
William H. 336
William T. 14

BONE
Abi S. 210
Agnes E. 210
Barbara Sue 118
G. W. 210
Hilda E. 32
Homer 32
W. Grady 210
William K. 210

BONNER
Dollie 32

BOON
A. 32
Edith 32
Priscilla S. 32
R. C. 32
Ratliff H. 32

BOONE
William Gilbert 44

BOONER
Curley 32
Joe 32
Johney 32

BORDERS
A. V. 196
B. 328
Bessie G. Newman 58
E. H. 58
Elizabeth Wilhite 290
Ella E. 196
Eugene H. 290
F. O. 196
Fannie O. 196.
Hiram H. 118
Hiram J. 118
Joseph D. 196
Regis A. 210
Rosa L. 328
S. L. 196
Thomas L. 210

BOWELS
Levina Smith 296

BOWEN
Mary L. 301

BOWLES
A. 181
Agnes 197
C. R. 181
Callie 58
Caroline Marie 58
Cicero 181
Clarence E. 58
Curtis 58
Elizabeth 181
Ethel 58
Frank 107
Garnett 58
J. B. 197
J. F. 107
J. J. 181
Martha I. 58
Mary 107
Mary L. 58
Mary R. 58
May 181
Nathan M. 197
Sarah E. 197
Tommie 58
W. H. 58
Zine May 181

BOYD
B. W. 210
Ben T. 210
Benjamin W. 210
Bertha L. 210
Bertha Little 210
E. W. 210
Effie 336
H. Oscar 336
James 336
Marie A. 210
Mollie E. 336
Nellie B. 336

BOYER
James W. 136

BRADBERRY
Arthur 210
Fred C. 127

BRADFORD
James Dean 80

BRADY
L. E. 14
M. M. 14
T. A. 14

BRANYON
Alta May 128
J. T. 128
M. E. 128

BRASELTON
Almeh H. 210
Annette Maughon 10
Clyde Royce 10
Frances Newell 11
Green 10
Green B. 10
Jacob 181
James Lewis Jr. 10
Joe B. 10
John Oliver Sr. 11
Lena 11
Margret B. 181
Mary 181
Mary Ann 10
Mary May Duncan 10
Pollie Darby 11

BRASELTON continued
Pollie Darby 11
Royce G. 10
Sarah B. 10
Steven W. 10
Susan F. 10
Susan F. 11
W. H. Sr. 10
William Henry 11
William McKiney 10

BRAY
Harvey F. 210
Willie R. 66

BREAZEALS
C. Norman 148

BREWER
Dellie Mae 14
Dennis O. 148
Dollie J. 211
Donald W. 211
Elich Tom 317
Holman 211
Lillie 14
Lillie Belle 317
Mannie Mae 317
Ruby B. 148
Weldon O. 211

BRIDGES
Ann 197
Ethel Gertrude 197
Eula M. 182
Georgia M. 182
H. Rev. 14
J. D. 197
J. Ernest 182
J. R. 182
L. C. 182
M. C. 197
M. R. 182
Martha A. 197
Mary A. 14
Mary Lee 197
Mary Rebecca 182
N. A. 182
Nancy A. 182
Nettie May 197
Roy W. 182

BRIDGES continued
T. W. 182
W. H. Jr. 197
William Fred 197

BROCK
Augustin Harrison 149
Barbara B. 211
Benjamin H. 81
Bernice T. 211
Bessie 81
C. A. 8081
C. A. O'Neal 331
Charles O. 149
Clara 331
Clifford W. 211
Arnold A. 261
E. S. 80
Elias G. 211
Elizabeth 261
Essa 81
Esther 81
Eula 80
Eulah 80
Fred S. 81
H. H. 8081
Henry H. 81
J. F. 211
J. T. (Jim) 262
J. lasure 211
James A. 107
James F. 211
Jason Mays 149
Jimmie 211
Julie Reed 261
Leila 211
Lou Dowdy 149
Lucy A. 107
M. F. 8081
Marshall G. 261
Mary F. Catlett 331
Mary P. 80
Miron H. 262
Nora T. 261
O. L. 80
Oma Estella 261
Ora 80
Parilee H. 262
Ralph 81
Roy 262
Sallie Simpkins 149

BROCK continued
Sarah 8081
Susan F. 81
W. L. 261
W. Larence 261
Willie Harrison 80
Woodie B. 261

BRONNER
Alice 310

BROOK
Brenda 341
Linda 341

BROOKS
A. F. 149
A. L. 149
Adolphus E. 149
Andrew L. 149
Annie Lucile 149
Annolevia 149
Bessie 149
Blondell H. 44
C. T. 81
Clifford N. 149
Clyde 149
Curtis P. 58
D. M. 182
Dell M. 149
Dorothy Ann 44
E. A. (Pat) 149
E. D. 44
Edward S. 149
Evelyn Elain 44
Gladys 44
Henry L. 149
Herbert 341
Howell 197
Ina Bell 197
J. L. 81
James L. 149
Joe Ira 44
Lila Mae Levell 149
Mary Jane 97
Mary Lila 149
Mauddell 149
Modena W. 211
Nancy 182
Nancy Elizabeth 81
Nancy Susie 81

BROOKS continued
Sammie 97
Sarah F. 149
Sarah L. 341
Thomas M. 149
W. H. 97,313
W. W. 81
Walter M. 149
William M. 211,341

BROOKSHIRE
C. L. 182
Elizabeth 182
Ellen 182
George L. 182
George M. 2
George T. 211
J. D. 182
Margie N. 211
Rebeckie J. Poston 182
Sally 2

BROOME
Pearl 211

BROWN
Charles L. 342
A. B. 44
Amanda 81
Andrey 44
Annie 44
Annie Lou 107
Ben C. 107
Billy Chandler 149
Charles E. 81
D. F. 108
Edward F. 14
Elisha H. 149
Eliza B. 107
Ernest A. 108
Ernest Harold 44
Evelyn 66
Flora Patrick 81
Freddie H. 267
Genie 136
Genie G. 136
Gladys D. 44
J. H. 44,211
J. M. 108
J. N. 136
J. Newt 136

BROWN continued
James E. 66
James V. 66
Jane I. 107
Joe 278
John 14
John T. 302
Julia Barber 302
L. H. 149
Lanora H. 211
Leighton Littleton 149
Lemuel T. 81
Lillian A. 32
Lydia J. 14
M. B. 328
M. C. 44
M. N. 44
Marion N. 149
Marshal S. 107
Mary A. 44
Mary E. 14
Mattie Samantha 107
May Ramsey 44
Mildred 107
Nell 107
Nellie 136
O. Belle 107
O. F. 108
Ollie G. 66
Omie 44
R. I. 107
Robert 278
Rufus C. 107
Sam Kenneth 211
Samuel Newton 81
Sarah 107
Susannah 14
T. C. 107
Tillman C. 107
Tillman C. Jr. 107
Tishie Marilla 136
Toy J. 136
Tressie 136
Uriah L. 107
W. G. 81

BRUCE
Annie E. 149
Roy 32
William F. 149

BRUMBALOW
Earley 197
Martin 197
Susan 197

BRYAN
Dora S. 44
Elzie A. 267
J. R. 44
Nancy 44
Noah J. 44
William P. 268

BRYANT
Andy 182
C. H. 44211
Caldoney 44
Charlie 44
Dennis H. 44
E. M. C. 197
F. O. Borders 197
James W. 182
Jane 44
Julian P. 45
M. J. 182
Martha J. Skelton 44
Paria F. 197
S. L. 197
Thelma 197
W. B. 44182
Waldo 182
Wince Rev. 44

BRYSON
Barbara 149
C. B. 149
C. T. 150
Charles L. 150
Gertrude E. 150
Pauline Winifred 150

BULLARD
Nora 32

BULLOCK
Vernie 67

BURGERS
Beatrice 211
L. J. 211
Lawton J. 211
Lettie Bird 211

BURK
Hushel 32

BURKE
Furd 33
Martha Twitty 150

BURNETT
John W. 212
Willie Mae 212

BURNS
Bessie 128
Buford A. 212
D. M. 128
David M. 128
Ella L. 128
Emma Powel 212
J. M. 128
Joseph Brantly 128
Maggie E. 67
R. B. 67
S. H. 128
Sallie C. 212
Sarah H. 128
Sarah L. 128
Susan E. 212
Thomas D. 128
W. J. 128

BURR
Victoria Wood 262

BURRELL
Andy L. 33
Mary Louise 33

BURROUGHS
Catherine 2
Julius C. 2

BURRUSS
Agnes D. 212
J. B. Jr. 212

BUSH
Elizabeth 150
Lucius T. 150
W. W. 150

BUTLER
Claudine 267
Dora 328
Fred 97
James 328
John T. 342
Judith A. 342
Reba Lee 267
Virginia 328
Zach T. 342

BYERS
Wellington 212

BYRD
Alton L. 212
Andrew J. 212
Evelyn 212
Hassie Byrd Edwards 212
John 290
Lula L. 212

CAGLE
Grocer 81
Jnett D. 81
Lilley 81
Mildred 81
W. J. 81
Willard 81

CAIN
Carl 108
Emma 108
Hilda Grace 45
James 317
Jesse 108
M. S. 108
Martha 317
Robert M. 108
Thomas 55

CALLAHAN
Abarilla 150
John 150
Linda 150

CAMP
B. L. 212
Bessie 299
Carlton 100

CAMPBELL
A. E. 150
Annie M. 45
C. C. 67
C. L. Rev. 45
Cora 108
E. A. 108
Elmer Carl 67
Estella J. 108
Eunice B. 212
Gipson 212
Herbert Gewel 182
Jaffie 67
Lola Estell 182
M. J. 108
Mandy 197
Mary J. 108
O. H. 150
W. D. 108
W. P. 108

CANTREL
Charlie J. 182
Nancy J. 182
Ralph Junious 182

CANTRELL
Sarah Loe 100

CANUP
Carl C. 108
Deamie 108
E. A. 108
Edmund D. 108
H. L. 33
Jessie L. 33
M. M. 108
Mary A. 108
Matison M. 108
Ozelle H. 108
Ruby G. 108

CAPES
Joseph B. 331
Ottice Lowe 331

CARDIDEN
Stella M. 303

CARITHERS
Clara Bell 33
James G. 331
Jennie 331
Jewel 150
Laura 331
Robert T. 150
Samuel R.
Sarah P. 150
T. A. 150
Talie 150
Virginia 331
William A. 331

CARLAN
Ira E. Jr. 118
Maulene M. 118

CARLISLE
M. 303
Tiny 303
William C. 303

CARLYLE
James Horace 314

CARLTON
Bealer Augustus 212
H. A. 212
Harrison A. 212

CARNEY
Arlena 331
C. G. 331
Etta 331
Gordon 331
Katie 331

CARPENTER
Lou Ellen 150
T. C. 150

CARRINGTON
Amanda Paralee 212
Arthur 299
Hal C. 212
Mattie Herring 212
Mattie Mae 212

CARRINGTON continued
William David 212

CARROLL
A. Boyd 150
Charles 81
Clyde 81
Daisy C. 67
Dell S. 81
Ernestine Barrett 67
Harvey R. 81
James Lewis 67
Jane 81
Lertrelle S. 150
Lillie H. 150
Robert Verdell 67

CARRUTH
Bob Anthony 33
Harvey R. 81

CARSON
A. Clarence 213
Bert A. 213
Bessie Love 213
Charles Maxey 213
Curtis C. 213
D. U. 213
David H. 213
George L. 213
George L. 213
George L. Sr. 213
Georgia Westbrook 213
Hortense 213
J. M. 213
Laurinda M. 213
Lizzie 213
M. C. 213
Mattie Holley 213

CARTER
Billy 151
Conie 151
Conie N. 151
David Augustus 150
Dock S. 213
E. E. 151
Edna 151
Elizabeth A. 151
Ethel 262
George Robert 82

CARTER continued
Grady 262
Homer 14
J. D. 14
J. Z. 82
James Zenous 82
John A. 82
John Orr 151
Loucinia Porter 151
M. V. 14
Martha 182
Monteen 108
Nora Tarrant 82
O. G. Washington 82
Ora 14
P. A. 150
Pratt A. 151
R. Earl 151
Ray 262
Robert Lee 82
T. W. 151
Theron Niblack 151
Thomas 151
W. J. 14
William 182
William Henry 151

CARLYLE
C. A. 14
C. Azalee 14
Grover Ansilum 14
J. M. 14
James M. 14

CARTLEDGE
John L. 290

CASH
America P. 284
Annie H. 262
B. W. 15
Eldred G. 284
Hoyt B. 132
John A. 302
John Sr. 284
Kay Broadus 15
Larry 183
Lucy Ann 14
Madeleine Elizabeth 284
Marion L. 284
Mathew 302

CASH continued
N. 284
Noah J. 262
Parilee E. 183
Phillip Bruce 183
Ralph M. 183
S. Adelaide 284

CASTELAW
G. O. Dr. 213
Pauline White 213

CATLETT
Caroline M. Polk 82
Clarence N. 136
Claude 151
Daisy G. 151
Ellie Grace 136
H. H. 82
J. F. 82
J. L. 82
Jasper 136
Leila B. 82
Louise 268
Martha N. 136
Mary Ann Wilson 82
Miram David 268
Roy P. 82
William L. 268

CAYLOR
Nancy 197

CEARLEY
C. C. 332
Mamie Lee 332
Martin 332

CHAMBERS
Alga A. Sgt. 15
D. C. 103
Mollie Belle 15
Patsy A. 15

CHAMBLEE
E. C. S. 132
Maud 132

CHANDLER
Calvin C. 290
Eunice J. 213
G. N. 67
Grace H. 213
Herbert 213
J. Edgar 213.
J. M. (Aunt Sissy) 317
J. M. 213
John Walter 317
M. J. 213
Mandy 328
Mary Irene 213
Mattie Ingram 213
Maxie L. 136
Rupert Clarence 213
Stacie Amela 118
Tresvan M. 303
Wheeler 328
Winford T. 213

CHATHAM
Mary Lizza Cartledge 290
W. G. 290

CHEATHAM
A. G. 290
Aaron 290
Allie Ruth 118
D. H. 290
G. H. 290
Kathleen Wofford 118
Philip 290
Thomas L. 118

CHEEK
Cora S. 136
Edney Isabelle Stephens 15
F. V. Rev. 15
Freeman Virgil 15
Henry M. 136
Infant 15
Lorena 15
M. A. 15
Major G. 15
Martha A. 15
Mary Maggie 303
Missouri A. 15
William 15
William C. Ga. Sgt. 15
William M. 15

CHEELY
Cynthia 336
G. M. 325
W. H. 336
Winnie 325

CHESTER
Isaac Thomas 118

CHESTNUT
Fred 2
Herschel G. 2
J. T. 2
John T. 2
Juna Belle 2
M. V. 2
Mary Vilula 2

CHILDERS
D. C. 108
Georgia A. 108
Goldie F. 45
Joe B. 108
Lon F. 45
Nina 108
Ted 45
Tom C. 45

CHILDS
Carrie L. 213
Curtis E. 151
Dewey W. 213
Dolia S. 213
E. D. 213
Edward M. 151
Jesse C. 213
Kitty W. 151
Lee R. 151
Lucy 213
M. Fannie 213
Marsha 151
Martha 151
Roy S. 213
Rufus 213
Sam H. 213
Stella 213
W. E. 213

CHRISTIAN
A. C. 33
Burdette 214
Burrell 214
Ida 214
J. L. 214
M. E. Shields 33
Sophie E. 33
W. D. 33

CHOCRAN
Amanda 45
J. Matt 45

CHRONIC
Agusta M. 132
Clarisa 16
Hazel 16
John H. 16
Lewis 16
O. M. Rev. 16
William T. 132

CHURCHWELL
Edward P. 58

CILLILAND
Mary 82

CLACK
Daniel L. 306

CLALK
Herman 15

CLARK
Addie T. 314
Carrie 183
E. D. 183
E. H. 326
Emma Mae P. 2
J. N. 183
James Coil 151
Jewell W. 2
Lamar W. 262
Linnie 183
M. W. 2
Moses 183
Omce Carroll 151
Royce Freeman 326
Ruby B. 314

CLARK continued
Selma C. 262
Tallulah 2
Wilbur C. 314
William M. 314
Willie A. 2

CLEGHOEN
Claud 214

CLEMENT
George C. 214
Kathleen 214

CLEVELAND
Alfred P. 262
Leeonia Bell 262
Mina G. 262
Nonnie J. A. 108
Velma Shubert 108

COBB
Alina T. 328
Harold 328

COCHRAN
Elijah Newton 100
Henry 214
Nathan M. 317
Sue 214
Willie Ruth 100

COFFEE
E. H. 214
Lucy Helen 214

COFER
Wanda Maxine 291

COKER
Amony 100
C. E. 108
C. Viola 15
Emory H. 15
Rosie 108
Thomas Clyde 214
W. B. 108

COILE
J. R. 282

COLE
A. Elie J. 214
Cecil W. 214
E. A. 136
Hoyt Otis 136
James Owen 214
L. J. 214
Luther N. 214
Soleda B. 214
T. 214
Theodore 214
W. C. 136
William C. 214

COLDMAN
Sallie F. 337

COLEMAN
Augustus A. 286
Carlton 214
Claude T. 276
Clifford L. 33
D. A. 214
Ella Stapler 276
F. A. 214
James Samuel 276
John Franklin 276
M. L. 276
Mary L. 214
Riley W. 284
S. A. 276
Samuel A. 276
Samuel A. 276
Thomas W. 276
Vassie 276
William S. 33

COLLIER
Andrew W. Franklin 317
B. Gregory 317
Benjamin H. 151
Curtis H. 151
Ettie Gregory 317
Frances V. 151
Frank 317
William D. 151

COLLINS
Allie E. 67
Clemmie B. 214
Edith D. 314

COLLINS continued
George H. Rev. 214
Henry 299
Janet G. 337
John H. 67
Levy 299
Lovie Aaron 67
Otto 314
R. A. 286
R. M. Presley 67
Stanley B. 67

COLLUM
E. R. 215
Guy 215

COLQUITT
Birdie H. 58
E. C. 58
Martha S. 58
William J. 58

COLVARD
Eunice A. 79

COMPTON
Charley D. 291

CONN
Thomas F. Jr. 215

CONNALLY
George W. 82
Martha T. Brock 82
Mary 82

COOK
D. C., Rev. 100
R. E. 306
W. A. 306
W. S. 306

COOPER
Ann Elizabeth W. 15
Annie Maud 16
Augustus 132
C. P. 132
Charles Curtis 183
Charles K. 215
Charlie 183
Claude R. 16

COOPER continued
Dewey 132
Early 16
Edna 16
Edna Cheek 16
Elizabeth 118
Etta 132
Flora S. 45
Florence 16
G. W. 97
H. M. Dr. 16
Hazel P. 45
Herbert 132
Hillyer Dr. 16
Hoyt T. 118
Ina L. 132
Ira Britt 317
J. C. 16132133
J. E. (June) 45
J. M. 16
J. O. 16
James C. 132
Jewel 133
John Hightower 215
John Millsap 299
Julia 16
Julia McEver 16
Lamar Jackson 215
Levie 97
Lillie Belle 16
Lizzie 16,132,133
M. M. 332
M. T. 16
Margaret S. 215
Marshall Tandy 16
Martha E. 16
Martha Veal 15
Mary Lue 133
Myrtie 133
Olive 132
Oswell P. 342
Ralph Monroe 16
Ruby 132
Sarah E. 324
T. L. 132
Thomas D. 45
Thomas Taylor 15
Thomas Wiley 197
W. Earl 197
W. H. 132
W. T. 132

COOPER continued
Willie Mae 317

CORBITT
Samuel B. 128

CORY
J. M. 133

COTRELL
A. R. 215

COTTON
Gibb Leroy 136
Theodosia 136

COUCH
Angie Marie 215
Esbon 33
Lettie Bales 303

COUNCIL
Willie S. 151

COWART
George E. 215
Tommie M. 215

COWLES
C. M. 215

COX
Bennie Arthur 303
Eleanor B. 109
Frances D. 118
John Thomas 303
Luther 303
Sarah Kass Anglin 303
Walter M. 215
William F. II (Kismet) 118

COY
Hettie L. Moss 125
Thomas 125

CRABLIE
Melvin 55

CRADDOCK
Sarah 278

CRAFT
Annie 310
Colene 16
J. E. 16
S. A. 16
William M. 152

CRAIG
Ernest E. 82
Guy William 82
Myrtie W. 118
Reba Vernell 151

CRANE
Alvin Thomas 136

CRAWFORD
J. Ben 215
Janie Lou 215
Joseph B. 215
Mary Lena 215
W. D. 67

CRENSHAW
Howard 119

CRIMMINS
Mary P. 152

CRISLER
Addison 55
Elizabeth 125
J. S. 125
Jeptha 125

CROCKER
Alan D. 216
Charles C. "Doc" 215
Clora 216
Clora Duckett 216
Curtis C. 216
Darald J. 216
Ethel M. 216
Fred J. 215
Guy G. 215
Hazel Jenett 216
Herman Young 216
J. P. 216
Mary Joe 216
Neadie R. 215
W. E. 216

CROCKER continued
William E. 216
Winett Elizabeth 216

CRONIC
Anna Mae 262
Arah L. 262
Billy M. 262
David Eli 262
Elvira 263
F. Maier 262
Frankie Lynn 262
J. Allen 262
Jane 306
Jasper P. 263
Jesse A. 262
John A. 306
John H. 262
Josie S. 262
June 306
Lewis V. 262
Mattie Lee 262
Minnie H. 262
Odom F. 263
Russell 306
S. H. 306
Simeon H. 306
W. B. 262
Warren W. 263
William R. 306
William R. 306
Worley 263

CRONIE
Joan Lavery 45

CROOK
Belle W. 109
Carrie M. 109
Comer A. 109
Earl Whelchel 109
Etta E. 183
G. W. 109
Hattie Tolbert 109
Henry 109
J. A. 109
James A. 109
Jeanette 109
John R. 109
Mary E. 109
Mary Evelyn 109

CROOK continued
Mattie L. 109
Pauline 109
Riley D. Sr. 109
Teddie Lee 109

CROSS
Elizabeth S. 198
Ethel 198

CROW
Alice Vinson 216
Annie L. 291
E. B. Jr. 216
Ernest Bartow 216
Fannie Elizabeth 317
J. N. 291
John H. 216
Mary Janice 216
W. H. 317

CROWE
Asbury Stephen 216
Emma Dalton 216
H. Luther 216
Napper 152
Ora 276
Thelma 276
W. 276
W. H. 276

CRUCE
Alvin 183
Charlie M. 3
Clarence C. 3
Dovie E. Roberts 183
J. M. 183
J. W. (Bose) 183
Jewell R. 183
John W. P. 16
Mattie A. Batchelor 183
Myrtice S. 16
Patrica Ann 3
Paul H. 183
Polly 183
Sam M. 183
Vesta F. 3
W. T. 183

CRUMLEY
D. Hershel 216
Dickie C. 152
Esco 152
Oeda B. 216

CULBERSON
Edgar 152
Mattie Sears 152
R. M. 152
Susan S. 152

CULPEPPER
Claude E. 109
Grace J. 109

CUNNINGHAM
Ansel 152

DADISON
Bessie (Dadisman) 152
Darlene (Dadisman) 152

DADISMAN
Doris Josephine 152
Howard D. 152
L. M. 152
S. E. 152
Stiles W. 152

DAILEY
E. S. 276
Eula Coleman 276
N. E. 276
Nesby Edgar 276
Tatum L. 119
Thelma 276

DAKES
L. A. 16
Marshal B. 16
W. 16

DAILEY
Filmore 303
H. J. 303
James F. 303
Palestine B. 303

DALE
Ann Phillips 216
Bobby 109
Eugenia H. 216
Harry Coil 216
John M. 216
Lena Ruth 216
Phillip 109
S. G. 216
Samuel G. 216
William A. 216

DALTON
Francis 268
Icie 216
Imojan 268
J. T. 216
L. N. 268
L. Nands 268
Leonard 268
Lola B. 67
Loy 216
Lula H. 268
M. C. 216
R. Ernester 268
S. J. 216
Vicky 152

DAMMONS
Claude Jr. 100
Geo. 100

DAMON
Patricia 328

DAMONS
Goldie 100

DAMOTH
Frank 109
Jessie B. 109

DAMRON
C. M. 289
Charley A. 342
Edward C. 289
Harriet 289
Mattie 289
Minty Ann 342
Shirley Eleen 289
Uriah 289

DANIEL
Artimisa V. 183
Bonnie Montine 67
Charley B. 68
Claude Y. 153
Emma J. Carter 152
Eulas 17
Fay E. 152
Floria 103
Forrest C. 67
George 103
Hoke L. 82
J. F. 291
J. Foster 291
J. T. 109
Lam H. 67
Lula Brown 109
Mamie L. 67
Nettie C. 291
P. A. 67
Roy C. 67
Russell 68
Sarah 109
Venie H. 67

DANIELS
Harlan H. 217
Mildred Mill 217

DARNALL
J. C. 268
Leila 268
Minnie L. 82
Nalda 82
S. J. 82
Tom B. 82
William W. 268

DARBY
James W. 3
Sallie Nowell 3

DARLEY
Alma S. 153
Harvey J. 153

DARNELL
D. E. 128
Felton Jay 128
G. A. 128

DAVENPORT
A. J. 133
Asbury J. 133
James W. 133
Joseph Archer 153
Martha J. 133
Mary J. Moore 133
Montine 133

DAVES
Charles J. 217
Priscilla Wofford 217

DAVIDSON
A. J. 128
Charlie Lee 128
Cora 128
J. Hosea 128
Ophelia 128
Russel Resine 128

DAVIS
Bertha P. 217
C. L. 183
Charles E. 83
Charles Edward 82
Chester A. 17
Cloub B. 153
Demaris Thurmond 68
Emma Mae M. 82
Emmie Ima 119
Ephraim 59
Esther 17
Flora B. 17
H. 183
Henry W. 153
J. Carlton 217
J. M. 17
J. Manley 17
J. Marion 17
Jane 183
Jenie H. 17
Joe Artis 17
John H. 17
John Henry 198
Joseph E. 17
L. M. 59
Lillian Lorene 217
Luther L. 217
Martha 17

DAVIS continued
Martha P. 59
Mary 17
Mary E. 153
Mary F. 17
Mary S. 17
Minnie Bell 17
Ola Pethel 198
Omer F. 17
Pink 17
S. A. 183
Thomas P. 337
Verne Luther 217
W. C. 59
W. Lyndal 17
W. Potts 217
W. T. 183
Zopporah H. 337
Sarah J. 268
Lou B. 263
John W. 263

DAVISON
Caroline 59

DAVISS
Glen 137

DAY
Curtis L. 153
Edward 109
G. T. 198
James R. 153
Margret G. 198
Robert Harold Jr. 153
Susan A. 109

DEADWYLER
Albert Bartow 217
Almeda J. Thurmond 217
Betty 68
Clyde 217
Cornelia C. Montgomery 217
Dora Carson 217
H. C. 68
Harriet A. 217
Harriet A. Wilhite 217
J. P. 217
John H. 279
Joseph P. 217
Josephine 279

DEADWYLER continued
Kyle T. 217
Lewis 279
Mamie E. 279
Theressa Miller 217
V. H. 217
Valentine H. 217
Willam T. 217
William V. 217

DEATON
Amelia Emmett 17
Desa 17
E. N. 17

DEAVORS
W. C. Rev. 68

DEAVOURS
Grady Hardy 291
J. Frances 342
William H. 342

DEE
A. C. 115

DE LA PIERRIERE
Angel A. Dr. 17
Bertrice Phillips 3
Edward Lee 17
Green Herschel Dr. 3
Herman Preston 3
Homer Clarence 3
Marie Belle 3
Mary Ann Smith 3
Otis Leon 3
W. P. Dr. 3
William 3
William Preston Dr. 3

DELL
Byrum C. 217

DELLINGER
Cora J. Parham 332
Jessie Lee 332
Nancy Lowe 332

DENNIS
J. 314
Karen D. 68

DENNIS continued
Marie A. 314
Sharon D. 68

DERRICOTTE
William 296

DICKSON
Dollie 153
Eliza 153
Hattie Potts 153
J. C. 153
Jeptha 153
Mary Elizabeth 153
Miss Ella 153
Taylor Jr. 153
W. W. 153

DIE
Willie 310

DILL
E. C. 217
Hilda 217
Seaborn E. 217
Wilburn 217

DILLARD
John Hansel 97

DILLS
Clyde W. 119
Fannie L. 217
John S. 217

DIXON
Loyle G. 217
R. Hubard 268
Ellie H. 268

DIAL
C. I. 33
Joseph S. 33
Lucy V. 33
Margaret 33
Nancy F. Archer 33
Sarah Lucille 33
W. M. 33

DICKERSON
A. J. 183
Mildred 184
Molly C. 184
William A. 183

DOCKERY
Elmer 332
J. W. 332

DODD
Johnie A. 34
M. N. 34
M. W. 34
Maedy M. 268
Marcus M. 34
Mary Mote 83
Nora N. 34

DONAHOO
May Sims 83
Doss P. 83
Wife of D.P. 83
R. B. 83

DOOLEY
Fred Leslie 298
J. C. 153
James Clifton 153
Martha Jane 153
Mattie J. 153
Pauline J. 298
Wilborn Cantrell 153

DOSS
Charles Jackson 83
Claude W. 83
George M. 83
India E. 83
Minnie 83
Thomas M. 83

DOSTER
Allen 97
Allen C. 184
B. F. 97
Bart 45
Birt 97
C. T. 97
Clyde 45
D. L. 97

DOSTER continued
David L. 4546
Dea 184
Dwight Raymond 184
E. T. 97
Eli F. 46
Essie B. 46
Evie S. 97
Fannie 97
Gladys 184
H. C. 97
H. J. 97
Henry Albert 45
Homer B. 97
Ida K. 45
J. A. Dr. 97
J. A. 45
J. F. 97,98
J. K. 98
James 97
James J. 46
James R. 184
John E. 184
John L. 45
Judge T. J. (Thomas J.) 153
Julia Dot 184
L. F. 97,98
Lona M. 97
Lucy Allen 184
Lula F. Roberts 97
Luther 97
Luther P. 97
Marcus J. 184
Mary 97
Mary E.45
Mattie D. 153
Melvie 45
N. C. 97
Nance 184
Nancy S. 184
Neta C. 45,46
Prudence Moore 97
R. 97
R. Frank 46
Rayfield 97
Raymon R. 184
Rhoda P. 97
Rosela Jane 97
T. J. 97
Virginia 97
W. B. 184

DOSTER continued
W. P. 98
William H. F. 46
William P. 45

DOTTERY
John W. 291

DOUGLASS
Thomas S. 59

DOWDY
Carl 68
Charlie 281
Dwayne D. Sr. 218
Effie 310
Estelle W. 218
F. D. 281
F. M. 281
F. W. M. 281
Fritz 68
Hosea 310
J. D. 68
James D. 69
Julia C. 310
Julia Denegan 68
M. L. 281
Mary E. 281
Mary Lou 68
Mattie 281
N. E. 310
Paul 281
R. J. 68
R. M. 281
Robert M. 281
Thelma 68
Thomas R. 59

DRAKE
Frank S. 68
Margaret M. 68

DUCK
Annie 18
Annie Kathleen 17
Bertie W. 17
Branton J. 18
Esther Allene 17
Evelyn 17
L. Gordon 17
Mae Cruce 17

DUCK continued
Margaret 18
W. Branson 17
W. J. Rev. 18

DUCKETT
Pearl C. 218
William D. 218

DUKE
B. F. 154
Billie 154
C. D. (Deck) 34
David H. Sr. 154
Dewey 100
Eliza G. 154
Fannie J. 34
Hattie Daggett 154
James Arthur 100
Matthew 329
Pross 329
Vannie 154
Will Henry 154
William Ralph 154

DUKES
C. S. 329
Lula V. 329

DUNAGAN
Ada S. 298
Ezekiel J. 298

DUNCAN
A. O. 268
Ammon M. 133
Anderson E. 18
Asler 133
Bessie 18
Columbus A. 218
E. 68
E. M. 18
Edwin 263
Ella Roberts 263
Elvin 263
Emory S. 263
H. H. 133
Henry H. 218
J. R. 68
J. Trammel 133
Jesse 68

DUNCAN continued
John L. 276
L. F. 18
L. G. 18
Lena Belle 18
Mary F. 18
Mary Frances 218
Mary M. 18
Matilda 18
Mattie E. Martin 68
Minnie B. 218
Minnie Lee 154
Naomie 133
Ola 18
Olen 218
Olivia Power 218
S. B. 133
Sarah 18
Tom 133
Walter 68
William H. 154
Zeb 18

DUNAGIN
Carl E. 326

DUNIGAP
A. L. 318
Jessie 318

DUNNAHOO
Eva H. 83
J. G. 83
J. H. 83
Jimmie 83
John G. 83
John J. 83
Lucy W. 83
M. L. 83
Marshall K. 83
Martha Jane Lemaster 83
Newt B. 83
Sallie M. 83
Sam E. 83
Thomas N. 83

DUNSON
Eula E. 218
George W. 268
J. Owen 218
L. J. 218

DUNSON continued
Lamontine Odell 218
M. R. 218
Sallie Rogers 218

DUPREE
George 279

DURHAM
Alma U. 314
Bonner M. 218
Columbus 314
Columbus A. 218
Grace S. 218

DURST
Florence Jackson (Dolly) 218
Fred E. 218

DYE
Beth Bennett 154
Coleman 311
Jesse L. 311

DYER
Barbara Lee 218
J. P. 218

EARHART
L. C. 59

EBERHART
Clyde 69

ECHOLS
Ella E. 154
H. U. Rev. 154
J. S. 154
Mamie R. 154

ECKLES
Cecilia 218
Coleman 218
Elizabeth Clay 83
Ellie Carter 69
H. 218
Henry C. 218
Joel Henry 218
John Douglas 69
John Foster 69
John W. D. 83

ECKLES continued
Martha Clevia Shankle 218
Mary Ann 83
R. A. 219
William F. 218

EDGE
Ava 18
Bartow T. 18
Catherine Ann 18
Cathrine Mc. 18
J. C. 18

EDINS
Alice L. 119
Charlie L. 119

EDMONDS
Florence S. 314

EDWARDS
A.E. 219
Arthur E. 219
Austine 137
D. F. 137
Durward R. 184
Easterly C. 219
Edna W. 83
Ernest G. 83
Eutaw B. 184
Fannie Parker 137
Farris 219
Frank Rudolph 219
George H. 119
Guy Norman 184
Hattie Hix 219
Henry Alvan 137
J. N. 137
J. P. 184
J. R. 184
J. Y. 137
James N. 125
James T. 125
James V. 137
John E. 219
Jonathan Lee 137
L. D. E. 137
Laurie 137
M. A. 184
M. J. 184
Maggie E. 125

EDWARDS continued
Mark A. 184
Mary E. 125
Mary J. 184
Mary M. 184
Mary N. 184
Mollie E. 137
Nancy E. 98
Orlena M. 219
Ottis Short 137
Robert 98
Rosa H. 184
Ruth 219
Samuel N. 219
W. M. 184
W. V. 184
William S. 219

EIDSON
Elizabeth Owling 219
R. S. 219

EKINS
Ethel Blackwell 184

ELDER
America A. 34
Bertha Estelle 34
Beulah 34
D. O. 34
David O. 34
E. H. 34
Eddie D. 34
Elmer H. 34
Emma H. 34
Ernest E. 34
Eula M. 34
G. K. 34
George Clifford 34
George Knox 34
Hettie 34
J. Louis 34
J. Sidney 34
James C. 34
John G. Dr. 34
John L. 34
Lucy A. 34
Martha 34
May 34
Melvin C. 34
N. T. 34

ELDER continued
Nathan 34
Ola 34
Omer G. 34
Sarah E. 34
Stephen 34
Susan Kittle 34
Woodie Lee 34

ELEY
Carrie M. 318
J. P. 318

ELLIOTT
Alma Watson 219
C. M. 219
Caroline Justice 219
Samuel J. 219

ELLIS
G. W. 154

ELLINGTON
John D. 154

ELROD
A. N. 84
Blondine 84
Bonnell 318
Cranford Pierce 154
E. Nat M. 84
H. I. 318
Hoke 110
Evie A. 303
J. E. 84
Jacob Edgar 84
James Terrell 318
Jesse B. 219
Judge H. 318
Laura E. 318
Luther F. 154
Margaret E. 303
Martha 110
Mary J. Brock 84
Maud Connally 84
Pat 110
Robert H. 303
Ruth Jacks 318
Sarah M. 84
W. D. 84
William E. 84

ELROD continued
Willie G. 303

ELLEN
Morgan 84

ELSESSER
Nettie J. 268

EMBRICK
Annie M. 219
Brenda Carole 219
Fannie 219
Richard 219
Robert L. 219

EMBRY
Emma C. 219
James T. 219

EMMETT
Charlie C. 18
Curtis 133
Grover 18
J. W. 18
Lillie L. 18
Lily 133
Martha Jane M. 18
Robert Lea Sr. 18
Roselee G. 133
T. A. 113133
Uniece 133

ENGLISH
Lois M. 154
Ulysses H. 154

ERDMAR
Mary Adelaide 281

ERVIN
Gaynelle 98
J. L. 98
Jennie 98
Mandy 98

ESCOE
J. D. Jr. (Jimmy) 154
James Daniel 154

ESPY
H. 155
M. 155
Robert 155
Sarah G 155

ESTES
Eliza Jane 282
J. W. 282
James Anderson 282
Jane 282
John W. 282
Marcus C. 282
S. E. 282
Thomas G. 282

ETHRIDGE
Ira Washington 155
Thomas A. 198

EUBANKS
G. H. 137
George H. 137
J. B. 137

EVANS
A.184
Allie 220
Alvin E. 84
Andrew 184,185
Annis 84
Atha 220
Benjamin S. 84
C. Robert 326
Calr 46
Carlton H. 46
Charlie F. 184
Clarence H. 220
Curtis E. 46
David L. 46
Diamond T. 269
E. L. 84
Eliza Ann 326
Ella F. 46
Ella S. 220
Ellaease 46
Emma C. 269
Eunice D. 84
F. C. 84
F. L. 185
Fannie 184

EVANS continued
Floyd C. 84
Floyd J. 184
Garnette 220
Geneva A. 84
Genie 46
Guss A. 220
Harin O. 220
Harriett Dorota 184
Hoke S. 125
Hubert H. 46
J. T. 220
H. Monroe 269
J. W. 46
James H. 184
Joel Selman 84
John G. 184
Jutson B. 184
Laura H. 220
Lillie 220
Lucile D. 184
Lula 185
Lula J. 184
Martha 185
Martha C. 268
Mary Dasie 84
Maryleen 125
Maudie Agnes 184
Mayrelle B. 184
Mollie R. 46
N. Hattie 184
Nettie 84
Nettie J. Stark 84
Mary M. 269
O. D. 268
Pearl E. 269
Raymond 46
Roy 185, 220
Royce M. 184
Rubin O. 269
Ruby B. 220
S. A. 184
S. C. 220
Samuel Philip 220
Sarah 184
Sarah Anne 184
Thomas A. 84
Virginia P. 185
W. C. 269
Wilda 269
William T. Rev. 184

EVERETT
James C. 155

EWING
Carrie B. Barton 19
J. B. 19
J. D. 19
J. W. 19
James B. 19
James Homer 19
Joseph 19
Joseph W. 19
Joseph William 19
Martha Louise 19
Mary Sue 19
Mary Sue 19
Nancy S. 19
Noah C. 19
S. E. 19
S. I. 19
Sarah 19
T. C. 19

FARABEE
Josie Belle 220
L. B. 220
L. J. 220
Luther B. 220
M. B. 220
Mauder M. 220
Roxanna Drusilla 220
W. C. 220

FARMER
Alton Ray 281
Evie M. 286
H. C. 286
H. D. 286
Henry G. 286
J. H. 69
J. M. 220
Joe Omar 281
M. E. 286
Martha E. 286
Mary Chandler 220
Mattie 286
Oza M. 286
Rupert T. 281
Thomas 286
Willie E. 286

FARR
B. F. 155
Bert Franklin 155
Raymond 155

FAULKNER
Candler 137
Carl W. 125
Essie P. 137
Eva Lou 137
George W. 137
John L. 185
John P. 220
Julie H. 137
Lizzie Oliver 137
Mary Alice 220
Mary P. 137
Minerva Jane 137
Pat S. 137
Rebecca O. 185
S. P. 137
William J. 137

FEAGINS
Dollie B. 185

FERGUSON
Bell B. 155
Callie M. 155
Charles L. 84
Dow W. 155
Gussie C. 84
Lillie Mae 119
Louisa 155
Nelson 155
William P. 119

FIELDS
Carrie 185
Columbia 98
Cora 198
E. C. 291
Ella 198
Emma 318
Emma Ophelia 291
Emma R. 46
Gladys F. 291
Harry L. 291
Herman T. 286
Indianna 46

FIELDS continued
J. A. 198
J. T. 98
J. W. 318
James M. 46
Jennie 291
John F. 291
Joseph E. 291
Linnie 98
Lonnie 291
Lula 291
Mandy F. 98
Ollie E. 46
Precilla 291
Robert O. 291
Ruby 291
Thomas 198
Thomas J. 291
W. W. 98

FIEVET
M. E. 35

FILE
A. J. 318
George W. 318
Nancy Gamlin 318
Solomon 318

FILLINGIM
Lonnie F. 220
Mary W. Eckles 220

FINCH
Alma V. 35
Annie H. 318
Charles S. 318
Corine Shields 35
Hoke S. 35
John F. 220.
Laura E. 220
Roy C. 318
Susie W. 318
Thomas A. 35
William G. 220
William Turner 220
Willie B. 300

FINTE
Carl Griffin 35

FITE
A. J. 318
Alice Armstrong 318
George Henry 155
H. S. 35
Henry Solomon 35
Willie M. 318

FITZGERALD
C. W. 287
Wayne 287

FLANIGAN
Allan J. 155
Allen M. 313
Effie 313
Eva M. 155
Susan M. 313

FLEEMAN
Addie May 276
B. F. 318
C. S. 276
Charles Edward 276
Charlie S. 276
Cora Sell 310
David 155
Denine 155
Dora 276
Eliza A. 155
Gail Pritchett 155
Lucile 318
Mamie 318
Mattie 276
Nezzie Eliza 276
Pauline 276
Tami 155
Timothy 155
Timothy David 155
W. H. 276

FLEMING
C. L. 332
D. Jewell 332
Ellen M. 137
Giles L. 332
Homer H. 137
Johnnie E. 332
Mabel 137
Sara F. 332
Sara Monica 291

FLEMING continued
Sarah Mitchell 84
Thomas M. 137
Vannah E. 137
William Adcas 332

FORD
Jane Anita 279
W. Cosby 119

FORRESTER
Flora 3
George 133
Guy 133
M. J. 3
Pearlie L. 133
R. L. 3

FORTNER
Louisa 54
Pink 46

FOSTER
Fannie S. 315
Jimmey D. Wight B. 128
Mamie Johnson 155
Roy C. 315

FOWLER
Paul B. 221
Clifford W. 332
J. C. 332
Lizzie B. 287
Lucy 98
Nettie F. 332
Roy 332
Ruby M. 221
Ward Timothy 221
William H. 287
Willis F. 332

FOX
Elizabeth 291

FRADY
Laura Hart 221

FREDERICK
George W. 221

FREE
Mary Brown 46

FREEMAN
A. Luther 35
A. 35
Ada 35
Alba 35
Alice 35
Bertha 35
Charles 35
Charles V. 36
Cynthia S. 35
Earley 35
Earley P. 35
Eliza A. 156
Emory 35
Ethel Mae 263
Ethel Mae W. 263
Eueric 263
Harriett E. 110
Hilda Grace 110
J. B. 35263
J. H. 110
J. L. 110
J. O. 35
J. S. 69
James Bascom 263
John H. 110
John R. 35
Julius O. 35
L. J. 35
Laura 35
Louisa N. 36
Louisa Neal 35
Loyce 263
Lula Bell 263
Lula P. 35
Luther C. 35
Mell 36
Mollie 35
Mozelle L. 35
N. E. 110
Nettie 35
Nettie H. 35
Ralph Dr. 3
Ruby Hanson 35
Ruby M. 35
Rufred 110
Sadie Dell 35
Susan 69

FREEMAN continued
T. A. 263
Thomas A. 263
W. Donald Sgt. 35
William 35
Henry Harrison 292
James Frances 292
Bonie Viola 277
Mamie 277

FRICKS
Clara Adel 3
James Marius 3
Robert Lee 3

FROST
A. A. 156
Alice Guest 156
Emory Carter 337
M. A. 337
Ruby E. 156
W. P. 337
William Clifford 337
William P. 156

FULCHER
Emily Lula Wright 319
G. C. 337
Ida . 319
J. F. 319
J. L. 319
J. Lillian 319
Jodie F. 319
John B. 337
Leb 319
Maggie 319
Marg L. 337
Pearl 337
Roy S. 319
Susie W. 319

FULLER
Dock J. 332
Lilly May 332
Malissa R. 332
Thomas S. 332

GABLE
C. E. (Bit) 19
E. M. 19
Emma 315

GABLE continued
J. L. 315
J. R. 19
Nettie A. 263
Russell G. 19

GADDIS
Fred A. 19
Nancy Wilbanks 125
Pearlie Mae Rider 198
Sallie 198

GAILEY
Claude H. 137
Hattie L. 138
Jeannette 137
John T. 137
Kittie V. 137
L. A. 69
L. T. 137
Nettie 137
Othel G. 138
W. D. 137
W. Jackson 137
William P. 137
Woodie M. 137

GAINES
Frances 311
Willie Mae 103

GARDNER
George 340

GARLEN
Jack M. 119

GARNER
J. Frank 319
J. M. 319
Jessie F. 319
S. E. 319
Sammie 221
Sarah B. 310
Thomas 221
Thomas A. 319
Thomas O. 319
Tony N. 221

GARRETT
Alexander 84
Bessie W. 59
Cora B. 84
Curtis Lawson 110
Eunice Simmons 185
G. D. 319
Gordon E. 84
Grand D. 46
J. Henry 84
J. L. 319
James A. 59
Jewel Allen 319
Jewel G. 319
Jud Stephens 46
Laura P. 59
Louis G. 59
Lucy D. 110
Mary Elizabeth 46
Methal L. 110
Millie 319
Millie V. 46
Virgil 59

GARRISON
Allene E. 119
Harwell Lee 119
Hilda M. 85
James E. 119
Mary J. 85
Robert E. (Bobby) 119
Samuel R. Rev. 185
Sara Walton 292
T. C. 84
T. W. 85
Thalma Pink 85
Thomas W. 84
William Don 221

GARRINGTON
M. G. 292
Mary 292

GARWELL
Jim 311

GARY
Annie M. Gary 286
Annie Maude 287
J. C. 286

GARY continued
John C. 287
Viola Maud 286

GASAWAY
J. C. 319
Johnnie 319
Lizzie R319
M. E. 319
Sumler Jewel 319

GATES
Betty 279
Charley 279

GEARIN
Louise F. 185
R. Boyd 185

GEE
A. J. Sr. 199
Berdie Pethel 198
Bonnie Fay 199
Bonnie Lou 199
Buddy Jr. 199
Callie 199
E. L. 198
Elizabeth 198
Frank 198
George W. 198
Golda Braskalou 198
Harold L. 198
Herman Dannel 85
J. H. 198
J. M. 198
Joe Lee 199
Lillie R. 198
Lollie 198
M. R. 198
M. T. 198
Myrtie M. 198
Nancy L. 198
Pam 198
W. F. 198
W. H. 199

GEORGE
Mattie E. 19
W. J. 19

GIBSON
Artemus G. 342
Cora A. 156
Duke 156
Lonnie 221
Mary 292
Mary D. 342
Nancy Garrison 221
Paul G. 342

GIDDENS
Esther 85
H. C. 85

GILBERT
Farris C. 156

GILLESPIE
Charles Ridley M. D. 11
Charles William III 221
Charles W. 221

GILLILAND
Canzadie 263
Corrie M. 263
Ethel 263
Gladis 263
Jesse M. 263
L. S. 263
Lake O. 263
Loy 263
Marie 263
Martha Brock 263
Minnie A. 263
Ola Mae 263

GILMAN
Mildred P. 221

GILMER
Woodie 101

GILMORE
Milton Johnson 264

GILSTRAP
Addie T. 156
E. Willie 156

GINN
Alfred T. 337
Elizie May 319
Emma 319
J. R. 319

GIPSON
Verner W. 119
Dona H. 119

GITTENS
Pearl P. 326
Adolphus 326
Minnie 326

GLAZE
Connie B. 47
Grady G. 47
M. Florence 47

GLAZNER
Kathleen Sharp 221

GLENN
Amanda A. 59
Andrew D. 59
Buford 59
J. H. 156
J. M. 128,156
Mattie Venable 69
Perry 128
S. N. 128,156
Talmade 69
William R. Sr. 69

GLOSSON
Lounita 69
Roy Homer 69
Temple 69
W. F. 69

GOBER
Allie S. 222
Amanda Owen 221
Claris 222
Clarrisa 222.
Delona 222
Eulah 222
Fletcher Estell 156
Fletcher Sanford 156
Frances Jane Bell 156

GOBER continued
Gertrude Glosson 221
G. W. 292
H. D. 221
Henry Jackson 156
James Thomas 221
John M. 222
Levi H. 222
Lora I. 222
Maggie 221
Marcus 156
Marvin 222
R. B. 221
S. D. 292
Thomas H. 221
Vira E. 138
W. Alden 221
W. J. 222
William J. 222
Willie 221

GODFREY
A. B. 103
John 281
John H. 281
Mattie I. 281

GOLIA
James C. 36

GOOCH
Arvey 47
C. E. 47
Carl S. 47
Desma 47
Estell H. 47
Ethel 47
Fred 47
J. H. 47
James Douglas 47
John Allen 47
Maynard 47

GOODIN
Annie Belle Hudson 222
C. A. 222

GORDON
Jerry Eugene 332
May 300
Thomas L. Jr. 332

GOSITT
Bud 222

GOSS
Elizabeth Ann 222
Florence 315
Jessie Helen 222
L. P. 222
Louise Parolee 222
Luther 279
Patricia Faye 279
Virginia 279
W. J. 222
William Judson 222
William Robert 222

GRACE
Bonnie C. 47

GREEN
Beulah Peeler 222
Daisey P. 222
Grace 222
J. F. 3
James R. 222
Martha Rebecca 3
Paul J. 222
Roy 222
Samuel M. 329
W. E. 222

GREER
A. L. 110
A. O. 110
Bessie E. 110
H. M. 110
S. L. 110

GREGORY
A. W. 185
C. D. 185
Charles D. 185
Elizabeth 185
G. D. 185
Grover C. 185
Harley 222
J. L. 319
John L. 319
Louise M. 185
M. E. 185

GREGORY continued
Martha Jane 185
Myrtle 319
S. E. 319
Sudie R. 319
Susie C. 138

GRESHAM
Dearon G. 340
Sylvia E. Dolan 340

GRIFFETH
A. O. 110
Amanda Hitchcock 85
Ann O. 110
Emma L. 110
Eula A. 110
J. W. 110
John 85
John W. 110
Julia 85
Maud 110
William 85
William B. 110

GRIER
Birt 20
Charlie J. 20
Cleve 156
Gordon Lee 156
Hattie 185
Hoke Smith 20
Jessie 185
Joseph 20
Laura 156
Mary I. 20
Nita Alline 69
Richard 185
W. H. 69

GRIFFIN
Alma M. 36
Claude Jr. 47
Edith L. 36
Elmer J. 120
G. W. 36
George Washington 36
I. W. 138
Inus Edmond 36
James L. 36
Lucy E. 36

GRIFFIN continued
N. D. 36
N. O. 36
Nancy Davis Elder 36
Patsy 156
Sara Ann 157
Wiley 311

GRIMES
Gabriel W. 69
Mae Omie 69

GRINDLE
Emma Mae Echols 157
Liley Mae 157
Roy John 157
Shirley Jean 157
Troy Lee 157

GRIZZLE
Lewis H. Jr. 157

GRUCE
Elijah M. 186
Jensie P. 186
Jessie L. 186
M. B. 186
M. M. 186
Myrtle Muhulda 186
N. B. 186
Ophelia 186
Peter 186
William J. 186

GUEST
Alice F. 337
C. B. 222
C. T. 222
Dellar W. 222
Dossie 222
E. H. 222
Ida Cleo 222
Ira 222
Lettie Jane 222
Nealie 222
S. M. 337
T. R. 337
Thomas 222
W. O. 222

GUNNELLS
Ella Montgomery 157

GUNNIN
A.L. 307
Arthur Jr. 307
G. E. 307
Georgia Ann R. 55
J. J. 55
J. L. M. 307
Lizzie Ophelia 307
M. F. 307
M. R. 307
Walker Edwin 307

GURLEY
Walter M. 223

GULLY
Lou C. 223

GUNNELS
Cora 223
J. H. 223

GUNTER
Annette E. 186
Billy J. 186
Brenda Carol 186
Eliza 69
Het Carson 223
J. E. 186
L. C. 69
Lester 186
Levi C. 69.
Martha 186
Wooda 69

HACKETT
R. Jack 47

HAGGARD
Annie C. 223
Arthur 223
E. S. A. 223
Genie 223
J. B. 223
Oscar J. 223
Rosa 223
Vernen 223
W. L. 223

HAINES
Elizabeth 133
Ella 133
Joseph B. 133
Joseph Burton 133
M. P. 133
Matthew 133
S. P. 133
Sarah 133

HALE
Alice 333
Allen 333
Elmer W. 157
Emory 329
George Glenn 333
Hoyt 333
Jack 333

HAMMOND
Elmer M. 320

HALL
Augustus G. 134
Bartow 186
Boston 223
Clifton E. 125
David 186
E. A. 125
Edna L. 125
Eliza Ann 125
Henry H. 199
James 36
Julia D. 157
L. C. 157
Mildred H. 315
Pauline D. 199
Ricky G. 47
Ruth 186
W. J. 125
Wilburn J. 315
William B. 186

HAMAKER
Frank 223
John 223
Katherine 223

HAMBRICK
Charles E. 120

HAMILTON
Royce 47

HAMMOND
Alvin Bryant 47
Delia 36
E. E. 269
Edwin E. 269
Franklin 269
James A. 36
L. 36
Lenora B. Wilson 269

HANCOCK
Claud 157
H. H. 157
Harold 157
Homer 157
Hugh Haroldson 157
Jack 223
John B. 157
Mary O. 157
R. J. 157
S. A. 157
Sarah Annie 157
Thomas Donald 157

HANLEY
John P. 223
Tammy Darlene 120

HANSON
Ada W. 157
Alia S. 157
David W. 157
J. Calvin 157
Kathryn R. 157
Lammoth Joe 103

HARDEN
Ada Pruitt 224
Joseph E. 224
Lawrence G. 224
Mary Adair 224
Mildred Barber 224
T. Colquitt Jr. 224
Thomas Colquitt 224
W. T. 224
William Preston II M. D. 224

HARBER
Homer R. 224
L. A. Jan 224
Lucy Henley 224
Lucy W. 224
Mittie Wright 224
W. T. 224
William Y. 223
William Y. 224

HARBIN
Robert Jr. 326
William Terry 326

HARDMAN
Elic Jackson 224
Emma Griffin 224
Ida Murrah Shankle 224
John Barnett 224
L. G. 224
Lamartine Griffin 224
Leona Wright Nelms 224
Nancy Trotter 224
Nora O'Neal 224
R. Clayton 224
R. L. 224
Van Payne 224
W. B. 224
W. B. M. D. 224

HARDY
A. Smith 224
Ada Q. 158
Albert M. 85
Albert Sidney Sr. 292
Alton 85
Anna N. 224
Annie S. 342
Artimus G. 292
Azzalee 307
Blanche C. 85
C. D. 158
C. Edward 158
C.H. 85
Charles F. 292
Charles H. 85
Clifford J. 224
Clifford W. 307
Clyde B. 158
Edward M. 292
Emma A. 342

HARDY continued
Ethel A. 307
F. M. 199
Fannie Dottery 292
Fannie E. 85
Fred J. 342
Harry P. 292
Henry J. 85
Hoke S. 342
Ida L. 199
J. Hubert 70
J. W. 292
J. W. Jr. 292
J. W. Sr. 292
James H. Moore 292
John G. 292
John W. 158
Joseph H. 292
Joseph W. Jr. 292
Julia A. Kenney 292
Julia B. 292
Laura C. 70
Laura Merritt 158
Lois B. 342
Lulah A. 292
M. A. 199
Lester Rufus 307
M. G. 292
Mamie E. 292
Martha S. Lee 303
Mary Ann 59
Mary Jane 292
N. C. 303
Nancy C. 292
Rosa M. 85
Ruby 85
S. E. 292
S. H. 292,303,342
S. W. 292
Samuel H. 292.
Samuel W. 292
Sarah E. 307
Spratlin William H. 158
Susan M. 292
William (Doe) 307

HARGNEWOOD
B. S. 224
Willie B. 224

HARGRAVE
Evelyn S. 158

HARMON
Francis C. 225

HARRIS
A. J. 225
A.F. 70
Abb Dorsey 225
Andrew J. 225
Chris C. 70
Clara P. 70
Emma Elizabeth 225
Essie Lenora 282
Frances Barber 225
Frank 329
Hoke S. 20
Hubbard Isaac 225
Ida Senora 70
Isaac Franklin 225
J. L. 70
J. R. 282
J. W. 225
James L. Jr. 70
Jane Vickie 282
Jesse N. 225
Jesse N. Jr. 225
Jesse Newton 225
John M. 70
John R. 282
Martha E. 282
Martha M. Morrison 70
Mary Cleghorn 225
N. 70
Nora 70
Pierce 120
Qullian Booth 70
Robert Lafayette 225
Robert Lafayette M. D. 225
Ruby Dunson 225
Sharon 311
Tina 225
Willie 279

HARRISON
Annie Lee 329
J. C. 158
James F. 103
John Rev. 128
Julious 20

HARRISON continued
Louisa 158
Margaret 128
Marion Barber 225
Mary Eliza 158
Mary Evelyn Roberts 103
Mary Frances 225
Sarah A. 158
T. P. 158
W. D. 287
William W. 225

HARTSFIELD
Ethel Stockton 158
Jesse 158

HARTLEY
Annie B. 225
Joe 20
William D. 225

HARVIE
Claud N. 85
Ethel 85

HARWELL
Clarnie 186
J. H. 186

HAULBROOK
G. F. 225
George Frank Jr. 225
Lovie 225

HAWKES
Ellis 281

HAWKINS
Annie G. 59
Athea Vernon Christian 59
Charles A. 59
Charles W. 333
Emma 158
Fred 158
J. B. A. 110
J. M. 59
James B. 48
John Milner 59
M. E. 110
Martha Elaine 158
Mary W. 48

HAWKINS continued
Mattie 48
Mattie L. 85
R. A. 199
Ruth M. 158
Susie E. 110
Thomas I. 59

HAWKS
Albert W. 225
C. E. 225
Cynthia Buckett 225
Eldridge 225
Floyd 225
H. Cal 225
Jessie M. 225
Obie 225
R. H. 225
Robert H. 225
Sarah Ruth 3

HAYES
A.L. 199
Aaron 315
Ada 320
Alvin 315
B. W. 320
Belah W. 60
Bell 199
Belle 315
D. C. 199
Dan I. 20
Dora 320
E. L. 320
Edmond Wiley 186
Emma 311
Florence 320
J. M. 199
Henry M. 307
James 320
James W. 199
Jane Boyd 60
Janice Lynn 327
Luther Glenn 199
M. Elie 337
Mamie 186
Martha H. 4
Mary 320
Mary R. 158
Master James Brent 327
Mattie E. 307

HAYES continued
Maybell S. 20
N. F. 98
Odessa 320
Olin H. 60
Omie 320
P. N. 199
Phoney C. 337
Robert H. 226
S. L. 320
Sarah Jean 327
Sarah Wilmer 320
T. B. (Toof) 98
Thedosia 199
Tommie 199
W. R. 320
W. W. 320
Wiley 186

HAYNES
Adam C. 311
Bailey 311
Claudee E. 226
Eliza 311
Emory Lee 226
Ernest 226
Etta 226
Ettie 226
Ettie C. 226
L. M. 226
Martha Ann 226
Mary P. 226
Mildred 226
R. L. 226
Robert 31
Robert L. 226

HAYNIE
C. G. 281
K. G. 281

HAYS
D. E. 48
T. B. 48

HAYWOOD
James H. 300

HEAD
A.M. 85
Arthur M. 85
Bernice 226
Bertha 199
Dessie Wilhite 85
Elizabeth Highfield 85
Ella Rogers 85
Emma Porter 85
G. W. 226
Hautelle 85
J. C. 85
L. J. 199
Lee 226
Lon J. 333
Mary L. 333
Minnie Lee 226
Naomi 4
Robert H. 4
Susan 226
W. C. 85
W. F. 85

HEALAN
A. L. 186
Annie Myrtle 186
Arminda L. 186
Arminda Missouri 186
C. F. 186
C. F. (Lum) 186
Curtis W. 186
Donald Devins 48
Dovie S. 48
H. William 48
H. William 48
J. F. 186
J. L. 186
J. M. 320
J. W. 186
J. Wilburn 186
James Hume 186
Joseph F. 186
Little Billy 48
Mary E. 186
Royce 48
Tyson D. 320

HEARN
Elizabeth G. 36
J. J. 36
M. L. 36

HEARN continued
Mary Lena 36

HECTOR
Jessie 279
Julia Thomas 79
Westley 279
William T. 279

HENDERSON
Lizzie 98
M. G. 320
Marrion 98
Mollie Jane 320
Ulysses S. 120

HENDRICK
Asa C. 138
John H. 138
Nancy B. 138

HENDRICKS
Edna 138
Elizabeth Harp 138
Howard 138
Ida W. 138
John J. Sr. 110
Mae Standridge 138
W. J. 138
William J. 138

HENDRIX
Earnest T. 110
G. T. 70
Gordon T. 70
J. J. 110,115
M. M. 110,115
Minnie 115
Roy 110

HENRY
A. L. 269
Amanda C. 269
Andrew Lafayette 269
Annie Dell 158
C. B. 158
Cleta A. 226
Eliza A. Keith 269
Fannie E. 226
James R. 269
Johnnie P. 269

HENRY continued
Joseph Patrick 269
Katie Lucile 158
Lovic B. 226
Permelia 269
W. Milton 269

HENSLEY
Allie 226
Ray 226

HERBERT
James E. 226
Vera B. 226

HERRING
Hoyt 226

HIGGINS
Angile 199
Chastine C. 199
Lacy 199
S. P. Rev. 199

HIGHFILL
Clara May 111
Claud 111
Frank 111
Harold 111
J. N. 111
J. T. 111
James Thornton 111
John F. 86
John F. 86
Mahala 111
Martha A. 86
Nancy 86
Nancy 86
Nancy Jane 111
Neva 111

HIGHTOWER
Beulah 227
Charles W. 227
Henry Linton 227
John Z. 227

HILDRETH
Walter A. 4

HILL
Anncybill 129
Annie Hugh 4
Archie F. 199
C. T. 129
Charles T. 129
Edith V. 129
Elmer T. 4
Emma 320
Frank D. 341
George 120
Henry Hoyt 129
Henry T. 320
Hugh W. 4
Jennings Bryan 129
Jewell T. 129
Lawrence Herndon 128
Lemento M. 341
M. V. 129
Maggie N. 4
Margaret E. 4
Marie 120
Minnie Viola 129
Oliver L. 120
Olivia W. 4
Ollie Belle 129
R. L. 4
Ray 300
Reba Joe 298
Robert L. 4
Tyson 4

HILLAND
Mary Frances 269

HINSON
Newton O. 36

HINES
Jesse 227

HITCHCOCK
E. T. 86
John W. 111
Martha L. 111
R. R. 111
Robert E. 111
S. L. 86
Sallie L. 111

HIX
Bertha O. 227
Grace T. 227
H. Beemon 227
I.R. 227
Jean C. 227
John F. 227
John R. 227
L. R. 227
M. L.227
Mattie R. Vandiver 227
Maurine W. 227
Raymond L. 227
Ruby J. 227

HOARD
Floyd G. 158
Harvey T. 158

HOGAN
C. A. 48
C. D. 48
D. C. 48
D. E. 48
Dora D. 48
E. M. 48
I. T. 2148
Lilla M.48
Lucy 48
Nell May 227
S. A. 21
W. E. (Dock) 48
W. T. 2148
Willie J. 48

HOGWOOD
Annie E. 227
Robert F. 227

HOLBROOK
Alice 227
Howell P. Jr. M. D. 227

HOLCOMBE
Jackson 86

HOLDER
Ada M. 159
Ben 48
Doris N. 48
Franklin Pendergrass 159

HOLDER continued
Grady Ben 48
Ina Oblevia 42
Infant Myrtle May 159
John 159
John M. 159
M. A. 42
Martha Angie 159
T. R. 42
Thomas R. 159
Thomas Rhodes 159
William W. 134

HOLEAD
Eliza Emeline 21
J. H. 21
N. B. 21

HOLLAND
Allen G. 86
Andrew Russell 20
Arch 200
Chrissey Adeline 20
Dora Davis 20
Elizabeth E. 227
Ethel C. 86
J. F. 86
J. H. 20
J. Tom 86
J. W. 20
J. William 20
James Marion 21
John H. 265
John Harvey 307
John Henry Maefield 20
Joseph Henry 20
Lillian M. Moon 20
Mary A. Hudson 20
Mary Ann 21
Mollie 20
N. D. 20
Norris R. 227
Nancy D. 86
Nolla 86
S. M. 20

HOLLIDAY
A. J. 138
A. M. 289
Alice 337
Angie Maudin 338

HOLLIDAY continued
Artimirre M. 289
Bertha Randall 138
C. P. 338
C. R. 338
C. T. 138
Charles Franklin 338
Claud E. 337
Claudia Wills 338
Crie Dell 337
Dovie Galvin 138
F. M. 289
Faye E. 138
G. W. 338
George 338
I. G. 338
Imagine G. 338
J. M. 338
John M. 337
John Martin 337
Joseph David 138
Key 337
L. W. 138
Mary Louise Strickland 338
Maude Pendergrass 159
N. E. 338
Nancy E. 337
Pauline 338
Pop 338
R. W. 337
Robert A. 159
Ruth 337
Sarah Sterling 338
Sophire 337
T. C. 159
T. G. 338
W. D. 338
W. J. 338

HOLLIFIELD
Esther M. 227

HOLMAN
Vera C. 307
David M. 307

HOOD
Addie 228
Adelia 228
Alice Owen 228
Ben 228

HOOD continued
C. J. 228
Bob L. 269
C. W. 228,269
C. Wilburn 269
Christiana Maley 228
Clement Dobbs 228
Clement Jefferson 228
Estelle 228
Eula M. 269
Eza 228
Farrer 269
Frances Suddath 228
George C. 228
Grace Goss 228
Istelle 228
J. L. 269
J. V. 269
James L. 269
James W. 269
John 228
Lewis O. 269
Luther M. 269
M. L. 269
Mattie H. 269
Melissa 228
Nettie Lorene Smith 269
Nora 228
Nora Hardman 228.
Olin Sharkle 228
Rachel M. 269
Samuel 228
V. F. 269
William Talm Sr. 228
Willie Clement 228
Woodrow 269

HOOPER
Charles F. 159

HOPE
Claude Durham 228
James Claude 228
Ollie Durham 228

HOPKINS
Addie Alma 86
C. Howard 138
D. A. 86
Hazel 311
John Clinton 138

HOPKINS continued
Kate Elder 36
L. M. 138
M. Lula 138
Mellie 138
Robert E. 36
W. D. 138
W. Dennis 138

HORGAT
Ludalia 11

HORNE
Effie N. 333

HOSCH
Agnes H. 120
Asbury Camp 4
Celestine Emma t
Elmer F. 120
Fannie Camp 4
Fannie Hosch 4
Flora 4
Fronie Harris 4
Gertrude Agnes 264
H. Omer 4
Henry Adrew 4
Henry Andrew 4
Janice Gale 187
John 4
John Henry 5
John R. 4
Lt. Henry 4
Mary 4
Mary Ann 4
Matilda 4
Mattie M. 5
Nancy 4
P. A. 264
Paul A. Sr. 4
R. A. 4
Russell Angel 4
Russell Brestone 4
Tabitha 4
Tabitha Hill 4
W. C. 187
Weldon H. 4
Ralph W. 228
Ellis 228
Russel F. 228
Mattie E. 228

HOSCH continued
Joanna 300
Ciceroe 300

HOUSE
Ionia J. 343
J. G. 70
Jessie L. 159
John C. 159
Margaret D. 70
S. J. 70
Sallie Jennings 159
Samuel S. 70
W. H. 70

HOWARD
Almedia Carruth 42
Beatrice 43
Booge 42
Frances Elizabeth 159
Frank 42
H. Thomas 42
Homer R. Capt. 42
J. Oscar 42
James Walter Sr. 43
Katie Ann 279
Lloyd E. 320
Lola Fleeman 42
Luke 31
Maebell 42
Martha E. 42
Maude L. 42
Robert Lee 42
Ruth Jeanette 43
Sallie A. 43
Wiley Chandler 159
Zack T. 43

HOWELL
Anne Randolph 159
Asa Jefferson 159
Donald 270
Elizabeth (Gilmer) 159
Frances Elizabeth 159
Glenn 159
Henry Raymond 159
Mary Belle 159
Robert S. 159
Wiley Chandler 159

HOWENSKY
Otis 228

HOWINGTON
Birdia 134
Charles P. 79
J. W. 134
John 264
Ola 187
Pearly M. 159
R. J. 187
Ralph J. 264
Sarah C. 264
Sybil E. 159

HUDGINS
Beverly Jane 264
Beverly P. 21
C. M. 5
Calena Bryan 315
Carl M. 5
Ilah Murphy 264
Maude Bridges 5
Virginia Lee 264
Wyatt Bevily 264

HUBBARD
Eudie P. 229
F. Marion 229

HUDSON
Ella 229
H. J. 229
J. A. 229
J. N. 229
J. P. 229
James P. 229.
James Thomas 229
Julius C. 229
Julius Fred 229
M. A. 229
Mattie A. 229
Minnie 187
Ormie 48
Sarah Jane 229
T. P. 229
Thomas P. 229

HUFF
Annie B. 159
George M. 320

HUFF continued
J. Herman 159
Mattie E. Howard 43

HUGHES
Arllie O. 111
John Dennis 229
John H. 229
Joseph 270
Loda Dunson 270
Mollie 111
Nellie Mae 229

HUGHEY
Howard 300
Royce 300

HULSEY
A. V. 264
Ada Virginia 264
Alma Mae 264
Dora C. 264
Estell Morgan 187
Eunice Arietta 187
J. I. 264
J. Paul Sr. 264
Jefferson I. 264
John O. 307
Lummie M. 264
N. H. 307
Nathan H. 307
R. A. 187
Ralph 264
Sabra A. 307
Thomas Wynn 264

HUMAN
Henry D. 160
Joseph Daniel 160

HUMPHREYS
Elmer 70

HUMPHRUS
J. V. 187
R. C. 187

HUNSINGER
Sherley Ann 48

HUNT
Beulah B. 60
Brother Lavater 60
C. Allie 60
Cortez O. 60
Ethyle D. 60
Etta F. 60
Eula S. 60
Janerio Toccoa 229
L. A. 70
Nelson P. 60
Opal K. 60
Rhoda Lou 60
Rhoda M. 60
Sister Inez 60
Tuc A. 60
W. J. C. 60

HUNTER
D. Glenn 125
Elizabeth Wier 160
Fannie M. 338
H. C. 160
Hubert D. 338
J. J. 264
John S. 160
Laura W. 125
Lillie 86
Martha A. 160
Minnie T. 86
Moriah H. 338
Robert J. 338
Sam William 338
Stark 338
Virginia Bell 338

HUNTSINGER
Callie Dale 160

HUTCHINS
Clara 70
D. W. 70
Ella D. 86
Ella O. 86
Emma J. 70
Ethel H. 86
Etta T. 111
George Bryan 111
M. E. H. 70
Mary E. 70
N. H. 86

HUTCHINS continued
Newton H. 111
W. W. (Bill) 70
William D. 111

HUTSON
Lizzie P. 49
Stephen 49
Stephen G. 187
William A. 49

INGRAHAM
Rufus 229

INGRAM
A. G. 229
Dora Wilson 229
E. H. 229.
Ezekiah H. Jr. 229
I. H. 229
J. W. 229
Joanne 229

IRELAND
Nancy 279

IRVIN
Alice 49
Ava 21
Charlie 21
E. A. 187
Eveline 21
George 21
J. (Nick) 49
J. F. 187
J. N. 98
J. O. 187
Lucindia 187
Lula H. 21
Marshal 21
Mattie P. 49
Rena 98
Samson 187

IRVINE
J. A. 333
S. J. 333

ISAM
Delay 21
George Thomas 21

ISAM continued
Jane Cosby 21
Sallie Johnson 21

ISBELL
B. M. 60
Daisy 60
L. B. 60
Lenton H. 60
Leon B. 60
Levis E. 60
Lou E. Shirley 60
Willie Maud 60

IVERSON
Alfred 293
Daisy 292
Frances 293
Jarvel 292

IVESTER
Katie Lou 120
W. Dennis 120

IVEY
A.J. 160
Alice Meade 160
Annie S. 120
Bannie B. 111
Beatrice 160
Betty Jean 270
Cora A. 187
E. G. 200
E. J. 160
Ella 160
George L. 21
Homer J.
Jim 160
Larry Lee 160
Loyd 187
Minnie A. 21
Pollie J. 200
Riley A. 120
Thomas C. 111
W. W. 270
Winifred Jr. 270

JACKS
C. S. 320
D. A. 340
E. L. 340

JACKS continued
Herbert P. 36
Janie 320
Lena 37
Lucy W. 37
Lunie Sheffield 37
Susie 340
Willie N. 36

JACKSON
Ada V. 70
Addie Lou 270
Albert 311
Anner B. 71
Annie Lou 71
Arthur D. 5
Beaulah 60
Bertha L. 230
C. S. 86
Candice S. 71
Carl Haynie 230
Charles Richard 21
Charlie H. 71
Claude E. 270
Edna 70
Elizabeth A. 71
Ernest W. 230
Fred 230
Gussie 70
H. S. 71
Hazie 101
Hershel 311
Horace Green 230
J. A. 111
Jesse 71
John 60
John G. 71
John William Jr. Dr. 11
Julius L. 70
Kate R. 160
Laurie 270
Leary M. 230
Lois H. 230
Lou Haynie 230
M. N. 111
Margie Wallace 86
Mary 71
Ned 71
Ned L. 111
Nellie 230
Olan 329

JACKSON continued
Robbie Evelyn 138
S. Wise 230
Savannah Christian 230
Sidney W. 230
Sterling 86
William P. 230
William Pirkle 230
Willie S. 270

JAILLETTE
Ada A. 5
Betty L. 5
Harriet C. 5
Mary E. 5

JAMES
Begar 230
Harvey A. 230
Henrietta 22
J. 230
Jane E. 22
Jesse E. 22
Jewell 22
John 22
John L. 22
Martha W. 230
Robert 230
Rufford Delain 111
S. B. 230
Samantha H. 111

JARRETT
Abrila 287
Ada V. 71
Addie 287
Alma 327
Bell 287
Clifford 71
Ethel Lorena 71
Eula M. 71
Foster Lee 302
Frances 71
G. Griffin 71
Irene 42
J. A. 71
James A. 160
Jeffie J. 327
Kate 327
L. D. 160
Mollie 286

JARRETT continued
Paul 302
Roy E. 302
S. E. 71
Sallie 287
T. W. 42
W. H. 287
W. N. 287
Whitson 287
William Henry 302

JENKINS
Clinton D. 98
E. N. 320
Emma H. 343
F. N. 98
Georgia 320
J. Wesley 343
M. W. 98

JENNINGS
George 129
J. E. 60
J. M. 60
Lucy V. 60
Mammie 129
Nora 340

JENNING
Alfred 312

JOHNSON
Albert S. 160
Alexander 22
Allen 160
Allen R. 160
Annie C. 22
Benjamin C. 49
C. W. 338
Capt. 161
Carey M. 37
Carlton E. 37
Carrie B. 61
Charlie 279
Cora J. 338
Ed 296
Ellis 22
Ellis R. 22
Emily 160
Farrie 37
Fred 37

JOHNSON continued
Freeman 22
George 338
Hattie 37
Henry G. 37
I. Sippie C. 49
J. A. 37
J. C. 37
J. D. 37
J. K. 160
J. M. 321
J. Monroe 37
J. R. 320
Jacob K. 161
James E. 160,161
James E. 338
James Monroe 321
Jeremiah 160
Joe A. 37
Joe C. 338
John M. 86
Julia 160
Leila 37
Julia E. 321
Louella 22
M. E. 160
Margaret W. 161
Martha Anne 22
Minnie 200
Nancey E. 37
Nancy A. 37
Nell 22
Ora Ruth 340
Parilee 37
Paul Henry 22
Pauline McRee 160
R. D. 160
Ralph 22
Martha Jane 320
Mary 320
Ralph Emerson 160
Resha 37
Richie B. 160
Robert 160
Robert D. 329
Robert David 160
Robert E. 160
Roberta 37
Ruby Davis 22
Safronia 37
Thomas S. 37

JOHNSON continued
Vera Mae 22
Vinnie L. 37
Mary Wood 320
Virginia T. 230
W. F. 22
Walter D. 340
Wanda J. 279
William 200
William C. 22
William Early 22
Willner V. 320
Young Joseph Sr. 230

JOHNSTON
Pauline H. 120

JONES
Amanda G. 111
Angie Belle Cape 230
Arrie 280
Beatrice B. 86
C. 49
C. A. 187
Cora 111
Decatur B. 230
Dod 338
Dorothy C. 120
Dorothy Loudell 187
Dorothy S. 230
Ed 230
Eliza R. 280
Frances Hanson 161
J. T. 37
J. W. 139
James H. 120
John Lewis 230
Julia Ann 230
Julia B. 139
Leary Baugh 230
Lola R. 49
Louise W. 338
Lula D. 187
Lula M. 230
Mamie L. 61
Marie T. 270
Mary E. 230
Pat Kessler 338
Phoebe B. 283
Robert T. 86
Roy 111

JONES continued
Roy F. 270
Roy H. 61
Thearon 111
W. (Hub) 230
W. H. 230
W. J. 280
W. Perry 187

JORDAN
Addie Mae (Coot) 121
Annielee 312
Delia P. 121
Earnest 312
Elijah 310
Geraldine 121
Gordon H. 121
Jimmie 312
Jodie 312
John T. 121
John T. Jr. 161
Joseph 312
M. O. 230
Margaret E. Stephens 310
Mattie O. 230
Robert 230
Sarah 230
Stephen Bandy 310
W. W. 230

JUSTICE
Allen 313
John Gillam 313
Mary 313
Susan 313

JUSTUS
George W. 187
Georgia Ruth 188

KEANUM
Jeannie Marie 270

KEITH
Cicero Harris 231
Clarence 270
Clarence C. 231
Emely B. 270
Lauren Harris 231
Lola W. 231
Marvin C. 270

KEITH continued
Nellie May 270
Rachel Angeline 270

KELL
M. P. 87

KELLEY
Clifford 71
Peat 71

KELLUM
Ambra Rogers 231

KELLY
A. J. 161
Idonia 161
May H. 161
Peggy Jane 161
Robert Judson 161
Sam 161

KENNEDY
Dan 296
Howard 22
Jane 296

KENT
Pearl Z. 112
Walter R. 112
William C. 304

KESLER
Annie Mae 287
Bethel T. 287
Bob D. 338
Boyd 71
Emma Lou 287
Ernest 71
Fannie 321
Frances Mary 71
G. F 71
G. N. 71
George F.71
Henry B. 37
Henry Melvin 71
J. B. 283
J. P. M. D. 71
Kenneth Wayne 287
Lam H. 321
Leota 37

KESLER continued
Lula 338
Martha 283
N. M. 71
Nancy M. 71
Ruby M. 71
Stanley 161
Thomas Martin 287
Thurman 161

KEY
M. Elizabeth 231
T. Erasmus 231

KICKS
Walter A. 161

KILEY
Bertha B. 22
Clifford M. 22
Jesse N. 22

KILGORE
Harve W. 321
Jod E. 308
Marvin T. 264
Mint M. 321
Myrtie H. 264
Nancy M. 321
Nevada F.
Solomon H. 321

KILPATRICK
Olivia 329

KIMSEY
C. L. (Duck) 101
Frances Bart 101
Pauline 101

KING
Allen 121
Berry 49
Daniel E. 270
Eva 270
Geneva 270
H. J. 270
John C. 231
Mary E. 231
Ola L. 121
Ruby 270

KING continued
Sallie N. 270
Sarah 270
Trelle 270

KINSEY
Emma A. 161
Louise Rees 231
Rosa Lee 161
William Earl 101

KINZEY
Nellie P. 71
W. J. 71

KNIPHFER
C. F. 264
Miranda 264

KININGHAM
J. L. 161
Joy M. 161

KINNEY
Alma B. 188
Claude 200
Elmer L. 188
Estelle Maddox 188
George Ann 188
George Washington 188
H. H. 188
J. H. 200
James M. 200
Jane Enerkube 188
Junions M. 200
Lula 200
Martha F. 188
Martha J. 200
Norma M. 188
Polly Ann 188
Sarah Frances 200
T. M. 200
Thomas 200
Thomas 200
Thomas M. 200
Thomas Norman 200
Virgil A. 188
W. F. 200
W. Garner 200
W. J. 200
Willie F. 200

KINNEY
Willie M. 200

KINZ
James C. 231
Ethel W. 231

KITCHENS
J. T. 161
John B. 121
Peggy 161

KITTLE
Cornelius F. 293
Fannie M. 293
R. 293

KIZE
A.D. 37
Eutha 37
Lona 37

KIZER
Herbert J. W. 162
Iva F. 162

KNOX
Samuel 162

KYTE
James Nelson 265
Margrett M. 265

LACEY
Barbara Lee 121

LACKEY
Andrew 200
Hannah F. 200
Julia Montino 129
Lizzie 129
W. B. 129

LACY
Edith Carol 139
C. W. 139

LAMAR
Julia D. 38
Muller B. 38
P. F. 38

LAMAR continued
Philip L. 38

LAMB
Bessie Smith 231

LANCASTER
Hannah H. 22
J. J. 315
James Walter 315
John 22
Lena Braselton 315
N. W. 2223
Parsada 23
T. W. 315

LANCE
Arthur Clayton 101
Caroline 49
Claudine P. 162
Eugene 101
Fred R. 162
L. C. 101
W. Asberry 49

LAND
F. 112

LANDERS
H. C. 188
W. W. 188

LANDRUM
Alma 271
Alma Minish 231
Alma R. 231
Ardellag 271
Cordelia 280
Dorie E. 271
E. D. 271
G. R. 271
Gartrell Riley 231
Riley 271
T. C. 271
T. Clarence 231
Winnie 271

LANE
B. Morsey 162
F. E. 162
M. 162

LANGFORD
Clyde 231
Luther A. 162
Mary S. 231
Mollie S. 5
Ralph A. 121
Thomas C. 5

LANGSTON
Albert C. 232
Clombus N. 87
Eliza G. 87
Eunice E. 271
Geneva 271
Gertrude 271
Gladys R. 232
Hoytie S. 121
James Odel 56
John 200
Lucy E. 271
M. J. 103
Norman D. Sr. 121
Obe L. 271
Oscar B. 271
R. L. 56
R. R. 56
Robert Livingston 271
Rosa Lee 271

LANKFORD
W. T. 304

LATTY
Stoy A. 112

LAWRENCE
M. T. 5
Vesta 5

LAY
Beulah 296

LEACH
Bessie Orpha 232

LEACHMAN
Gertrude 232
Mattie 232
Willie 232

LECKIE
Gussie 112
Harrison Newell 112
Sammy Columbus 112
W. C. 112

LEDFORD
Alice Johnson 162

LEE
Annie H. 112
Curtis E. 188
Emma M. 49
Floyd 188
Floyd 188
George W. 49
Hannah 265
Henry 265
Hessie 112
Lilli 188
Lilly 188
Lula Ann 49
R. 162
W. 112
Zelar Wilson 188

LEMLEY
Katie Bell 112
M. V. 112
V. C. 112
Victoria 112

LENDERMAN
Robert D. 271
Ora H. 271

LENRY
Beulah 293
Jim 293
Roy 293

LESLER
Rosie 296

LESTER
Fannie 312
Lamb 312
Lillie D. 329
Mary G. 340
Ola M. 329

LESTER continued
S. M. 312

LEVANS
Mary 5

LLEWELLYN
Joseph 71
Maybell L. 71
N. C. 71
Nannie M. 71

LEWIS
Mildred B. 232
Richard Lee 232
T. S. 232

LILLY
James Rufus 5

LINCEFELT
Bessie 134
W. H. 134

LINDERMAN
Dewitte 232
Ella F. 232
J. H. 232
Jack Hampton 232
John F. 232
Lola P. 232
Ora Hudson 232

LINDSEY
James 162
Jane M. 162
Mary Caroline 162
Samuel Middleton 162

LITTLE
Annie 265
Claud 232
Claude 232
Cora Q. 232
Cora Quillian 232
Fannie S. 265
Frank Quillian 232
Gracie 265
H. P. 232
Henry 296
Howell Park 232

LITTLE continued
J. Tom 265
Lois 232
William Howard 265

LITTLEFIELD
G. B. 321
Robert A. 321

LOCKMAN
Howard 232

LOGAN
B. M. 333
Benjamin M. 333
Elvina R. 333
F. M. 333
Henry Asco 333
Jessie C. 333
John F. 333
Mattie P. 333
Mellie Arminda 333
Minnie Parham 333
William R. 333
Winnie 333

LOGGINS
Charleston L. 112
Christine L. 121
Hope E. 121
Ida 271
J. B. Sr. 112
Julitt O. 112
Luther 271
Maggie Montine 56
Mary E. 139
W. R. 112
William R. 112

LONG
Alice Griffeth 162
Annie 129
Annie 162
H. J. 129
Hazel Pittman 162
John Anderson 162
John David 162
N. C. 129
Robert A. 162
T. Frank 162

LORD
Bolen 232
Charlie G. 139
Charlie W. 233
Charlotte Jane 233
Clementine 232
Clyde V. 232
D. M. 251
E. A. 87
Easter A. 139
Emory S. 163
Fletcher 139
Florence P. 139
George Grogan 139
Gerald W. 233
Gladstone E. 139
Gladys 87
Gwynell 233
Helen R. 163
Hewlett Ellis 233
Ina I. 233
J. E. 87
J. E. J. 139
J. M. 233
Jack B. 139
James W. 163 232
Jesse L. 233
Jessie M. 233
John H. 163
June Charlotte 233
Lavina P. 163
Lois E. 233
Luther 233
M. E. 139
Mack (N. G.) Jr. 233
Maggie H. 233
Mary H. 139 233
Mary Maude 139
Nelia Vaughn 233
Sybil 139
Verner Gwynell 232
Victor 251
W. F. 139
W. French 232
W. N. 233

LOTT
Andrew T. 134
Darwin A. 134
Dean S. 5
Ella H. 5

LOTT continued
Fannie Marlowe 134
George W. 5
H. J. 6
Isaac Fred 134
J. J. 134
J. P. 134
J. T. 134
John H. 5
Jurelle G. 5
Leila 6
Lena L. 134
Lester Judd 5
Margaret C. 134
Mary 134
Olivia 6
Olivia Bell 6
Ralph 6
Walter N. Sr. 134
William L. 134

LOVE
Cora L. 61
George D. 61
Mary 233

LOVEL
Lizzie 112

LOVERN
Estelle Stone 284

LOVIN
Johnie Elizabeth
Nancy A. 233
W. P. 233

LOWE
Charles R. 87
Doris Nell 333
Georgia Parham 333
M. L. Jr. 333
Marion L. 333
Mary W. 333
Winfred M. 333

LOWERY

Randall Kenneth 87
Thomas E. Jr. 87

LUMPKIN
John 280

LUND
Agnes Cameron 43

LUTHIE
Charles E. 233
Eva Collins 233
George C. 233
Jessie M. 233
Minnie P. 233
R. Ellis 233
W. H. 233
William Henry 233
William M. 233

LUTHER
Henry A. 23
Maudie I. 23

LYLE
A.J. 341
Anna 321
C. W. 321
Caroline C. 321
Elma B. 121
G. W. 321
Guy 321
Hester J. 200
I. H. 200
J. H. 321
James Henry 321
Jesse B. 321
John B. 321
L. W. 321
Louise 321
Lula Wall 321
Luther J. 121
Malinda 321
Mary E. 321
Mary Elizabeth Holliday 338
Mary J. 200
R. H. 321
W. C. 321
Willie A. 321

LYLES
Elizabeth 321
J. B. 321

LYNN
Sarah Elizabeth 163
G. W. 163

McCAIN
Claudie E. 321
Jessie Henry 321
Louise Waddell 321
Washington W. 321

McCLESKEY
Cora Mack 312
James W. 293
Lou Wier 293
Lucile 312
Lucretia 293

McCLURE
Grady H. 235
Rennie D. 164
Wayne W. 164
William H. 235
Winnie B. 235

McCONNELL
Katharine Adams 235
Melissa Hood 235
Noel 235
W. F. 235
William Felton 235

McCOY
Alexander F. 165
Eva E. 165
George Otis 122
James B. 164
James Benjamin 165
John 164
John C. 164
Malissa Adeline 165
Mannie H. 164
Minnie 164
Montine 164
Roy Ledford 126
Susan C. 164
William P. 235
Wilmath A. 164

McCURRY
Estell S. 129
Ray 129

McDANIEL
Elizabeth 265
Frances 104
James A. 265
Julia Marie 50
Lester 304

McDONAL
Jerry E. 165

McDONALD
Alvin H. 61
Belle B. 11
Belle Braselton 11
C. T. 265
Charles Tate 265
E. M. 11
Edward Monroe 11
Edwin A. 61
Ella 298
Grace M. 235
H. H. 61
Jessie E. 298
Joan 298
Kathryn 235
Mae 322
Marian Lanelle 11
Pattie 265
Ronny O. (Ron) 122
Sarah Jane Nix 61
Sherry Ann 265
Thomas J. Dr. 61
Walter A. 322

McDOUGALD
Alice 50
Arminda 50
Eddie 50
F. J. 50
Floyd 50
R. J. Jr. 165
R. L. 165
Tina 165
William J. 50

McDUFFIE
William Penn 236

McELHANNON
Ida 165
J. M. 38
James E. 165
John Emory 165
John Monroe 38
Johnie H. 165
M. H. 38
Martha Shields 38
Mary Lee 165
S. E. 165
T. A. 165
Thomas Asbury 165
William Andrew 38

McELROY
Flora R. 139
Lester P. 139

McENTIRE
Edith 236
J. C. 236
Paul 236
Selina 236
Vesta 236
W. E. 236

McEVER
A. R. 24
Ada M. 24
Alis Cleo 24
Amanda 24
Andrew
Annie E. 24
B. E. Rev. 190
C. C. 24
Caldonia 24
Carrie L. 236
Charlie 190
Cora E. 24
E. C. 190
Ellen Roberts 24
Emeline 322
Fred 24
Hugh 24
J. A. 190
J. D. 24
J. F. 24
J. H. 190
J. M. 24
Jake W. 236

McEVER continued
Joe D. 24
John A. 322
John F. 24
Joseph C. 24
Joseph C. 24
Julia 24
Laura 24
Laura S. 24
Lillie M. 24
Lula E. 190
Lyman B. 24
Marguerite S. 236
Memph M. 236
Mary Haynes 24
Minnie Craft 24
Miron 190
N. J. 190
N. J. Batchelor 190
Nancy 322
Nicy J. 24
P. A. 24
R. B. 24
Robert A. 190
Robert A. 24
Rossie Bell 24
Sallie Boyd 24
Sallie White 24
Sarah Bell 24
Sarah J. 24
Thomas E. 24
W. T. 24
Walter W. 24
William W. 24

McGALLIART
Florence P. 236
Robert P. 236

McGANTS
Effie Eugenia 6
William B. 6

McGARITY
Pearl 165

McGINNIS
E. Young 236
Fred 139
Frederick Hutcheson 139

McGINNIS continued
G. D. 236
J. Reuben 139
Lamartine H. 139
Lillie R. 236
Lowena Ray 139
Mary F. 139
Richey J. 236
Susan 236

McGINTY
Henry E. 304
J. A. 304
John A. 304
Julia L. Moore 304
Mary Alexander 293
Will 293

McGUIRE
Charles J. 322
Dorris V. 322
Mattie 322
Oliver 236
William F. 322

McINTYRE
C. C. 113
Mattie 113

McKINLEY
Nathan 280

McLARY
Marsisia 114

McLESTER
Cynthia 56
James G. 56
William M. 56

McMULLAN
Ethel J. 165
James L. 165

McMURRY
Flora 277

McNAIR
Ruby Irene P. 283
William Green 283

McNEAL
B. E. Rev. 190
Bessie H. 190
Cora 190
D. S. Jr. 190
Didlard 190
E. C. 190
Elizabeth 190
J. A. 190
J. D. May 190
J. H. 190
Jack 190
John T. 190
Jurell 190
Lula E. 190
Maggie R. 190
Nancy 190
T. M. (Bus) 190
Voy Jeanette 190
William 190
William A. 190
William Ed 6
William Hoyt 190
Willie 190

McPHAIL
J. D. 236
Lizzie Pilsbury Ward 236

McREE
William Jefferson 165
Arthur H. 165
Beulah B. 165
Caroline 72
Clyde Walker Jr. 72
Frank W. 72
Jessie V. 72
L. M. 72
Lula Pittman 165
Marcus V. 72
Robert Lee 72
W. J. 72

McWOOD
Dane 236

MABRY
Eva Leila Carithers 163
Mary Alice 163

MACK
Henry 312
Lewis E. 312
Martha 312

MADDOX
A. Jackson 188
Annie D. 188
Beretha Bell 189
Bertha Mae 189
Charley 189
Charley 23, 189
Charley C. 188
Clayborn D. 189
Daisy Mae 6
David Claude 189
Doris Daniel 72
Edd 163
Elizabeth 188
Elizabeth Areleane 188
Emory Anthony 233
H. R. 189
Fronie 265
H. E. 265
Harold 101
Harrison 188
Harrison T. 265
Herbert H. 189
Hester R. 265
Hoyt M. 189
Ina 189
Ina T. 188
India 188
J. Arthur 87
J. Cecil 233
J. H. 189
J. W. 188
Jack 189
James H. 189
James L. 188
Jannie Mae 265
John W. 23
Julia A. 23
Julia H. 134
L. C. 188 189
L. F. 188
Lenard C. 188
Lovie Lee 189
Lula Frances 188
Madelyn 188
Margaret C. 23

410

MADDOX continued
Martha Adeline 189
Martha E. 188
Mary 189
Maude T. 189
Minnie Wilson 297
N. L. 188
Olive M. 163
Ralph E. 233
Ruby E. 233
Seaborn M. 189
Sebe 188
T. S. 188,189
T. T. 265
Talmadge C. 265
W. G.134
W. H. (Burster) 189
W. H. 6
Walter G. 134
William H. 6
Wilma L. 233

MAHAFFEE
Helm 233
J. F. 233
Lois 233
M. T. 233

MAHAFFEY
Alexander M. 6
Cornelia H. 6
Evie C. 163
J. A. B. 163
James F. 6
James H. L. 163
John Spruell 6
Lewis N. 129
Lurlie 163
William H. 129

MacKEAN
Maud Britton 11

MALEY
Barnett G. 121
Bessie Evans 129
Guy T. 121
J. H. 61
Johnny Lee 139
Mattie 61
Sara B. 121

MALEY continued
Sarah A. 61
William Henry 129

MALOCH
R. C. (Pat) 49
Sadie W. 49

MALOOK
Edd 163
Jessie Freeman 163

MANDERS
James J. 234
Mary C. 234

MANGUM
Darell D. 234
Docia D. 87
Ellie Mae 234
Henry W. 234
Hoyt J. 87
Kathrin 234
Mansel 87

MANLEY
Candis S. 234

MANUS
Ann 189
Estelle H. 163
J. B. 6
J. Hubert 189
J. W. 189
James M. 308
Jewell T. 189
John W. Jr. 189
Mary Jane 6.
Pearl 189
Rome J. 163

MARION
Ransom O. 112

MARLER
Aunt Betty 103
D. P. 113
David P. 113
John E. 87
Sarah E. 113

MARLER continued
W. Mansel 87

MARLIN
Claypus Hope 49

MARLOW
A.D. 113
Ada L. 113
C. E. 113
Catherine 113
Christina 234
Cynthia E. 113
D. J. 23
D. M. 113
D. R. 113
D. W. 113
David J. 6
Delonie D. 113
Donnie S. 113
Edna R. 113
Edward James 234
Emma 23
Emma M. Moon 6
Essie L. 113
Evelyn 113
F. F. 113
F. G. 113
F. W. 113
Grady W. 113
H. Henry Jr. 234
Hubert R. 113
Irene 113
Jane Margaret 234
Johnnie Claude 113
Lena E. 113
Levie M. 113
Lizzie 113
Lizzie A. 189
Lizzie E. 113
Louise S. 113
Lovie 112
Lum 113
M. L. 113
Mannie H. 113
Martha M. 113
Maude 113
Mose S. E. 189
Neeby Donald 163
Ollie 113
Paul F. 113

MARLOW continued
R. B. 113
R. M. 113
Ransom C. 113
Richard Dewey 113
Roxie 49
Susan 322
Sylvey Lee 113
Tilithia C. 113
W. H. 113
W. J. 113
W. L. 113
W. Lee 112
W. M. 113
William H. 322
William M. 189
William M. 322
Woddie B. 113

MARLOWE
Betty Sue 104
H. C. 104
Susie P. 104

MARONY
Ellen 234
W. B. 234
Z. B. 234

MARSINGILL
Corine 327
Dewey E. 327
H. Alonzo 327
Mary H. 327
Patricia 327
Ralph 327

MARTIN
Alvin 164
Artie A. 339
Augusta Harber 234
Azzylee 164
Bealah 201
Beatrice 38
Bert 50
Beulah May 200
Byrd 339
Clara Williamson 164
Cleo Evans 87
D. Ben 339
Dennie 87

MARTIN continued
Dorothy Lanell 234
Doyle 234
E. B. 339
E. T. 339
Elisha B. 339
Elisha Byrd 339
Elizabeth McCarty 38
Elizabeth T. 293
David B. 334
Egbert A. 315
Emma G. 87
Emma H. 50
Emma T. 339
G. H. 87
Gabriel Pierce 234
George 163
George Hampton 87
Guy 50
H. L. 38
Herby 50
Hettie Inez Williamson 293
Hollis 50
J. Lee 87
Joe Sharp 234
John 339
Joseph Garland 164
Joyce Ann 50
Julia 189
Julia B. 339
Julia Fannie 87
Lee 234
Lenard P. 298
Levi 339
Levi G. 38
Malachi 38
Margaret D. 234
Marion 234
Mary 234
Matilda 72
Max Hilda Jess 293
Mendell 189
Myrtle L. 87
N. G. 339
Nellie G. 339
Nettie Mae 315
Octavie I. 339
Otis E. 315
R. B. 164
R. R. 87
Reed W. 234

MARTIN continued
S. W. 200201
Samuel Walter 201
Tiney 164
Lillie May 72
W. D. 293
Weyman Jarrett 164
William C. 87
William D. 196
William James 163
William L. 234

MASHBURN
Althia J. 334
B. G. 334
B. J. 334
Bettie Jean 334
Edgar William 334
Edna Burr 334
Fannie B. 334
J. Clifton 334
Ruth 334

MASON
Emmie 234
Rucker 234

MASSEY
Agnes Freeman 277
Bertha 140
Claud 234
E. A. 277
E. R. 140
Elizabeth 125
Ellen O. 235
Harold 140
Herman 140
J. C. 234
J. H. 277
J. N. 72
J. W. 235, 277, 287
James A. 140
James E. 125
Jessie M. 277
Kate Roberts 164
Leonia Bells 72
Lizzie 287
M. L. 72
Madison Thomas 235
Mae Potts 277
Mildred Ruth 304

MASSEY continued
Milo H. 164
Nela Chandler 235
Ollie M. 72
Onie 235
Pearl W. 304
R. N. 277
Robert T. 72
Ruby C. 235
Rufus N. 304
Swep D. 140
Tommie A. 234
Vester F. 72
W. R. 287
Walter J. 72
William Curt 140

MASSINGILL
H. A.134
J. A. 134

MATHEWS
Anzy M. 288
Ashby 288
Carrie 308
Eva 308
Homer L. 288
Homer Milton 288
Huiett 308
J. B. 308
J. N. 308
Jessie 308
John T. 288
Lewis 308
Lillie Mae 288
M. H. 288
M. J. 308
Martha 308
Martha Jane 308
Martha S. 308
Mary 235
Monteen 308
R. F. 235
W. J. 235
Willie 308

MATHIS
A. W. 88
B. H. 201
Bartow Hale 322
Belle 201

MATHIS continued
Callie 88
Guy Thomas 322
Ina 201
Laura E. 88
Lou C. 88
M. G. 201
Maggie M. 88
Mary L. 201
Nettie Belle 322

MATTHEWS
Ada 235
Alice B. 284
Alyce H.164
Birtie Miriam 88
Carol Sue 287
Frances 293
J. M. 189
J. W. 88
Milton Edward 287
Nina Lou 235
Paul B. 164
Pollie McEver 189
Richard Earl 235
Robert 287
Sarah E. Glenn 61
William S. 61

MAULDIN
Allen D. 164
Azilee Ray 164
Basiel L. 129
Clarence L. 23
Coleman 164
Dora M. 38
Fannie J. 72
James 164
James G. 164
L. W. 38
Lester Gibson 129
Lewis C. 122
Nancy H. 129
Ola H. 164
Ora A. 164
Ruth S. 122

MAXEY
Cora 297

MAXWELL
A. E. "Tom" 122
Annie Lou H. 122
C. P. 62
Carlton 62
Clombus P. 62
Cumi 62
Della W. 62
Edman B. 62
Emma J. 235
H. Douglas 38
Herbert Earl 61
J. W. 61
Jessie 62
Jessie B. 62
Jessie Blanche 62
Jim A. 235
John W. 61
L. G. 62
L. Gratt 62
Leola M. Benton 62
M. L. 61
Mamie Christian 164
Mary E. 62
Mary Nunn 61
Mollie Lee 61
Norman 62
R. B. 164
Sarah P. 61

MAYFIELD
Eula D. 312
Lillie 304

MAYNARD
James 308

MEALOR
Lillian Ann 236
T. C. 236

MEDLEY
Billy Lee 237
Eulous G. 237
Frank Henry 237
George W. 237
Gertrude 237
H. J. 237
Henry B. 237
J. E. 237
Louis Lord 237

MEDLEY continued
Myrtle 237

MEEKS
M. S. 237
N. L. 237
Nellie Anglin 237

MERCER
Bertha G. 288
O'Neal W. 288
Sidney 288
William 288

MERCIER
A. Louise 237
B. F. 237
Ethel G. 237
May Zelma 165
Obed B. 237
Susie E. 237

MERK
Alice Alexander Cheatham Roberts 293
Alva G. 88
Claude H. 88
D. S. 88
Dilmus L. 88
E. Hoyt 88
E. Jurell 88
J. W. 88
John Wesley 88
M. E. 88
Marcia T. 88
Mary E. 88
Starky H. 88

MIDDLEBROOKS
Herman T. 166
Ila Roberts 166
Lucille N. 166
Thomas P. 166

MILFORD
Florence W. 271
W. Brantly 271

MILLER
Addie L. 343
Carrie E. 88
Fannie E. 288

MILLER continued
James 304
Jane M. 343
Jim R. 288
Joe C. 343
John H. 288
Lillia 288
Robert M. 343
W. H. 288

MILLIKIN
Mamie A. Chandler 72
R. K. 72

MILLS
Walter B. 79

MINISH
Bonnie Lavorne 237
Dwayne A. 237
Edna Louise 237
Ella H. 237
Joe B. 237
Milton H. 237
Rita B. 237
Robert L. 237
Terry W. 237
Thomas Aubrey 62
Tinie Benton 61
Victor B. 61
Walter N. 237
William H. 61

MITCHELL
A. Grady 72
Alice 166
Alice R. 88
C. T. 166
Carrie M. 50
Charlie R. 88
Cynthia S. 88
Dora 88
Fannie G. 88
Frank Elijah 237
G.L. 88
John James 88
Maud Coleman 237
Vassie 88

MIZE
Charles Allen 237
Cora Lee 38
Ella Neal 237
Inez 38
Joseph 38
Leila Ritchie 237
Louise T. 238
Robert F. 38
Rupert E. 343
Samuel A. 237
Theron N. 237
William S. 237

MOBLEY
H. J. 166
H. L. 166
H. Lewis 166
Henry Isham 166
Jacqueline 166
Louise Pendergrass 166
Mildred 166

MOM
Rufus 329

MONTGOMERY
B. T. 322
C. L. 166
Carrie Deupree 166
Claude 238
Elizabeth Griffeth 238
John 322
John Oliver 238
Katy 322
Lizzie Harber 238
Mattie Lillian 238
Ruby Ritchie 239
Thomas E. 166
Walter C. 166

MOODY
H. Art 238
Murwyn M. 238
Pamela L. 238

MOON
Annie E. 283
Calvin E. 300
Donald 300
Ella D. 23

MOON continued
Emma 166
Frances 101
Frances 322
Georgia A. 23
Griggs M. 300
Lonnie B. 166
M. G. 166
Macon A. 300
Mary 300
Thomas J. 23
W. P. 300
William J. 23

MOORE
A. Hal 166
Alva Appleby 166
Calderwood Harrison 166
Donald Roy 304
Emma 304
G. W. 304
George F. 238
George W. 304
Hattie E. 238
Heppie B. 238
John S. 304
John W. 201
Letitia Sander 166
Lilliam B.
Milliard Fillmore 166
Millie 304
Millie Freeman 304
N. Ross 304
R. D. 166166
Sarah Ethel 166
Thomas A. 238

MORGAN
D. D. 56
Elizabeth H. Dunson 56
J. E. 201
J. P. 238
James R. 238
L. M. 334
Linda 334
Maybelle H. 238
Nancy M. 334
Pauline 201
Thomas J. 238

MORRIS
Betty Ann 88
David Tillman 271
Ellis 88
Glen 88
John D. 190
John H. 88
R. V. 271
Rabun Gilmore 293
Susan E. 190
Wayne 88

MORRISON
Alice C. 238
Annie P. 23
Christian Ann 166
David P. 122
Emma 300
James 23
Jessie J. 238
Leary Fillmore 166
Lester B. Rev. 122
Minnie Head 166

MOSELEY
John N. 327
Manteline Bailey 327

MOSLEY
H. L. 167
L. P. 167

MOSS
Celia Bell 6
Delia G. 140
E. A. 140
E. C. 140
Emma R. 140
F. W. 140
Jack 140
Laura Frances 140
N. A. Rev. 6
W. T. 140
William T. 140

MOTE
Will M. 114

MOTES
C. G. 89
Lula 89

MOTES continued
Martha 89
Thomas T. Madison 89

MULLINS
Blanche V. 238

MUNDY
Isabelle Robert 23
Z. T. 23

MURPHY
A. J. 201
Andrew E. 201
Annie Mae 191
Charles Terrell 201
Clyde 201
D. E. 201
E. L. 201
Eliza S. 201
Emma Love 201
Este 201
F. T. 201
Floella 201
Franklin D. 201
Fred 201
G. T. 201
Gartrell 201
Idea E. 201
J. M. 190
Janette 201
Jerry W. 201
Julia Mae 201
L. G. 201
Lily Mae 190
Lucy 190
Lycurgus G. 201
M. E. 201
Martha A. 190
Martha E. 190
Minnie Mae G. 201
Natalie 201
Neola 201
Nora 201
Nora Foster 201
Polly Ann 190
Raborn Lee 190
T. 191
Terrell 190
Tinie 26
Ula Mae 190

MURPHY continued
William J. 190
William P. 201
Zemily G. 201

MURRAY
David D. 283.
Elizabeth Potts 277
Eula 277
Hattie Mozelle Jarrett 302
Horace E. 277
Lucy B. 271
Mamie 271
Robert Lett 277
W. Columbus 277
W. T. Jr. 277
William J. 271
William T. Sr. 277

MURRY
Cleo Ofus 277
Emeline 277
L. B. 277
Mary Belle 277
W. T. 277

NABERS
M. D. L. 167

NALLEY
Annie Frances 89
B. H. 89

NALLY
Grady 114
Harriett Susan 114
Webb 114

NASH
George O. 114

NEAL
Augusta Ann 25
James T. 25
Jennie Lee 315
Sarah Jo 315
Wingfield 312

NELMS
Charles H. 238
Francis M. D. 238

NELMS continued
Harriet L. 238
L. B. 238
Leonidas 238
Lydia Elbert 238
Mary Hamaker 238
V. L. 238

NEW
Barbara Ann 122
Eugenia T. 271
James M. 271
William L. Jr. 122

NEWBERRY
Ada M. 191

NEWMAN
Francis A. 62

NIBLACK
Alice Hardy 167
Virgil Augustus 167

NICHOLS
J. W. 6
Jessie 6
Louis 6

NICHOLSON
Alma L. 89
Cam C. 325
Etta S. 89
Henry F. 89
Howard E. 239
J. R. 89
John Otis 89
Juanita 167
Lula W. 325
Morgan R. 89
Pearl R. 272
S. C. 325
T. S. 89
Thomas F. 272
Wilma Lilly 89

NICKELSON
Annie N. 322
B. B. 322
Dock S. 322

NICKELSON continued
John A. 322

NIMMONS
Ammer A. 239
Waymon A. 239

NIX
Andrew J. 167
B. 114
Bonnie S. 62
Claud 239
Cora Lee Bland 239
D. B. 62
D. M. 62 239
Dillard M. 239
Dilmus H. 62
Dora Bennett 62
Dovie Hammons 323
Dusty 50
Edd 50
F. J. 239
Frances R. 62
Francis 114
Gladys 89
Howard M. 38
Hymer L. 239
J. M. 62
J. Nelson 239
Jesse H. 38
Jessie 50
Joe W. 38
John A. 114
John Morgan 62
L. M. 239
Lillian M. 62
Lizzie Lurene 62
Lloyd M. 239
Lucile 62
M. E. 114
M. F. 114
Martha A. 38
Mary E. 114
Mary Gray 239
Norma Lee 62
P. J. 239
Permelia Jane Mitchell 62
Richard 239
Richard M. 239
Robert C. 62
Rosana A. 167

NIX continued
Tennelle 62
Walter 89

NORRELL
Drusilla 114
John F. 114

NORRIS
James Jr. 280
Jessie C. 114
Joseph 89
Sarah C. 114

NORVILLE
Clevia W. 89

NOWELL
A. N. 7
Malvin 7
Matilda 7
William F. 7

NUNN
A. T. 89
Bennie 89
Betty H. 89
C. C. 89
C. G. 89
Charles Patrick 272
Clay 89
Crawford M. 239
Crofford C. 89
Dora H. 167
Drucilla 140
E. S. 89
E. T. 272
Elijah G. 89
Elizabeth H. Porter 140
Elizabeth S. 272
Eunice C. 89
Ezra B. 239
Fannie Evans 89
Folia D. 272
G. L. 140
George L. 272
Hattie 239
J. M. 272
Jim T. 239
Joseph O. 272
Louie 89

NUNN continued
Louise 89
M. J. 140
Martha 56
Martha A. 272
Martha Ann 90
Mary Janne D. 272
Minnie E. 140
Norman R. 140
R. C. 89
Mary Arlisa 89
Mattie A. 89
Mollie 89
R.C. 89
Reuben C. 272
Robert M. 272
S. J. 89
Samuel 140
Sammie J. 89
Sandy 89
Thomas J. 239
V. L. 140
Valley L. 140
W. T. 140
William 272
William H. 167

NUNNALLY
Nancy G. 334

NUTTAL
Leah 122
Robert H. 122

O'CONOR
Minnie S. 239

O'DILLON
James A. 38
Lillie Elder 38

O'KELLEY
Thomas Randolph 272

O'REAR
Charles W. 239

ODUM
John Thomas 90

OLDHAM
A.J. 325
Augusta 325
C.G. 325
Cynthia 325
J. Weldon 325
John M. 325
Mary 325
Sarah Lu Tiller 325
Wildey 325

OLIVER
A. N. 104
Amanda A. 104
Armineda T. 191
Charles N. 104
Charlie H. 343
Delphia 191
Doris 343
Eugene B. 304
Fannie E. 104
Gladys Smith 343
Helen A. 343
Henry J. 191
J. C. 104
J. Thomas 104
Laura 191
Lila B. 104
Lula Reynolds 104
Mary Ann 191
Maud M. 343
Nell Ford 343
Theodocie 104
Worth 104

OLSEN
Elizabeth Smith 239

ORR
Fannie G. 167
John J. 167

ORRA
Elizabeth K. 56

OTT
Kenneth W. Sr. 239
Mary Elizabeth 239

OWEN
Barbara Sue 25
Mary Elizabeth 239

OWENS
Floyd 280

OWENSBY
Charles W. 240
Hattie B. 240
Mamie Iola Ray 140
Roscoe H. 240
Ruth 283
William Gordon 140

PACE
E. O. 72
Effie B. 283
Emma 72
Ewsial 72
George R. 283
Georgia 72
J. H. 272
Mary Jane 272
Sidney J. 272
W. H. 72

PAGE
Am 240
Clarence A. (Tater) 240
Howard H. 240
Lou Willie 240
Mary A. 283
Mildred R.
PALMER
Randall K. 191
James F. 240
Pearl Barber 240

PAGGETT
Jake 297
Mattie 297

PARK
Hiram L. 62
Icie D. 62
John Russell 7
Lorenza D. 62
Lucius 62
M. W. 7
Mattie Mae 7

PARK continued
Maude 7
Robert D. 101

PARKER
Charles W. 104
D. L. 104
George N. 63
Jessie 272
Lelia Hayes 63
Mollie 90
Sara J. 72
William M. 73

PARKS
Buck Leo Howard 265

PANTHER
W. W. 90

PARHAM
D. A. 334
Emily J. 334
Frank S. 334
H. Ralph 334
J. C. 334
James Thomas 334
Jimmie 334
John H. Neal 334
Mary A. 334
Maude S. 334
Reed D. 334
Thelma L. 334
Thomas Jefferson 334
W. L. 334

PARNELL
C. 293
Charity L. 240
E. P. 293
G. R. 293
Julia E. 293
Junus L. 293
M. 293
Rupis N. 240

PARR
Michael H. 343

PARSONS
E. D. 114

PARSONS continued
Nettie Louise 114
Nettie Marler 114

PARTAIN
Charles O. 240
Sara Q. 240

PARTRAM
Joseph A. 240
Savannah P. 240

PATMAN
Willie 312

PATRICK
Annie Bradley 7
Coly 90
Emma Brock 90
Gladys H. 167
J. B. 90
John B. 167
John Henry 167
Josephine S. 167
L. Estelle 104
Lizzie Carter 167
Lola Drake 7
Lonnie 167
Martha H. 104
Mary M. 167
Miles J. 167
Noble M. 167
Samuel 114
T. W. 90
Thomas L. 104

PATTERSON
Lantia V. 140
Wister T. 140

PATTON
Amanda A. 39
J. Tolbert 240
Jack 280
Robert L. 39
Robert L. Jr. 39
T. D. 240

PAUL
H. C. 240
Hinton G. 240

PAUL continued
Nancy 240

PAYNE
Alice B. 73
Carrie G. Gunter 73
Daniel 73
Edna 73
Edna F. 73
Ethel 240
Eunice P. 191
Flora M. 300
J. D. 334
J. L. 191
L. E. 240
Martha J. 334
Myrtle 73
Nola Harriett 73
R. L. 73
R. L. Jr. 73
William Brad 73
William Thomas 73

PEAR
Jessie Annie Pear 135

PEARCE
Carrie 7
James W. 7
Jesse L. 7
Martha A. 7

PEEBLES
Albert Jr. 50
Jazel M. 50

PEELER
B. M. 241
C. E. 241
Ettie Williams 241
Henry 241
Margaret W. 241
Noel Clifford 241
Ruth 241
William Henry 241

PEEPLES
Edna A. 241

PENDERGRASS
Alva Nathaniel P. 167
Alva W. 168
Bessie 241
Harold 168
Hillard 339
J. B. 168
James E. Jr. 168
Franklin L. 168
James Bascomb 168
Joseph 168
Martha E. 42
Martha Elizabeth 168
Mary Lou 168
Mattie Dell Heath 168
N. H. 42
N. M. 168
N. N. 167, 168
Nathaniel H. 42
Ned Nixon 168
Nellie E. 168
Phillip Trout 168
S. B. 168
Thomas Nathaniel 168
W. 399
W. B. 399
W. T. Rev. 241
Wesley 167
William Lane 168
William Lane 42
Worth H. 168

PEPPERS
Adelia 114
Davy 7
Emma 7
Jesse 7
M. C. 7
M. W. 7
Manolia B. 114
Rosella De La Pierrier 7
W. K. 114
Winnell 265

PERDUE
Carl 191

PIERCE
Early 191
Peark K. 191

REDDICK
Robert E. Lee 192

PERRY
Charlotte S. 168
Eula D. 298
Helen T. 90
James J. 90
M. P. 298
N. H. 241
Newton H. 90
P. O. 90
Ruth L. 241
Sarah G. 90
W. Carse 298

PETHEL
Edgar J. 202
Fred 202
Gannie J. 202
Grace 202

PETTY
P. 101
Stoy 101

PETTYJOHN
E. H. 168
Helen 101
J. J. 168
James E. 168

PHARR
John Young 104
Mannie Roberts 104

PHILLIPS
A. W. 99
Ada Doster 99
Albert W. 51
Alp 99
Augustus 191
Bessie Lyle 99
Bustell 51
C. P. Rev. 241
Caroline Lyle 99
Charles M. 51
Charlie 99
D. L. P. 99
Donald E. 191

PHILLIPS continued
Eddie B. 50
Edward 191
Effie 99
Elizabeth B. 50
Ella T. 241
Emily J. 99
Estell G. 241
Fannie P. 51
Finnie 99
Flora S. 241
Florence S. 51
Frances M. 50
Frank 51
Fred Davis 99
Genie Brown 99
Greg 312
Grover 241
H. (Miss) 90
J. H. Jr. 51
J. Homer 51
J. Robert 191
Hugh 99
James 51
James H. 312
Johnnie L. 241
L. W. 99
Latimer 241
Laurabell 51
Lewis 241
Lula H. 312
Lula Mathews 191
M. Frank 312
Martha 241
Martha Elizabeth 191
Martha Oralee 51
Mary E. 191
Mary J. 51
Mary W. 51
Maud S. 241
Miles 99
Minnie 241
Minnie Lee 191
Myron Russell 191
Onie 191
Pete 51
Reba S. 51
Robert Lawson 99
Robert T. 99
Roxie 00
Russell 191

424

PHILLIPS continued
Sallie F. 99
Sanford J. 50
Sara 241
Sindy Adell 99
Thomas 51, 99
Tommie G. 51
Tommie W. 50

PICKENS
Lillie E. 241
Walter R. 241

PICKRELL
Benjamin F. 90
C. W. 104
Croff Y. 104
J. N. 105
Kathie Sue 104
Lucy W. 90
Mattie E. 104

PIERCE
Mary Louise 73

PIKE
E. A. 285
Estelle Adelaide 285
Estelle C. 285
Henry 168
J. D. 285
Jefferson D. 168
Lucy A. 168
Margaret 308
Montine 285
W. I. 168
W. S. 308

PINION
Alice C. 90
George W. 90
James G. 90
Jim 90
Joyce C. 90
Linda 90
Webster C. 90

PINSON
Charlie W. 168
Dell Pharr 130
Ina Lindsay 168

PINSON continued
Ina Lindsay 168
Mary born 294
Mattie O. 168
W. A. 168
William Worth 130

PIRKLE
Avarilla 7
Claude 168
Della 7
Edward L. 169
Green H 7
Green H. 308
Jane Smith 308
Oscar 7
P. P. 308
P. Parks 7
Pearl A. 169
Robert N. 169
Etrich Sr. 280
H. H. 283
Susie 283

PITTMAN
Alfus R. 241
Amy J. 170
Charlie O. 73
Clarence C. 241
Clarence E. 242
Clarence W. 241
Frances B. 242
Georgia F. 73
Lowell J. 192
May McRee 170
Lillian Augusta 242
Mordecia Monroe 170
N. 170
Oliver 242
Pamelia Hilley 242
Pleasant Owen 242
Ulee 242
W. Kenneth 241
Wilmer Owen 242

PITTS
Angeline 272
Jessie J. 272
Jessie O. 272

POE
Buford 140
Ethel G. 63
J. F. 140
John Ferd 140
Mattie Lee C. 140
Paul 63

POLLARD
B. F. 51
Darlene 51
Grady 51
Maydia Juanita Bell 297
Vennie 51

POLTS
J. D. (Jake) Sr. 122
Thomas K. 122

POMEROY
Richard S. 55

POPE
Lillia 308

PORTER
Anna V. 39
Annie 91
Annis 73
Arthur N. 39
Boyd 272
C. G. 91
C. M. 91
Carlton Floyd 242
Carrie Sue 73
Columbus B. 140
Cora Irin 272
Earl O. 272
Emma Head 242
Evie O. 101
Florence M. 115
H. P. 73
Harold Crawford 91
Henrinelle 73
Henry Eugene 272
Homer Ralph 327
J. H. 39
Jim 115
L. O. 91
Lena Mae 39
Lenard 169

PORTER continued
Lester 130
M. L. 73
M. S. 272
M. S. Sr. 73
M. T. 272
Marion S. 140
Mary Lou Hayne 73
Mary W. 169
Maude 91
Melvin 313
Mollie T. 140
Ora B. 39
Ralph 91
Robert B. 91
Robert L. 169
Roy M. 91
Ruth Sonia 327
Samuel Asbury 169
Venie Venable 73
W. T. 39
William T. 39

POTTER
Dilmus 169
G. P. 323
G. W. 323
Hattie Jack 323
J. W. 323
J. W. 323
Jack 323
John H. 323
L. C. 323
L. L. 323
Lillie M. 323
Lottie 323
Lucious W. 323
Martha E. 323
Nancy 323
Nora Gilbert 169
Pinkie 323
Ralph Brightwell 323
Thomas Richard 323
Trudie Lee Berryman 323

POTTS
A. W. Potts 277
Amy Kathryn 73
Bonnie B. 74
C. C. 74
C. G. 63

POTTS continued
C. H. 74
Carrie 74
E. F. 63
Edna M. 130
Ellie Myrtice 73
Emily Mae 73
Ernest L. 130
Ervin D. 130
Florence S.63
Frances Elizabeth 74
Frank 73
G. L. 74
Henry J. 74
Homer O. 74
J. D. 63
J. M. 130
J. N. 73
J. T. 277
Jack 63
James M. 73
James Rockwell 73
Jim Henry 130
John D. 63
Julia C. Gathright 74
Kate Eckles 73
Katie 73
Leila Mae Eckles 73
Little Potts 25
Lou E. Murray 277
Lula Mae C. 73
Lummie 74
Martha A. 73
Mary C. 74
Mary E. 63
Odell 130
Rockwell Eckles 73
Scina Barnett 25
Sidney Walter 73
Sumner S. 63
Thomas A. 74
W. M. 74
William B. 63
Willie Ruth 73

POWELL
Celia Carnes 242
James Clyde 242
James Horace 242
Lula H. 339
Oliver Lonzo 339

POWER
Annie Williford 242

POWERS
Ella Josephine Wood 242
W. B. 242

PRESSLEY
Albert T. 98
Bertie L. 98
Betty Ann 51
Edd 51
Genie 98
Harvey S. 51
Ida Mae 51
Martin Jr. 51
Rachel 51
Roger 51
W. D. 51
Wiley Vandiver 51

PRICE
Estella 130
W. W. 130

PRICKE
J. H. 242
Olin Hester 242
P. R. 242

PRICKETT
A. P. Rev. 126
Fay 56
J. F. Morgan 56
N. C. 56

PRITCHETT
Edward 122
Roy 63
William Larry 63

PRUITT
Bertie Lee 105
C. A. 334
C. T. 105
Celia M. 169
Dock Harvey 242
Eula Ethel 242
Hartley Paraham 335
J. W. 91

PRUITT continued
James M. 63
John J. 242
Johnny 105
Larry E. 242
Lee Roy 169
Lucy G. 91
Mandy 91
Mollie T. 63
Nezzie M. 242
R. D. (Bud) 11
Ruth L. 11
T. C. 334
W. A. 91
William C. 169

PUCKETT
Albert Floren 285
Juday Malinda 304

PUGH
Anna Bell Howington 134
Betty Corene 272
Carrol 242
Corrie L. 242
John 242
Lizzie 242
Martin Pugh 134
Ollie L. 272

PURCELL
Bessie L. Hughes 273
Corene 273
Elbertice 243
Elvira F. 243
Harold L. 169
Hugh C. 141
John H. 243
Lam H. 141
Lavina Kesler 141
Mildred 273
Nora M. 141
O. S. 273
Odis S. 273
R. T. 141
Vivian H. 273
W. Odell 243

PURDY
Albert Haskell 243
C. Haskell 243

PURDY continued
Etta B.

QUATTLEBAUM
Fred 8
Harry C. 8
M. E. 8
Mary E. 8
Paul 8
Stafford 8

QUEEN
E. C. 39
E. V. 25
Minnter Juel 25
S. J. 25

QUILLAN
Mr. 64

QUILLIAN
Clarissa 243
Clarissa Dean 243
Fletcher Rev. 243
Joseph A. 243
Kasiah Malissa Meadors 243
Mary C. 243
Ophelia 243
Robert T. 243
S. N. 243
Sadie C. 243
T. F. 243
Thomas F. 243
William Anthony 243

RAGAN
Alice C. 115
John A. 115
Lee 115
W. L. 115

RAGSDALE
Leonard 243
Margaret 243
Nannie Emma Lord 243

RAIDEN
Docia F. 39
George B. 39

RAINEY
Wilma Wylene 265

RAKESTRAW
Anna L. 313
Hannah 313
O. L. 313
Stella 313

RAMEY
Marvin J. 141

RAMSEY
Howard D. 243
Mattie Lee 243
Millard C. 243
Susan E. 243
Will N. 243

RANDALL
Charles W. 51
Mary 141

RANDOLPH
Ann 297
Cornelia Moon 169
Eliza 25
Elizabeth C. 169
Fannie May 169
Fletcher Jr. 341
H. J. 25,169
Hilliard J. 25
J. H. C. 25
James E. 169
Joshua H. 169
Mollie 25
W. R. 25

RATLIFF
Myrtle 335

RAVENDER
Edna Mae 39
J. L. 39

RAY
Allene 74
Eula Estelle 243
Harriet A. Patton 74
Hubert J. 141
Hugh 74

RAY continued
Katie M. 141
Lillie Gailey 141
Maggie L. Ragsdale 74
Margaret 74
Martin 243
Nellie May 74
O. G. 74
Olevie 74
Owen 74
RAY
Reba H. 74
Rosa N. 141
Ruby W. 74
S. Gibson 141
S. R. 141
Samuel Sylvestus 141
William C. 74

REDD
Charles 74
Leah O'Donald 74
William D. 74

REDDICK
Alvin Jeff 266

REDMON
Bessie S. 244
Betty Gene 244
Elice S. 244
G. Wiley 244
George 244
H. J. 244
J. O. 244
J. R. 244
Joe 243
John 244
John Richard 244
L. 244
Leila 243
Lenear B. 244
Lonie 244
Mandy Baker 243
Richard Bud 243
Wiley 244

REECE
Mamie F. 141

REED
Dora I. 25
Flora L. Nelms 244
H. Grady 25
Logan 335
Moses Wesley 244
Rose H. 202
T. Gilford 202
W. H. 335

REEVES
Becky 135
Emory E. 74
Eula Lee 74
Eula V. 74
F. E. 74
J. D. 135
John Pittard 74
Sharon Wesley 343

REIDLING
Beatrice G. 244
James O. 122
Mae Bell 122
Ola H. 122
Olcy F. 122
Thomas D. 122

REINHARDT
Jewell L. 8
S. Gertrude 8

REYNOLDS
A. J.192
Aby Myrtle 192
Andrew Jackson Rev. 192
Arthur William 105
Ava 192
Bennie Donald 192
C. H. 192
Claude 115
D. A. 192
Dave A. 192
E. M. 141
Edward M. 141
Ernest 192
Ernest C. 192
Estelle S. 192
Eula Waddell 105
Fannie M. 52
G. W. 192

REYNOLDS continued
George C. 115
Hattie S. 192
Helen 52
James D. 192
Jane S. 192
Jeremiah 51
Johnnie 192
Larry J. 192
Lena M. 192
Mary M. 192
Minnie 115
Minnie L. 327
Minnie V. 141
N. J. 192
Paula Jean 141
Steve 52
Susie Bryan 115
Thomas William 105
William E. 327
William H. 192

RHODES
Dozier B. 244
J. R. 244
James M. 244
Julian G. 244
Leila C. 244
Mary J. 244

RICE
Allen P. Jr. 244
Allen P. Sr. 244
Claudia C. 244
George T. 244
Homer Hoot 244
John G. 244
Marion H. 244
Nelle 244
Nelle Harber 244
Ola H. 244
Pearl Power 244
W. B. 244
William Brannon 244

RICH
C. E. 294
Carrie E. 294
Cordelia F. 294.
Edna E. 294
W. W. 294

RICHEY
Annie T. 245
Bessie May 245
C. O. 245
Charlie B. 245
Charlie H. 245
Cordelia Lord 245
E. W. 63, 244
E. W. P. 63
Evelyn P. 245
Garner R. 245
H. M. 245
Henry T. 245
J. O. 245
J. S. 245
J. S. P. 245
James R. 245
James R. 245
John Olin 245
L. F. 345
L. S. 245
Lola 245
Lola Benton 244
Lou Eaton 245
Lydia Gertrude 63
M. A. 244
Mary Etta Nix 63
Mary Ruth Allen 245
Merdelle H. 245
Otis Samuel 245
Pearl 245
Roy V. 63
Sarah 245
William T. 245

RICKELS
B. P. 323
John 323
Lora 323
Ruby Lee 323
Sarah E. 323

RIEVES
T. J. 192

RICHARDSON
Augusta K. 192
C. C. 202
Charlie 202

RICHARDSON continued
Charlie Herbert 202
Clara Mae 192
Clarence 192
David L. 245
David R. 192
E. C. 192
E. Clyde 192
Henry C. 316
J. M. 25
J. W. 192
Johnnie 192
Julian L. (Foxie) 192
Lena W. 316
M. Lula 192
Margie H. 192
Margie R. 192
Marshall H. 192
N. C. 25
Ola 202
S. F. 192
Sarah Frances 192

RILEY
Eddie D. 102
John 330
Margie 330
Mattie 300

RITCH
Ella 294
J. E. 294
Jewell V. 294

RITCHIE
Frank Telford 245
Georgia Usry 245
Susie Evans 245
Thomas Evans 245

RIVES
Ava Hogan 52

ROACH
J. Nelson 123
Marion Fay 245
Randall 245

ROBERTS
A. Scott 39
Ada 105

ROBERTS continued
Aisa 105
Alvin E. 266
Arthur 135
Arthur William 105
Callie 105
Charlie
D. C. 308
D. H. 105
Darenda 105
Dave 52
Desma M. 266
E. L. 323
Early U. 266
Edward H. 105
Effie Jane 266
Elizabeth 91
Ellie May 39
Emily 42
Emma F. 323
Essie E. 39
Esther D. 266
Evie 105
Exie S. 273
Frances 266
Frank 169
Fred 99
George D. 52
Georgia Ann Winston 25
Grace 266
Hubert Jefferson 266
J. B. 104 105
J. Davis 135
J. R. 105
J. Rainey 273
J. W. 323
J. W. Jr. 323
James E. 273
John S. 308
Josiah 52
Leila H. 323
Louella 323
Lucile 323
Mandie E. 135
Marcus A. 8
Margaret J. 105
Martha 99
M. F. 308
Major C. 245
Mary A. 105
Mattie Bell 169

ROBERTS continued
Maude 52
Nannie E. 105
Pearl W. 126
R. L. 39
Ralph B. 8
Rhoda 266
S. C. 105
Sarah Eliza 52
Stephen 105
Susie M. 52
Vada Skelton 266
W. C. 105, 323
W. D. 99
W. F. 323
W. J. 25
W. W. 105
Worth 323
Zilly 52

ROBINSON
Amanda E. 245
Homer 343
James Henry 343
Sallie Walden 343
Samuel Ernest 335

RODGERS
J. W. 26
W. M. 26

ROE
Loyce S. 266

ROGERS
A. A. 245
Henry Jewel 339
James T. 246
Marion Irene 245
Martha Elizabeth O'Kelly 246

ROSS
Charles 169
E. C. 169
Elenor Caroline 169
John N. 169
Lucy Whitehead 169
T. L. 169
Tommie 169

ROUSE
Mattie E. 26

ROY
Henry L. 246
Lilliam P. 246

ROYAL
Irene 294

RUSSELL
Stiles 246

RUTHERFORD
Anna 309
Elizabeth Ann 308
William B. 308

RYLEE
E. J. 246
Elizabeth 246
Wilkie 246

SAILERS
Carrie Lay 246
Deloney 246
Ethel P. 246
Frances Chandler 91
George W. 141, 246
Harvey F. 123
Jacqueline W. 343
Jane S. 141
Joe 246
Laurie Ingram 246
Mae Onie 123
Obe O. 246
W. Carl 246
W. Lamar 123
Walter Henry 123

SAILORS
Bernice 105
Bessie G. Douglas 63
Christine L. 170
Cora 26
Cordelia D. 273
E. M. 105
Henry M. 193
Hubert P. 105
J. Lou 273
J. M. 273

SAILORS continued
J. W. 56
Jack 273
James 56
John W. 273
Joseph E. 56
L. M. 56
Linton 56
Martha J. 56
Marton B. 56
Nancy 273
Robert S. 105
T. G. 56
Tallulah G. Short 273
V. A. 56
W. C. 273
W. C. Jr. 273
William C. 105
Y. Z. 170
Young 273

SALORS
C. C. 26
Curtis C. 26
Ida 26

SEAGRAVES
Mary Sallie 298
William Hoyl 298

SAMPLES
Ishmael DeWitte 170
Mary D. 170
R. M. 170
R. W. 170
Raymond Jr. 170

SANDERS
Ada B. 246
Ann 130
Bessie E. 91
Billy 288
D. Gwinn 246
Donald J. 246
Eliza Barnett 346
George W. 246
Howard 246
Ida P. 288
James B. 246
James Willie 288
Lastus M. D. 246

SANDERS continued
Lenard C. 288
M. Tharpe 246
Mary Bennett 246
Nellie A. 52
Plumer S. 246
R. L. 246
Ralph 288
Robert L.246
Ruth Denham 246
T. Poullain 246
Turner H. 246

SARGENT
Benie 74
D. D. 74
Irene 74
Mary Ray 74
Maver I. 74
Shirley C. 74

SATTERFIELD
Ann 52
Clyde 52
H. W. 52,323
Henry W. 52
Jeffrey D. 170
Pearl 52
Ray 52
Royce David 170
Royce H. 170
Tonia S. 170
William Clyde 52

SAULS
G. W. 193
Malitt 193

SAYLORS
Parina H. 193

SAXON
Grady W. 247
H. E. 247
Lewis 247
Mary G. 247
Mary S. 247
Maybell J. 247
Rena G. 247
Willie M. 247

SCARBOROUGH
Elmer A. 126
Geneva N. 126

SCOGGINS
C. M. 247
Claud 247
Elma C. 282
Emma Greer 247
Harriet Arminda 247
J. H. 247
J. M. 282
John Jr. 247
Levi Lincoln 130
Mark W. 282
Mary E. 247

SCOTT
Jack Shelnutt 170

SCRUGG
Ruby Dora Joan 301

SEABOLT
Dexter Lee 91
F. H. 91
J. W. 91
Lillie A. 91
N. A. 91
Rudolph 91

SEAGRAVES
Bernice 123
Berr A. 247
Claude 247
Iva F. 247
J. B. 123
Nezzie W. 247

SEARS
Arthur G. 247
M. Evelyn 247
Mary Garrison 91
Olevia 91
T. W. 91
W. R. 91

SEAY
W. J. 170

SEBOLT
John H. 335
May 335

SEEGARS
Otis 280

SEGARS
Ada N. 344
Georgia A. 344
John J. 344
Olive Florian 344
Ray 344
Simon A. 344
Thomas Leon 344

SELF
D. T. 202
E. H. 130
Eva 202
Floella G. 39
Ina Estelle 52
Lee Earnest 39
Roy Ernest 202
Stacy M. 52

SELL
Angie M. 310
B. Elmer 309
Celia 310
Dorothy Hill 9
Howell Jackson 9
James 310
Julia Anderson 9
L. Frank 310
Lucious C. 310
Sarah L. 310

SELLARS
Emma Brady 247

SELLERS
J. 313
Louoll Harris O'Neal 301

SEWELL
Monroe 301

SEXTON
Rafe. 115

SERODING
Eugenia M. 247
Norbert R. 247
Ruth B. 247

SEYMOUR
C. F. 248
C. T. 248
Charlie T. 247
Claud F. 248
Francis O. 247
Glenn Rondol 248
Louise C. 247
Malcolm H. 247

SHACKELFORD
Dessie 297

SHANKLE
Andrew Marvin 248
Lovic P. 248
Minnie B. 273
Nana Johnson 248
Olin E. 248
Pearl Bush 248
William 273

SHANNON
John F. 248

SHARP
Anna 248
B. B. 248
C. H. D. 302
Clara Mae 248
E. H. 130
E. J. 130
Edmond J. 74
Esther Lee 248
L. H. 248
L. J. 248
Margaret 130
Mary 74
Nelly N. 248
Pauline S. 248
W. T. 302

SHARPE
Anne Lou 280
J. W. 280

SHARPE continued
Mae 280
Momme 280
Sara 280

SHAW
Betty A. 193
Boyd 202
George W. 106
H. Foster 193
H. W. 106
Herbert 202
Hubert 202
J.P. 202
Mary Evie 106
Rache 202
Sarah A. 202
Tom Pinson 106
W. B. 106

SHED
J. J. Sr. 26

SHELL
Henry Hilliard 248
Willie McCurdy 248

SHELNUTT
Lena H. 63
William M. 63

SHELTON
Berry 52
Mary 52

SHEPHERD
Grace 330
J. W. 248
Rosalie Smith 248

SHEPPARD
Iva 248
J. J. 248
Margaret Shankle 248
Rosena Maret 248
William Daniel 248

SHERARD
Cornelia 170
S. W. 170

SHERIDAN
Marvin 52
Sinthia 52

SHIELDS
A. S. 40
Annie Elder 40
Annie Mae 248
B. S. 330
E. S. 39
Ella 170
Emanuel Scott 170
Emma 170
Emma S. 40
Emory H. 40
Helen Anice 39
J. C. 40
J. T. 39
James 330
James T. 40
Jewiel 330
John W. 248
Joseph R. 39
Lazunia 330
Lilly Alice 40
Lula 330
Luther 102
Ola F. 39
Sarah J. 39
Victoria 330
W. S. 40

SHIFLETT
Alexander 294
Claude 294

SHORE
Cander 249
Luther C. 249
M. E. 249
Odell 249
Salome H 249
T. H. 249
Tempy B. 249

SICOLS
Lener 249

SILMAN
Henry M. 171
J. B. 171

SILMAN continued
James B. 171
James Paul 249
Jane Yearwood 171
Kathleen Couch 171
Robert Ralph 171

SHIRLEY
Anna Carol 123
B. T. 64
Betty Colquitt 64
C. P. 42
D. T. 64
Edward W. 327
Irene 42
Jasper W. 64
Leo B. 64
Mary A. 64
Richard Butler 64
Sallie 42
Thurza Ann 64

SHOCKLEY
Cynthia 171

SHORT
A. F. 142
Ada Ray 142
Clyde 142
D. G. 126
Dooly C. 142
Dovelee B. 141
Etherlinda L. 126
Ethleen 142
Frank Olin 142
George L. 126
Hattie 141
James H. 126
Jane M. 141
Jesse Williams 126
Johnie L. 126
Joseph D. 141
Keff 142
L. E. 126
M. J. 142
Martha E. 142
Mary A. 123
Maudie 126
Minnie Lou 123
Obie 123
Ola D. 91

SHORT continued
Retha F. 142
V. Alberta 142
W. H. 142
William Grief 141
William H. 141
Woodie 91

SHROPSHIRE
Lucius A. 171

SHUMAKE
Emma W. 171
Emory Gordon Sr. 171
Laura Lee 171

SIKES
Carrie E. 194
Exa F. 40
George E. 171
Joe Talmadge 40
John Bell 171
Lillian Lorane 171
Mary Ruth 194

SIMMONS
Albert C. 202
Annie Mae 202
Bashia S. 202
Belle B. 202
Carroll J. 171
Ellen 202
Emma Mozelle 202
H. G. 202
H. G. 202
Harriett Eviline (Whitmire) 202
J. Anderson 202
Laura J. 193
Nina 202
Northern 202
Rachel Y. 202
Truman T. 202
W. P. 171
William P. 193
Winford 202
Woodie 202

SIMPSON
Talmadge Brock 171

SIMPSON
Fletcher 203
Kate 203
William N. 203

SIMS
Alice B. 106
Alma R. 64
Annie 106
Carlton C. 64
Cora W. 64
Ella Colquitt 64
Henry C. 64
Jeanett H. 249
Joe 91
Joe 91
John Clark 64
Lammie C. 64
Lawrence S. 64
Matilda C. 193
Myrtle 91
Nathan 330
Paul H. 249
W. S. (Bill) 193
Woodie Callie 115

SKELTON
A. Virgil 53
Berry 53
Estell 53
Estelle Roberts 266
Eunice May 26
G. W. 26
George W. 193
Ila 53
J. B. 193
J. H. 266
J. M. 193
J. V. 53
J. W. 53
James Edward 53
James S. 53
John H. 53
John H. 53
Lola 53
Martha Ellen 193
Mary Ann 26
Mary J. 53
Mary L. 53
Nancy L. 53
Sarah E. 26

SKELTON continued
Spurgeon 26
W. J. 26

SLATER
Earlie T. 249
J. A. 249

SMALLWOOD
Ada Belle 249
Agnes M. 172
Debra Ann 249
Drucilla G. 249
E. L. 249
Elisha Litt 249
Ethel E. 250
Grady 249
Howard R. 53
Howard R. Sgt. 53
J. L. 171
James D. 249
John H. (Jake) 171
John T. 249
Lizzie 171
Lou 249
Loy 171
Lucius Littleton 249
Luke L. 250
Martha E. 249
Mary T. 53
Mattie 171
Mellie 172
Minnie B. 249
Newt 171
Odessa V. 249
R. A. 249
Roxie T. 249
Roy D. 249
Ruby 171
Ruzell 53
Susan Elizabeth 249
T. N. 249
Thomas P. 249
W. E. 171
Willie Pearle 249
Wilton M. 171
Youle F. 171

SMITH
A. 340
A. A. 56
A. E. 26
A. N. 26,27,266
A.J. 273
Alford H. 316
Alice R. 316
Allen 250
Andrew T. 273
Annie L. 115
Annie L. 250
Annie Mae 250
Antine 27
Anza 288
Arnold Randolph 172
Asa L. 250
B. Paul 273
Benjamin C. 203
Bobby 250,273
Buell 301
C. Eugene 75
C. P. 172
Carl E. 250
Charlie Emery 294
Clark Howell 172
Claud 203
Claude P. 53
Clyde S. 266
Cordelia 26
Cornelia Thurmond 250
D. B. 172
Daisy W. 64
Dee 26
Donald Brooks Jr. 172
Dora E. 273
Eliza 340
Elizabeth 250,324
Emma 250
Emma Walton 250
Ethel D. 53
Etta W. 250
Eulla 305
Evie 301
F. A. 250
F. C. 323
F.115
Fletcher 142
Flora Hardy 294
Florene James 250
Frank 99

SMITH continued
G. C. 115
G. M. 826
George 8
George Erwin 172
Grocer 64
Grover E. 8
Gus 266
H. C. 26
H. M. 250
H. N. 26
Hark 340
Harry Lee 250
Hazel J. 250
Henry M. 250
Hoke 203
Hollis 250
Homer L. 316
Icie Cornelia 250
Idea 340
Isaac S. 115
J. 340
J. A. 172
J. Almond 26
J. Chester 172
J. F. 92
J. H. 2627
J. L. 273
J. N. 56
J. R. 26
J. W. 26
James Henry 115
James W. 323
Jeptha A. 250
Jessie L. 250
Joe B. 282
Joe Fred 64
John C. 194
John L. 294
John W. 250
Johnnie Louise 203
Julia Hardy 294
Julia W. 250
L. C. 8
L. G. 26
Lamb B. 250
Lee V.250
Leila B. 8
Lena S. 250
Lenora 26
Lewis W. 316

SMITH continued
Lillie FC. 142
Lizzie 266
Lucile G. 250
Lucy F. 250
Lula 324
Lula A. 273
M. O. 250
Margie E. 250
Martha M. 250
Mary B. 250
Lola 115
Lula Elizabeth 26
M. M. 250
Margaret F. 194
Martha 340
Mary 64,115
Mary E. 115
Melinda Jane 316
Michael Eugene 53
Milton 26
Minnie 340
Mittian Lola 27
Mittie G. 273
Myra Thompson 172
Myrt Park 8
Nancy L. 323
Nettie Miller 64
Nezzie 250
Ora Dyaman 172
Otis 250
Patricia 64
Paulina C. 8
Pearl 92
Pearl C. 203
R. C. 75
R. Earl 75
R. L. J. 250
Ransom 340
Robert Lee 294
Roberta 316
Rosa 250
Rosa B. 250
Robert D. 64
Ruby 273
S. J. 172
S. P. 26
Sally 250
Sam 64
Selwyn J. 250
Stephen Lester 323

SMITH continued
Susie Ester 335
Terry Lee 115
Theodocia Victoria Dill 305
Venie 26
Viola 92
W. G. 250
W. Gordon 250
W. H. 172
Walter C. 172
William 115
William D. 288
William Floyd 250
William G. 250
William H. 172
William Henry 172
William L. 250
William M. 8
William P. 27
Willie 340
Willie Rich 294
Zora T. 266
Zuline T. 250
Mattie J. 309
W. M. 309
Martha 309
David 309

SNIPES
Fannie G. 251
Hoyt Allen 251
Parker 251
Ray 273
Thomas E. 123
Wilma C. 273

SOLOMON
Jake 172

SORRELLS
Carrie 251
Wyley 251

SORROW
Castellaw B. 251
Harber D. 251
J. H. 251
James V. 251
Lila L. 251
Lonnie M. 251
Olia S. 251

SORROW continued
Rilla I. 251
Samuel Carlos 251
Sidney L. 251
W. O. 251

SOSEBEE
E. H. 251
Louise 92
M. B. 92
Nancy 251

SPAIN
Adeline 27
Cynthia A. 27
F. A. 27
Roseller 27
Thomas A. 27

SPEALMAN
Angel D. 27
Mae Etta McDaniel 266
Mary Antionette 27

SPENCER
Claude W. 294
Ella J. 115
Finley B. 294
John Tillman 294
Odie I. 294
Robert J.
S. C. 294
Sallie G. 294
Sarah A. 115
Thomas J. 294
W. M. 294
William 115,294
William M. 294
William W. 294

SOSEBEE
Cora E. McGee 172
J. B. 203
Mattie Hulsey 172
Ralph Lee 203
Richard T. 203

SPRATLIN
William T. 172

SPRUELL
John W. 27

STADLEY
L. T. 313

STAGNER
Susie B. 251

STANCIL
Eli 193
H. 193
Ila Mae 193
J. H. (Mollie) 193
J. H. 193
Junius A. 193
Malvin 193
Mollie 193
N. E. 193
Thomas H. 102
Tirza Loucile 193

STANDRIDGE
Alice 251
Clara M. 316
Clyde Joe 251
Dallas 251
Henry G. 316
Hettie R. 251
Isaac B. 172
J. B. 251
Jessie P. 251
John M. 92
Leona M. 251
Luke
Mary Helen Lacy 123
Riley 251
Ruby C. F. 251

STANRIDGE
Dillard 203
Docia 142
Dozier 203
E. T. 203
Ella T. 203
Hettie 142
Hilda Runa 142
Howard 142
Isaac 142
J. A. 142
J. C. 142

STANRIDGE continued
J. D. 142
J. H. 203
J. P. 203
James H. 203
James J. 142
Julia Jarrett 142
Mamie B. 283
William C. 142
William Preston 142

STANLEY
G. W. 172

STAPELER
Katharine 277
Katharine Hale 277
L. A. 277
Thomas 277

STAPLER
D. T. 278
Floyd 278
Frances A. Jennings 278
Harriet B. 251
Hoyt 251
John M. 277
John O. 278
Joseph Archibald 278
Leonora E. 278
Margaret Edmondson 278
Myrtie 278
Robbie A. 278
Robert B. 252
Susannah M. 278
T. A. 278
T. J. 278
T. T. 278
Thomas J. 278
Timothy T. 278
W. T. 251

STARGEL
Iola R. 53
Jones C. 53

STARGIL
A. T. 194
M. M. 194
Mary 194
Mary E. 194

STARK
Aldine 252
Arabella Brown 252
Cicero D. 252
Clara F. 252
D. M. 172
Evelyn 252
G. D. 252
Grade Elizabeth 252
Hope 252
Kathrine 252
Lula Helen 252
S. L. 252
Susan 252
Thelma 252
W. W. 252
Weldon F. 252
William Weldon 252

STATON
Frank Christopher 172
Lizzie Segars 172
Thomas C. 173

STEADMAN
John B. 252
Rosa L. 252

STEELE
Roy R. 252
Sarah B. 252

STEPHENS
Addie 252
Alexander 335
Annie 27
Brisey A. White 27
Canon 335
Cleo Weathers 335
Crawford 173
Elizabeth F. 53
Ellis 27
Etta J. 27
George Garner 252
J. A. 27
J. E. 252
J. N. 27
Joe W. 27
John Newton 27

Joseph A. 27
STEPHENS continued
Julia 27
Julie E. Vaughlin 27
Levie E. 27
Lindsey S. 173
Nancy Ann 27
Nolan 27
Ray J. 27

STEPHENSON
Baby Joan 252
Hattie R. 252
Jim U. 252
Kathleen W. 273
Lula J. C. 252
Tom B. 252
Willie O. 252

STEPP
D. E. 54
Dora A. 324
Eliza Caroline 324
G. L. 54
J. W. 324
Julian N. 53
Ralph 53

STEVENS
Anna 280
C. M. 75
Charlie O. 75
Homer 280
L. G. 75
M. E. 64
Martha E. 64
Mattie E. 64
W. C. 64
W. T. 64

STEVENSON
Jessie Merle 252

STEWARD
David 297

STEWART
Alice E. Hutchins 75
Amanda C. 253
Annie Lou 309
Belle W. 344

Cammie A. 28
STEWART continued
Carlton 297
D. O. 194
D. W. 309
Daniel W. 123
David 309
David Oscar 309
David W. 309
Eliza 203
George H. 194
J. N. 75
James B. 203
John M. 344
Louisa Stewart 54
Mamie L. 253
Myrtle Belle 309
Parks 309
R. T. 309
Ransom R. 54
Rosa Telula 309
S. C. 309
Sarah A. 194
William Ed 28

STOCKTON
Arline 92
B. B. 92
Carlton Patrick 92
Edna L. 142
Edward 142
Fannie 92
Hulda 92
J. E. 115
J. O. 92
J. W. 92, 173
James W. 92, 173
John Oscar 92, 173
Leila B. 173
M. M. 115
Mae 142
Mary M. 142
Mary Patrick 173
Miller 294
Runa W. 294
Sarah Joe P. 115
Minnie 92
W. M. 142

STONE
Alton Luther 285

Annie 285
STONE continued
Cleo Evans 8
Curtis 142
E. A. 285
E. B. 285
Eunice L. 285
Gwyn 285
J. A. 285
Jim E. 285
John F. 8
John R. 285
Mamie B. 92
Margie R. 285
Marvin A. 285
Mary G. 285
Mary Lee 142
Nilda 285

STOREY
Annis 8
Belle P. 8
Calvin T. 173
Dell McRee 173
Dorothy 8
Hoyt E. 130
Hugh H. 173
James A. 130
James M. 8
Jessie Frances 154
Martha M. 173
Martha R. 130
William Jackson 173

STORY
Caroline 131
James A. 131
Morgan 330
Woodie 131

STOVALL
Albert B. 253
James Thomas 173

STOVER
David Gordon 173
Leila Emmett 173

STOVER
Grady 92

STOWE
Grace B. 253
H. DeWitt 253
Susan H. 253
Willis M. 253

STRANGE
J. R. 194
J. W. 28
John G. 28
M. E. 194
Martha 28
Martha E. 194
Mary J. 28
Octavia Dunahoo 194
Ora May 194
W. N. 194

STRAYNGE
James A. 8
Emma E. 8

STREETMAN
A. F. 126
Allie M. 305
B. L. 126
Edward B. 75
Guf. 53
J. W. 142
Larman 142
N. C. 142
N. M. 53
Robert B. 305
Thomas C. 53
Toilet 126

STRICKLAND
Arlie 173
Arlie C. 173
Brant W. 253
Charles 115
Emily H. 253
Guy 173
James E. 173
James H. 173
John W. 173
Nancy E. 173
Permelia Farabee 253
Sarah A. Marler 115
Virginia G. 123

Wilbern 253
STRICKLAND continued
William H. 253

STRINGER
Anna A. 106
Dewitt S. 116
Gary Sean 106
Infant of Millard 106
Millard A. 106
Oscar D. 116
Sarah M. 116
Scott 116
William P. 106
Willie 106

STROUD
Martha M. 75
Samuel J. 75

SULLIVAN
Earnestine 173
J. P. 173
James E. 173
James W. 253
Janell 173
Martha M. 253
Pearl 173

SUTTON
C. N. 65
E. L. 65

SWAIN
Annie L. 92
Charles H. 92
Hazel 92
Walter C. 92

SWAN
Charlie V. 40
Corrie F. 40

SWANGIM
K. E. 75
M. E. Eberhart 75

SWEATMAN
Robert M. 327
Savannah E. 327

SWINDLE
Hoyce M. 253

SYKES
Reba B. 174

SYRAN
Carlbel H. 253
T. J. 253
Thomas J. 253

TALLENT
Agnes L. 253
Edward D. 253
Mark A. 309
Mary L. 309

TALMADGE
Leta Montgomery 174

TANNER
Billy George 194
Bunyon 203
Carrie Jane Love 274
Elizabeth 203
George D. 123
Jane Davidson 123
Joyce E. 92
L. P. 274
Otis 194
Roy 266
Ruby Dean 266

TATE
A. D. 99
Alvin C. 54
Artie H. 102
Ineze 253
Irvin M. 253
Julia E. 203
Lucy S. 253
Mary J. 54
Melvin C. 54
Myrtle 54
Rawlin S. 99
S. P. 99
Sadie P. 54
Thomas R. 203
Tobe 54

TATUM
Hoyt J. 174
Hubert 174
Minnie S. 174
William O. 174

TAYLOR
C. B. 194
Donnie Clyde 174
Grady W. 174
Joe Henry 297
Laurence 281
Mary Lee 174
Milledge 174
Z. O. 194

TEAGUE
Mary 7

TEAL
Ernest 116
F. A. 116
S. F. H. 116

TENCH
Bular Mae 254
Celia H. 254
Clyde 254
Fannie Annabell Hicks 254
Guy 254
J. B. 254
M. B. 254
Mack B. 254
Margaret Lois 254

TERRY
Annie Dotson 324
Rufus 324

THRELKELD
Virginia L. Hanson 106
G. W. 106

THOMAS
A. Paul 254
Bashie M. 254
Belinda R. 313
Clara D. 299
Columbus 299
Dea Clifford (Sark) 340

Elizabeth C. 9
THOMAS continued
Estell 340
George C. 340
J. E. 203
J. Luther 266
J. W. 254
L. W. 9
Norris Emory 203
Onie Bridges 203
Pearl W. 266
Prince 340
Rosie E. 203
Sarah 203
Susan 254
Susan Lockhart 254
Vassie 340
William 203
Willie T. 313

THOMPSON
Americus 324
Annie Mae 93
Charlie 93
Dr. James A. 324
Francisa 174
Fred C. 75
Gordon G. 75
Ida Anderson 9
J. N. 9
Jacob D. 324
James M. 75
Jasper L. 324
Jasper Newton 9
John 324
Mamie V. 75
Mary L. 324
Milton 174.
Pearlie 93
Phoebe L. 324
Plonia G. 75
Robert E. 143
Robert G. 143
Tibbie A. 324
Vernard 93
William S. 174

THORNTON
Eugenia 285
Ira G. 285
J. Glover 285

J. Mark 285
THORNTON continued
Jessie H. 285
Mark 285
Sarah E. 93
W. A. 93

THREATT
Odell G. 254

THURMON
C. V. 93
J. B. 93
J. B. Jr. 93
John B. Sr. 93
Little Ruth 93
Mary A. C. V. Sailers 93
Mollie W. 93
Ottico M. 65

THURMOND
Alvin 254
Alvin H. 254
Annie Mae 344
Bertha I. 124
Cohen E. 344
Delyon Elwanda 254
Frank 254
Franklin W. 28
Gussie F. William 75
J. M. 194
Jessie 254
Jessie Rhodes 254
John A. 124
Julian 9
L. E. 254
Mattie C. 274
Ollie I. Potts 75
Rhodes 254
Rosie B. 194
Samuel Preston 28
Sarah Ella 28
W. M. 274
W. R. 75
William Reuben 75
Woots O. 124
Y. L. 254

TILEER
Tommie Lou 174

TIMBS
Chesley 194
Elizabeth 204

TIMMS
Dukie? 267
Edd 267
Tracie Runa 267

TITSHAW
E. M. 28
F. B. 28
Fannie M. 28
J. T. 28
James T. 28
John 267
L. W. C. 928
Mary 267
Mary A. 28
Mollie 28
S. W. 28
Serena 28

TOLBERT
Allis H. 254
Annie Pauline 93
Charlie A. 174
E. M. 93
Emma W. 174
Eula T. 174
H. H. 254
James D. 174
James W. 174
Martha 254
Ruby L. 174
William T. 254

TONEY
Dora Holliday 339
Mary E. 93
Milton G. 93
Ruby W. 79
Thurston S. 79

TOOKE
Charlton Clinton 254

TOUCHSTONE
Thomas B. 254

TOW
Charlie 131
Lula 131
William 131

TRACY
Ruth 9
S. T. 9
Sadie Darby 9

TRAMMELL
Donna Marie 75
Floyd A. 75
Mattie D. 76
N. G. 131
O. A. 131
Ralph 131

TRAWICK
Paul B. 254

TREADWELL
Essie Mae 330

TRIBBE
J. E. 174
Susie Thompson 174

TROUT
Florida B. 175
Laura L. 174
Nancy Myrt 116

TRUITT
Nathan Wylie 255
Susan Virginia Barbara 255

TUCK
J. A. Dr. 40
James M. 40
Lucile 40
Lucy E. 40
Neva 40

TUCKER
Homer Allen 274
Julia V. 274
Leolane 124
Mary F. 255
Merle Ginn 274
Milton 124
TUCKER continued
Vera E. 274
Virginia 274
W. A. 274
W. A. Jr. 274
William A. 274

TUGGLE
J. L. 255
Milissia A. 255
Sallie 9

TURK
George 102
Tishie 102
Henson Sims 102

TURNER
Calhoun 255
Caroline M. 54
Carrie Gober 255
Charles H. 93
Clara L. 204
Clyde Hancock 175
F. Marion 204
Fannie E. 93
Harold Lee 106
Homer J. 54
Fannie K. 131
Hugh H. 106
Ida Mae 131
Ila Eurene 175
Inese B. 131
Iva L. 54
J. A. 175
J. Marion 131
Jennie Ann 175
Joe J. 65
John Collier 175
John M. 131
Kittie B. 106
Mary 255
Mattie 93
Minnie Lee B. 65
Mitt W. 126
P. W. 93
R. H. 131
Robert Louis Jr. 65
William 126

TURPIN
Earnest Jack 175
James H. 255

TWIGGS
Artie 54

TWITTY
Jasper Newton 175
Mary Carithers 175

TYRON
Art 340

UNDERWOOD
David P. 116
Sarah S. 116

USHER
Paul 102

VANDIVER
Arthur 94
Arthur Hettie 93
C. L. 93
Cecil L. 93
Cecil R. 65
Claudia C. 175
E. Foshia 93
Emaline 93
Eula S. 94
F. Dillard 93
Foster M. 175
G. C. 93
George C. 93
Gertrude 93
Hattie 93
J. H. 93
Jacob Warren 94
Octavia L. 94
Randy Lee 175
Sarah L. 65
Vivian L. 93
William H. 93
Williard T. 94

VARNUM
Alvin D. 175
Deana 175
George W. 175

VAUGHN
Albert 28
Boyd Carey 274
Curtis C. 143
Dosia A. 143
Emory 255
Herman 143
J. Boyd 143
John F. 143
Keith 255
Levonia Catlett 143
Logan 28
Martha J. 274
Mary Lou 143
W. A. 28
W. Z. 274
Z. 274

VEAL
Virginia Elizabeth 28

VENABLE
A.L. 314
Ada J. 76
Albert M. 76
Albert Ned 76
Alice Pittman 175
Allen L. 324
Alma Ruth 314
Clara 76
Daniel H. 314
Claud 76
Cleo V. Register 76
E. M. 76
Easter M. 255
Elmer J. 324
Emma W. 76
Emory Alva 76
Ethel 40
Eula M.255
Fred 76
Gilbert R. 76
Grover C. 255
Herman C. 324
Hoyt W. 76
Ida Elizabeth 76
Iris Gayle 76
James Leslie 175
James T. 76
Jean W. 335

Jesse M. 76
VENABLE continued
Joe Richard 76
John A. 175
John J. 255
Kate 324
Lela 76
Lona Mae 76
M. E. 314
Maggie 324
Martha A. 314
Martha J. 76
Martin 76
Mary 76
Mary Elizabeth 76
Mattie 314
Max 76
Mays A. 76
Mollie. 314
Ned Jr. 76
Nelle 76
Oscar E. 175
Richard 76
Robert Tuck 76
Sadie M. 324
Sara F. 314
Sarah E. 175
Sumnie R. 335
T. W. 76
Thelma M. 76
Thomas W. 335
Walter L. 40
Wiley 76
Zora 76

VENERABLE
Lottie Wade 175
Okie Long 175

VERNER
John Clark 255

VERNON
James T. 274
Nettie E. 274

VICKERY
Grover W. 274
Herman 274
Jack 274
James V. 274

Ruth 274
VICKERY continued
Ruth W. 274

VIDICE
George 28

VOYLES
Erastus M. 274
Florence 143
George O. 143
Laura S. 274
Lessie P. 176
M. B. 94
W. G. 94

WELLS
Larkie Etta 274

WADDELL
Agnes 255
Bobbie Scott 324
C. E. 29
Dursor 29
Eliza 94
Frank 94
Franklin 94
George E. 324
Gordon Hushel 94
J. F. 29
James A. 29
James F. 29
Johnson 29
Lillie C. 255
Lottie Bell 94
Lucille 29
Marion B. 255
Mollie 29
Ned 29
Patrick 94
S. L. 29
Sophronia Elrod 94
Wendy 324

WADE
Elizabeth S. 54,195
Emma May 195
Emmie 54
Erastus C. 256
Henry D. Sr. 54
Hobson M. 54

John 274
WADE continued
Marion 54,195
Marion B. 54
Mittie C. 256

WAGES
Andrew 325
Brooks B. 326
E. G. 325,326
Ellis B. 299
Elzy J. 325
Irmine M. 299
James B. 325
Jasper I. 325
Jessie F. 299
June E. 299
Lucille P. 256
Mary A. 326
Mattie F. 325
Maud Z. 299
Nannie 326
S. C. 326
Steven 326
Susan M. 325
Suzy Thomas 299
Wayman 326
William Andrew 299
William S. 325

WAGNON
Leila 256
W. B. 256

WAIR
Annett 341
William 340,341

WAITS
John F. 326

WALDEN
Lonnie W. 99

WALDROP
Cora R. 256
Guynita S. 256
H. Eugene 256

WALDROUP
Sam W. 256

WALKER
Charles M. Jr. 256
Cynthia A. Austin 288
Emma Martin 288
Ernest M. 335
Eula Roba 335
Frank Lee 335
Grace L. 256
Jesse Y. 335
Jesse Young Jr. 335
John B. 288
Lenora 77,278
Lonnie M. 288
Martha A. 285
Marvin 256
Mary 77
Naomie Smallwood 256
Robert Joe 77
Sallie Z. 335
Samuel A. 288
Usuler A. 285
W. D. 256
Zack F. 288

WALL
Martha A. 29
C. C. 327
David Olin 176
Edna W. 176
H. Thomas 29
Nancy E. 339
Ola 106
Richard H. 176
Robert D. 195
Thelma 106
W. J. 339
W. M. 339
William C. 256
William Calvin 327

WALLACE
Duncan 76
G. A. 54
Henry 54
James O. 278
John H. 99
Johnnie C. 278
Lizzie 54
Lucy Brewer 54
Nancy Brewer 99

O. F. 94
WALLACE continued
R. E. 100
Sarah A. 94
Willie 100

WALLIS
John J. 314
Sarah G. 314
Virginia V. 314

WALLS
Delmus W. 305

WALTERS
C. O. 295
Oscar 295
S. F. 295

WALTON
Annie Grace 344
H. F. 344
Henry F. 344
Irene A. 344
Lizzie M. 305

WANDECK
James 256
Sammie 256

WARD
Annie Mae 124
Arthur I. 256
Bertha 195
Candler 195
Clifford Clay 256
Eddie C. 256
Emma L. 256
Forrest A. 124
Jerry Melton 176
Lillie Mae 256
Mamie L. 256
Melinda S. 79
Nancy 116
Roscoe 256
W. L. 9,116
William 195
William Lewis 9
Z. A. 116
Zimmer A. 9

WARDLAW
A. J. 257
Amanda J. 257
Anna D. 257
B. F. 257
Benjamin F. 257
Benjamin Franklin 257
Corrie Estell 257
Dairo Resta 257
Esther Lucille 257
Jason C. 257
Jason C. Jr. 257
Jesse Calvert 257
L. G. 257
Mary R. 257
Rufus Franklin 257
Sarah A. Howard 257
Walter M. 257
William Franklin 257

WASHINGTON
Alice Smith 341
John 341
Teresa R. 341

WATERS
Candler G. 77
Carson C. 257
Dorothy 124
Larry Harrison 204
Oma A. 9
Urcy 257
Willie Mae R. 257

WATKINS
Alford 65
C. C. 116
Essie B. 116
F. M. 116
Fannie Mae 116
George T. 116
Laura C. 116
Lillia A. 54
Robert A. 116
Rodney 195
Ronnie 195
Roy 282
Sarah Ann 116
Wayne 195
William S. 54

WATLINGTON
Slover 11

WATSON
Billy Ray 204
Callie Eloise 176
Elijah B. 257
Ella C. 328
Gussie Long 176
Hannah H. 204
Harrie A. 176
J. D. M. 29
J. David 257
J. H. 29
Jessie M. 29
John Henry 313
Johnny 204
Laura Owen 257
Louise 204
Martha J. 176
Mary Elizabeth 176
Minor H. 328
R. L. 29
Robert 204
Samuel Alexander 176
William Anderson 176
Zilla C. 257

WEATHERFORD
Clara 195
Earley 195

WEATHERLY
Davis C. Jr. Capt. 29
Davis C. Sr. 29
Ella Davis 29
Frederick Elma 29
Georgia D. 324
John S. 324
John Stanford 324
R. A. 77
Rhoda Elizabeth 324
Russie Alice 77
W. F. 77
Walter R. 77

WEBB
A. P. Pye 116
Americus S. 257
Annie Lord 257
Curtis W. 116
WEBB continued
Cymenthia L. 257
Faye C. 116
Frank 77
George W. 257
Josie M. 77
Markers F. 77
Martha L. 257
Martha Susan Allen 257
Olah W. 176
Pearl 77
Pearl E. 257
Perry E. 257
T. W. 176
Vella 257
W. L. 176
W. M. 257
William Albert 257

WEHUNT
Farris H. 328
Lois G. 328
Lula M. 328

WEIR
Alice May Jackson 176
Della C. 176
Fred B. 176
Jessie A. 176
John Gordon 176
Maud 176
T. W. 176
William J. 176

WELCH
Eugenia 302

WELCHEL
Esther A. 344
Ned H. 344

WELLS
Wesley L. 258

WEST
Chester R. 65
Susie Bishop 258

WESTMORELAND
George W. 176

W. R., Rev. 77
WESTMORLAND
B. Clyde 258
George 258
Henry 258
Ida B. 258

WHEELER
Charlena 275
Claude 275
Dan J. 94
H. W. 275
Horatio 275
Horatio W. 275
Ida D. 94
M. A. 275
M. L. 177
Martha Ann 275
Minnie 258
W. J. 258

WHELCHEL
Amanda 116
Coyle B. 177
Edward Darwin 305
H. 305
Hattie B. 177
James H. 177
Julis B. 177
L. E. 305
L. P. 177
Lucy 177
Martha Elizabeth Huff 305
Martha Kelton 305
Mattie Lee 305
Ned C. 177
Nedy U. 177
R. E. 177
R. F. 116
R. J. 116
Robert Eugene 177
S. N. 305

WHELESS
Fannie L. 336
Paul Darel 336
W. H. 336

WHITE
Agnes Hood 258
Alice T. 258

Andrew Jackson A. 29
WHITE continued
Anna G. 94
Annie 143
Annie H. 77
E. R. 29
Emma R. 29
Eugenia 94
Eula M. 40
Eula May 94
G. W. 94
Hillie J. White 29
Hoyt 94
J. W. Jr. 258
James J. 94
Jesse 94
Jesse White 94
John 29
John Sr. 29
John Wesley 258
Joshua 30
June W. 30
Lillie 94
Lois Elizabeth 177
Lucious 30
Martha E. 95
Marvin 258
Mattie 94
N. A. 94
Nancy Mae 30
Mae Parker 258
Nicie 29
Polly Chamblee 29
R. J. 40.258
Reba 40
Rillam 30
Robert B. 94
Robert F. 77
Robert J. 40
Roxie Ann P. 77
Sallie L. Bailey 94
Sara B. 258
Sarah A. 177
T. W. 29
Tandy 94
Thomas W. 30
W. E. 95
W. F. 95,106
William F. 94

WHITEHEAD
Annie 258
Berner 258
Bessie Archer 336
Claude C. 283
E. B. 336
E. D. 258
Elijah D. 258
Emma 258
Eugene 283
Eva 258
Fannie P. 283
G. N. 325
George Bee 258
Hautie 278
Hessie Lee 117
J. G. 258
Jerry Ann 177
Jimmie 283
John 258
Leala S. 283
Lizzie Wood 40
Margaret E. 258
Mary Holland 258
May 284
Mildred 325
R. A. 258, 339
Robert H. 339
Sallie 117
Stephen Theo. 40
W. O. (Pete) 177
W. T. 278
Walter T. 278
William H. 278
William T. 258
Willie 283

WHITFIELD
Boyd 258
Grover C. 258
J. P. Sgt. 77
Janet E. 258
Lavender P. 258
Michael B. 258

WHITLOCK
Georgia Ann 65
Guy Jr. 95
Hiram M. 65
Jacob 102
Janice M. 95
WHITLOCK continued
Jim 102
Lillie C. 102
Nancy 65
William 95

WHITLOW
Julia McKie 259
Vera Pauline 259
William A. 259

WHITMAN
David 177
John B. 177
Lorena J. Callahan 177

WHITMIRE
Beulah 204
Beulah W. 177
Eddie Omer Sr. 177
Kate M. 95
L. F. 95
Laura Dell 95
Lee F. 95
Ludie Frank 204
Mildred Nunn 95
Myrtie J. 204
O. C. 95
Ola C. 95
Otis 95
Sarah Caroline 95
Sophie 177
T. E. 177, 204

WIER
Alice 10
Annie Mae 77
Arlie 77
Bessie M. 95
Charlie Reese 295
Clarende E. 77
Don E. 10
Elizabeth Wilhite 295
H. L. 9
Henry T. C. 77
I. 10
Ida Pinson 295
Idalia 9
J. Frank 344
James 295

James B. 95
WIER continued
Lamissie 295
Lizzie R. 77
Lovic L. 10
Myrt C. 77
Nina Eckles 77
Robert W. 295
S. B. 10
Samuel D. 295
Sarah J. 295
Wesley 295

WIGINGTON
E. G. 131
Harriet E. 131

WILBANKS
Aubrey W. 259
Betty 143
Billy J. 177
Broadus 143
Carole 143
Eddie 126
Edna 126
Ella 143
Grady O. 259
Guy 143
Henry W. 177
Hoke D. 124
Huldah N. 143
Ida E. 259
Isaac 259
J. H. 126
J. M. 127
Jackie 177
James E. 126
Jeff C. 126
John Sr. 124
John W. 126
Josephine 126
Kathryn J. 177
Laura Wi259n
Lillian 143
Mary Johnson 126
Nettie L. 124
Oliver B. 143
Ora W. 177
Patricia 177
Patricia 177
Roxie Mae 177

W. L. 143
WILBANKS continued
William L. 143
William M. 143

WILBORN
Nelie 301

WILBURN
Elex 301
Offie Blakely 301

WILCOX
Joseph Dillard 56

WILDER
H. W. 259
Sharon 259

WILHITE
Angeline Doss 178
Doss T. Sr. 178
J. C. 178
Jean Moran 178
M. G. 178
Myra 259
Myrtle 178
S. V. 178

WILKERSON
Maggie 117
R. 117

WILEY
Clara 309
Edna 309
Ethel Orem 309
J. E. 309
J. W. 143
James D. 95
J. D. 309
John 78
John D. 309
Joseph E. 309
Lee 313
M. C. 10
M. E. 309
Maggie 309
Margaret 309
Margaret S. 309
Mary E. 309

Ola 309
WILEY continued
Omer Lee 309
R. L. 309
Robert Cobb 309
Robert Lee 309
S. G. 309
Susan S. 95

WILHITE
A. A. 95
Blanch 95
Clara Belle 95
Clementine 95
M. C. 95
M. E. 95
M. G. 95
Mamie M. 131
Mary E. 95
Mattie L. 95
Morgan 131
S. T. 95
W. T. 95

WILKES
A. L. 285
Alline D. 78
Audrey F. 78
Benjamin A. 285
C. Herbert 78
Charles E. 78
Claude T. 78
Daniel Parker 78
Ellison 285
Fannie I. 259
George Edwin 78
George S. 78
Gerome C. 78
J. Edd 78
J. O. 285
John A. 78
L. Jeff 78
Lorenzo D. 259
Lowery Grant 178
M. Josephine 285
Mary E. 78
Murley Mae 285
Myrtis 78
R. H. 78
Radford H. 78
Rosa G. 78

S. C. 78
WILKES continued
Sadie 78
Sarah S. 78
Steven Allen 78
Thomas S. 78
Valna Pauline 78
W. A. 78
Waymon A. 78

WILKS
Charlie D. 78
Dorris Laconia 78
L. J. 78
S. F. 78

WILLIAM
Willis 178

WILLIAMS
A.B. Dawson 259
B. P. 259
Billy 259
Callie 204
Charlie 281
Clarence 204
Cora May 204
E. B. 259
Elma H. 143
Emma 259
Emma L. 305
G. T. 259
George T. 204
H. Odell 259
Hattie 259
Henry Eugene 259
Hilda M. 143
J. Billy 259
J. D. 259
Jim E. 305
John K. 305
J. S. 204
Joe 204
Joyce 259
Lillie C. 259
Lonnie L. Jr. 259
M. C. 204
Mattie L. 316

WILLIAMSON
A. J. 78, 79

A.G. (Sporty) 305
WILLIAMSON continued
Anna Belle 344
Bertram C. 295
C. F. 295
Carl 65
Caroline F. 78
Charlie R. 79
Cranston B. 79
Dillie 260
Eliza J. 79
Ethel T. 259
Ethleen 259
F. Hoyt 344
Floy 295
Floy Juanita 295
Frances A. 295
Fred H. 259
George Earl 295
Hettie C. 295
Hilda Marie 295
J. P. 295
James G. 295
Jamie Polk 295
Julius Donald 295
Julius P. 295
Junie 330
G. L. 78
Hazel Lee 260
J. 78
J. David 79
J. L. Jr. 178
Jennie H. 344
Josephine Freeman 79
Junius H. 78
Junius S. 344
L. M. 305
M. G. 295
M. Glenn 295
M. M. 295
Mattie M. A. 295
Nancy L. 78
Nathan 78
Nathaniel J. 305
Nelle B. 79
Oscar 305
Robbie T. 295
Robert O. 344
Sallie Mae 79
Talm 295
Thomas Ray 79

Thomas Ray Jr. 79
WILLIAMSON continued
V. M. 260
Violet M. 259
W. B. 305
W. Donald 259
Woodson Lafayette 259

WILLIFORD
Carrie Head 261
Henry Oscar 261

WILLS
Clara M. 178
Edna Wood 339
Florence 178
Frances Olivia Holliday 178
J. E. 178
J. Herman 124
J. W. Jr. 41
J. W. Sr. 41
James A. 178
Jim 339
Laura C. 178
Lizzie 41
Mary Lou 178
Ola Mae 124
W. C. 178
W. M. 41
William Crofford 178

WILSON
A. Grady 275
Addie C. 178
Alice 95
Allen D. 275
Allie J. 275
Andrew 297
Angeline E. 178
Arthur C. 178
Benjamin F. 10
Bessie B. 65
Betty Jo 275
C. C. 275
Caroline 131
Catherine H. 178
Columbus W. 55
Crawford C. 275
D. W. 95
Daisy Bean 10
Daniel W. 95

Dea John 297
WILSON continued
Deacon Andrew 297
Dewey H. 275
Effie W. 30
Emma Lou 275
Ethel R. 275
Eunice V. 275
Fannie G. 297
Fred C. Gurley 178
G. C. 275
G. J. N. 178
G. S. 275
George 297
George N. 275
Rosa 297
George Noble 275
Grover 275
Guy 178
H. V. 96
Harold W. 261
Harvey Valentine 96
J. B. 275
J. S. 95
James Weldon 275
Jessie Knight 41
John B. 124
John L. 41
Johnie 275
Johnnie 275
Joyce 95
L. C. 41
Lawson 56
Leila L. 275
Lillie B. 275
Lillie Brown 275
Lottie R.178
Lucy 96
Lucy Boswell 96
Mae Maddox 10
Martha A. 275
Martha C. 178
Martha J. 41
Martha Rosetta 65
Mary Elizabeth 275
Mary Lanier 275
Mattie Belle 131
Minnie L. 95
Minnie Mae 131
Minnie T. 275
Morn 95

Nancy E. 178
WILSON continued
Nina S. 95
Ninie 275
Nora F. 55
Olin 275
Olline M. 275
Ora K. 124
Paul 30
Paul F. Sr. 178
R. B. 275
Robert R. 178
Rosa Leo 275
Ruby C. 275
Sallie Dickson 178
Samuel Wright 178
Sanford 275
W. W. 275
Willie W. 275
Summie 65
Tallulah H. 261
W. L. 275
Willie 275
Woodrow 275

WINBURN
A. A. 179.
William 179

WINGFIELD
Levi 305

WISE
B. S. 260
F. W. 260
Jessie Mae 260

WITT
Ann Oliva 179
Ann Olivia Middleton 179
Bell 301
David 179
Joe 301
Nancy 179
William 179

WOFFORD
Cynthia Jill 260
Daniel Lamar 260
Hugh M. 260
J. W. 260

WOOD
Alice B. 284
Annie W. 41
Aretha E. 260
Barbara 260
Beulah E. 143
C. O. 260
Caleb Mack 260
Cary 260
Charles O. 260
Charlton N. 195
Cornelia A. 41
D. C. 260
Dee 30
Dewitt 41
E. 195
Edna Moody 260
Ellen B. 204
Emory Speer 260
Ethleen T. 260
Eveline 260
Fannie 260
Fannie Epsy 204
Fletcher 179
Green L. 41
Guy L. 55
Henry M. Sr. 30
Hester B. 284
Howard 267
Hoyt C. 267
Hoyt D. 143
Ida 260
Irial E. 143
J. A. 179
J. C. 41,275
J. G. 41
J. N. 260,336
J. P. 260
J. T. 325
J. W. 41,204
James K. 260
James M. 41
James R. 41
Jeff 41
Johnnie Ray 336
Julia 41
Julia E. 41
L. Hinton 55
Lassie Mae Lowe 336
Jasper Lee 260

Jasper Newton 260
WOOD continued
Jesse P. 260
Laura Lumpkin 325
Lavina Whitmire Bowles 204
Lenora W. 55
Lillie J. 30
Lou E. 267
Lula Cronic 267
Marshall 41
Mary A. 41179
Mary E. 41
Maude 41
Maude J. 41
Mildred 275
Minnie Bell 41
Mollie 41
Nancy N. 336
Odie G. 260
Omer Odell 260
Pelina Loggins 260
R. C. 204
R. L. 41
Raymond A. 336
Ruth Sykes 30
S. A. 260
Sallie 275
Sam 284
Shirley Ann 124
T. L. Jr. 143
Thelma M. 267
Thomas N. 336
Tyria L. 143
W. P. 204
W. Tom 41
Walter Mitchell 204

WOODALL
Ronald E. 260
Walter Gene 179

WOODS
Charlotte Ethel Jane Wilson 298

WORLEY
Annie Ruth 96
Arizona 267
Artie S. 96
Charlie 261
Frank 96
Hannah L. 96

John R. 96
WORLEY continued
M. A. 96
Mellie P. 179
S. R. 96
Sarah Cantrell 96
Sim R. 96
Thomas G. 96
Thomas H. 96
Tom D. 179

WORSHAM
E. A. Giddens 96
Elizabeth Evilene 179
J. L. 96
W. A. 179

WRIGHT
Almeda J. Thurmond 260
Barbara C. 195
Benjamin L. 117
C. F. 117
Edde A. 96
Harve J. Jr. 117
Howard 117
Ila G. 117
James W. 260
Jim W. 117
L. A. Nell 117
Lelar T. 117
Maggie 117
Magnolia 117
Mamie Sudderth 179
Marion W. 117
Noria S. 117
Ruth Mae 117
S. M. 117
Sarah M. 117
Sue T. 260
T. Frank 65
T. N. 117
Thomas 117
W. H. 260
William 260

YANCEY
Bonnie Carter 180

YARBROUGH
Alma R. 261
Arthur C. 276

Bessie Moena 295
YARBROUGH continued
Blanch H. 261
C. D. 295
Cora C. 180
Ernest 295
Henry D. 295
Jimmy D. 261
L. G. 295
Lemon 295
Lottie Caroline 295
Luther J. 180
Marie 295
Mollie P. 276
Owen 295
R. D. 295
Thomas N. Jr. 261
Thomas U. 261

YATES
John Lacy 124

YEARGIN
J. C. 57
John J. 57
Martha E. 57
S. J. 57

YEARWOOD
A.T. 195
Avis S. 132
B. F. 195
Clara Barnett 131
Eli 195
G. E. 131
George A. 41
Helen 131
Ida E. 195
Katherine 131
Little A. T. 41
Lizzie 41
Oscar 195
Rachel 131
S. J. 195
Sarah J. 195
W. C. 41

YONGE
Frankie 96
Jack R. 96
John R. 117

YOPP
Georgiana 204
James E. 205
Joseph E. 204
Martha J. 204
Mattie 204
Minnie O. Morgan 204
S. D. 204
Samuel D. 205
Velmer 205

YOUNG
E. L. 10
F. B. 10
Henry Velvin 10
Lottrell Chandler 330
Loyd Kirby 10

END

www.ingramcontent.com/pod-product-compliance
Lightning Source LLC
Chambersburg PA
CBHW050425240426
43661CB00055B/2274